The second edition of *Guide for Alternate Route Teachers: Strategies for Literacy Development, Classroom Management and Teaching and Learning, K–12* features a new chapter on Using Technology to Support Literacy Instruction. Here are some great online resources you will turn to again and again! This table can also be found in Chapter 9, pages 206–207.

Table 9.1

Literacy Skill	Site	Activities
Reading		
Decoding	www.readingrockets.org	Reading readiness activities, letter recognitions, e-books
	www.starfall.com	
	www.abc-match.com	
Phonics	www.abcfastphonics.com	Practice word sounds
	http://pbskids.org/lions/	Play phonic skill games
	http://meddybemps.com/letterary/index.html	Interactive phonics activities
Fluency	www.voki.com	Create animated talking characters (multiple languages)
	www.bookpop.com	Read along with animated text
	www.talkingpets.org	Text-to-speech
	www.shidonni.com	Student drawings come to life (talking, dancing, playing)
Guided Reading	www.bedtime-story.com	Read and listen to stories
	www.webpop.com	Read and respond to stories, print books
Independent Reading	www.drscavanaugh.org/ebooks	Read and respond to books online
	www.storyplace.org	Read and listen to stories, interactive activities (English and Spanish)
	www.magickeys.com/books	Read books independently
Comprehension and Critical Thinking	http://interactivities.mped.org/view_interactive.aspx?id=127&tit=	Create organizational webs (cluster, cause & effect, hierarchy)
	www.eduplace.com/graphicorganizers/pdf	Create graphic organizers
	www.abcteach.com/reading/storygrammar.htm www.palmbeachk12.fl.us	Create story grammars
	http://old.escambia.k12.fl.us/schscnts/brobm/te...	Create summaries of texts
	www.kizoa.com	Create slide shows
	www.voicethread.com	Talk about and share images, documents, etc.
Vocabulary Development	www.wordle.net	Create "word clouds"
	www.vocabulary.com/wordcity.html	Develop and practice new vocabulary words
	www.readwritethink.org/constructaword.com	Construct new words
	www.puzzlemaker.school.discovery.com	Create crossword puzzles
	www.bbc.co.uk/skillwise	Practice prefixes, suffixes, roots, letter patterns
	www.funbrain.com *or* www.spellingbee.com	Play spelling games
Writing	www.readwritethink.org	Create newspapers, brochures, flyers, booklets
	www.storybird.com	Create stories with text and pictures
	www.glogster.edu.com	Create interactive posters
	www.kerpoof.com	Create storybooks, paintings

PEARSON

ALWAYS LEARNING

Dr. Frances A. Levin

Introduction to Teaching
A Guide for New Jersey's Alternate Route Teachers

Adapted for the 24-Hour Course
Required for a Certificate of Eligibility (C.E.)
to Teach in New Jersey

Second Custom Edition

Selections taken from:
A Guide for Alternate Route Teachers, Second Edition
by Frances A. Levin and Mary Alice McCullough

Pearson Learning Solutions, 501 Boylston Street, Suite 900, Boston, MA 02116
A Pearson Education Company
www.pearsoned.com

Printed in the United States of America

000200010271308017

TF

ISBN 10: 1-256-65514-7
ISBN 13: 978-1-256-65514-5

Contents

List of Models

Preface

This book was written with the intention of providing valuable information, models, and resources to help guide teacher candidates who have made the important decision to teach children in the state of New Jersey. The state has recently added new regulations for alternate route teachers which require that candidates take a 24 hour course, called "Introduction to Teaching", designed to provide a foundation and background knowledge in teaching. This book will take the new teacher through all of the topics and concepts necessary to help candidates feel more prepared and confident in their new profession.

The topics chosen for this book address the issues that have the most immediate concern for new teachers, such as teacher expectations, classroom management, assessment, unit and lesson design, and so on. Chapter 5. "Literacy Instruction K-12" and Chapter 6, "Literacy Across the Curriculum" are specifically dedicated to literacy development. Those chapters were important to include because literacy skills (reading, writing, interpreting, viewing, speaking, and critical thinking) play a major role in advancing student learning in *all* grades and in *all* content areas. For this reason, examples were chosen to further clarify the strategies and methodologies in this book primarily from the language arts. The thinking was that all our readers would then have an understanding of the language arts, which would enable them to accommodate the procedures and strategies to their own content areas. After all, students have to learn how to read a book efficiently and effectively, whether it is a chemistry book, a history book or a novel. As the saying goes, "All teachers are teachers of reading".

This book further supports teachers' understandings by providing relevant research and by placing the major educational issues with which they will be confronted within their historical contexts. In addition, we provide lists of websites and texts that teachers can access to broaden their scope and knowledge base.

We wish you success in your new career in teaching and hope that each year brings you joy and continued inspiration.

**INTRODUCTION TO TEACHING: 24-HOUR
PRE–SERVICE PROGRAM TO QUALIFY FOR AN
INSTRUCTIONAL CERTIFICATE OF ELIGIBILITY (C.E.)**

 Introduction

This pre-service component recognizes that, for many participants, this course begins the process of accepting vast changes in their personal and professional lives. Respecting their expertise, the goals for the pre-service component are framed around two critical areas: an overview of and preparation for the skills and tools needed for the teaching profession; and essential attitudes and dispositions needed to maintain poise as novice teachers in diverse communities.

The program's primary intention is to provide a snapshot of teaching. For instance, it addresses concerns related to personal expectations and actualities. Moreover, the program prepares participants to begin their search for a new job. For many, this means understanding what schools are looking for in teachers, recognizing education buzz words and preparing demonstration lessons.

As part of the 24 hours, the program should provide the participant with a "clinical" opportunity through structured observations in a school setting. Collaboration with school districts will provide both a window of opportunity for the candidate and a potential recruitment tool for the district.

The program of study is organized by "sessions" of which each is approximately two (2) hours in length. An additional four hour "clinical" experience will afford the potential candidate the opportunity to gain true insight into the school environment. Possibilities for the format of the 24 hours include:

- 10 sessions of 2 hour classes plus 4 hours of classroom observation, or
- 5 sessions of 4 hour classes plus 4 hours of classroom observation, or
- 4 Saturday classes of 5 hours each with 4 hours of classroom observation, or
- Blended online classes with 2-4 class meetings.

At the conclusion of the 24 hours, the candidate must complete the following assessments to receive a Certificate of Completion for submission as part of the application for certification:

1. Classroom Observation Report

- All candidates will observe for 4 hours in a classroom that matches their intended Certificate of Eligibility. Elementary candidates will observe literacy and content areas in an elementary school.
- Middle and secondary candidates will observe several classes in the four hour time period in their intended content area.
- Each candidate will use the General Observation Form (See last page)

  Observation Report Assessment Includes:
- General Observation Form
- Interview with a teacher or administrator – Suggested topics for interview:

  Challenges of teaching

  School mission

  Classroom management

  Family involvement

  Assessment
- Reflections

2. Lesson Plan

3. Showcase Portfolio

- Includes:
- Resume
- Cover Letter
- Lesson Plan
- Philosophy of Education Statement
- (Certificate of Eligibility, after course when issued by the D.O.E.)

4. Attendance/Participation

Completion of entire 24 hours is required.

The following ten (10) sessions serves as a model of a prescribed program of study both in scope and sequence.

Session 1: Overview of the Teaching Profession

The purpose of this session is to provide candidates with an understanding of teaching as a profession, focusing on the culture of schools, including expectations and the transitioning necessary for alternate route teachers.

Topics for Discussion:

- Expectations in today's schools
  Personal • State • Parents • Students • Supervisors • Administrators • Colleagues
- Professional Time Management
- The Importance of Reflective Teaching
- Professional Standards for Teachers
- Transitioning to a teaching career
- Credentials- Taking the Praxis and the 2.75 GPA
- Description of the Alternate Route Program – regulatory requirements for eligibility

Reading Assignment: *Introduction to Teaching: Guide for New Jersey's Alternate Route Teachers,* Levin & McCullough (2011). Pearson Education. *Chapter 1*

Assignment/Assessment: Response to the readings. Group Activity: If you could interview a teacher or administrator, what questions would you ask?

Instructor's Resources: D.O.E. Webinars
Do You Believe In Me? (YouTube video)
"My Mother's Gravy" Phil Delta Kappan, 2001

Professional Vocabulary: word wall, professionalism, professional development, confidentiality, humility, knowledge, skills, dispositions, highly qualified, accountability, Certificate of Eligibility, provisional and standard license, Provisional Teacher Program

Professional Standards for Teachers – Standard Six: Learning Environment, Standard Eight: Communication, Standard Ten: Professional Development

Session 2: Classroom Management Workshop

The purpose of this session is to provide candidates with information related to procedures and routines in a classroom as well as behavior management. This session will focus on creating a positive learning environment in all classrooms.

Topics for Discussion

- Classroom Management
- Procedures
- Routines
- Classroom Design
- Managing Time and Instruction
- Teacher Dispositions
- Managing Paraprofessionals and Co-Teaching
- Motivation – Intrinsic vs. Extrinsic
- Behavior Management Plan
- Assertive Discipline
- Conflict Resolution

Reading Assignment: *Introduction to Teaching: Guide for New Jersey's Alternate Route Teachers,* Levin & McCullough (2011). Pearson Education. *Chapter 2*

Assignment/Assessment: Written response to the reading.

Each candidate will write a description of an ideal classroom, including procedures and behavior management.

Instructor's Resources: Classroom vignettes and Case Studies from MyEducationLab (MyEducationLab is an online site from Pearson Education that includes a variety of information ranging from videos on many educational topics, such as class management, educational research, classroom vignettes, booklets on topics ranging from literacy to special education, job searching skills, and much more).

Professional Vocabulary: environmental design, classroom design, passion for teaching, co-teaching, paraprofessionals

Professional Standards for Teachers: Standard Three: Diverse Learners, Standard Four: Instructional Planning and Strategies, Standard Six: Learning Environment, Standard Seven: Special Needs

Session 3: Assessment

The purpose of this session is to provide a clear understanding of the use of assessment as a tool to inform instruction. Candidates will learn about a variety of assessments that are used in districts across New Jersey.

Topics for Discussion:

- How-to-use Assessment tools in your classroom
- Types of Assessment (standardized tests, running records, anecdotal records, content area tests, projects, informal assessment, etc.)
- Using Rubrics in Your Classroom
- Using Portfolios
- NJ Core Curriculum Content Standards

Reading Assignment: *Introduction to Teaching: Guide for New Jersey's Alternate Route Teachers,* Levin & McCullough (2011). Pearson Education. *Chapter 4*

Assignment/Assessment: Do a KWL on assessment – elements of a good lesson, how to engage children in the assessment process

Instructor's Resources: MyEducationLab– portfolio samples, Classroom vignettes

Professional Vocabulary: intrinsic, extrinsic, corporal punishment, community of learners, New Jersey NJASK, SRA, HSPA, assessment, authentic assessment, portfolios, rubrics, observation

Professional Standards for Teachers: Standard Four: Instructional Planning and Strategies, Standard Five: Assessment, Standard Six: Learning Environment, Standard Eight: Communication, Standard Nine: Collaboration and Partnerships

Session 4: Lesson Planning Workshop Part 1

This session will offer candidates the opportunity to learn to write and implement lesson plans as part of a unit study. Candidates will learn the elements of a good lesson and how to accommodate the individual needs of their students. The lesson will be appropriate to the age and subject matter that the candidate desires to teach.

Topics for Discussion:

- Presenting a Lesson as Part of a Unit of Study
- Provide Candidates with Samples of Good Lessons and Do Lesson Plan Analysis
- Elements of a Good Lesson
- The Importance of a Strong Introduction (examples)
- Strength and Weaknesses of a Lesson
- Clear Objectives
- Sample Format
- Assessment
- New Jersey Core Curriculum Content Standards

Reading Assignment: *Introduction to Teaching: Guide for New Jersey's Alternate Route Teachers,* Levin & McCullough (2011). Pearson Education. *Chapter 3*

Assignment/Assessment: Write a group lesson plan addressing content area and differentiating instruction.

Instructor's Resources: Sample Lesson Plans from MyEducationLab
Web sites for models for lesson plan
www.masterteacher.com; www.educationworld.com;
www.teacher.scholastic.com; www.adprima.com

Professional Vocabulary: Standards, objectives, assessment, learning styles, modifications, differentiated instruction, anticipatory set, Do Nows

Professional Standards for Teachers: Standard Four: Instructional Planning and Strategies, Standard Five: Assessment, Standard Seven: Special Needs, Standard Eight: Communication, Standard Three: Diverse Learners, Standard 6: Learning Environment

Session 5: Literacy Instruction – Content Area Literacy

This session is designed to provide all teachers, elementary, middle, and secondary, with the strategies and understandings to teach students to read effectively. Candidates will learn how to teach students to efficiently read a textbook and to foster a love of literacy.

Topics for Discussion:

- All Teachers are Reading Teachers
- Components of a Balanced Literacy Classroom
- Content Literacy in Middle and High School: How to read the text
- Using Literacy Strategies for Successful Reading
- Differentiating Instruction

Reading Assignment: *Introduction to Teaching: Guide for New Jersey's Alternate Route Teachers,* Levin & McCullough (2011). Pearson Education. *Chapters 5 and 6*

Assignments/Assessment: Create a file of literacy strategies for your content area. Collaborative Peer Review

Instructor's Resources: "Literacy Activities in the Classroom" Vignette. MyEducationLab

Professional Vocabulary: balanced literacy, writing process, read-alouds, language arts block, differentiating instruction, literacy strategies, content literacy

Professional Standards for Teachers: Standard Three: Diverse Learners, Standard Four: Instructional Planning and Strategies, Standard Five: Assessment, Standard Six: Learning Environment

Session 6: Professional Responsibilities: Finding a Teaching Position

This session, which is midway through this course, addresses the issues and tools involved with securing a teaching position in New Jersey.

Topics for Discussion:

- Applying for the Certificate of Eligibility (C.E.)
- The role of the N.J. Department of Education (D.O.E.)
- Resume Writing
- Interviewing Skills – Role-playing
- Job-hunting Resources
- Showcase Portfolios
- Philosophy of Education
- Personal Improvement Plan (PIP)
- Provisional Teacher Program

Assignment/Assessment: Write a statement explaining your philosophy of education.

Instructor's Resources: NJ DOE web site, NJHire, MyEducatioLab (online resource for resume writing and interviewing skills)

Professional Vocabulary: Professional development, provisional certification, standard certification

Professional Standards for Teachers: Standard Ten: Professional Development, Standard Eight: Communication, Standard Eleven: Ethics

Session 7: The Many Faces of Diversity

The purpose of this session is to provide candidates with a clear understanding of the tremendous diversity that teachers face in classrooms every day. Candidates will learn the importance of accommodating instruction to meet the needs of students.

Topics for Discussion:

- Cultural Diversity
- English Language Learners

- Challenges of the Urban Experience
- Teaching the Gifted and Talented
- Teaching Students with Special Needs
- Teaching Students with Alternative Lifestyles
- Classifications of Special Education- Special Ed laws
- Multiple Intelligences

Reading Assignment: *Introduction to Teaching: Guide for New Jersey's Alternate Route Teachers,* Levin & McCullough (2011). Pearson Education. *Chapters 7 and 8*

Assignments/Assessment: Group activity developing lesson plans that reflect the needs of diverse learners.

Instructor's Resources: MyEducationLab booklet,"What Every Teacher Should KnowAbout Special Education" article, "Good Teaching Matters". Thinking K-16. A Publication of the Education Trust. Summer 1998.

Professional Vocabulary: English Language Learners (ELLs), IEPs, multicultural literature, disability, handicap, 504 Plan

Professional Standards for Teachers: Standard Three, Diverse Learners, Standard Four, Instructional Planning and Strategies, Standard Five: Assessment. Standard Six: Learning Environment, Standard Seven: Special Needs, Standard Ten: Professional Development, Standard Eleven: Ethics

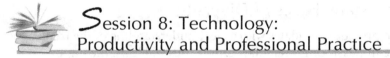

*S*ession 8: Technology: Productivity and Professional Practice

This session will address the importance and practical use of technology in the classroom. Candidates will incorporate technology into their activities.

Topics for Discussion:

- Integrating Technology (finding the best tools for your grade/subject)
- Using the Internet in Your Classroom

- Technology and the NJCCS
- 21st century Literacies
- Technology Resources (freeware, grants, set-up)

Reading Assignment: *Introduction to Teaching: Guide for New Jersey's Alternate Route Teachers,* Levin & McCullough, *Chapter 9*

Assignment/Assessment: Each candidate will edit a Word Document, create a graph from a spreadsheet, create a 5 slide PowerPoint, and email documents to the instructor.

Instructor's Resources: MyEducationLab

Professional Vocabulary: web 2.0, web quests, digital story, podcast, search engine, URL, flash drive, blog

Professional Standards for Teachers: Standard Ten: Professional Development, Standard Five: Assessment, Standard Six: Learning Environment

Session 9: Lesson Plan Workshop Part 2

This session will provide candidates with the opportunity to present their lesson plans to their peers. Candidates will receive recommendations from their instructor as well as their colleagues.

- Each candidate submits a Lesson Plan
- Candidates present their Lesson Plans in small groups of 3-4 and bring copies for their group (Instructor provides rubric for written lesson plan.)
- Group members complete a lesson plan checklist.
- Instructor asks for a few volunteers to do demonstrations lessons in front of the class.
- Class critiques.

Assignments/Assessment: Each candidate will create a Lesson Plan and present it to a group of colleagues.

Instructor's Resources: MyEducationLab lesson plan samples

Professional Vocabulary: reflective practitioner, rubrics, peer mentoring

Professional Standards for Teachers: Standard Three: Diverse Learners, Standard Four: Instructional Planning and Strategies, Standard Five: Assessment, Standard Six: Learning Environment, Standard Seven: Special Needs, Standard Eight: Communication, Standard Nine: Collaboration and Partnerships,

Session 10: Home-School Connection/Wrap-Up

This session will be divided into two sections. The first half is designed to help candidates create and foster a positive ongoing relationships between the school and the home. The last section of this class is designed to help candidates assemble their Showcase Portfolio.

Topics for Discussion:

- How Can Teachers Promote Family Involvement?
- Teacher Conferences
- Building Trust
- Continued Communication
- Class Newsletter

Reading Assignment: *Introduction to Teaching: Guide for New Jersey's Alternate Route Teachers,* Levin & McCullough (2011). Pearson Education. *Chapter 10*

Assignments/Assessment: Candidates will assemble and showcase their portfolios to their colleagues.

Instructor's Resources: MyEducationLab digital portfolios

Professional Vocabulary: newsletters, mutual trust, student-led conferences

Professional Standards for Teachers: Standard Eight: Communication

What Are the Expectations for Teachers in Today's Schools?

Making a life change can be at once exciting and exhilarating and daunting and exhausting. Knowing in advance what will be expected of you will lessen the anxiety and confirm that your decision to enter the field of education is a good one for you. A good place to begin is with a cursory glance at teacher expectations and how they have changed over the years.

 ## Changes in Teacher Expectations

Teaching and learning have changed radically over the past forty years. At one time, teaching expectations were limited to presenting lessons and grading papers. Preparation was minimal because programmed lessons with answer keys and objective tests

were purchased along with the textbooks, making it possible for teachers to easily satisfy their responsibilities during their contractual nine-to-three workday. Classroom discipline was generally not a problem because teachers had both parental and administrative support. Most students actually feared a trip to the principal's office because of the additional consequences they knew they would face once they got home. Curriculum and standards were determined by local boards of education, and accountability rarely went beyond the building level. This, you will find, has all changed.

A major change is in the academic, performance, and professional expectations for teachers. Research in teaching and learning, technology, and globalization has changed the face of teaching. The responsibilities of teachers and administrators continue to increase exponentially in an effort to keep up with the ever-growing internal and external demands placed on schools. Unlike educators in the past, teachers today have as their primary responsibility to prepare their students with the skills, concepts, and knowledge base that will enable them to compete in a demanding global environment that requires that they not only *know more* but also be able to *apply what they know* to the unknown. To accomplish this, teachers are being asked to introduce curricular skills and concepts much earlier and in much more depth. Consequently, young children are starting to learn how to read and write in preschool; middle school students are taking algebra and biology; and high school students are taking college-level classes for credit. These curricular demands require that teachers themselves have not only a strong content area background but also a strong knowledge base in teaching pedagogy that would enable them to teach students in a way that would maximize their understanding and ability to apply what they have been taught.

Another change is society's expectation of who should be taught. Until the middle of the twentieth century, the focus of the school's attention was on the academic preparation of those entering the professional fields. Advanced courses such as foreign languages, abstract math, chemistry, and physics were exclusively reserved for those who were college bound. The other students were given general courses such as applied math, nonacademic English, and earth science, which did not require students to go beyond literal understandings of the texts they were reading. These students, most of whom entered the workforce right after graduating from high school, were being prepared for jobs that were characteristically regimented and systematic. The advent of computers changed all of that. Not only did computers change the way we communicated with each other, they also changed the way goods and services were produced, marketed, and delivered. This new technology began to rapidly replace unskilled laborers, forcing millions to be reeducated in order to compete for jobs. Today's jobs and the jobs of the future require that employees have advanced technological skills and the ability to think critically and develop new ways to use those skills. For example, auto mechanics today must be technologically savvy to be able to diagnose and solve problems embedded in an automobile's complex computer systems. This shift in technology has had a tremendous impact on schools and teachers, who, seemingly overnight, have become responsible for preparing *all* students—not just a select few—to think critically. This was the impetus for radical changes in curriculum and required that the doors to those advanced courses, focusing on critical thinking as well as on content, be opened to all students. Within a short period of time, this drive to educate all of our students with the same advanced skills and concepts had gone beyond the social implications to become a national economic imperative. To ensure that all students were being given the skills and concepts they needed, state and national standards were set and tests were developed to measure attainment of those standards. This change in focus had a tremendous impact on teacher expectations. Teachers are now not only expected to teach the content and skills identified by the standards, they are also being held accountable for their students' mastery of those skills and concepts.

A final change in teacher responsibilities happened as a result of the vast amount of research that has been done in the areas of teaching and learning. For a long time, students were taught with methods based on the stimulus-response-reinforcement learning theories posed by Skinner's (1974) research with animals. The problem with this method is that it trained students, like animals, to respond to, not to think or be able to generalize information in other areas of their lives. Thanks to the researchers and scholars who have followed Skinner, we now know a great deal more about how students learn and what strategies teachers can use to maximize their students' learning. We know, for example, that:

- Children learn at higher levels and at greater rates when they are actively engaged in their own learning (Piaget, 1995; Vygotsky, 1986).

- Comprehension is increased significantly if students are given problems to solve and the opportunity to use talk to negotiate meaning to solve those problems (Reader-Response Theory) (Beach 1993; McCullough 2002; Rosenblatt, 1976; Vygotsky, 1986).

- Tracking doesn't work. Children who are tracked into remedial classes rarely advance to the next level (Gamoran, 1986; Goodlad, 1984; Wheelock, 1992).

- Teaching vocabulary with lists without multiple opportunities to use the words in different contexts doesn't work. Students learn best when given multiple contextual strategies, for example, clustering (Marzano & Marzano, 1988), word mapping (Blanchowicz, 1986), collaborative word selection (Fisher, Blanchowicz, & Smith, 1991), and word play (Nagy & Scott, 2001).

- Children will read if they are given texts that interest them (Harkrader & Moore, 1997; Huck & Kuhn, 1968).

- Comprehension and retention are increased significantly if students are given opportunities to make connections and apply what they know to their own lives (Rosenblatt, 1976).

- Just because children can read words with accuracy and fluency doesn't mean they understand what they are reading (Allington & Cunningham, 2002).

- A child's literacy development is enhanced significantly when taught with a balanced approach to literacy instruction (Clay, 1985; Strickland, Galda, & Cullinan, 2004).

- Students learn best when their learning style matches their teacher's teaching style (Gardner, 1983).

- Student failures can be minimized when student weaknesses are identified prior to the failure with assessments that are varied, frequent, and ongoing (Clay, 1991; Galda, Cullinan, & Strickland, 1993).

Most important, current research continues to show that, although some people believe that quality education is in direct proportion to funding, the most important influence on student learning is not money or computers or even books; it's their teachers (Barnes, Britton, & Torbe, 1989; Fish, 1980; McCullough, 2002). For this reason, teachers today have the responsibility, expectation, and moral obligation to provide their students with a quality education using strategies and methodologies that are grounded in scientifically based research.

What Do Administrators Expect of New Teachers?

Administrators, who are supported by content area supervisors, are primarily concerned with issues dealing with faculty, discipline, safety, and school operations. In addition, they are accountable to the state and to their local boards of education for their students meeting local, state, and national academic standards. Administrators (K–12) will expect new teachers to do the following:

- Come to school every day prepared to teach lessons that will prepare students to meet standards on state and national tests.

- Be punctual. (Report to school on time and remain in the building until the designated leaving time; arrive at classes, duties, and meetings on time, etc.)

- Present themselves as role models by dressing, speaking, and acting in a professional manner.

- Attend and participate meaningfully in monthly faculty meetings, Back-to-School Nights, parent-teacher conferences, and other events.

- Keep accurate and up-to-date academic and attendance records.
- Maintain a safe physical and emotional student environment both inside and outside the classroom, which includes protecting students from both physical attacks and verbal abuse as well as exposure to hazardous areas or substances.
- Maintain a neat, orderly, and inviting physical environment for students.
- Take charge of students during drills for fire, bomb threats, and terrorist attacks, which includes taking and reporting attendance.
- Maintain classroom discipline and decorum.
- Report suspected physical and/or psychological abuse of students.
- Enforce the school's discipline code and report infractions (e.g., drug and alcohol use, excessive tardiness, insubordination).
- Comply promptly with requests from parents, staff, or other administrators for information or reports.
- Submit grades and progress reports on time.
- Provide accommodations for students with special needs.
- Administer standardized tests.
- Report punctually to and supervise assigned duties (such as hall, cafeteria, bus, lavatory).
- Serve on special committees (i.e., discipline committee, Back-to-School Night committee, prom).

Note: Some administrators may expect that all new teachers will take on additional responsibilities such as coaching a sport or advising a club.

What Do Content Supervisors Expect of New Teachers?

Content area supervisors' concerns are primarily academic. They are responsible for ensuring that students receive a quality education and that teachers are given the support they need in the form of materials, equipment, mentoring, and professional development to make that happen. In return, content area supervisors will expect the following of new teachers:

- Be familiar with local, state, and national standards.
- Develop units of instruction using scientifically based teaching strategies that support local, state, and national standards.

- Be prepared every day to present lessons that are differentiated, student-centered, challenging, active, and interesting.
- Use teacher-developed assessments and standardized test results to inform instruction.
- Use ongoing and varied assessment tools to evaluate student learning.
- Be reflective practitioners who allot time each day to reflect, assess, and make necessary modifications to the day's activities (lessons; interactions with students, parents, and colleagues; new policies or procedures, etc.).
- Submit weekly detailed lesson plans in the required format.
- Design learning centers and bulletin board displays to support unit objectives (K–6).
- Work closely with the Child Study Team to develop lessons for students with special needs. The Child Study Team is a team of professionals who set and manage the educational and behavioral programs of students with disabilities.
- Attend and participate in a meaningful way in monthly department meetings.
- Submit written requests for books, materials, and supplies.
- Maintain accurate and up-to-date grade and attendance books.
- Keep parents informed of their child's progress via phone calls, email messages, newsletters, progress reports, or letters home.
- Serve on committees to develop curriculum and review new materials for possible purchase.
- Remain current by continuing personal professional development by taking graduate courses, attending professional meetings and conferences, participating in teacher mentoring programs, and so on.
- Be kept informed of both problems and successes that you are having.

Note: In smaller school districts, the roles of the building administrator and the content area supervisor are often assumed by the same person.

What Do Students Expect of Their Teachers?

Students, regardless of age or feigned indifference, come to school each day with high expectations of the teachers, who for many of them are the people with whom they spend the majority of their day. A sad reality is that some students have more contact hours with their teachers than with their own parents. This may account for the change over the years in what students expect from their teachers—from being primarily impersonal and academic to being more personal as well as academic. When asked, students responded that they expected the following of their teachers:

- Know who they are.
- Like them and like teaching.
- Come to class every day prepared to teach lessons in a way that is personable and understandable.
- Be knowledgeable, current, clear, concise, and consistent.
- Be approachable, flexible, and open to opposing ideas.
- Be good role models with a sense of humor.
- Be fair, encouraging, sensitive, and nonthreatening.
- Return work in a timely manner, preferably the next day.
- Be more than "correctors." Acknowledge the students for something done well.
- Maintain discipline in the classroom.
- Participate in school activities (coach, attend sporting events, buy fund-raising candy bars, etc.).
- Be available and genuinely willing to provide extra help or counseling when needed.
- Advocate for them when they have problems.
- Keep them safe from physical and psychological attacks.

What Do Parents Expect of Their Children's Teachers?

Because many students live in a single working-parent home or in a home where both parents work, there is an increasing demand on teachers' time. More and more, parents are expecting teachers to accept responsibilities that would have traditionally been theirs. Many schools have accommodated parental requests by expanding their curriculum to include courses in sex education, parenting skills, and values clarification with the expectation that teachers will teach them. In addition, parents expect teachers to do the following:

- Value and nurture their children.
- Have their children's best interests at the heart of each action and decision.
- Be competent, current, and effective.

- Teach the content needed for their children to succeed on standardized tests and in the classes that follow.
- Academically challenge their children with lessons that will move them beyond their current grade level.
- Be sensitive, understanding, and attentive to children's individual needs.
- Provide extra help when needed.
- Provide educational experiences beyond the classroom (class trips, guest speakers, etc.).
- Keep them informed (for example, through phone calls, email messages, notes home, progress reports).
- Be a positive role model.
- Keep their children safe from physical harm and from the potentially psychologically debilitating taunts of bullies.

 ## What Should You Expect as a New Teacher?

It's important that you not only have a good idea of what is expected of you as a first-year teacher, you should also have an idea of what it is that you should expect. Your list of first-year teacher expectations should include the following:

- A safe working environment.
- Administrative support. If you have a problem with a student or parent that you have been unable to handle on your own, you should expect intervention and backing from the administration in some form (such as conference, detention, letter home, suspension). You should also expect to be advised of the outcome of the intervention.
- Supervisory support. It is understood that no one comes to teaching fully prepared or equipped for the task. You should, therefore, expect ongoing support from your supervisor through frequent classroom observations and follow-up conferences.
- Ongoing mentoring with a master teacher, which is typically arranged by the content area supervisor. New teachers should expect the mentor to meet with them at regularly scheduled meetings to (1) offer constructive critiques of their lesson plans and classroom practices; (2) share materials,

strategies, knowledge, and experience; and (3) be a sympathetic listener and counselor.

- Professional development opportunities and, in some cases, funding.

- Materials, tools, and equipment necessary for you to deliver the course content.

- Pertinent information about students in your class (Individualized Education Plans [IEP] for special needs students, lists of students with health issues or chronic discipline problems, etc.).

- Pertinent information about the school (faculty manual listing duties and responsibilities; schedules; discipline code; curriculum guide; academic performance standards; calendar of events; procedures and forms for ordering materials and for making health, guidance, and special services referrals).

What Are Your Personal Expectations?

Now that you have had a chance to see some of the things that will be expected of you, take some time and reflect on what you expect from teaching and enter those expectations in your journal. Specifically, you want to consider what you expect from

- Your principal
- Your content area supervisor
- Your mentor
- Your colleagues
- The parents of your students
- Yourself

What Can New Teachers Do to Meet Expectations?

At the beginning this may all seem somewhat overwhelming; however, there are steps that you can actually take prior to entering the classroom and throughout the school year that will help reduce your burden, lessen your anxiety, and help you meet these expectations. First, it's important that you be cognizant of exactly what is expected; then, be proactive in meeting those expectations.

Before School Begins

- Meet with your supervisor and/or building administrator and get the following:
    - A printed list of their expectations for you. If one is not available, take notes at the meeting and send a copy to your supervisor or administrator via email as a follow-up to ensure that you have the same understanding.
    - Copies of the texts and lists of materials, tools, and equipment available that you can use to support your teaching throughout the year.
    - A planning book so that you can begin immediately to plan for the year.
    - A list of audiovisual aids and technology available to you and clarification of how you can access them. It's also a good idea to get the name of the person who is responsible for the care and upkeep of the equipment and the procedure for having equipment repaired.
    - A class roster with student addresses, phone numbers, and assigned guidance counselors.
    - A list of students with special needs in your class and their IEPs.
    - A copy of the discipline code and procedures, the name of the individual in charge of discipline, and where the disciplinarian can be located and accessed.
    - A map of the school.
    - A copy of the school calendar, noting holidays and special events.
    - A list of dates students will be absent from your classroom for such activities as student assemblies, state standardized testing, health exams, pep rallies, guidance scheduling, midterm and final exams, and scheduled class trips.
    - A curriculum guide for your grade or content area.
    - A copy of the local, state, and national standards. (Refer to Table 3.1 on page 51.)
    - A roster of school personnel and where they are located. If you are going to work in a school district that has a large population of students who speak English as their second language, be sure to ask who you should contact to have communications (letters, conferences, directions for students, etc.) translated.
    - Copies of pertinent forms (such as discipline, health, guidance, and Child Study Team referral forms, lesson-plan format, requisition forms for supplies, and additional texts).
    - The procedure and forms for reporting absences.

Note: All of this information should be readily available and easy to access.

- If access to your classroom is possible, set up your classroom with attractive bulletin boards, learning centers, seating arrangements, personal areas for students (cubbies), designated storage areas for books and materials, and so on.
- Develop your classroom academic and behavioral expectations and post them in a highly visible location (grades K–6) or have them printed, ready for distribution (grades 7–12) on the first day. (See Chapter 2, Models 7 and 8.)

- Develop a list of classroom management routines for turning in homework, going to the nurse, going to the lavatory, handing in late work, taking attendance, storing materials and equipment, and so on. (See Chapter 2, Models 5 and 6.)

- Prepare letters of introduction to parents and have them ready for mailing on or before the first day. (You can be sure the parents will be impressed.) (See Chapter 10, Figures 10.1 and 10.2 on pages 210 and 215.)

- Prepare a welcome letter to your students and post it prior to the opening of school. (See Model 1: Welcome Letter to Students.)

- Use your plan book to develop an academic game plan. Map out the units of instruction for the year. These can, of course, be modified during the year. This plan will help you see the "big picture," lend continuity to your teaching, and allow you to order materials, books, and equipment in advance. (See Chapter 3.)

- Set up your grade book.

- Develop your first unit of instruction and prepare the first two weeks of lesson plans, including assessments and scoring rubrics. (See Chapter 3.)

- List the supplies and materials you will need for your first unit so that you can submit your requisition form on or before the first day of school.

- Develop an agenda for your first day. (See the next section for suggestions.)

- Prepare student name tags and put names on student folders.

- Develop and organize a substitute teacher folder or binder. Being a substitute teacher is very difficult, particularly in the upper grades where many students have turned "getting over on the substitute" into a fine art. Although administrators know this, they still expect substitutes to come into your classroom and provide meaningful instruction and good classroom management in your absence. You can help your substitute meet this expectation by providing a three-ring binder or an accordion folder with all the information that would be needed throughout the day. (See Model 2: Checklist for Substitute Teacher Folder and Model 3: Substitute Teacher Classroom Evaluation Form.)

Throughout the School Year

- Ask your supervisor to set aside time each quarter to review with you your progress toward meeting the expectations set for you.

- Maintain a weekly journal where you can record your thoughts, reactions, successes, disappointments, and reflections on how you can improve your teaching practices; your interactions with students, parents, and colleagues; and so on.

- To stay current, join a local, state, or national professional organization and subscribe to its journal.

- Attend a professional development meeting or conference. Most major conferences are posted in the professional journals and on their websites.

- Use rubrics to facilitate returning student work promptly. (See Chapter 4, pages 79, 83–85, and 91.)

At the End of the School Year

- Revisit expectations set for you and by you for the past school year. Identify those you met and reflect on ways you can meet the goals you were unable to reach.

- Meet with your supervisor to discuss your reflections and to get suggestions for helping you meet next year's expectations.

- Reward yourself for a job well done.

- Begin to prepare for the next year.

The First Day: Setting the Expectations

As the saying goes, you only have one chance to make a first impression. What you do on the first day will set the tone for the days that follow. For this reason, it is considered by many teachers as the most important day of the year. You want students to leave your class with the impression that you are a kind, interesting, organized, knowledgeable person who has a great deal to offer them. Most important, you want them to think of your class as an event that they won't want to miss. A carefully planned first day is the first step to ensure this reaction. To this end, we strongly recommend you enter your classroom on the first day with a huge smile and a written agenda. What follows are some of the things you may want to include on your first day.

- A formal greeting, welcoming students to your world.

- A short introduction of yourself. Make it fun and interesting. Don't talk about your degrees or your philosophy of education—boring!

- Take attendance and assign seats. Having the seating chart completed before class begins saves a lot of time and makes you look very organized.

Suggestions for Introductory Activities

An introductory activity is a good idea for the first day, particularly in classes where the students do not know each other. It gives students an opportunity to be recognized without the pressure of thinking of something interesting to say, which usually accompanies those dreaded requests by teachers for students to introduce themselves. A well-planned introductory activity will also help you begin the process of personalizing your students in a fun and interesting way.

These activities are intended to be introductory only; therefore, each should be time limited. It's a good idea to bring a stopwatch to help you manage the time.

Activity 1 Student-to-Student Introductions

In pairs, have the students conduct mini-interviews of each other for five minutes. At the end of that time, have each student stand up and formally introduce his or her partner using the information garnered from the interview. Prior to the interviews, instruct the students to find out a minimum of four interesting things about their partners.

Activity 2 Most and Least Activity

Separate the class into pairs and give each student a list of most and least favorites to fill in for their partners. The list might include such items as candy bar, movie, actor, video game, and car. After five minutes, move around the room and ask students to share what they found out about their partners. Using an overhead projector and a transparency, a whiteboard, or a chalkboard, record common class likes and dislikes.

Activity 3 Beat the Clock

Divide the class into teams of three or four and give each team the same crossword puzzle to solve. After ten minutes, have the teams share results. You may want to award a prize (candy bar, extra credit points, stickers, etc.) to the winning team.

Activity 4 Me in a Bag

Give each student a paper lunch bag, four squares of paper, and a magic marker. Then, ask the students to draw something on each one of the squares that tells something about themselves and their interests. Students can either switch bags and guess the interests of their partners or share the contents of their own bag with the class.

Activity 5 Who or What Am I? (grades K–4)

Cut out pictures (famous people, animals, things) and tape a different picture on the back of each student. Then, give the students the opportunity to ask three people in the room for a hint to the identity of the person or thing in the picture. End the activity by bringing each child to the front of the room to guess the identity of the picture on his or her back.

Activity 6 Scavenger Hunt (grades K–4)

Divide the class into teams and give the teams a list of things that can be found in the classroom. Without moving from their seats, they must use their eyes only to find each item. Give the teams five minutes to find and record the locations on their answer sheets. For nonreaders, the answer sheets should be two vertical rows, one with a picture of the item to be located and the other with the picture of the location. Students should be directed to draw a line between the item and its location.

- Have an introductory activity. This is a great way for you to begin to identify and personalize your students. (See Suggestions for Introductory Activities.)

- Collect pertinent student data (grades 4–12). Use three-inch by five-inch index cards. They're easy to store and easy to transport. Save time by having the information you want on the cards already listed on the board (e.g., name, address, phone number, email address, emergency contact person and number, guidance counselor, homeroom). Handing cards out at the door as the students walk in also saves time. (See Model 4: Student Information Card.) To get this information from nonwriters, send the data form to the parents for completion along with their introductory letter. When asking for student information, only ask for information that you need and never ask for personal information that might be embarrassing for some students (e.g., What does your father do for a living? Can your parents read and write? Do you have your own bedroom?).

- Present a slide show of pictures of key personnel in the school (such as principal, vice principal, nurse, librarian, crossing guards, reading specialist, cafeteria staff, and bus drivers).

- Take Polaroid or digital photos of students to be used to personalize cubbies or assignment charts.

- Review procedures, routines, and expectations. For grades K–6, these should be displayed on a large poster in a prominent place in the room. For grades 7–12, these should be printed and distributed.

- Distribute and review the syllabus for the first month (grades 9–12).

- Distribute a student interest survey. (See Chapter 4, Model 23.)

- Assign jobs (grades K–5). Have students on a rotating basis be responsible for collecting homework, monitoring the hall, passing out paper, and other tasks.

- Distribute texts and cover books.

- Give students their first assignment.

Meeting expectations is integral to every aspect of teaching. From this day forward, you will be about the business of meeting expectation—expectations set for you by your building administrators, your immediate supervisors, your students and their parents, and, most important, expectations of competency and exemplary teaching that you will hopefully set for yourself.

Advice from the Field

The following is advice for new teachers garnered from a survey of 150 seasoned teachers with a total of 3,855 years of teaching experience.

- The more planning and busywork you can do before school begins, the more time you will have during the day and throughout the year to spend on what matters most—teaching children and working toward becoming an exemplary teacher!

- When setting up your grade book and game plan, include holidays and days your students will not be in your class.

- To avoid being distracted by students who arrive after class has started on the first day, it's a good idea to make up in advance five packets of everything you are going to distribute that day.

- Use your preparation period wisely. Have units done well in advance of their delivery. Make modifications immediately to lessons taught so that they will be ready for the next teaching year.

- Stay clear of faculty room gossip. It will always come back to haunt you.

- Make friends with the administrative and custodial staff. They're wonderful allies.

- Use the first few months of department meetings to quietly listen and learn. Seasoned teachers are quickly turned off by inexperienced teachers telling them what they should do.

- Develop a class website that parents and students who miss class can access to stay aware of class assignments and activities.

- To keep parents informed, use the school computer system to send a newsletter via mass mailing or send personal email messages to parents to apprise them of student problems or successes. Ask your administrator or supervisor if approval is needed in advance for mass mailings. Be sure to keep hard copies of everything you send.

References

Beach, R. (1993). *A teacher's introduction to reader-response theories.* Urbana, IL: National Council of Teachers of English.

Blanchowicz, C. L. Z. (1986). Making connections: Alternatives to vocabulary notebooks. *Journal of Reading, 29,* 643–649.

Clay, M. M. (1991). *Becoming literate: The construction of inner control.* Portsmouth, NH: Heinemann.

Clay, M. M. (1985). *The early detection of reading difficulties* (3rd ed.). Portsmouth, NH: Heinemann.

Fish, S. E. (1980). *Is there a text in this class?: The authority of interpretive communities.* Cambridge, MA: Harvard University Press.

Fisher, P. J. L., Blanchowicz, C. L. Z., & Smith, J. C. (1991). Vocabulary learning in literature discussion groups. In J. Zutell & S. McCormick (Eds.), *Learner factors/teaching factors: Issues in literacy research and instruction* (40th Yearbook of the National Reading Conference, pp. 201–209). Chicago: National Reading Conference.

Galda, L., Cullinan, B. E., & Strickland, D. S. (1993). *Language, literacy and the child.* Orlando, FL: Harcourt, Brace.

Gamoran, A. (1986). Instructional and institutional effect of ability grouping. *Sociology of Education, 59,* 185–198.

Gardner, H. (1983). *Frames of mind: The theory of multiple intelligences.* New York: Basic Books.

Goodlad, J. (1984). *A place called high school.* New York: McGraw-Hill.

Harkrader, M. A., & Moore, R. (1997). Literature preferences of fourth graders. *Reading Research and Instruction, 36*(4), 352–399.

Huck, C. S., & Kuhn, D. Y. (1968). *Children's literature in the elementary school.* New York: Holt, Rinehart and Winston.

Marzano, R. J., & Marzano, J. S. (1988). *A cluster approach to elementary vocabulary instruction.* Newark, DE: International Reading Association.

McCullough, M. A. (2002). Influences on how readers respond: An analysis of nationality, gender, text, teacher, and mode of response in four secondary school literature classrooms in the Netherlands and the United States. Unpublished doctoral dissertation, Rutgers University, New Brunswick, NJ.

Nagy, W., & Scott, J. (2001). Vocabulary processes. In M. L. Kamil, P. B. Mosenthal, P. D. Pearson, & R. Barr (Eds.), *Handbook of reading research* (Vol. 3, pp. 269–283). New York: Longman.

Piaget, J. (1995). *The essential Piaget.* H. G. & J. J. Voneche (Eds.). Northvale, NJ: Jason Aronson.

Rosenblatt, L. (1976). *Literature as exploration* (4th ed.). New York: Noble & Noble.

Skinner, B. F. (1974). *About behaviorism.* New York: Random House.

Strickland, D. S., Galda, L., & Cullinan, B. E. (2004). *Language arts: Learning and teaching.* Belmont, CA: Wadsworth/Thompson.

Vygotsky, L. S. (1986). *Thought and language.* Cambridge, MA: MIT Press.

Wheelock, A. (1992). *Crossing tracks: How untracking can save America's schools.* New York: New Press.

Welcome Letter to Students

Dear Sandra:

My name is Ms. Bartlett, and I am going to be your third-grade teacher this year. I have a lot of wonderful and exciting things planned for you and your classmates. We're going to be learning math, science, history, and geography. We're also going to be reading some fascinating books about children your age who live in other countries. You're even going to be given a personal pen pal so that you can write to a boy or girl in another country. I will share the other fun things we will be doing together when I meet you on September 15.

I am enclosing a special name tag for you to wear on the first day of school. I will be wearing the same name tag with my name on it so that you will be able to recognize me.

I'm looking forward to meeting you. Till then, have a good rest of the summer!

Sincerely,
Ms. Bartlett

Checklist for Substitute Teacher Folder

Include the following items in your substitute teacher folder:

_____ schedule and room assignments

_____ class roster and seating chart

_____ copy of homeroom and classroom procedures

_____ list of students in the class who require special attention and specific directions for accommodating those needs

_____ list of classroom monitors

_____ bus assignments and procedures

_____ lesson plans with clear and specific directions (Typically five days of plans are required, with all assignments photocopied in advance for the substitute.)

_____ map of the school and copy of the school calendar

_____ list of key personnel (principal, nurse, guidance staff, Child Study Team, disciplinarian, etc.) and where they can be located

_____ discipline report form

_____ hall passes

_____ list of emergency procedures

_____ substitute teacher evaluation form (See Model 3: Substitute Teacher Classroom Evaluation Form.)

Substitute Teacher Classroom Evaluation Form

Thank you for taking charge of my class for the day. It's important to me that my class runs smoothly in my absence. Therefore, I would appreciate your taking a few minutes to share with me your impressions of the day.

Thank you,
Ms. Bartlett

Name: _____ Date: _____

Class: _____

1. Did you find the Substitute Folder helpful?   Yes ___ No ___

2. Were the lesson plans complete and easy to follow?   Yes ___ No ___

3. Did you have the materials, texts, and equipment needed to
    teach the lesson?   Yes ___ No ___
    If not, what was missing? _____

4. Did any interruptions prevent the lesson from being completed?   Yes ___ No ___
    If so, please explain. _____
    _____

5. Were the students cooperative and well behaved?   Yes ___ No ___
    If not, please explain. _____
    _____

6. Please identify the students who were problematic. _____
    _____

7. Please identify the students who were particularly helpful. _____
    _____

8. What did you enjoy most about your day? _____
    _____

    Comments and suggestions for improvement: _____
    _____
    _____

Student Information Card

Information Card (Front)

Name_____ Homeroom_____

Student ID number_____

Address _____

Telephone number _____

Email address _____

Guidance counselor_____

Emergency contact person_____ Phone number_____

Information Card (Back)

Period	Room	Teacher	Subject	M	T	W	Th	F
1	B12	Johnson	English 1	X	X	X	X	X
2	C18	Jacks	Music		X		X	
3	GYM	Anderson	PE	X	X	X	X	X

Classroom Management

The Importance of Good Classroom Management

Classroom management is important for three very good reasons. One, a well-managed classroom means the difference between loving your job or leaving at the end of each day feeling defeated and depressed; two, a well-managed classroom maximizes your instructional time and sets the stage for you to be able to teach effectively; and three, a well-managed classroom speaks volumes when it comes to being asked to return the following year. No matter how brilliant you may be or how strong your credentials, if you can't manage your classroom, you probably

will not be asked back. Teachers and administrators may disagree about many things, but on the importance of classroom management, they are in total agreement. Professionals in the field come to understand very quickly that effective teaching and learning can only happen in a well-managed classroom.

What makes classroom management so important is that it encompasses so many facets of a teacher's day. At one time, the concept of classroom management referred to classroom decorum and discipline. This definition has been expanded over time to include how teachers organize and manage instruction; the physical layout of the classroom; daily classroom procedures and operations; instructional and noninstructional time; texts, equipment, and support materials; and, in some cases, paraprofessional assignments.

*I*dentifying Your Management Needs

Becoming an effective classroom manager, like everything else, happens over time and requires planning that is both strategic and reflective. The most successful teachers have a clearly defined management plan in place, which they review and modify each year, prior to entering the classroom.

Because teachers are individuals with different tolerances, expectations, personalities, and ways of interacting with people, there is no one absolute management system that works for everybody. Therefore, as a new teacher, you need to develop a system for managing your classroom that works best for you. A good way to approach this is with a reflective self-assessment to identify the optimal conditions (both physical and behavioral) under which you anticipate you can teach with a high degree of effectiveness. Knowing in advance exactly what will make you successful will allow you to plan for success instead of just hoping that it happens. Begin your self-assessment by listing your needs:

- *Environmental needs* (e.g., a round table for conferencing, ample storage area, filing cabinets)

- *Instructional needs* (daily newspapers, computers, supplemental texts, state and national standards, etc.)

- *Student behavioral needs* (list of rules; for example, students need to [1] be on time, [2] follow directions, [3] be respectful, [4] complete homework assignments)

- *Personal needs* (e.g., a break every two hours, released time for doctor's appointments, a room with air conditioning)

- *Professional needs* (released time to attend graduate school, registration fees for professional conferences, ongoing mentoring, etc.)

Note: This assessment is specific to you and must support your personal comfort level. It stands to reason that if you are not comfortable in your environment, you will be less capable of managing it effectively. Once you have identified your needs, you can begin to explore possible ways to meet your needs before you actually begin teaching.

Managing Instructional Space

Classroom design depends largely on the physical size of the room as well as the size and the amount of furniture and equipment that you need to accommodate within that space. Regardless of how much or how little you have, you need to consider the following when organizing your classroom:

1. When organizing the student seating, make sure that you have an unobstructed view of *all* of the students at *all* times.

2. Arrange seating so that all of the students have a comfortable view of you. Students become distracted and frustrated when they have to constantly shift in their seats or crane their necks to see what is happening.

3. For safety, make sure that both you and the students can move freely between the desks or tables.

4. Make sure students can easily exit the room in an emergency. (The doorway should be clear at all times, and the window ledges should be able to be easily cleared.)

Note: Arranging desks and equipment is only a part of managing classroom space. The physical appearance of the room is equally important. It sends a message to everyone who enters the room about your feelings about the importance of the space and the things that go on within it. Plants, pictures, posters, and student artwork will make the room more interesting and inviting to everyone, including yourself.

Organizing Space for Instruction

For optimal learning, arrange student seating within the classroom to support your instructional activity.

- *Rows* are good for any activity that requires that you have the students' undivided attention (during direct instruction, modeling, testing, etc.). Because rows limit students' line of vision, they are not an optimal design for class discussions.

- A *large circle* provides a clear line of vision between students and is good for activities in which you want students to interact with each other (during performances, exhibitions, demonstrations, class discussions, or meetings).

- *Small groups* of three to four students provide for optimal participation because they afford everyone the opportunity and time to speak. For this reason, they are ideal for small-group discussions and projects.

Note: Changing the classroom design is a winning teaching strategy. It adds interest and stimulates participation, while it accommodates and supports the lesson objectives. However, like everything else in teaching, for this strategy to be effective, it needs to be planned. To save time and avoid confusion, have the room set up in the formation that supports your teaching for the day *prior* to the students' entering the room. If you want them to sit in designated seats, photocopy a seating chart and hand it out as the students enter the room. This way they can go directly to their seats so that you can begin class on time.

Organizing Space for K–5

In addition to considering how the desks will be organized for instruction, K–5 teachers who support their teaching with literacy centers must also consider how to organize these centers within the classroom (see Chapter 5). Typically, these centers are set up around the perimeter of the room. Because many teachers do not have a large enough room to accommodate multiple learning centers, they need to *create* space for students to work. Keep in mind that literacy centers are places where students go to practice the skills and concepts taught in class and that the centers change throughout the school year as the lessons and units change. You don't always need a lot of space to have productive literacy centers. The following suggestions may help you create literacy centers with very little space:

- Put a tablecloth for students to sit on, books, materials, and directions into a book bag for an instant literacy center.

- Attach metallic letters or numbers to the side of a metal filing cabinet for a literacy center where students can practice their math or word skills.

- Fill a large cookie tin or colorful gift bag with flashcards and provide large placemats or carpet squares for students to sit on, and you have a literacy center.

- Place a small blanket or carpet squares, tape recorders, headsets, and audiotapes next to an outlet to create a listening center.

- Empty a low cabinet and put in it the materials needed, directions, and a sectioned piece of colorful material for students to sit on, and you have a literacy center.

- Provide an overhead projector, transparencies, and oil pens to create a literacy center where students can collaborate to compose a story or make a puzzle or word game they can share with the class.

- Fill a plastic crate with interesting books and a blanket for students to sit on, and you have a literacy center.

- Cover a part of a wall or the back of a closet door with construction paper and give students words printed on cards backed with double-sided tape, and you have a literacy center where students can practice grammar and sentence construction.

Note: You don't need a lot of space to have meaningful literacy centers. You just need to look at the space that you have differently. Children are perfectly happy sitting on the floor, as long as they have something that they can sit on that defines their individual space (such as a carpet square, a placemat, a segment of a piece of material, a blanket, or a tablecloth that has been sectioned with a magic marker or masking tape, etc.).

Managing the Daily Operations of Your Classroom

Being well organized saves time, eliminates stress, and keeps students focused. In addition, a well-organized classroom makes students feel safe, comfortable, and secure. Knowing what to do and when and how to do it eliminates confusion and the possibility of error, which inevitably results in frustration and contention. Here are some helpful suggestions.

For Grades K–5

- Create and post a daily or weekly schedule of activities, and assign time frames to the activities to help students learn how to manage their own time.

- Assign monitors for classroom duties such as watering the plants, shutting down computers, collecting assignments, and distributing class work. (See Model 5: Duty Management System: Helping Hands.)

- Create guidelines and procedures for bathroom breaks, handing in class assignments and homework, moving between classes, participating in class discussions, and getting your attention when you are working with other students. (See Model 6: Classroom Procedures for K–5.)

- Identify for students where materials are to be stored and the procedure for putting things away.

- Hang a poster of behavior expectations in the front of the room and review it frequently. (See Model 7: Behavior Expectations for K–6.)

- Provide written instructions and review directions and performance expectations at the beginning of each assignment.

- Provide models for all student assignments so that they have a clear understanding of what they are expected to do.

- Provide activities for students to choose from during free time.

- Clarify for students how to get extra help.

- Print in-class and homework assignments on the board each morning before class and make reviewing the assignments a part of your daily routine.

- Provide an opportunity for students to have input into classroom organization, either with a suggestion or comment box or during a scheduled class meeting.

For Grades 6–12

- Provide students with a syllabus at the beginning of each unit, identifying goals, expectations, assignments, and due dates.

- Clarify for students how the class will be run. For example, you may want to begin each class with an objective quiz, which will be followed by student discussions in small response groups. If you change formats, alert the students the day before and provide them with detailed instructions. If the change requires a change in seating, provide a seating chart to save valuable class time the next day.

- Provide models and scoring rubrics with each assignment so that students will have a clear understanding of what they are expected to do before they begin the task.

- Provide students with a written explanation of the grading procedures.

- Provide students with a printed summary of their grades at the end of each quarter.

- Review policies regarding tardiness and absenteeism, class trips, and so on.

- Clarify behavior expectations. (See Model 8: Classroom Expectations for 6–12.)

- Clarify the guidelines for fire drills, lavatory breaks, makeup work, and so on.

- Identify a specific time and place you will be available for extra help. Provide a sign-up sheet with designated times so that students won't be wasting valuable time waiting for a conference.

- Provide an opportunity for students to express their opinions and make suggestions regarding classroom activities and procedures. This could be done by providing a suggestion or comment box, by holding an informal class meeting, or by having students comment in their journals.

$\mathcal{M}$anaging Time and Instruction

Managing time and instruction, two topics that are interrelated and integral to good classroom management, are discussed in context in Chapter 3, "Planning for Success."

$\mathcal{M}$anaging Paraprofessionals

A survey of chief school officers conducted in 1999 by the National Resource Center for Paraprofessionals indicated the existence of more than 500,000 full-time paraeducator positions in all content area programs in schools throughout the United States (Pickett, 1999). This number continues to increase significantly as schools turn to paraprofessionals to support academic teachers and their schools' federal mandate to leave no child behind. Although schools have employed teacher aides for over forty years, what has changed markedly is the services these men and women provide each day to support the classroom teacher. No longer limited to keeping records, preparing materials, maintaining equipment, or monitoring students in lunchrooms, hallways, or lavatories, teacher aides now are seen as paraprofessionals who participate in the learning process and in the delivery of direct services to learners and their parents (Moshoyannis, Pickett, & Granick, 1999). Today, paraprofessionals instruct learners in small and large groups, assist with assessment activities, administer standardized tests, and document learner performance (Moshoyannis et al., 1999; Pickett, 1999).

Should a paraprofessional be assigned to work with you, keep in mind that you are the primary teacher in the classroom. Paraprofessionals are there to assist and support teachers. They are not intended, nor are they qualified, to develop curriculum and instruction or to be the sole implementer of an instructional program. In addition, keep in mind that not all schools have prerequisites for paraeducators that include coursework in classroom management or in teaching and learning. It is important that you find out what the school policy is and what the academic preparation of your assistant is before making decisions about how you want the paraprofessional to support you and your teaching. If paraprofessionals in your

Suggestions for Managing Paraprofessionals

1. Meet with your paraprofessional prior to the opening of school to make decisions about how the paraprofessional's time will be spent. Prior to this meeting, list the roles, duties, and responsibilities you would like the paraprofessional to have in your classroom and ask that the paraprofessional bring a similar list to the meeting. This way, you will both have a clear vision of each other's expectations as well as talking points, which you can use to negotiate a common understanding.

2. Following the meeting, provide the paraprofessional with a written description, explicitly detailing the roles, duties, and responsibilities that you have agreed on. Copies of this description should also be given to your supervisor and building administrator to ensure that everyone has a common understanding.

3. Provide the paraprofessional with copies of your lesson plans in advance so that he or she can prepare. Share any difficulties you foresee students having and discuss the paraprofessional's role in resolving the problems.

4. Discuss with the paraprofessional your philosophy about classroom decorum and discipline and provide a copy of your behavior-management plan.

5. Meet at least once a week with your paraprofessional to ensure that you agree on your goals and expectations. It's important to designate a specific time each week for this meeting and to include it in your weekly agenda to ensure that the meeting does, indeed, take place.

6. Provide the paraprofessional with constructive evaluations of his or her work. Unless you have supervisory credentials and authorization from your school, these evaluations should be handled as informal discussions, identifying both strengths and weaknesses. It is important that if something needs to be remediated, you offer specific suggestions for doing so.

7. Provide training for your paraprofessional. For example, if you want that person to lead the class in a book walk, you need to provide instruction clarifying exactly how to do a book walk, or if you see a professional conference or a course that would be beneficial, ask your supervisor or administrator to arrange for your paraprofessional to attend.

8. Always treat your paraprofessional as a professional. Be sure to make requests, not dictate orders. Don't hesitate to solicit his or her opinions and suggestions. Although the person may not be degreed, many paraprofessionals have years of valuable experience in the classroom that you could use to enhance your teaching and classroom management skills.

Defining Paraprofessional Duties and Responsibilities

When meeting with your paraprofessional to identify duties and responsibilities, you may want to consider the following:

Instructional Duties and Responsibilities	Noninstructional Duties and Responsibilities
Conduct book walks and read-alouds.	Manage record keeping (attendance, grades, hall passes, etc.).
Assist students with research and projects.	
Help students edit their work.	Manage equipment.
Respond to student questions.	Monitor students in the lavatory, hallways, and lunchrooms.
	Prepare materials (photocopy, collate, organize, etc.).
Document student learning using rubrics.	Set up literacy centers.
Tutor students individually and in small groups.	Attend to students who have special needs.
Research and provide background information on given topics.	Attend to students who are disruptive.
	Manage classroom organization and clean-up.
Listen to and monitor children as they practice skills.	Organize and attend class functions and trips.
Ask probing questions that will assist student understanding of texts.	Order materials requested by the teacher.
	Escort students to the office, library, gym, pull-out classrooms.
Assist with the administration of tests.	
Help students select activities once they have completed their work.	Prepare bulletin boards and student work displays.
Monitor and support student work in literacy centers.	Monitor and manage students' makeup work.
	Help monitor students during schoolwide drills.
Participate in parent-teacher conferences.	
Participate in Child Study Team meetings.	

school district have a negotiated contract that outlines the parameters of their work assignments, be sure to review the parameters before you ask a paraprofessional to do something that would be in violation of the contract.

Note: As you are working with your paraprofessional to define and establish the expectations and boundaries of your relationship, keep in mind that the ultimate goal is to create a positive work environment for you, your paraprofessional, and the students you both serve. This can best be accomplished through clearly defined roles, mutual respect, and a strong commitment to the educational process.

 # Managing Behavior

Identifying Your Management Style

Before you begin to develop your personal classroom management plan, you need to consider some important issues. One very important issue is how you plan to interact with your class. Inexperienced teachers often make the mistake of using strategies that intimidate and control student behavior. They clearly do not understand the monumental difference between controlling a class and managing a class. Nor do they understand the ramifications of opting for control. Control is used to obtain compliance and blind obedience and is easily accomplished with the use of threats and intimidation, which most often are executed with the basic *if–then* declarative statement. Sometimes these threats invoke the wrath of a higher authority: "If you don't sit down, I'm going to send you to the office" or "If you don't stop talking, I'm going to call your parents." Sometimes these threats involve the possibility of punishment: "If you get out of your seat one more time, you're not going on the field trip tomorrow" or "If I have to speak to you again, I'm deducting points from your grade." Sometimes these threats are veiled in questions that give the illusion that the student has a choice: "Remember what happened the last time you didn't finish your work?" or "Do I have to give you more work to keep you quiet?" Regardless of how these threats are presented, they are the least effective way to manage a classroom. Threats always set up an adversarial relationship between the student and the teacher, one in which the teacher may appear to win; however, the win is a hollow victory. You may get the child to comply, but the child, being human, will respond to the threat by being upset or angry. In either case, your student will not be in the frame of mind necessary to learn, which is, after all, your primary objective as a teacher.

A more effective way to manage your class is with challenging lessons that are interesting, active, and student-centered. Children who are actively engaged in their own learning are less likely to create problems. You will find that problems erupt quickly when children are bored or frustrated. Equally important, students need to feel successful. No one wants to feel like a failure, no matter what the age. If you see that a student is having difficulty, address the issue immediately *before* it becomes a failure. Having ongoing assessments will quickly alert you to problems in student learning so that you can give the student extra help and avoid unnecessary failure. (See Chapter 4 for suggestions.) This will also validate for your students that you care about them and about their learning, something all students, whether they will admit it or not, want from their teachers. The bottom line is success feels good, and children who feel good about themselves will want to come to your class every day and they'll want to please you and themselves by completing their work and by being a valued member of the class.

Developing a Behavior Management Plan

Like knowing what will make you successful, knowing what will impede your success is equally important. A vital step in this developmental process, then, should be to identify possible student behaviors that you think will be deterrents to your success. Once you have identified potential problems, begin to organize your personal management plan in three parts. Under Part 1, identify those conditions that would interfere with your ability to be an effective teacher. No condition should be considered too trivial to make this list. Teachers often find that it's the little things that are most irritating and distracting to their teaching. Under Part 2, identify what measures you could take to prevent the interference. You will find that many problems can be avoided or at least minimized by simply putting in place preventive measures at the onset of the class. Finally, under Part 3, identify what action you would take should the preventive measure not work. See Table 2.1 for a sample behavior management plan.

It's important to remember that a behavior management plan is a work in progress. You will need to revisit and reevaluate your plan frequently to identify procedures that worked well for you and to modify those that did not. Understand that it will take several years to shape your plan into a reliable document that you can refer to with confidence.

Teaching Good Behavior

At the beginning of the school year, in addition to giving students classroom procedures and guidelines, it's a good idea to give them actual training in good classroom conduct. You can't always assume that children understand what good classroom conduct is. Nor can you assume that they have a repertoire of behavioral alternatives. Having student-centered lessons dedicated to behavior gives

Table 2.1 **Behavior Management Plan**

Undesirable Conditions	Preventive Measure	Corrective Measure
Students running around room	1. Give students expectation of walking on the first day and clarify the danger to students and others. 2. Verbally reinforce behavior expectations daily at the beginning of class until learned.	*First offense:* Correct verbally with explanation. *Second offense:* Time out. *Third offense:* Behavior conference with student, self-assessment, and monitoring.
Students interrupting (calling out inappropriately)	1. Give students expectation of not interrupting on the first day. 2. Verbally reinforce behavior expectations daily at the beginning of class until learned. 3. Model behavior.	*First offense:* When student calls out, reiterate the rule with explanation and call on someone else for the response. *Second offense:* Behavior conference. *Third offense:* Time out and call parent.
Students bullying other students (verbally, nonverbally, physically)	1. Show film on bullying on second day of class and discuss the seriousness of bullying. 2. Model respectful behavior.	*First offense:* Detention, behavior conference, and call home. *Second offense:* Send to principal's office.
Students not staying on task	1. Check that the assignment is not too difficult and that students have the skills in place to be successful. 2. Make sure directions are complete and understandable. 3. Check student records to identify students who may have problems in this area and monitor them as they are doing the assignment to help them stay on task.	*First offense:* Conference with student to determine the source of the problem. *Second offense:* Behavior conference, student self-assessment, and monitoring. *Third offense:* Contact guidance counselor for suggestions and support.

Undesirable Conditions	Preventive Measure	Corrective Measure
Students coming to class unprepared	1. Discuss the importance of coming to class prepared on the first day. 2. Require students to keep a homework to-do list in the front of their notebooks. 3. Inform parents that students will be receiving nightly assignments and ask for their assistance in checking that they are done. 4. Come to class prepared every day.	*First offense:* Conference with student to see if there is a problem. *Second offense:* Contact parent or guidance counselor for suggestions and support. *Third offense:* Detention.
Students not paying attention	1. Do not begin speaking until everyone is paying attention. 2. Stand by students who tend to not pay attention. 3. Check student records to identify students who have had this problem in the past and make sure you have their attention before beginning.	*First offense:* Conference with student. Give student personal cue that could be used to redirect attention. *Second offense:* Contact guidance counselor for suggestions and support to help student focus. *Third offense:* Notify parents of the problem.
Students destroying property	1. Clarify expectation for respect of property on the first day. 2. Model respect for student property.	*First offense:* Send to principal's office and notify parents.
Students coming to class late	1. Discuss expectation on the first day. 2. Always be on time and start class on time every day.	*First offense:* Verbal warning. *Second offense:* Behavior conference. *Third offense:* Detention, contact guidance office and parents.
Students refusing to participate	1. Ensure students understand the rationale and benefits of the assignment and for participating. 2. Sit students next to students who will participate. 3. Give students a specific task or job.	*First offense:* Conference to determine why the student does not want to participate. Provide student with strategies for participation. *Second offense:* Joint conference with guidance counselor. *Third offense:* Parent conference.
Students who do not work cooperatively in groups	1. Assign everyone in the group a specific task.	*First offense:* Conference and mentor student and provide cooperative learning strategies.

students an opportunity to think about behavior and learn new ways of conducting themselves while at school. Your lessons could include the following:

1. Lead a class discussion about behavior, beginning each segment of the discussion with "What should a student do if . . . ?"

2. Give students scenarios and ask them in small groups to discuss how the student behaving badly could solve his or her problem in a more productive way.

3. Give groups of students scenarios and ask them to write and act out two skits, one showing a negative behavior and the other, an alternative way to behave.

4. Give students a list of problems. Next to each problem, provide a negative strategy for dealing with the problem and ask them to think of a more appropriate alternative behavior.

5. Invite a guest speaker or a panel of speakers who are authorities on behavior (school psychologist, social worker, local psychiatrist) to come into your high school class to discuss behavior and why people behave the way they do.

Correcting Behavior Problems

Very often, you can resolve a minor problem such as inappropriate talking by merely moving toward and standing next to the offender, or standing quietly waiting for the class's attention, or using cues such as raising the volume of your voice or holding your hand above your head. Sometimes, a simple "May I please have your attention?" is enough to bring the class to order without resorting to a disciplinary action. Intuitive students will actually observe you modeling good behavior and follow suit. Other times, however, you will have to take more direct action. Before you do, make sure that the corrective measure is appropriate for the offense. Talking in class, for example, merits a less extreme corrective measure than does verbally attacking another student. Take time to consider what will be minor and major offenses in your class and what corrective measures you are going to attach to each offense. The following are some options to consider for minor offenses.

■ *Assign Time Outs.* Having a private area in the classroom where children can be sent to "cool off" is particularly effective for students who have been managed with time outs at home. Students should be required to be reflective during time out. A condition of leaving time out should be either a verbal or written acknowledgment of the offense and possible alternative ways the student could have handled the situation.

- *Enter into a Behavioral Contract with the Student.* This strategy, which requires that the teacher and student meet and negotiate behavior, is an effective way to have students take responsibility for their own actions. The teacher and student agree on the desired behavioral outcomes and time lines as well as the rewards and penalties for meeting or failing to meet the contractual obligations.

- *Change Classroom Seating.* Sometimes, just rearranging the seats in the classroom, separating students who negatively influence each other, is an easy resolution to discipline problems.

- *Have Offenders Self-Monitor.* This strategy engages students in monitoring and correcting their own behavior. The teacher meets with the student regularly to review and discuss the student's self-monitoring record and to explore alternative ways of managing the problems that led to the offender's undesirable behavior. (See Model 9: Student Self-Monitoring Record.)

- *Send the Students to Their Guidance Counselors for Behavioral Counseling.* This is an appropriate strategy for students who need more time and more in-depth counseling than you are able to give.

- *Hold Class Meetings.* This is a wonderful way to have the members of the class participate in managing classroom decorum and discipline. Giving students the opportunity to engage in an open dialogue regarding appropriate behavior and penalties empowers them by giving a sense of control and a vested interest in conforming to the guidelines they helped develop.

- *Acknowledge Good Behavior.* Everyone enjoys recognition and praise. Acknowledging students individually for their good behavior is possibly one of the simplest and most effective ways of managing classroom discipline.

There may be times, however, when these remedial strategies do not work. When that happens, you need to resort to more punitive measures. *Note:* Punishment is only in order when you have exhausted *all* other options.

Punitive Measures

- Take away school privileges such as going on a class trip or participating in sports or after-school activities. Participating in activities is not, as some students think, a right; it is a privilege that must be earned with good grades and good behavior.

- Assign detention after school.

- Send students to in-school detention or suspension.

- Have the student removed from the classroom until a joint conference is held with the parents, student, and school administrator.

- Send the student to the principal's office. Although necessary at times, it should be your last option.

There are three important things to remember about punishment. (1) The goal of punishment should be to correct behavior. Whatever the punishment, it should be temporary: students should know that they have the opportunity to regain their privileges with remediated behavior. (2) Academic work should NEVER be used as punishment. Punishing students by having them read an extra book or by writing an essay, for example, sends the wrong message. We want students to see academics as fun and rewarding, not punitive. (3) Whatever choices you make regarding punishment, make sure they are consistent, fair, and within the framework of your school's policy.

Handling Severe Discipline Problems

In a perfect world, there would be no severe behavior problems, but unfortunately, that's not the world teachers live in. At one time or another, every teacher, regardless of experience, encounters discipline problems that cannot be handled with mediation. It is important to be prepared. Read the discipline code and procedures *before* you enter the classroom for the first time. Find out who is in charge of discipline in your school and how you contact that person should the need arise. Don't wait until you have a volatile situation in your class to find out what you should do or who you should contact. For your safety and the safety of your students, you need to have an action plan in place for major infractions. Discuss this plan with your supervisor and the person who is in charge of discipline to ensure you are all in agreement.

Dealing with Students Who Are Out of Control

There may be times when you might encounter a student who is either belligerent or out of control. When this happens, an immediate response is necessary. Most important, you need to remain calm. A screaming teacher exacerbates the situation and gives the other students the impression that the teacher is also out of control. What you want to do first is try to isolate the student who is causing the disturbance in a nonconfrontational way. This can usually be accomplished by asking the student to step outside the door, which will give you the opportunity to get the student calmed down so that you can find out what happened and begin working on a resolution to the problem. If the child refuses to comply, you will need to call the office for assistance. Even if the problem is resolved, it is important that you follow up on the incident. Approach the student, either later in the day or the next day, to discuss what happened and to explore alternate strategies that the student could have used to resolve the problem that led to the disturbance. Sometimes students act out because they need help and they don't know how to ask for it. An unfortunate reality is that you will probably have students at one time or another who are living in abusive or destructive environments over which they have no control. In these cases, acting out is often a cry for help. If the student continues to present problems, you need to find out why. The guidance office and the principal's office are two good places to start to see if a history of discipline problems exists. You should also consult the Child Study Team and the school nurse to see if a medical problem or learning disability may be causing the child to act out. Talking with other teachers who have had the student will also give you valuable insights and possible strategies for handling future problems. You could also ask your department supervisor for advice. Once you have an understanding of the student's background, you need to contact the parents and ask them to come in for a conference, which should be attended by all the interested parties. For example, depending on the problem, the interested parties could include the student's guidance counselor, the discipline officer, the nurse, or the school psychologist. The student should also be invited to participate in this meeting. The important thing to remember is that you are not expected to resolve severe discipline problems on your own. You are, however, expected to be proactive and ask for help when you need it.

Rewarding Good Performance and Behavior

Too often, teachers are so busy with the demands of the job that they limit their teaching to correcting poor student behavior and performance. While it is important to make corrections, it is equally important to remember to let students know when they are doing something right. These rewards can come in different shapes and forms. Simple forms of acknowledgment such as applause, smiles, and high fives are easy to distribute and fun to give and to receive. Here are some other suggestions for showing your appreciation and approval.

For Grades K–6

1. Give students tokens and invite them to deposit one in a container at the front of the class each time they do or say something that deserves recognition. When the container is full, treat the class to a popcorn or an ice-cream party.

2. Send Performance Certificates home once a week to applaud good work or behavior.

3. Don't limit your phone calls to parents to those dealing with problems. Call them with good news and let them share in the joy of their child's success.

4. Give out Student of the Week awards and make sure everyone makes the list.

5. Reward the class with a class trip. Trips don't always have to be someplace special. A picnic on the school grounds can be just as much fun.

6. Give the class a homework-free pass for the weekend.

7. Place decorative stickers and stamps on work, which is always welcome.

For Grades 7–12

1. Make a special effort to see the student outside of class to compliment his or her work or behavior.

2. Send a special progress report home or call parents directly to share good news.

3. Reward the class with a special trip, guest speaker, or pizza party at the end of the quarter.

4. Ask students' permission to use their work as models for other students.

5. Make a point of having a conversation with your students about something other than class work. Find out what your students' interests are and make a point of showing your interest in them.

6. Reward the class for good work during the week with a homework-free weekend.

7. When talking to students about their work, remember to include compliments as well as criticisms. Whenever possible, try to express criticisms in the form of corrective suggestions. If you identify weaknesses in red ink, try highlighting strengths in blue or green so that students can see and take pride in the positives in their work.

Managing English Language Learners

1. Be sensitive to the possibility of cross-cultural miscommunications. Students may be responding to what they think you want them to do, which may not be the same as what you intend for them to do. An easy way to address this issue is by simply asking them to explain what they think the assignment is before

they begin. It's always a good idea to be prepared to give students directions in a variety of ways (verbal and visual) until you see that they understand.

2. Understand that communicating in a different language is tiring. After a period of time, your students may lose focus, not out of disinterest but out of exhaustion. These students may need more frequent breaks or some quiet downtime to regroup.

3. Engage your students in meaningful activities. Like all students, busy students are less likely to present problems. Have a host of planned activities at your fingertips that will promote their English language development.

4. Make sure that your language, tone, facial expressions, and gestures match the message you are communicating. Students with limited language proficiency depend on nonverbal cues to understand. They may misinterpret *loud* for *reprimanding* or a *rushed* expression for *annoyance* and become upset and then shut down.

5. Be aware that not understanding can lead to frustration, which can, in turn, cause English language learners to act out or shut down. When you see students becoming frustrated, approach them immediately and try to help them overcome whatever it is that is causing them difficulties.

 ## Advice from the Field

- Always enter your classroom with a smile. Everyone responds favorably to a smile and a warm welcome. Your students are no exception.

- Introduce classroom and behavior management practices the first day of class and reinforce daily for at least the first two weeks of classes to ensure students have a clear understanding of how they will be operating for the remainder of the year.

- Always treat your students with respect. Always say "please" and "thank you" and expect your students to do the same. A good rule of thumb is to treat your students as you would like your own children to be treated.

- Always be clear. Say what you mean and mean what you say. If you want your students to sit down, do not ask them, "Do you want to take a seat?" With this question, you're inviting a response that most likely will be "no," rather than what you really want.

- Always be consistent. Students feel comfortable when they know what to expect.

- Always take an interest in your students. Make your students feel they are important. Ask about their activities outside the classroom. Notice when they're absent. Give them compliments.

- Always begin the term by assigning seats. One, this creates a degree of comfort for children by eliminating the "sit by me" syndrome that for popular students is a natural part of their day, but for the unpopular students never is; and, two, it helps you learn names quickly and expedites taking attendance.

- Always begin your class on time and insist that students arrive on time. This sends an immediate message to your students that what is going to be happening that day is important, and there's no time to be wasted.

- Always have something planned that contributes meaningfully to student learning. You can be sure that a free period or a movie that is unrelated to what is being learned will be interpreted as you not having anything planned. If you expect your students to come to class prepared, you must set the example by doing the same.

- Always make your expectations, both academic and behavioral, clear on the first day of class.

- Always explain the rationale for each expectation. If you don't have a better reason than "because I say so," it's a good idea to drop the expectation. Students, regardless of age, who understand why they are being asked to do something are more likely to comply if they see the wisdom in the request.

- Always be supportive. If you tell children they *can*, they *will*. Keep raising the bar and challenge your students to reach it. If students respect you, they will rise to the level of your expectations.

- Always applaud good work and good behavior.

- Don't scream. It's ineffective and it makes you look ugly.

- Don't ever put your hands on your students. Throwing objects at or near students is also a big no-no.

- Don't invade your students' space unless invited. Keep a professional distance. Unless there is a problem, stay out of their personal business.

- Don't be rude or sarcastic. Remember, you're the role model and students are quick to mimic what they see.

- Don't humiliate students. Don't post or read grades out loud. Don't call on students who you know don't know the answer. Don't make snide comments when they are wrong.

- Don't allow your students to harass other students. Never tolerate rude comments, snickers, laughs, or inappropriate eye rolling when another student is participating.

- Don't put yourself on a pedestal. If you make a mistake, admit it and move on.

- Don't be inflexible. There's often more than one way to do something. Applaud students who think out of the box instead of doing things exclusively "your way."

- Don't negotiate discipline. Make consequences clear on the first day and then stick to them.

- Don't allow yourself to say "If you do this one more time . . ." because that tells the student that he or she can commit the offense one more time.

- Don't try to be like your students. If you want to be respected, you have to command respect. Dress, act, and speak like an adult if you want to be treated like one. Remember: You can be with them but not of them.

- Don't be alone with students in your classroom without being clearly visible from a door, which should *always* be open. This invites misunderstandings that can lead to problems in and outside the classroom. Students, regardless of age, are impressionable and can easily misread your interest in them. The open door sends a clear message that your meeting is strictly professional. If you are going to be working with students after school, it's best to let someone in the office know.

- Don't be afraid to show that you have a sense of humor. Teaching is fun. Don't be afraid to show your students that you enjoy being with them and that teaching and learning gives you great pleasure.

Remember that your students have the same feelings you do, and they, like you, have good days and bad days. Respect their feelings. Give them space when they need it and support when they ask for it. Make your classroom a safe, comfortable, inviting place to be. If you think of your students as your guests and your classroom as a party where you're serving a plethora of academic goodies, you will find your classroom a pleasure and a place that you can easily manage.

Additional Resources

Bianco, A. (2002). *One-minute discipline: Classroom management strategies that work.* San Francisco: Jossey-Bass, Inc.

Cangelosi, J. S. (2000). *Classroom management strategies.* New York: Wiley.

Emmer, E. T., Evertson, C. M., & Worsham, M. E. (2000). *Classroom management for secondary teachers.* Boston: Allyn & Bacon.

Evertson, C. M., Emmer, E. T., & Worsham, M. E. (2000). *Classroom management for elementary teachers.* Boston: Allyn & Bacon.

Mackenzie, R. J. (2003). *Setting limits in the classroom: How to move beyond the dance of discipline in today's classroom.* New York: Random House.

Payne, Ruby K. (2003). *A framework for understanding poverty.* Highlands, TX: Aha! Process Inc.

Online Resources

Answers.com—www.answers.com/topic/classroom-management
4 Faculty—www.4faculty.org
Pro Teacher—www.proteacher.com
Electronic Learning Community—www.pgcps.org/~elec/gameplan.htm

References

Moshoyannis, T., Pickett, A. L., & Granick, L. (1999). *The evolving roles of education/training needs of teacher and paraprofessional teams in New York City Public Schools.* New York: Paraprofessional Academy, Center for Advanced Study in Education, Graduate Center, City University of New York.

Pickett, A. L. (1999). *Strengthening and supporting teacher and paraeducator teams: Guidelines for paraeducator roles, supervision, and preparation.* New York National Resource Center for Paraprofessionals in Education and Related Services, Center for Advanced Study in Education, Graduate Center, City University of New York.

Duty Management System: Helping Hands

Assignment	Responsibilities	Helpers
Teacher's Assistants	Pass out and collect papers, books, and materials.	Alan, Paula
Line Leader	Leads the line when students pass between classes.	Fred
Line Ender	Ends the line and ensures no one gets lost.	Alison
Door Holder	Holds door when class is coming and going.	Phileppe
Lavatory Monitor	Monitors behavior in boy's room and reports problems to teacher.	Richard
Lavatory Monitor	Monitors behavior in girl's room and reports problems to teacher.	Morgan
Refuse Collector	Passes trash can through the room at the end of the day.	Andrea
Librarian	Checks books in and out of class library during free time.	Ling
Horticulturalist	Waters the plants on Monday morning.	Roberto
Board Cleaner	Erases the blackboard at the end of the day.	William
Ichthyologist	Feeds the fish every morning.	Cassandra
Errand Runner	Runs errands for teacher.	Adam
Desk Monitor	Checks desks at the end of the day to ensure they are in place and have no writing on them.	Ryan
Time Keeper	Alerts teacher when it is time to clean up for the day.	Jared
Bulletin Board Attendant	Posts student work on the bulletin board.	Jeanette
Equipment Manager	Passes out and collects equipment during recess.	Peter
Substitute (1)	Substitutes for helper who is out.	Ken
Substitute (2)	Substitutes for helper who is out.	Maria

Classroom Procedures for K-5

What Do I Do If . . .

I want to ask a question?	**Raise your hand and wait patiently to be called on.**
I want to go to the lavatory?	**Sign your name in the lavatory book, take a pass, and walk quietly to the lavatory.**
I want to go to the nurse?	**Raise you hand and ask for a pass to the nurse.**
I want extra help?	**In class: Raise your hand and ask for help. After class: Extra help is available every Monday from 3:00 to 4:30. Just come in.**
I want a book to read?	**During Free Time, you can check a book out with our class librarian.**
I want to hand in my homework?	**Put your homework in the homework box as soon as you come into the class.**
I want a drink of water?	**Unless it is an emergency, please wait until break time.**

Behavior Expectations for K-6

Good Classroom Behavior

1. Always be polite. Say "please," "thank you," and "excuse me."

2. Always be respectful of other people's feelings. No mimicking, name-calling, making funny faces, or laughing at other classmates.

3. Always wait your turn. Raise your hand and wait quietly to be called on. Your turn will come.

4. Keep your hands to yourself. No touching, pushing, shoving, or hitting other students.

5. Always use your soft voice in the classroom.

6. Be where you are supposed to be when you are supposed to be there. No wandering around or getting lost.

7. No temper tantrums. If you are having a problem, talk to me and we will work together to solve the problem.

8. Stay in line with hands to your sides when we are moving between classes.

9. Always be safe. No throwing anything in the classroom.

10. Never bring anything dangerous to school like a knife, a gun, or an object with sharp edges.

Classroom Expectations for 6-12

I expect that all of my students will

- Come to class eager to read, ask questions, challenge, and debate the material presented.
- Challenge the limits of their own thinking.
- Be responsible for their own learning.
- Be open to other students' beliefs and opinions.
- Treat every member of our classroom community with sensitivity and respect.
- Work cooperatively in Reader Response groups.
- Work to develop strong literacy skills (analytical reading, writing, speaking, viewing, etc.)
- Be seated and ready to begin when the second bell rings.
- Come to class prepared *every day* with books, pens, notebooks, and journals.
- Complete and submit all assignments *on time*.
- Come in for extra help *immediately* when a problem arises.

Students can expect that I will

- Come to class every day prepared with a meaningful lesson.
- Provide instruction that supports local, state, and national standards.
- Begin and end class on time.
- Be open to conflicting arguments and opinions.
- Be fair and nonjudgmental.
- Provide a minimum of one week's notice prior to an exam.
- Return all written work within one week of receiving it.
- Provide scoring rubrics for all written assignments, projects, presentations, and so on, at the time the assignment is given.
- Be available for extra help in my classroom every Wednesday from 3:00 to 5:00.
- Provide students with grade sheets at the end of each quarter.
- Treat my students with respect.

Student Self-Monitoring Record

Name: _____

Behavior needing correction: _____

Date	What happened?	What caused it to happen?	How did you handle the problem?	How might you handle a similar problem in the future?

3

Planning for Success: Unit and Lesson Planning and Design

 ## Why Plan?

Exemplary teaching doesn't happen by accident; it happens as a direct result of careful, thoughtful planning that is informed by content area expertise, a wide range of pedagogically sound strategies, and a clear understanding of how students

learn best. Although there are many reasons why teachers spend so much of their time planning, the most compelling reason is time. Once you begin the planning process, you will see very quickly how little instructional time you actually have in relation to the volume and scope of material you are expected to teach your students. When one thinks of 180 to 200 days, it may sound like a lot of time, but when you factor in holidays (Spring recess, Christmas recess, Thanksgiving, Rosh Hashanah, Yom Kippur, Martin Luther King Day, Memorial Day, Presidents' Day, etc.), educators' professional conference days, state testing days, parent-teacher conference days, days lost to inclement weather, half days for Back-to-School nights, and midterm and final exam weeks, your actual teaching time is greatly reduced. Add to that, time lost for class meetings, health screenings, assemblies, guidance appointments, fire drills, and scheduling for the following year and you will undoubtedly see the urgency in planning. Teachers who do not put the time and necessary effort into effective planning inevitably find themselves at the end of the year with a monumental list of things they "didn't get a chance to cover."

Another equally important reason for planning is that it allows teachers to visualize the content of their courses to ensure that all of the skills and concepts required by local, state, and national standards have been taught and that the individual learning styles and capabilities of all of their students have been given consideration in each unit of instruction. In addition, being able to visualize their teaching agenda helps teachers quickly see gaps in instruction, which impede the natural flow and continuity of the course. Ordering and scheduling are also made much easier with long-range lesson plans. Teachers who wait until the last minute to order materials or to schedule guest speakers and field trips often find that their needs cannot be accommodated.

Teachers also find that written lesson and unit plans, in addition to providing documentation accounting for curriculum and instructional practices, provide strategic talking points for one-on-one conferences, with mentors or supervisors, that are personal and class-specific. Teachers and supervisors tend to agree that conferences based on actual practices and curricular choices are much more satisfying and more productive than conferences based on generic comments or observations.

A final reason for teachers to plan effectively is a more personal one. Having instructional plans is like taking a trip with a clearly defined road map and itinerary, particularly for new teachers. Like any new adventure, you will find that traveling with a good map and a well-thought-out itinerary will provide you with a sense of comfort and security by reassuring you where you're going, when you're going, how you're going, and ultimately why you're making the trip.

Where Do I Begin?

The process of instructional planning should begin the moment you are given your teaching assignment. Once you know what you will be teaching, you need to immediately begin collecting all of the relevant information, sources, and materials that you will need to begin putting your program together. This list should include the following:

■ A three-ring binder and a box of three-ring plastic binder sleeves for lesson plans and support materials. A binder is a great way to keep all your lesson plans, assessments, handouts, and support materials together. Having a separate binder for each unit makes it easy to access, store, review, and organize information for the following year.

■ A ten-month working calendar for the school year.

■ A copy of the school calendar for the year.

■ Copies of all the textbooks you will be using throughout the year.

■ Lists of the supplies and equipment available for your use.

■ A list of the audiovisual materials available for your use.

■ A list of the computer programs available for your use.

■ A list of the current library materials available, which will be helpful when planning research and library assignments.

■ A list of external sources (such as guest speakers, possible field trips, movies, documents) that you would like to incorporate into your program.

■ A copy of the school's curriculum guide. *Note:* If the school does not have a written guide, use the state and national standards to guide your curricular choices.

■ A list of the state and national standards. If your school does not have copies of the standards available for you, you can access them online at the following sites:

   ■ *Individual state standards:* www.statestandards.com
   ■ *National standards:* See Table 3.1 for a list of websites.

Now that you have everything you need, you are ready to begin the fun part—the actual planning process!

Table 3.1 National Teaching Standards

Discipline	Developers of Standards	Website
Art (visual and performance)	The American Alliance for Theater and Education, National Art Education Association, and the Music Educators National Conference	www.artsedge.kennedy-center.org/teach/standards
Economics	The National Council on Economic Education	www.ncee.org
English/Language Arts/ Reading	The National Council of Teachers of English, the International Reading Association, and the University of Illinois Center for the Study of Reading	www.ncte.org
Foreign Languages	The American Council on the Teaching of Foreign Languages	www.actfl.org/14a/pages/index.cfm?pageid=3324
Geography	The Association of American Geographers, the National Council for Geographic Education, and the National Geographic Association	www.nationalgeographic.com/education/standards.html
Health	The Committee for National School Health Education Standards	www.aahperd.org/aahe/pdf_files/standards.pdf
History/Civics/Social Studies	The Center for Civic Education and the National Center for History in the Schools	www.sscnet.ucla.edu/nchs/standards
Mathematics	The National Council of Teachers of Mathematics	www.nctm.org/standards
Physical Education	The National Association of Sports and Physical Education	www.aahperd.org/naspe
Psychology	The American Psychological Association	www.cnets.iste.org/teachers/+_stands.html
Science	American Association for the Advancement of Science, the National Science Teachers Association, and the National Research Council's National Committee	www.nsta.org/standards
Technology	International Technology Education Association	www.apa.org/ed/topss/homepage.html

Step 1. Date your working calendar for the entire school year.

Step 2. On your working calendar, identify all the full or partial days that you will *not* be teaching (such as holidays, parent-teacher conference days, educator's conference days, professional development days, exam days). Be sure to identify days that have activities scheduled that will take students out of your classroom (such as pep rallies, assemblies, class scheduling, health screening days).

Step 3. Identify the units that you will be teaching. Schools typically identify in the curriculum guides the units you are expected to teach as well as the specific skills and concepts and the estimated time each unit should take. If your school does not have a curriculum guide, you will need to go to the state and national standards to identify the skills and concepts and organize them into logical, coherent units of study.

Step 4. Plot the units on your working calendar. There is no rule governing the length of a unit. Units can vary from being a week long to a month long or even longer, depending on the content and skills that need to be taught. These dates are best guesses. You won't know how long it will actually take you to teach a unit until you teach it. The actual start and end dates will most likely change. What plotting does is give you a game plan. Remember, when plotting your units, to consider the importance of continuity. For example, you wouldn't want to start a unit on a day before a special event (such as prom day, track-and-field day, yearbook day), the day before a holiday, or the day before students will be out of class for an extended period of time (such as for standardized testing) and expect they will come back with the same enthusiasm for their studies. For the same reason, you wouldn't want to begin a new unit on a Friday.

Note: Make sure you are familiar with the skills and concepts being tested on the standardized tests required by your school or state, and teach the units that focus on those skills and concepts prior to the administration of the tests. Remember, it is your responsibility to prepare your students to do well on those exams.

Planning Units of Instruction

Once you have identified the units you will be teaching, you are ready to begin laying out the content you want to cover in each unit. In doing so, consider the following:

1. How you want to organize your unit (that is, chronologically, thematically, sequentially, or another way).

2. What instructional goals will be addressed in the unit.
   Note: Instructional goals are learning competencies that students are expected to achieve. To ensure compliance with the federal No Child Left Behind (NCLB) Act, most schools are using state and national standards as their target instructional goals. It is not necessary that you teach to all the state and national competencies in every unit; however, you will be expected that you address all of them over the course of the year.

3. What instructional objectives are going to be addressed in the unit.
   Note: Instructional objectives are measurable behavioral expectations that support the unit instructional goals. They identify exactly what students will know and be able to do at the end of the unit.
   Note: Instructional goals are learning outcomes that are expressed in general terms and reflect the "big picture," whereas instructional objectives are learning outcomes that are specifically identified, such as the following:

   > *Instructional goal:* To provide opportunities for students to listen, read, write, think, and speak critically (New Jersey State Department of Education, Core Curriculum Standards 3.1, 3.2, 3.3).
   > *Instructional objective:* To read "A Fool's Paradise" and identify themes, patterns of imagery, symbolism, and character motivations.

4. What type of assessment tool you want to use to identify your students' instructional needs. (See Chapter 4 for suggestions.)

5. What texts are going to be used to meet the goals and instructional objectives. Units should contain a wide range of materials, including texts (textbooks, novels, short stories, plays, poetry, lyrics, nonfiction accounts, news and magazine articles), film, musical selections, artifacts, graphs, charts, pictures, computer programs, guest speakers, class trips, documents, experiments, models, interviews, surveys, presentations, etc.

6. How much time you are going to assign to each text. There are no hard-and-set rules about time. Curriculum guides typically provide estimated time frames, but these are just estimates. Two different classes taught the same lesson by the same teacher could, because of student differences, conceivably take different lengths of time to complete. If you do not have a guide to follow, good resources for time frames are content area supervisors and teachers who have either taught the course or taught the students who will be in your class. Another source is lessons in your content area that are available online. Reviewing a few of these will give you an idea of how much time other teachers are taking to cover similar material. (See Model 11: Lesson Plan for

suggestions.) Once you have taught your first unit and have become familiar with the pace of your students' learning as well as the pace of your teaching, you will have a realistic basis for timing the rest of your units. In general, it is better to overplan than to underplan. Unit and lesson plans should be seen as flexible guidelines. Multiple modifications and revisions throughout the year are anticipated and expected.

7. Identify how you plan to assess your students' learning. Remember that units must include multiple forms of assessments. (See Chapter 4 for suggestions.)

8. Evaluate your unit to ensure you have included all the necessary components.

9. Decide the order in which you want to teach the texts.

10. Develop daily lesson plans to support unit goals and objectives. (See Model 10: Unit Plan.)

*P*lanning Unit Lessons

Lesson planning is all about decision making, creativity, and passion for your discipline. It's where you get to use your expertise to make critical choices that will empower students with not only an understanding but also hopefully with an interest in your content area that will continue beyond your classroom. While the instructional goals are determined for you, how you help your students reach those goals is in your hands. You get to select and sequence the texts, strategies, activities, assignments, and assessments that will literally bring what they're learning to life for them.

Step 1. Note the theme or focus of the unit.

Step 2. Identify the unit instructional goals the lesson will be supporting.

Step 3. Identify the texts you will be using for the lesson.

Step 4. Identify the instructional objectives of the lesson. Remember, instructional objectives are lesson specific and must be measurable. For example, "students will enjoy the story" is certainly a desirable outcome, but because it cannot be measured it would not be a suitable instructional objective.

Step 5. Identify the learning-style focus of this lesson. Most teachers tend to use strategies that are compatible with their own learning style, which is fine for the students who share the same learning style but disastrous for students who learn differently. (See Chapter 4.) Noting the learning styles addressed on each lesson plan will help you see gaps in your instructional strategies, which need to be addressed in order to accommodate the learning needs of *all* the students in your class.

   Note: It is unrealistic to assume that all learning styles will be addressed in every lesson; however, all the learning styles of your students should be given consideration over the course of the unit. Knowing the learning styles of the students in your classroom and being aware of the styles addressed in the lesson will alert you to disconnects and identify for you the students who may have difficulty meeting the expectations of the lesson. Knowing this in advance, you can prepare to assist these students with differentiated strategies so that they too can be successful.

Step 6. Identify how you are going to teach to the goals and objectives—the lesson. Cohesive lessons are presented in three parts: the introduction, learning activities, and closure.

- A strong *introduction*, which makes the immediate connection between the students and what they are going to learn, will pique your students' interest and make them want to participate in the activities that follow. The best introductions help the students personally connect with the subject matter, giving it relevance and meaning, which will translate for them into a reason to learn.

  Examples of weak introductions
  a. "Students, turn to page 14 in your books and begin reading about the beach."
  b. "Today we are going to study the beach."

  Examples of strong introductions (early grades)
  a. Bring in a tape of the sounds of the beach and ask students what they hear or what it reminds them of.
  b. Hold up a picture of a beach scene and ask students to tell you what they see, what they hear, what they smell.
  c. For students who have never been to the beach, bring in a bucket of sand and a bucket of dirt and bottles of salt and fresh water. Let the students touch and smell the sand, dirt, and water so that they can tell you the differences and similarities. Bring in seashells and pictures of sea creatures and ask them to match the sea creatures to the shells and tell you the criteria they used to make the matches. Ask them to tell you what the shells tell them about what life must be like under the sea.
  d. Show students a clip from a movie or television show with a beach scene and ask them what they see and hear and what inferences they can make

about people who like or dislike the beach or ask them what they like or dislike about the beach.

e. Ask them to think about what it would be like to live on the beach or ask them to tell you what they think the pros and cons of living on the beach would be. What makes going to the beach fun? What takes away from the fun?

f. Use K-W-L (Ogle, 1986): A strategy that asks students to identify what they know (K), what they want to know (W) about a topic before they begin their reading, and then what they learned (L). (See Chapter 6.)

Examples of strong introductions (6–12)

a. Give students a prompt related to the subject matter of the lesson and five minutes to respond in their journals. This will give them an opportunity to identify and formulate their opinions on the topic before they are asked to share them.

b. Ask a provocative question that will connect the students personally with the subject (e.g., Has anyone here ever witnessed an act of prejudice either inside or outside of school?).

c. Show a clip from a movie or television show dealing with the same subject and ask for reactions.

d. Present a scenario and ask the students in small groups to come up with a solution or tell you how they would have handled the same situation.

e. Share a recent newspaper article or clip of a newscaster reporting on a situation similar to one you'll be considering in your lesson.

f. Use K-W-L, which is equally effective with students in the upper grades.

■ A list of *activities* tells what your students will do during the lesson. Next to each activity, identify the learning style being addressed.

■ The *closure*, like the introduction, is equally important as the lesson itself. It is in this part of the lesson that you help students make sense of the activities. You can't assume that students will see the "big picture" and make connections on their own. You must help them understand the usefulness or meaning of what they have just learned. A good idea is to literally ask them how what they have learned can be seen in or applied to their lives outside of the classroom.

Step 7. Identify the student's homework assignment. The purpose of homework is to reinforce skills and concepts taught in the lesson. Therefore, the homework assignment should always be directly related to the content of the lesson. It is another way for you to assess whether your students have understood what was taught in the lesson. Reviewing homework will inform you of the skills and concepts that need more attention before you move on to the next lesson. For this reason, it is important that the homework be given attention the next day.

Note: Never use homework as punishment. It is also important that when you are assigning homework you be sensitive to the amount of time it will take students to finish the assignment. Remember, students have already spent six to seven hours in a classroom. Asking younger students to spend another two to three hours on homework is unreasonable. An easy way to check to see if the amount of homework you're assigning is reasonable is to ask students and/or their parents how much time is being spent on homework each evening. You can be sure they will greatly appreciate your intuitiveness and sensitivity.

Step 8. Identify the materials or equipment you will need for the lesson. If you need special materials, supplies, or equipment that are not normally housed in your classroom, order or reserve what you need for that day at least a week or two in advance. Ask your supervisor at the beginning of the school year what the procedures and time lines are for ordering and reserving. There is nothing worse for teachers than to have a great lesson and not have the resources to teach it because they were remiss in scheduling equipment or ordering materials.

Step 9. Identify how you are going to assess whether your students understand the skills and concepts taught in this lesson. Students run into trouble when their teachers move ahead to the next lesson before they have had an opportunity to master the skills and concepts taught in the previous lesson. Assess students' mastery at the conclusion of each lesson to prevent this from happening. See Model 11: Lesson Plan.

Note: Asking students if they understand is not a viable assessment tool. Many times students *think* they understand when they really don't. For that reason, you need to use an assessment tool that accurately identifies and documents your students' learning. (See Chapter 4 for suggestions.)

Step 10. It is important that at the end of each lesson, you take the time to review your lesson and the performance of both you and your students. Understand and accept that becoming an exemplary teacher doesn't happen overnight. The best teachers are those who are constantly reflecting, self-evaluating, and looking for ways to improve their teaching. An easy way to monitor your lessons and teaching is with a self-assessment tool that can be personalized, duplicated, and placed in your unit binder at the end of each lesson. You will find these extremely helpful when you review and modify your units for use the following year. See Model 12: Teacher Reflection and Self-Assessment.

Online Resources

Over time, you begin to develop a teaching style that will be entirely your own. The way you interact with students, the way you move about the classroom, the way you look at students and communicate nonverbally, the way you use the tone and inflections of your voice to articulate and accentuate ideas, the way you question students, and the way you pace your lessons are all characteristically unique. No two teachers are exactly the same. For that reason, you should not expect that you could use another teacher's lesson plans and get the same results. You will find that teaching from plans that are taken verbatim from books or websites will be less satisfying because they will not be entirely compatible with your teaching style. You should, however, look at other teachers' plans to see what they are thinking and doing. There are places online, for example, that you can go to get ideas that you could modify to accommodate your teaching style and incorporate into your own plans. Table 3.2 lists websites that you should consider visiting.

Planning for English Language Learners

If you have English language learners (ELLs) in your class, you will have the additional responsibility of teaching content skills and concepts to "English language learners in strategic ways that make the concepts comprehensible while promoting the students' academic English language development" (Short & Echevarria, 2004/2005, p. 10). Without question, this is a formidable task, especially for teachers who have limited experience with languages and cultures other than their own. You can, however, take steps that will help you meet this challenge. The first is to make ELL accommodations an integral part of your planning process.

This process should begin with the collection of information about your students. Research showed us early on that when students' first language is valued

Table 3.2 Websites for Lesson Models and Ideas

Discipline	Website
Art (visual and performance)	www.lessonplanspage.com www.teacher.scholastic.com www.mcrel.org/lesson-plans www.bestwebquests.com www.smithsonianeducation.org/educators
Economics	www.mcrel.org/lesson-plans www.bestwebquests.com
English/Language Arts/Reading	www.lessonplanspage.com www.teacher.scholastic.com www.mcrel.org/lesson-plans www.bestwebquests.com
Foreign Languages	www.mcrel.org/lesson-plans www.bestwebquests.com www.nwrel.org/sky/index.php www.eduref.org
Geography	www.nationalgeographic.education.com www.mcrel.org/lesson-plans
Health	www.lessonplanspage.com www.teacher.scholastic.com www.mcrel.org/lesson-plans www.nwrel.org/sky/index.php
History/Civics/Social Studies	www.civiced.org www.lessonplanspage.com www.teacher.scholastic.com www.mcrel.org/lesson-plans www.bestwebquests.com www.smithsonianeducation.org/educators
Mathematics	www.nctm.org www.lessonplanspage.com www.teacher.scholastic.com www.mcrel.org/lesson-plans www.bestwebquests.com
Physical Education	www.teacher.scholastic.com www.mcrel.org/lesson-plans www.nwrel.org/sky/index.php
Psychology	www.eduref.org/cgi-bin/lessons.cgi/social_studies/ psychology

(continued)

Table 3.2, Continued

Discipline	Website
Science	www.lessonplanspage.com
	www.teacher.scholastic.com
	www.mcrel.org/lesson-plans
	www.bestwebquests.com
	www.smithsonianeducation.org/educators
Technology	www.lessonplanspage.com
	www.teacher.scholastic.com
	www.mcrel.org/lesson-plans
	www.smithsonianeducation.org/educators
	www.bestwebquests.com

and fostered ELLs are more successful academically because they are allowed and encouraged to call on their established knowledge base and personal experiences to support their learning (Hakuta, 1986). For this reason, it is important to consider student backgrounds and interests when planning lessons. If you provide ELLs with specific examples from schema they understand, they have a better chance of understanding new concepts. This will require that you spend time talking to them (either one on one or through an interpreter) to collect information that you can use to plan your lessons. When planning, make it a practice to do the following:

1. Incorporate an *explicit* ELL vocabulary component into your daily plans, which will provide students with the language they will need to navigate the lesson (that is, content-related vocabulary; directional words such as *compare*, *contrast*, *dissect*, *support*, *argue*, etc.; colloquial expressions you may use in your teaching). An easy way to determine language beyond the content that students will need is to tape-record a few of your classes and note the kind of language and language patterns you tend to use when teaching.

2. Present key concepts in multiple modes so that ELLs can "learn by seeing concepts demonstrated, by hearing them described, and by participating in activities that show the concepts in action" (Carrier, 2006, p. 131).

3. Include *explicit* language objectives (reading, writing, speaking, viewing, etc.) for ELLs in all your lessons.

4. Plan activities that will give students opportunities to extend their academic talk both individually and in groups.

5. Plan support for each lesson (e.g., anticipation guides, visual aids, vocabulary lists with definitions, chapter outlines) that students can be given in advance of the lesson so that they can prepare to learn.

*P*utting Planning into Perspective

The necessity for unit and lesson planning should be clear. Academically and pedagogically sound plans legitimize your practices, while providing purpose, direction, and focus to your teaching. Walking into a classroom without a well-thought-out lesson plan is like a coach sending his or her team onto the field without a game plan. The probability that either of you will come home a winner is not great.

*R*eferences

Carrier, K. (January/February 2006). Improving comprehension and assessment of English language learners using MMIO. *The Clearing House, 79*(3), 131–136.

Hakuta, K. (1986). *Mirror of language*. New York: Basic Books.

New Jersey State Department of Education. (Fall 1998). *New Jersey core curriculum content standards*. Retrieved January 2, 2006, from www.state.nj.us/njded/cccs/

No Child Left Behind Act, § 20 U.S.C. 6301 et seq.

Ogle, D. M. (1986). K-W-L: A teaching model that develops active reading of expository text. *The Reading Teacher, 39*(6), 564–570.

Short, D., & Echevarria, J. (December 2004/January 2005). Teacher skills to support English language learners. *Educational Leadership, 62*(4), 8–13.

*O*nline References

PBS Teachers—www.pbs.org/teachers
Moodle—http://moodle.org
Teacher Resources—www.learnReturn.com
A-Z Teacher Stuff—www.atozteacherstuff.com/Model 13

Unit Plan

Unit: Things are not always the way they appear. **Grade:** 9 Language Arts

Learning Styles: Visual, verbal, auditory, independent, social, applied

Instructional Goals:

1. Provide opportunities for students to listen, read, write, think, and speak critically (New Jersey State Department of Education, Core Curriculum Standards 3.1, 3.2, 3.3).
2. Provide opportunities for students to critically read and respond to a variety of texts (New Jersey State Department of Education Core Curriculum Standards 3.4, 3.5).

Instructional Objectives: At the end of this unit, students should be able to

a. understand the difference between appearance and reality.

b. analyze character actions for motivations.

c. evaluate advertisements for credibility.

d. begin understanding the following literary terms: theme, symbol, image.

e. contribute meaningfully to discussions within groups.

f. write a cohesive essay.

g. respond to objective questions designed to test reading comprehension.

h. critically respond to their readings with journal entries.

i. expand their vocabulary with twenty new words from their reading.

Pre-teaching Assessment Tool: *T* or *F* inventory on literary terms and concepts developed in the unit.

Texts:

a. Nonfiction: "A Fool's Paradise" by Floyd Dell

b. Poetry: "A War Prayer" by Edgar Allen Poe

c. Film: *Murder, She Wrote*, starring Angela Lansbury

d. Advertisements from magazines and television commercials

e. Fiction: *A Separate Peace* by John Knowles

f. Film: *A Separate Peace*

g. Artifact: Body biographies (*A Separate Peace* characters)

h. Graphics: Survey and graph of perceptions of betrayal

Estimated Time Frame: 30 Days

a. "A Fool's Paradise"	3 days
b. "A War Prayer"	2 days
c. *Murder, She Wrote*	5 days
d. Advertisements	5 days
e. *A Separate Peace*	15 days

Teaching Strategies:

a. Reader Responses	f. Journals
b. Surveys	g. Open-ended questioning
c. Q&A	h. Body biographies
d. Student presentations	i. Read-alouds
e. Direct instruction	j. Journal responses

Assessments:

a. Participation in Reader Response groups	f. Objective reading quizzes
b. Essay responses	g. Student-teacher conferences
c. Journal responses	h. Homework responses
d. Analysis of survey responses	i. Responses to direct questioning
e. Teacher observations	j. Student presentations

Lesson Plan

Title of Unit: Things are not always as they appear. **Grade:** 9 **Time Frame:** 2 days

Learning-Style Focus: auditory, social, verbal

Text(s): Print: "A Fool's Paradise"

Instructional Goals: To provide opportunities for students to listen, read, write, think, and speak critically (New Jersey State Department of Education, Core Curriculum Standards 3.1, 3.2, 3.3).

Instructional Objectives: Students should be able to
1. read "A Fool's Paradise" critically and understand the difference between appearance and reality.
2. identify theme.
3. identify character motivations.
4. make predictions based on textual information.
5. understand the meaning of *respectability, deceptive, evasion, comparative, immaculate, currency, arrogant, anxiety, bewilderment, renunciation,* and *tendrils.*
6. write responses to text in their journals.
7. talk about the text in response groups.

Lesson:

Introduction: Students will be asked to respond to the following prompt in their response journals: Do you think your parents should always tell you the truth or are there times when you think it is acceptable for them to keep the truth from you?

Activities: [Next to each activity, identify the learning style(s) addressed.]
1. Q&A: Students, in pairs, will listen to me read the first paragraph. At the end of the paragraph, students will each write one question that they have about the events in the first paragraph. Students will then ask their partners the question and record the answer given. Questions and answers will be shared with the rest of the class. This activity will be repeated with the rest of the story. (verbal, auditory, social)
2. Students will return to their response groups to collectively consider the following questions: (auditory, social, verbal)
    a. What decisions made by the parents were good ones? Which ones were bad?
    b. How was the boy helped by their decisions? How was he hurt?
    c. Should the boy have been told the truth? Why or why not?
3. Students will share group opinions with the class.

Closure: Teacher-led discussion: What do you think the author was trying to tell us through this story? Can you see that there was a difference between the way things appeared and the way they actually were? How can you see this being helpful in your own lives?

Homework Assignment:
In your journals, make a list of ways you predict the decisions of the parents will affect the boy in the future. Next to the effect, explain why you think this might happen. (independent, verbal)

Materials Needed: Paper, pens, short story "A Fool's Paradise"

Assessment: Student understanding will be assessed by (1) meaningful participation in share-pair and response groups and (2) written responses in journal.

Reflection/Self-Assessment:

Teacher Reflection and Self-Assessment

Lesson: _____ Date: _____

1. What went well, and why? _____
_____
_____
_____

2. What didn't go well, and why? _____
_____
_____
_____

3. Which instructional objectives were met? _____
_____
_____
_____

4. Which instructional objectives were not met?_____
_____
_____
_____

5. Which students had difficulty with the lesson?_____
_____
_____
_____

6. Which students had no difficulty with the lesson? _____
_____
_____
_____

7. What can I do to improve the lesson? _____
_____
_____
_____

Evaluating Student Knowledge and Performance

How Student Evaluation Has Changed

The past twenty years have witnessed significant philosophical and pedagogical changes in our thinking about *how* we measure, *what* we measure, *when* we measure, and *why* we measure student competencies. Arguably, the most significant change has been in *how we measure* student learning, which has pedagogically moved from exclusively administering objective tests to following an evaluative process that has been redefined to include assessment, evaluation, grading, and application.

Step 1. Assessment is the process by which information about student learning is gathered. To accommodate student differences in learning styles and to ensure an accurate and a balanced appraisal of student knowledge, understanding, and abilities, a wide range of assessment tools must be used, which includes traditional testing as well as alternate forms of assessment (such as performances, projects, teacher observations).

Step 2. Evaluation is the process of interpreting the information gathered on the assessments. This is typically done with rubrics, which identify and clarify learning and performance goals.

Step 3. Grading is the process of assigning a quantitative value to the evaluations. Grades are an important step in this process because they give us a systematic way to visualize, discuss, and compare student progress in relationship to previous assessments, to other students' performance on assessments, and to state and national standards.

Step 4. Application is the process of taking the results of the assessments and using them to monitor current practices and to inform future instruction (individual and/or whole class).

What we measure has also changed significantly. While objective tests measured what students recalled, they didn't account for students' understandings or for their ability to apply what they knew. Therefore, evaluations had to be modified to include the measurement of student comprehension, which, in order to provide a more accurate and comprehensive view of student learning, required the use of alternate evaluative instruments (e.g., performance, portfolios, projects) in addition to traditional objective testing.

When we measure, like our belief in what should be measured, has also changed dramatically. Traditionally, teachers tested student learning at the end of the lesson or unit taught. Once the tests were administered and scored, the teachers moved on to their next set of lessons. This was fine for the students who did well on the tests; however, for the students who did poorly, this presented problems, particularly if the information tested was necessary for them to understand the skills and concepts being taught in the units that followed. These students were essentially doomed to fail. To prevent this from happening, teachers now are encouraged to administer a wide range of assessments throughout the unit. These ongoing assessments help teachers identify student misunderstandings so they can be corrected before the student fails.

Our understanding of *why we measure* has also changed. At one time, assessments were used exclusively to identify and validate learning and to determine student placement. After reviewing the assessments with the students, they were typically filed and only used, if needed, to clarify grades to interested parents and administrators. No longer filed away, assessment tools are now used by teachers to inform their instruction. Assessments identify very quickly for teachers which students need additional tutorial support and what skill and concept misunderstandings need further attention prior to moving on to the next unit of instruction.

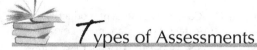

Types of Assessments

Table 4.1 lists some of the tools you can use to assess your students' learning. It is important that your assessment be ongoing and varied enough to account for all of the learning styles of the students in your classroom.

Table 4.1 Types of Assessments

Assessment	Characteristics	Examples
Summative	Given at the end of the unit to measure student learning. Always graded.	Objective and subjective exams, reports, projects.
Formative	Given periodically during the learning experience to identify student progress and identify student misunderstandings and errors so that they can be corrected prior to the summative assessments. Can be graded, but need not be.	Quizzes, graphic organizers, worksheets, interviews, conferences, student questioning, rough drafts.
Norm-referenced	Based on standards, compares students with other students in the same grade level.	State and national standardized tests, SAT, Iowa Test of Basic Skills.
Authentic	Mirrors kinds of activities students experience outside the classroom.	Presentations, performances, experiments, inventions, conferences, interviews, surveys, debates, exhibitions.
Text-based	Developed directly from curriculum-based texts.	Essays, objective quizzes and exams.
Teacher-developed	Developed by teachers to supplement information from authentic and text-based assessments.	Essays, objective quizzes and exams, research projects, graphic organizers.

(continued)

Table 4.1, Continued

Assessment	Characteristics	Examples
Computer-based	Developed by computer companies to reinforce classroom learning, skill- and concept-based, providing more complex questions as the student responds correctly.	Tutorials, skill and concept drills.
Portfolios	Collection of pieces of representative individual student work.	Collection of student products (essays, poems, art, music, etc.).
Teacher observations	Observations of students engaged in classroom activities. Can be academic or behavioral. Recorded, dated, and used to clarify student needs or behavior.	See Model 17: Teacher Observation Form.
Teacher questioning	Used to assess student knowledge and understanding.	Literal and probative questions about readings, experiences, and applications.
Peer reviews	Using a rubric, peers evaluate specific aspects of each other's work.	Edit or evaluate peer work (writings, presentations, artwork, performances).
Self-assessment	Using self-assessment tools, students evaluate their own learning and learning needs.	Journals, learning logs, self-evaluation forms. See Model 19: Self-Evaluation Form.

Selecting Appropriate Assessments

Before you begin the process of designing an assessment, you must first identify exactly what you want to know and what each type of assessment can tell you about your students' learning. (See Table 4.2.)

When selecting assessments, think in terms of units of instruction. Use the following checklist to ensure fair, complete, and accurate assessment of your students' knowledge and understanding. Each unit should include assessments that

_____ Are ongoing, purposeful, and meaningful.

_____ Reflect what has been taught.

_____ Tell you what students know, what they understand, and how they relate what they know and understand to the world outside the classroom.

Table 4.2 Assessment Chart

Assessment Goal	What Assessment Measures	Examples	Assessment Tool
To assess content knowledge and information	Students' ability to recall objective information and data (what, when, where, how)	Formulas, spelling, definitions, grammar facts, details, rules, addition and multiplication tables	Objective tests/quizzes, summaries, retellings, worksheets, researched reports, book reports, oral presentations, computer-assisted programs
To assess comprehension	Students' understandings based on objective data and information (why)	Cause and effect, character motivations, relationships, implications, interpretations	Essays, graphic organizers, Reader Response groups, learning logs, projects, presentations, inventions, journals, analytical research papers, debates
To assess transference of knowledge	Students' ability to apply the data and their understandings to life outside the classroom (application)	Activities mirroring life outside the classroom	Portfolios, presentations, inventions, conferences, interviews, surveys, performances, original writings, exhibitions
To assess reading (K–4)	Students' reading levels, decoding skills, and reading behaviors	Miscues, omits words, substitutes words, self-corrects, asks for help	Running records, anecdotal records, retelling, developmental checklists
To assess student perceptions	How students perceive what they know, what they need to know, and what they want to know	Student's belief that he or she has understanding, which may or may not be true	Learning logs, journals, teacher questioning, student-teacher conferences

____ Align with the goals and objectives of the lesson and unit.

____ Align with state and national standards.

____ Use multiple texts (novels, poetry, drama, short stories, nonfiction, documents, film, television, newspapers, computer programs, audio, surveys, interviews, class trips, etc.).

____ Require students to use multiple strategies (writing, speaking, listening and responding, performing, drawing, interpreting, reviewing, building, etc.).

___ Allow for a variety of responses (objective, interpretative, authentic).

___ Correspond to student learning styles.

___ Include opportunities for students to self-assess.

___ Provide information about student learning that you can use to monitor and evaluate your own teaching.

Developing Effective Test Questions

Objective Tests (Multiple Choice, True/False, Matching, Fill in the Blank)

An objective test is one that requires no judgment by the scorer when it is being marked. The most important attribute of an objective test is *content validity*, which exists when the test measures what the teacher wants it to measure; that is, the questions match a set of predetermined objectives. A second important attribute of an objective test is *reliability*, or consistency. A reliable test is one that would produce similar results if it were administered again to a similar group of students. Objective testing has both advantages and disadvantages as noted in the following list:

Advantages	**Disadvantages**
Tests can be used to measure a broad content area.	Tests are time consuming to construct.
Tests can measure thought-process levels, from recall to critical thinking.	Students' responses are subject to guessing. Teachers don't know if a right answer is a result of knowledge or a lucky guess.
Tests are highly reliable. Scoring standards are fixed.	
Tests can be machine scored.	Slow or weak readers operate at a disadvantage.
	Tests cannot assess students' ability to write.

Guidelines for Developing Multiple-Choice Questions

Multiple-choice questions typically provide students with a stem (a complete or partial question or statement) and four response choices that will make the information in the stem true or accurate.

- Ask significant questions that reflect students' understanding and knowledge.
- State the question clearly and concisely in the stem so that students know what the question is asking.
- Order the responses in a logical way.
- Avoid putting grammatical clues to the answer in the stem.
- Avoid giving 3/1 or 4/1 splits in responses where one response is overtly different from the others.
- Avoid using "all of the above" or "none of the above."
- Provide responses that are uniform in length.
- Make all of the responses plausible.
- Make choices parallel in structure.
- Try to avoid a negative format in the questions.
- Provide one clear answer.
- Randomize the position of the correct answers.

Adapted from *The AP Vertical Teams Guide for English*, 2002. New York: College Entrance Examination Board.

Examples of common errors made in writing multiple-choice questions

1. Asking questions that provide no insights into what the student knows about content.

    Example: The author's first name is
    A. Sam   C. Bruce
    B. Alex   D. John

2. Providing answers that are absurd and obviously incorrect.

    Example: The word *limpid* has the same meaning as the word
    A. cold   C. stupid
    B. clear   D. snowy

3. Putting grammatical clues in the stem.

    Example: The words "Lolling dogs droop in dead doorways" are an example of an
    A. alliteration   C. simile
    B. metonymy   D. pun

4. Writing questions that are unclear, lacking enough information in the stem for students to understand what is being asked.

   Example: The character is
   A. unhappy   C. successful
   B. intelligent   D. creative

5. Providing answers that are obvious 3/1 or 4/1 splits, where one answer is completely different from the others.

   Example: The tone of the first stanza of the poem is
   A. calm   C. joyful
   B. casual   D. exhausting

6. Providing answers that differ in length.

   Example: The phrase "dead doorways" implies that buildings are
   A. very hot   C. cool
   B. locked   D. deserted and totally empty of all life

Guidelines for Developing True/False Tests

True/false tests are relatively easy to construct, administer, and score. Keep in mind the following four things when developing the questions:

1. Make sure the questions are worth asking.

   Example: What is the author's middle name? is not worth asking.

2. Write the questions clearly and concisely; avoid unnecessary language.

   Example: In the question, *Thomas Jefferson was a wealthy landowner who wrote the Declaration of Independence*, the first part of the question is unnecessary.

3. Make sure each question is either clearly true or clearly false.

   Example: Farmers are given subsidies by the government.

   Explanation: Although some farmers are given subsidies, not all are, making the question sometimes true and sometimes false, but not clearly either true or false.

4. Don't mix facts in the question.

   Example: A square is a <u>geometric shape</u> that has <u>three sides</u>.

                          Fact 1   Fact 2

Guidelines for Developing Matching Tests

A matching test consists of two lists of items. These exams are used by teachers to test their students' ability to see *relationships* between the items in the two lists. The following is important when developing a matching test:

1. A clear relationship must exist between the two lists (such as causes and effects, novels and characters, tools and their uses, terms and definitions, problems and solutions).

2. The directions must clarify the relationship between the two lists.

3. One list should be longer than the other to encourage reasoning rather than the process of elimination.

Guidelines for Developing Fill-in-the-Blank Tests

Fill-ins require that students use textual clues and recall as well their understanding of the material world and reasoning skills to answer the questions correctly. When developing fill-in-the-blank tests, you need to do the following:

1. Indicate in the directions if more than one answer could satisfy the question.

2. Include questions that assess students' comprehension as well as their ability to recall details.

   Example: Jane was angry with her father because _____.

3. Provide enough information in the stem to enable the students to answer the question.

   Poor: _____ went _____ to find _____.

   Better: Directly following play practice, Sally went _____ to find _____.

4. Structure the sentence so that the appropriate word when placed in the blank will make the sentence grammatically correct.

   Poor: Following his trip abroad, Sam suffered from an *rare* disease.

   Better: Following his trip abroad, Sam suffered from a *rare* disease.

Subjective Tests (Essay Exams)

Subjective tests require that scorers use their judgment when marking the tests. There's not always a "right" answer and, like objective exams, they have advantages and disadvantages associated with them.

Advantages

Tests are relatively easy to construct.

Tests can examine a topic in depth.

Tests give students an opportunity to show what they know.

Tests can assess students' ability to reason and write.

Disadvantages

Reliability of scoring tends to be low.

Tests can be laborious to score.

Students with weak writing skills are disadvantaged.

Tests measure a limited content sample.

Guidelines for Developing Essay Tests

- Ask significant questions that reflect what has been taught.

- Ask students to develop an *in-depth* response to only *one* idea.

- Remind students that responses require a topic paragraph with a thesis statement, supportive paragraphs, and a concluding paragraph. *Note:* Short answers are not essays!

- Include exam directions that require students to support their opinions with specific examples from their texts, their learned knowledge, or their experiences.

- Limit questions enough to be answered in-depth within the testing period. (Rule of thumb: one question per 45-minute period.)

- Build time into the testing period for students to organize and edit their responses.

- Provide students with an essay format prior to the test. (Teachers primarily interested in responses permit students to have a copy of the format on their desks during testing.)

- Use test-specific rubrics to score exams to ensure scoring reliability. (See Figure 4.1.)

Figure 4.1

Rubric for Scoring Writing Assignments (Grades 4–5)

Name: _____ Date: _____

Class: _____ Assignment: _____

Skill	Excellent (3)	Good (2)	Needs Improvement (1)	Score
Topic Paragraph	Topic paragraph is well developed and includes summary details and a main idea.	Topic paragraph has summary details and main idea but needs to be developed with more information.	Topic paragraph is missing summary details and main idea, or needs to be developed with more information.	
Supporting Paragraphs				
Topic Sentences	All of the topic sentences support the main idea.	Most of the topic sentences support the main idea.	Most of the topic sentences do not support the main idea.	
Supporting Sentences	All of the sentences support the paragraph topic sentence.	Most of the sentences support the paragraph topic sentence.	Most of the sentences do not support the paragraph topic sentence.	
Concluding Sentences	All paragraphs have concluding sentences.	One paragraph is missing a concluding sentence.	More than one paragraph is missing a concluding sentence.	
Concluding Paragraph	Paragraph summarizes the main ideas in paper.	Paragraph summarizes most main ideas.	Paragraph is missing or fails to summarize main ideas.	
Content	Content has three excellent ideas that support the main idea.	Content has three good ideas that support the main idea.	Content has fewer than three good ideas or has errors in information presented.	
Neatness	Paper has margins and is neat.	Paper has margins, but may have some marks.	Paper is missing margins and/or is messy.	
Organization	Ideas are presented in a logical order.	Most of the ideas are presented in a logical order.	Ideas are not presented in an organized way.	
Spelling and Word Usage	All of the words are used correctly without any spelling errors.	Most of the words are used correctly. There may be one spelling error.	The errors in word usage and/or spelling make reading and understanding difficult.	
Capitalization	Capital letters are used appropriately.	There may be one capitalization error.	More than one error in capitalization exists.	
Sentence Structure	All of the sentences are complete and correctly structured.	Most of the sentences are complete and correctly structured.	Many sentences are incomplete and/or incorrectly structured.	
Total Score				

Scoring: A=30–33; B=26–29; C=22–25; D=19–21
Comments/Suggestions:

Types of Essay Questions

- *Closed-ended questions* are those in which the teacher has predetermined what information is expected to be found in the answer—for example, "Identify and describe five different ways we use water in our community."

- *Open-ended questions* are those that allow students to use their own thoughts, reasons, and experiences, in addition to textual knowledge, in the answer. They have no predetermined "correct" answer. Open-ended questions ask students to make connections between what they have learned and their own lives. *Note:* Personalizing the question makes it more understandable and easier for students to respond to. For example, instead of asking students "What would it be like to be blind?" ask "If you suddenly lost your sight, how would your life change?"

Developing Good Essay Questions

Keep the following in mind when writing essay questions:

1. Keep the question simple. Be clear and concise. Avoid unnecessary language that may confuse students' understanding of what is being asked.

   Poor: Write a descriptive essay concerning the functionality of computers.

   Better: Describe the different ways computers are used today.

2. Include directional words in the question that will clarify what students need to do (*compare, contrast, identify, describe, defend, refute, explain, support, clarify,* etc.).

   Example: Defend or refute the idea that countries benefit from war. Give reasons and examples from history to support your position.

3. Clearly identify any specific information you want in the response.

   Example: Describe the major contributions President Richard Nixon made while in the White House. Include specific examples of political, economic, and social contributions in your essay.

4. Limit the question to make answering it possible within the testing period.

   Poor: Discuss the Civil War.

   Better: Identify the major events that led up to the Civil War and explain the significance of each event.

5. Include only ideas directly related to the main idea of the question.

   Poor: Identify the major themes in *Death of a Salesman* and explain why you chose them and in what other texts you have seen them.

   Better: Identify the major themes in *Death of a Salesman*. Give specific examples in the play to support your opinions.

Note: When developing tests, it's always a good idea to take the test yourself before giving it to your students. This way, if there are any problems with the questions, you can sort them out before they become major problems on test day.

Making Sense of Subjective Assessments

One of the problems that new teachers frequently have is how to translate subjective assessments, once they have them, into usable information that they can call on to support their students' learning and to validate their own subsequent curricular decisions. For many, developing interesting assignments that are also creative and provocative is the easy part. The difficult part is to figure out a way of grading the assignments that is fair and consistent with the goals and objectives of the assignment itself. The solution to this problem is to develop and use rubrics. A *rubric* is a set of criteria that identifies the expectations for a completed product. "Rubrics require a Likert-type scale to quantify decisions about performance and a semantic scale to describe different levels of learning for a particular activity" (Stanford & Reeves, 2005, p. 18). Rubrics do the following:

- Eliminate confusion for students by explicitly identifying the knowledge and performance expectations of the assignment.
- Simplify the grading process by focusing the evaluator's attention on specific information and skills.
- Objectify the evaluation by assigning competency levels (1–3) to specific outcomes.
- Ensure that all student work is evaluated in the same way, which eliminates real or imagined teacher biases.
- Visually display student strengths and weaknesses, which makes for easy monitoring for both students and teachers.
- Provide a quick and easy way to check the alignment of the assignment to lesson/unit and/or state and national standards.

Figure 4.2

Rubric for Scoring Analytical Writing

Name: _____ Date: _____

Assignment: _____

Category	Excellent (3)	Adequate (2)	Unacceptable (1)	Score
Title Page	Correctly structured.	Title page has minor errors in form and structure.	N/A	
Introduction and Conclusion	The paper has a strong introduction and conclusion.	The paper includes a weak introduction and/or conclusion.	The paper is missing either an introduction or a conclusion.	
Topic Sentences	All supportive paragraphs have topic sentences that support the thesis.	N/A	Most topic sentences do not support the thesis.	
Supporting Sentences	All supportive examples are complete and support the topic sentence.	Most of the supportive examples are complete and support the topic sentence.	Supportive examples are incomplete and/or do not support the topic sentence.	
Paragraph Explanations	All paragraph explanations clearly explain how the example supports the topic sentence.	Most of the paragraph explanations clearly explain how the example supports the topic sentence.	Paragraph explanations do not clearly explain how the example supports the topic sentence.	
Completeness of Response	The paper has five supporting paragraphs.	N/A	The paper is missing supporting paragraphs.	
Tenses	All of the verbs are in proper tense.	Errors in tense are not excessive.	Errors in tense are excessive.	
Transition	Appropriate transition exists between all paragraphs and within paragraphs.	Appropriate transition exists between most paragraphs and within most paragraphs.	Transition is weak and/or missing between paragraphs or within paragraphs.	
Direct Quotes	All direct quotes are appropriate and complete.	All direct quotes are appropriate, but some are incomplete.	Has inaccurate and/or missing quotes. Quotes cited may be incomplete.	
Grammar and Punctuation	The paper is nearly free of grammar and punctuation errors.	Errors of grammar and punctuation do not fall into patterns and are not excessive.	The paper exhibits patterns of errors in the areas of grammar and/or punctuation.	
Spelling and Vocabulary	The paper is free of spelling and word-choice errors.	Errors in spelling and word choice are minimal and not repetitive. Errors do not inhibit meaning.	The paper exhibits patterns of errors in spelling and word choice. The errors are excessive and/or inhibit meaning.	
APA Format	The paper follows APA style guidelines.	Errors in APA formatting are minimal.	Errors in APA formatting are excessive.	
Total Score				

Scoring: A=32–36; B=28–31; C=25–27; D=23–24; F=Below 23
N/A: not applicable

Figure 4.3

Rubric for Scoring Reflective Journals

Name: _____ Date: _____

Skil	Excellent (3)	Adequate (2)	Unacceptable (1)	Score
Format	Entry is correctly formatted with identification of response, page in text where it can be found, and the response.	N/A	Entry is missing the page number and/or identification of the response.	
Quality of Response Selection	Response selection is relevant and significant to the meaning of the text.	Response selection is relevant but is not significant to the understanding of the text.	Response selection is superficial and does not contribute to the understanding of the text.	
Quality of Response	Response evidences thinking that is literal, analytical, and makes connections between the text and the reader's experiences.	Response attempts to analyze the text but does not attempt to make connections between the text and the reader's experiences.	Response is literal.	
Length of Response	The ideas evidenced are fully developed.	Most of the ideas are fully developed.	Most of the ideas need to be developed with more information.	
Grammar, Punctuation and Word Choice	Entry is written in complete sentences and is nearly free of grammar and punctuation errors. All of the words are used correctly.	Entry is written in complete sentences. Some errors in grammar and punctuation exist, but they do not appear to be in a pattern nor do they inhibit the understanding of the response.	Entry may not be written in complete sentences and/or may have excessive errors in grammar and/or punctuation. Errors in word choice inhibit the understanding of the response.	
Total Score				

Scoring: A=14–15; B=12–13; C=10–11; D=8–9 **Grade:** _____
Note: The total grade will be lowered for journals that are missing assigned entries.

Steps for Designing an Effective Rubric

1. List the learning outcomes of the assignment. Specifically, what do you want your students to know and be able to do? (For example, you may want your students to research and present an oral report on a given topic; use support materials and props; have good eye contact; and use appropriate body language, expression, and volume.)

2. List the formatting criteria that you expect to be followed in the assignment (such as introduction, supportive details, conclusion).

3. List the usage and grammatical criteria that you have for the assignment (e.g., use of complete sentences, spelling, punctuation, correct use of scientific terms).

4. For each criterion, determine what will be regarded as Excellent (3), Adequate (2), and Unacceptable (1). *Note:* There must be *discernible differences* between the expectations of each criterion. Problems arise when the differences are slight. (For example, a clear difference should exist between an excellent and adequate performance.)

5. Convert the scores into grades, following your school's grading policy. (For example, a student who scores 24 out of 27 points in a school that has 90–100 as an *A* would receive an *A* on the assessment.)

Once you have set up your original rubric, you can easily modify it to address the specific criteria for each assignment, which is preferable to using a generic rubric that may not account for what you are assessing.

Note: Always distribute and review scoring rubrics with the students when you give them the assignment to ensure that the performance expectations are clear *before* they begin the assignment. To eliminate confusion and possible misunderstandings, it's a good idea to give students a sample assignment, ask them to score it using the rubric, and discuss their scores in relationship to your own. To help you get started, Figures 4.2 and 4.3 on pages 78–79 provide sample rubrics for you to consider.

Designing Authentic Assessment Tools

Not all students test well for a variety of reasons. Some students have difficulty with the format of objective tests. Some students overthink the test questions and lose sight of what the questions are asking. Some students freeze when faced with a test and literally shut down. For students like these, what they produce during an examination period speaks only to their test behaviors, not to what they know or to what they are capable of doing. To properly and fairly assess these students, teachers need authentic, alternate forms of assessment that allow students to demonstrate their knowledge using a format that is understandable and accessible to them. Authentic assessments closely mirror the kinds of activities that students will experience outside the classroom. They are usually performance based and are often collaborative. Activities such as formal presentations, performances, portfolios, experiments, inventions, movies, computer animations and games, journals, original writings, PowerPoint presentations, research, interviews, exhibitions, surveys, and debates would fall into this category.

Note: While authentic assessments clearly benefit poor test-takers, they are equally beneficial to good test-takers. Authentic assessments give all students opportunities to collaborate, develop, and practice good critical-thinking skills, while at the same time providing opportunities for students to explore ways they can apply what they are learning to the world outside the classroom.

Guidelines for Developing Authentic Assessments

1. Activities should be challenging, meaningful, and tied to instruction.
2. Activities should be clearly defined (what the activity is, what skills or concepts will be demonstrated, time frame, etc.).
3. Activities should be aligned to the student's learning style.
4. Students who are capable should participate in the selection, design, and planning of the activity.
5. Students should be given a rubric prior to the beginning of the activity to identify performance expectations.
6. Student progress should be monitored throughout the activity to ensure that the student's work is on target.

Steps for Designing an Authentic Assessment

Step 1. Clearly define the project. It is important that both the student and the teacher have the same understanding of what the student is being expected to produce. Having a written agreement between the student and the teacher that clearly defines all aspects of the project is a good way to ensure that this happens. The most successful projects are those that are designed and developed collaboratively by the teacher and the student. When defining the project, be sure to include the following information:

■ What it will be or what form the project will take (such as presentation, PowerPoint, survey, dramatization, movie, research).

- What skills, concepts, or body of knowledge will be exhibited in the project. These skills and concepts should be aligned with your instruction.
- The scope of the project. For example, if the project is a survey, how many participants will be included; if there is an expectation of research, how many sources will be included.
- How the project will be used to determine the quarter or semester grade.
- The time frame for the project, including when the project is due.
- When the student will work on the activity.
- What materials or equipment will be needed and who will assume the responsibility for getting those resources.
- If students are collaborating, how they will be working together, what responsibilities each will assume, and so on.
- How, when, and to whom the project will be presented.

Step 2. Set up an ongoing assessment schedule. It's important that the student's progress be checked periodically throughout the project to ensure the work is on target. Divide the project into segments and assign each segment a due date when you will meet with the student to assess what has been done to date.

Step 3. Develop criteria for scoring. Rubrics are ideal for scoring authentic assessment because they can be easily customized to accommodate differences in projects. When you meet with students to develop a scoring rubric, bring a list of the specific criterion that you want this project to exhibit.

Step 4. Develop a tool for student evaluations. If the projects are going to be presented to the class, it's a good idea to guide students' responses with specific questions instead of just asking, "What did you think?" When designing a student evaluation form, frame the questions in a way that would give the presenter *positive* feedback. For example, "What did you like most in the presentation?" or "What did you learn?" or "What would you like to know more about?" are more sensitive and more helpful than asking "What would you have done differently?" or "What would make this presentation better?" It's also a good idea to stay away from having students rate each other's performance (poor, good, very good, excellent, etc.). These evaluations typically tend to reflect how the students feel about each other rather than provide useful feedback on the work being presented. See Model 13: Authentic Assessment.

Using Portfolios to Assess Student Learning

A portfolio is an assessment strategy that can be used to measure student growth over time and over projects. The portfolio is a collection of an individual student's work that is systematically collected at regular intervals and exemplifies his or her expertise in a given area. The portfolio can be used to collect and evaluate varied sources of information that demonstrate a student's learning and competence in terms of process (*how* the student reaches a goal) and product (*what* the student produces). Both teachers and students value portfolios as a form of assessment because they allow for a more complete and comprehensive view of a student's abilities and competencies. Unlike some tests, which only show what a student recalls, portfolios provide students with the opportunity to *demonstrate* not only what they know but also what they can do and how well they can apply what they know to other areas of their lives. In addition, portfolios reflect the student's ability to set and achieve learning goals, something that is not readily seen in a single exam.

Guidelines for Developing Portfolios

1. The contents of the portfolio should be challenging, meaningful, and tied to instruction.

2. Teachers and students are partners in the educational process. They work together to assess student strengths and weaknesses, establish learning goals, select products to be included in the portfolio, and evaluate portfolio contents.

3. The contents of the portfolio are clearly defined (learning goals, pieces to be included, how the pieces demonstrate the learning goals, how the portfolio will be assessed, time frame for completion, etc.).

4. Portfolios are multidimensional, taking into account student interests, learning needs, experiences, and goals.

5. Students are required to be reflective and to self-assess.

6. Students are evaluated against themselves, not against other students.

7. Assessment is systematic and ongoing.

8. Samples are collected systematically over time and are used to measure student growth.

Implementing Portfolio Assessments

Keep in mind when developing your portfolio assessment strategy that it is an ongoing decision-making process. Some of the decisions should be made collaboratively with the student or students who will be responsible for the portfolios (contents, goals, assessments, organization, etc.) and some of the decisions should be made in advance of your first collaborative meeting (what learning their portfolio will demonstrate, logistics, due dates, when students will work on their portfolios, etc.).

Because portfolios are unique assessment tools, there are no set rules about what shape a portfolio takes. Some portfolios are housed in folders, some in crates or boxes, and some electronically. Likewise, there are no rules about what goes into the portfolio. They are collections, representative samplings of the student's work. They can be collections of writing, art, musical compositions, artifacts, experiments, and so on. It is important that the student and the teacher have a written description of the project that reflects their common understanding. Some of the decisions you and your students need to consider when implementing portfolio assessments include the following:

- The purpose of the portfolio.
- The kinds and number of learning samples that should be included.
- The skills, concepts, and knowledge that will be demonstrated in the portfolio.
- What the portfolio will assess (types and quantities of errors, thinking and problem-solving strategies, ability to apply skills and concepts, ability to edit, process, final products, etc.).
- The logistics (where the portfolio will be kept, how often students will work on the portfolio assignments, when students will work on their portfolios, due dates, etc.).
- The lessons that need to be taught to support student success with the portfolio assignments.
- How the portfolio will be organized.
- How the portfolio will be assessed.
- When conferences will be held to review portfolio progress.
- How evaluations of the portfolio will be used.
- How students will self-assess.

Portfolios can be multidisciplinary and represent work over the course of an entire year; however, it is not necessary to begin your portfolio assessment agenda on such a grand scale. Until you become comfortable with the process, it's advisable, when first starting out, to limit the scope of the portfolios, with the understanding that they can be expanded with new learning goals and activities once previously set goals have been met. Model 14 is an example of an initial writing portfolio that was limited to five samples. Models 15 and 16 give students the opportunity to reflect on and self-assess the work included in the portfolios. Figure 4.4 provides a rubric for scoring portfolios.

The key to success when using portfolios as assessment tools is organization. Having clearly defined expectations, procedures, and activities will reduce the anxiety and ensure an exciting and productive learning experience for both you and your students.

Figure 4.4

Rubric for Scoring Portfolios (Grade 6)

Name: _____ Date: _____
Assignment: _____

Learning Goals	Topic Paragraph	Supporting Paragraph	Conclusion	Neatness	Organization	Spelling and Word Usage	Total
Sample 1							
Sample 2							
Sample 3							
Sample 4							
Sample 5							

Scoring: 3=Excellent; 2=Good; 1=Needs Improvement
     27–30=A; 24–26=B; 21–23=C; 19–20=D

Topic Paragraph
    3: Well-developed with introductory information that clearly explains what will be discussed in the rest of the paper.
    2: Needs to be developed with more information.

Supporting Paragraphs
    3: Complete with topic sentence, supporting details, and conclusion.
    2: Complete, although some paragraphs need more supporting details.
    1: Incomplete and/or missing supporting details.

Conclusion
    3: Summarizes ideas presented in the paper.
    2: Summarizes most of the ideas presented in the paper.
    1: Missing and/or fails to summarize main ideas.

Neatness
    3: Has margins and is neatly presented.
    2: Has margins but may have marks.
    1: Missing margins and/or is messy.

Organization
    3: Ideas are presented in a logical and an understandable way.
    2: Most ideas are presented in a logical order.
    1: Ideas are not presented in an organized way.

Spelling and Word Usage
    3: All words are used correctly without any spelling errors.
    2: Most words are used correctly. There may be one spelling error.
    1: Errors in spelling and/or word usage make reading and understanding difficult.

*U*sing Assessments to Monitor Student Progress and Inform Instruction

Learning is a lifelong *process* that is continuous and subject to change. Ongoing and student-centered assessments will bring students to this understanding in a very real and personal way. In the past, when assessments were given at the end of a unit, students who failed or did poorly had no opportunity to modify their understanding before teachers moved on to the next unit. Now teachers understand the importance of assessing throughout the unit to identify and address student weaknesses so that students don't fail. These ongoing assessments can take a variety of forms. Anything that gives you information regarding your students' knowledge and understanding can be used as an assessment tool. For example:

- *Homework and class assignments* can help identify student strengths and weaknesses in a particular area. To quickly identify areas that need more instruction, ask students to self-assess assignments by identifying those questions or problems that gave them difficulty and the reasons why or at what point they experienced difficulty. Also ask students to identify problems or tasks they felt were particularly easy.

- *Objective quizzes* given at the beginning of the period help assess reading comprehension quickly and easily. These quizzes need not be long. Five questions (typed) will tell you very quickly if students understand what they read. These questions should be significant to the meaning of the text (How did John react to the news of his friend's death?) as opposed to identification of trivia (What was John wearing when he was told of his friend's death?). *Note:* If a student indicates that he or she is doing the reading but is still performing poorly on the quizzes, refer the student to the reading specialist for an evaluation to see if a reading problem might be preventing the student from understanding.

- *Response journals* help assess student understanding. Ask students to write a reflective response to something in their reading that resonated for them to help you see disconnects in understanding or interpretations that may not surface in class discussions. Through response journals, teachers can sustain the assessment by dialoging with students via written personalized responses to the students' responses.

- *Graphic organizers* help students to organize concepts and data in a visual way. Because the information is typically displayed in words or fragments, they provide a quick and easy way to see if or how students are connecting ideas. (See Chapter 6 for examples.)

- *Teacher observations* help capture information that escapes formal evaluation. Teachers *see* behaviors or responses that could affect or explain student performance (in either a positive or a negative way). These observations, which could be either academic or behavioral, should always be recorded, dated, and used by teachers to inform decisions about a further course of action. (See Model 17: Teacher Observation Form.)

- *Teacher questioning* is a classic strategy and is used by teachers to assess student knowledge and understanding and their academic strengths and weaknesses. Ask both literal questions (that assess knowledge) and probative questions (that assess comprehension and ability to apply information) during class discussions or informally during casual conversations.

- *Student-teacher conferences* are an effective way to ascertain information regarding your students' learning. Most students feel more comfortable sharing difficulties with their teachers one on one rather than in a whole-class setting. To maximize conference time, both you and your students should bring a written list of issues you want to discuss. Keep a record of each meeting, documenting the discussion and the decisions made during the meeting. (See Model 18: Conference Report Form.)

- *Student writings* give teachers a great deal of information that can be used to inform instruction. These writings don't have to be long. A ten-minute writing in response to a prompt prior to beginning a unit or lesson will reveal issues students are having with their writing and organizational skills as well as their knowledge, beliefs, or positions on issues that are integral to the lesson or unit. Mid- and post-teaching writings are also good ways to monitor student progress and learning.

- *Student self-assessments* help teachers get a more complete picture of student learning, needs, and related issues. Journal entries, learning logs, and self-evaluation forms are typical tools used for this type of assessment. (See Model 19: Self-Evaluation Form and Model 20: Learning Log for Self-Evaluation). Students should self-assess frequently; they need practice being reflective. Many teachers ask students to self-assess at the end of each class period as a strategy for informing their next day's lesson.

- *Peer reviews* can be seen as a teaching tool as well as an assessment tool. Having students evaluate other students' work reinforces their own knowledge and understanding, while honing skills they can use for their assessment of their own work. *Note:* For peer reviews to be productive, students must be given a rubric to clarify and guide their review of another student's work. The use of a rubric gives the students a sense that their papers are being evaluated fairly. They also provide talking points for students to use to discuss their evaluations with each other and with you following the reviews.

Assessing Young Readers

Reading is the bottom line to all learning. Good readers are advantaged with the vocabulary, skills, and strategies that allow them to access all the content areas; poor readers, regardless of ability, are conversely disadvantaged. They are like tennis players competing in a high-stakes match without a racket. They can't succeed. For this reason, how reading instruction is addressed in the early years is critical to a child's success in school and to the range of possibilities and opportunities that follow.

As a classroom teacher, you have the social, ethical, and professional responsibility to teach *all* the children in your class to be good readers. This can happen with a sound reading program that includes a wide range of assessments that are systematic, are administered frequently, and identify individual strengths and weaknesses. This system of assessments could include, for example, informal reading inventories, running records, anecdotal records, story retelling, and developmental checklists, and writing assessments in addition to interest surveys, reading logs, journals, portfolio assessments, writing samples, teacher questioning, and conferencing. Maintaining an assessment portfolio throughout the year for each student will make it easier to assess each student's performance and progress comprehensively and reliably.

Informal Reading Inventories

It's important that students be given reading materials that are appropriate for them, materials that are challenging but not so difficult that they would frustrate and shut down the reader. Informal reading inventories (Cooter, 1990) help teachers identify the reading level of each student so that appropriate texts can be selected. These assessments, which identify a student's ability in graded or leveled reading materials such as basal readers or books used for guided reading, characterize reading levels as independent (easy to read), instructional (ideal for teaching), or frustration (too difficult). Periodic administration of these inventories helps teachers assess student progress and informs the teacher when the student is ready to be moved to the next level of reading. Among the inventories that are frequently used in schools today are *Classroom Reading Inventory* (Silvaroli, 1986), *Developmental Reading Assessment* (Beaver, 2001), *The Flynt/Cooter Reading Inventory for the Classroom* (Flynt & Cooter, 1998), and *The Flynt/Cooter English*Español Reading Inventory* (Flynt & Cooter, 1999).

Running Records

A running record (Reutzel & Cooter, 2004), which is taken by the teacher as the student is reading, identifies the student's decoding development as well as what the student can do both independently and with teacher support. The teacher sits beside the student while the student reads a 100- to 200-word passage and records what the student does during the reading. A coding system developed by Marie Clay (1972, 1993a, 1993b) is used to identify how the child responds to each word read (for example, reads it correctly, substitutes an actual word with another word, asks for help, recognizes error and self-corrects). This coding system takes about two hours of practice to master. Most teachers find that the time spent learning the codes is negligible compared to the benefits to their students. The results of the assessment tell the teacher with 90 percent reliability if the book the child is reading is appropriate. Giving a child a book that is too difficult frustrates and demoralizes the child, which often translates into the child being turned off to reading. Conversely, giving a child a book that is too easy will quickly bore the child and cause him or her to lose interest in reading. The goal is to help children become independent readers and lovers of books. Giving students books that are challenging, interesting, and manageable is the first step in making that happen.

Running records also help teachers group students effectively for guided reading. By taking frequent running records, the teacher knows when the student is ready to move to another group. A final benefit is that while running records help teachers monitor the progress of their students, they also verify for them the success of their own intervention strategies. Teachers monitor the progress of their students; they also verify the success of their own Intervention Strategies. For procedures for taking, scoring, and analyzing Running Records, see *www.readinga-z.com/guided/ runrecord.html* or *www.eworkshop.on.ca/edu/pdf/calculatepercentaccuracy.pdf.*

Anecdotal Records

Anecdotal records (Winograd, Flores-Duanas, & Arrington, 2003) are informal observations made by the teacher as the students are working. These records are helpful in identifying behaviors that do not present themselves on traditional tests and assignments, behaviors that may be impeding student success. For example, Ms. Anderson, while taking anecdotal records during learning-center time, noticed that Alex was having difficulty getting started. By the time he finally began working productively, most of the other children were finished. Had his teacher not been observing Alex, she may have misinterpreted his failure to complete the assignment as inability, disinterest, or inattentiveness when the real problem was his weak organizational skills, something she now knows she has to address.

Although there are no steadfast rules about taking anecdotal records, many teachers find it helpful to select a focus for a particular set of observations (such as organization, comprehension, interactions with other students, time-on-task).

Because these records are informal and individualized, it is not necessary to observe all of the students on the same day. It is necessary, though, that the same behaviors or competencies be observed multiple times during the year so that you can monitor both student progress and the success of your intervention strategies. See Model 21: Anecdotal Record.

Story Retelling

Story retelling can be used to assess students' comprehension and ability for literal recall (Fountas & Pinnell, 1996) and to identify their sense of story structure. This assessment, which usually immediately follows a student's reading of a story, requires that the student retell the entire story in sequence, as the teacher notes the recollections. You may want to look for the following skills and concepts during this assessment:

- the accuracy of the sequencing
- the accuracy of the events being recalled
- evidence of elements of structure (beginning, middle, end)
- accurate identification of major events in the story
- accurate identification of minor events in the story
- accurate portrayal of characters
- references to elements of text (theme, setting, plot, etc.)
- inferences and judgments made by the reader
- recollections of supporting details
- connections readers make between the text and their own lives

Your analysis of the students' retelling will help you identify what areas of instruction need more attention. Like all assessments, to accurately assess student growth, conduct retelling assessments several times during the year. See Model 22: Story Retelling.

Developmental Checklist

A developmental checklist will help you monitor individual or group progress. The best checklists, which are teacher developed and focus on a particular set of skills or behaviors that can be easily observed, are simple to develop and can easily be used to monitor students' progress on a weekly basis. The checklist in Model 23: Developmental Checklist was created to monitor student behaviors before, during, and after reading.

Assessing English Language Learners

As the numbers of limited or non-English-speaking students continue to increase in classrooms throughout the United States, teachers in larger numbers are being faced with the challenge of developing strategies that will enable them to assess these students in ways that will yield high degrees of reliable information that they can use to inform their instruction. What confounds this problem for most teachers is their inability to converse with their students in their native language and their understanding that it is impossible to obtain accurate information about student knowledge if that knowledge is being assessed in a language or a format the students don't understand. To compensate for the disparity in languages, teachers are rethinking how they assess their students and providing alternate forms of assessments and/or modifications to their existing assessments and procedures. These modifications could include the following:

1. Replace traditional testing with authentic, performance-based assessments.

2. State the questions in active rather than passive voice (for example, change "If a man left his family . . ." to "If you left your family . . .").

3. Align materials and texts to students' language proficiency level.

4. Allow students to use a list of terms or vocabulary words with definitions that would help them understand the expectations of the assignment or test.

5. Provide the questions or directions in both the student's native language and English.

6. Give students extra time to complete the tasks.

7. Test students separately to alleviate the discomfort and distraction of taking more time than their English-speaking classmates.

8. Provide students with models of test questions and responses.

9. Simplify the test questions, removing all unnecessary language.

10. Allow students to use bilingual dictionaries.

11. Give assessments that rely on graphic and visual content and verbal responses instead of on dense texts.

12. Allow students to be assessed as part of a collaborative group.

Sharing the Results

Keep the lines of communication open between parents, teachers, and students, particularly when it comes to grades and student performance. While teachers understand that grades are just a small piece of the big picture, parents and students continue to see grades as the most important piece. You can diffuse unnecessary student and parent anxiety about grades by simply being open about your grading procedures and by sharing student progress throughout the year with periodic updates in addition to the report cards. Like rubrics, progress reports objectify grades and make it clear to parents and students *how* the grade was determined.

Progress reports should be specific. For example, reporting that Tom has missed four of the last six assignments has more meaning than "Tom's weakness is homework." A standardized form is best for these updates. They don't take much time to fill out, and they're easy for students and parents to read and understand.

The frequency for sending progress reports is up to the teacher. Many K–5 teachers find sending them weekly is a good strategy for keeping the students on target and for keeping the parents involved in their children's learning. Should you decide to do this, alert parents in advance of the day they should expect their children to bring these reports home. For middle and high school teachers, because of the number of students, it is more realistic to provide these reports at the middle and at the end of each marking period.

The Power of Assessments

Although we would like students to think of assessments in positive terms, as tools that are used by their teachers to make curricular decisions that will in turn lead to their successful learning, the truth of the matter is that most students think of assessments as being punitive. Undeniably, assessments hold a great deal of power for students at all levels of learning, and this power is felt at an early age.

Inadvertently, teachers and parents condition children to view assessments as being negative by the very language and behaviors they use to discuss and respond to assessment results. As early as kindergarten, answers are designated as being either right or wrong, with the *right* answers being rewarded with smiles, smiley faces, and hugs, which, at home, children receive for *good* behavior. As children proceed through school, they come to understand that for them to move forward with their friends, they have to do well on tests and assessments. They understand that not to do well means they will be left back. In addition, for many children, parental approval and consequent social life and privileges are connected to their performance on assessments. A poor report card could easily translate into weeks of staying in on Saturday nights until the grades improve. In high school, the power of tests is felt even more as students come to understand that their ability to get into the college of their choice or to receive scholarship support will be predicated on how well they perform on school-based and standardized tests and assessments.

The probability that you can change this perception is low. However, you can be sensitive to the stress and anxiety that students experience with testing. Understand that students do take test results personally, even if they don't acknowledge it. Understand the ramifications testing can have on students' self-perceptions, and understand that you can make a difference in *your* class by assessing frequently and by working with your students to use those assessments to improve their learning and consequent summative results.

Advice from the Field

- If a significant number of students do poorly on an assessment, check to see if the instrument is flawed before making the assumption that the students didn't study or that they didn't understand the material.

- If an assessment is going to be graded, make sure you give students ample notice so that they can study. It's a good idea to give students at least a week's notice for a major exam.

- Always set your students up for success. Make sure they have the skills in place *before* they are tested.

- Always find something good to say about a student's work or performance.

- Always begin and end assessment conferences with something positive.

- Don't use tests or the threat of tests to control your students. It sends the wrong message about the function of testing.

Additional Resources

Butler, S. M., & McMunn, N. D. (2006). *A teacher's guide to classroom assessment: Understanding and using assessment to improve student learning.* San Francisco: Jossey-Bass, Inc.

Clay, M. M. (1985). *The early detection of reading difficulties* (3rd ed.). Portsmouth, NH: Heinemann.

Clay, M. M. (1997). *Running records for classroom teachers.* Portsmouth, NH: Heinemann.

Harp, B. (1994). *Assessment and evaluation for student-centered learning.* Norwood, MA: Christopher-Gordon.

Stiggins, R. J., Arter, J. A., Chappuis, J., & Chappuis, S. (2007). *Classroom assessment for student learning: Doing it right—using it well.* Upper Saddle River, NJ: Prentice Hall.

References

The AP vertical teams guide for English (2nd ed.). (2002). New York: The College Entrance Examination Board.

Beaver, J. (2001). *Developmental reading assessment.* Parsippany, NJ: Celebrations Press.

Clay, M. M. (1972). *Reading: The pattern of complex behavior.* Exeter, NH: Heinemann.

Clay, M. M. (1993a). *An observation survey of early literacy achievement.* Portsmouth, NH: Heinemann.

Clay, M. M. (1993b). *Reading recovery: A guidebook for teachers in training.* Portsmouth, NH: Heinemann.

Cooter, R. B., Jr. (Ed.). (1990). *The teacher's guide to reading tests.* Scottsdale, AZ: Gorsuch Scarisbrick.

Flynt, E. S., & Cooter, R. B., Jr. (1998). *The Flynt/Cooter reading inventory for the classroom.* Scottsdale, AZ: Gorsuch Scarisbrick.

Flynt, E. S., & Cooter, R. B., Jr. (1999). *The Flynt/Cooter English*Español reading inventory.* Upper Saddle River, NJ: Merrill/Prentice Hall.

Fountas, I. C., & Pinnell, G. S. (1996). *Guided reading: Good first teaching for all children.* Portsmouth, NH: Heinemann.

Gardner, H. (1983). *Frames of mind: The theory of multiple intelligences.* New York: Basic Books.

McWorter, K. T. (2000). *Guide to college reading.* New York: Longman.

Reutzel, R. D., & Cooter, R. B., Jr. (2004). *Teaching children to read: Putting the pieces together* (4th ed.). Upper Saddle River, NJ: Pearson.

Silvaroli, N. J. (1986). *Classroom reading inventory* (5th ed.). Dubuque, IA: William C. Brown.

Stanford, P., & Reeves, S. (March/April 2005). Assessment that drives instruction. *Teaching Exceptional Children, 37*(4), 18–22.

Winograd, P., Flores-Duanas, L., & Arrington, H. (2003). Best practices in literacy assessment. In L. M. Morrow, L. B. Gambrell, & M. Pressley (Eds.), *Best practices in literacy instruction.* New York: Guilford.

Online Resources

Edutopia—www.edutopia.org/assessment
Teacher Vision—www.teachervision.fen.com/assessment/resource/5815.html
Center for Teaching—http://cte.umdnj.edu/student_evaluation/evaluation_cat.cfm
Rubrics for Teachers—www.rubrics4teachers.com

Authentic Assessment: Grade 10 Language Arts

Name: _____ Class: _____

Teacher: _____ Date: _____

Project: Write an original short story, five to eight typewritten pages, about a conflict between two characters that thematically shows man's insensitivity to man. The story will include description and dialogue and will be written in complete sentences that are free of grammar and punctuation errors.

Project Participant(s): John Arlington

Skills/Concepts/Knowledge: The story will demonstrate an understanding of the progression of plot (exposition, rising action, climax, falling action, and conclusion), conflict, theme, paragraph development, grammar, and punctuation.

Scope: N/A

Time Frame: Four weeks; project due 2/22

Work on Project: Work on the project will be done during class on Fridays and at home.

Resources needed: None

Project Review Dates: Teacher-student conferences will be held during class on Mondays and after school by appointment.
       Conference 1: Outline Due—2/1
       Conference 2: First Draft Due—2/8
       Conference 3: Second Draft Due—2/15

Presentation of the Project: The story will be shared with the class during an oral reading on 2/22.

Evaluation of the Project: The project will be evaluated with a rubric developed by John and Mr. Peters.

How the Project Will Be Valued: The story will be 20 percent of the second-quarter grade.

Sandra's Writing Portfolio

Title Page

Letter to the Reader (describing the goals and contents of the portfolio)

Baseline Sample
> Title: My Bedroom
> Assessment of Strengths and Weaknesses

Descriptive
> Title: A Day at the Beach
> Personal Comments (explaining why the piece was selected,
>   what specific goals were being addressed)
> Rough Draft
> Self-Assessment

Expository
> Title: How to Plant a Rose Garden
> Personal Comments
> Rough Draft
> Self-Assessment

Narrative
> Title: The Day My Brother Was Born
> Personal Comments
> Rough Draft
> Self-Assessment

Persuasive
> Title: A Dress Code Is Needed at Selby High School
> Personal Comments
> Rough Draft
> Self-Assessment

My Best Piece
> Title: Shopping with My Grandmother
> Personal Comments
> Rough Draft
> Self-Assessment

Portfolio Reflective Self-Assessment

Name: _____ Date: _____

Title: _____

1. My goals for this piece were _____
   _____.

2. The goals I met were _____
   _____.

3. The goals I did not meet are _____
   _____.

4. What gave me the most difficulty on this piece was _____
   _____.

5. What I did to solve the problems I was having was _____
   _____.

6. What I would do differently on the next piece is _____
   _____.

7. What I like most about this piece is _____
   _____.

8. What I have learned is _____
   _____.

9. What I would like to know is _____
   _____.

10. What I need help with is _____
    _____.

Portfolio Final Self-Assessment

1. What goals did you set for your portfolio?

2. What goals did you meet?

3. What goals did you not meet?

4. What problems did you have while working on your portfolio?

5. How did you solve each problem?

6. What did you find easy while working on your portfolio?

7. What did you enjoy most about working on your portfolio?

8. What would you do differently the next time?

9. How could your teacher be more helpful to you?

10. What are your goals for your next project?

Teacher Observation Form

Teacher: _____		Class: _____	
Date	Student's Name	Observation	Action

Conference Report Form

Date: _____ Conference Site: _____

Conference Participants: _____
_____
_____

What Was Discussed:
_____
_____
_____
_____
_____

Decisions Made:
_____
_____
_____
_____

Conference Follow-up:

What Student(s) Will Do:
_____
_____
_____

What Teacher Will Do:
_____
_____
_____

What Parent Will Do:
_____
_____
_____

Date for Follow-up Conference: _____

Self-Evaluation Form

Name: _____ Class: _____

Date: _____ Lesson: _____

What I learned today:

What I thought was most interesting:

What I thought was least interesting:

What I found confusing:

What I would like to know more about:

Learning Log for Self-Evaluation

LEARNING LOG

Name: _____ Class: _____

Date	What I Learned	What I Don't Understand	What I Want to Know More About

Anecdotal Record

Teacher: _____

Student: _____

Guided Reading	Writing Workshop	Learning Center	Independent Work Time	Free Time	Action Needed

Comments:

Story Retelling

Sequence of events in the story
1. _____
2. _____
3. _____
4. _____
5. _____

Supporting details
1. _____
2. _____
3. _____
4. _____
5. _____

Recollections of characters (physical, behavioral, attitudinal)
_____
_____
_____

Identification of conflicts
1. _____
2. _____
3. _____
4. _____
5. _____

Setting
_____
_____

References to literary devices (theme, tone, plot, etc.)
_____
_____

Inferences/judgments
_____
_____

Connections made between text and student's personal experiences
_____
_____

Teacher's observations/comments:

Student strengths:

Student weaknesses:

Developmental Checklist

Group: _____ Date: _____

Text: _____

Behavior	Sally	Tom	Andy	Pam	Sara
Before Reading					
Begins immediately					
Makes predictions based on title and cover					
Shows enthusiasm for reading					
Asks questions about the text					
During Reading					
Uses visual information to support comprehension					
Questions during reading					
Makes predictions					
Self-corrects					
Rereads to confirm accuracy and/or understanding					
After Reading					
Draws conclusions					
Makes personal connections with story					
Connects story elements with other stories					
Asks questions					

Comments:

Learning-Style Assessment

To score your assessment, record the total number of *As* and *Bs*.

Part 1

_____ 1. I would prefer to follow a set of
   a. oral directions
   b. written directions

_____ 2. I would prefer to
   a. attend a lecture given by a famous writer
   b. read a story written by the writer

_____ 3. When I am introduced to someone, it is easier for me to remember the person's
   a. name
   b. face

_____ 4. I find it easier to learn new information by
   a. reading about it
   b. seeing pictures or examples

_____ 5. I prefer classes in which the teacher
   a. lectures and answers questions
   b. uses films and videos

_____ 6. To follow current events, I would prefer to
   a. listen to the news on the radio
   b. read the newspaper

_____ 7. To learn how to operate a fax machine, I would prefer to
   a. listen to a friend's explanation
   b. watch a demonstration

Part 2

_____ 8. I prefer to
   a. work with facts and details
   b. work with theories and ideas

_____ 9. I would prefer a job where I
   a. follow specific instructions
   b. figure out what needs to be done

_____ 10. I prefer to
   a. solve math problems using numbers
   b. solve math problems using theories

_____ 11. I would prefer to write a term paper explaining
   a. how a process works
   b. a theory

_____ 12. I prefer tasks that require me to
   a. follow careful, detailed instructions
   b. use reasoning and critical analysis

_____ 13. For a criminal justice course, I would prefer to
   a. discover how and when a law can be used
   b. learn how and why it became law

_____ 14. To learn more about how an airplane works, I would prefer to
   a. take a model plane apart
   b. understand the principles of aerodynamics

Part 3

_____ 15. To solve a math problem, I would prefer to
   a. draw or visualize the problem
   b. study a sample problem and use it as a model

_____ 16. To remember something, I
   a. create a mental picture
   b. write it down

_____ 17. Assembling a bicycle from a diagram would be
   a. easy
   b. challenging

_____ 18. I prefer classes in which I
   a. handle equipment or work with models
   b. participate in a class discussion

_____ 19. To understand and remember how a machine works, I would
   a. draw a diagram
   b. write notes

Learning-Style Assessment

_____ 20. I enjoy
    a. drawing or working with my hands
    b. speaking, writing, and listening

_____ 21. If I were trying to locate a new friend's house, I would prefer
    a. a map
    b. written directions

Part 4

_____ 22. For a grade in biology lab, I would prefer to
    a. work with a lab partner
    b. work alone

_____ 23. When faced with a difficult personal problem, I prefer to
    a. discuss it with others
    b. resolve it myself

_____ 24. Many teachers could improve their classes by
    a. including more discussion and group activities
    b. allowing students to work on their own more frequently

_____ 25. When listening to a lecture or speaker, I respond more to the
    a. person presenting the idea
    b. the ideas themselves

_____ 26. When on a team project, I prefer to
    a. work with several team members
    b. divide the tasks and complete those assigned to me

_____ 27. I prefer to shop and do errands
    a. with my friends
    b. by myself

_____ 28. A job in a busy office is
    a. more appealing than working alone
    b. less appealing than working alone

Part	Choice A Total	Choice B Total
1	Auditory	Visual
2	Tactile	Conceptual
3	Spatial	Verbal
4	Social	Independent

Interpreting Learning-Style Scores

Part 1: This score indicates whether you learn better by listening (auditory) or by seeing (visual).
Auditory learners tend to learn more easily by hearing than by reading.
Visual learners have strengths with visual modes of learning such as reading, studying pictures, reading diagrams, and so on.

Part 2: This score describes the types of learning tasks and learning situations you prefer and find easiest to handle.
Tactile learners prefer tasks that involve real objects and situations. Practical, real-life examples are ideal for you.
Conceptual learners prefer to work with language and ideas. They do not need practical applications for understanding.

Part 3: This score reveals your ability to work with spatial relationships.
Spatial learners are able to visualize or mentally see how things work or how they are positioned in space. Their strengths may include drawing, assembling, or repairing things.
Verbal (nonspatial) learners lack skills in positioning things in space. Instead, they rely on verbal or language skills.

Part 4: This score reveals whether you like to work alone or with others.
Social learners prefer to work with others, both classmates and teachers, closely and directly. They tend to be people-oriented and enjoy personal interaction.
Independent learners prefer to work alone and study alone. They tend to be self-directed or self-motivated and often goal-oriented.

Adapted from K. T. McWhorter. (2000). *Guide to college reading.* (New York: Longman).

5

Literacy Instruction K–12

A variety of methods and materials may be used to teach literacy K–12. Highly effective teachers must teach students to read with comprehension and fluency, to write using the writing process, to listen effectively, and to speak comfortably and correctly. Studies have shown that it is neither the materials nor the methodology but rather the teacher that makes the difference in literacy instruction (Paterson, Henry, O'Quinn, Ceprano, & Blue, 2003). Arguably, some materials and methods are better than others, but believing in your purposes and your goals and knowing the important basic components of an excellent literacy program will guide you in your teaching of literacy.

This chapter begins with a discussion of balanced literacy because it has implications for all readers and writers. It includes the essential components of literacy that may be adapted for all levels of instruction. Although teachers often associate balanced literacy with elementary students, its components and tenets can easily be incorporated into all lessons in middle and high school as well.

Secondary teachers can benefit from a deeper understanding of how students learn to read. Many middle and high school students are unprepared to read grade-level content material. This may be extremely frustrating to teachers who expect that the students will understand the text and their lectures. Students with learning disabilities, reading issues, and/or English Language Learners (ELLs) have needs that must be addressed by middle and high school teachers. Most traditionally prepared teachers who have had many education courses have a difficult time teaching their content to all students; for alternate route teachers, it presents a more difficult challenge. We believe that providing a framework such as balanced literacy, which explains a successful way to teach literacy, will benefit teachers of all grade and content levels.

Balanced literacy represents what scholars in the literacy field have learned over the past fifty years, which is that literacy instruction must consist of a balance or combination of various approaches to be effective and to meet the needs of students. Much has been written about phonics or skills-based instruction versus whole language or a more holistic approach that focuses on the use of great literature. That debate has raged for years, but it is now understood that both of these approaches have great merit and should be incorporated into all literacy instructional programs. Students need a variety of approaches that can provide a well-rounded approach to learning. Different types of learners need different approaches and balanced literacy offers a variety of instructional modes, which is a key to its success.

What Is Balanced Literacy?

Balanced literacy is a literature-based framework for teaching literacy behaviors, attitudes, and skills to children. It is a comprehensive approach to teaching students how to read, write, speak, think, and view. The ultimate goal of balanced literacy instruction is to foster a love of reading and writing that will inspire and challenge students to develop as lifelong learners who naturally think of themselves as readers, writers, speakers, and thinkers. This is accomplished by using authentic reading and writing experiences to teach students how to use literacy strategies and skills and by giving them many opportunities to apply what they have learned. This process is used at all levels of instruction.

Advocates of balanced literacy instruction (Cooper & Kiger, 2003; Mazzoni & Gambrell, 2003) believe that for students to develop as good readers, writers, speakers, thinkers, and viewers, the teaching strategy must include the following:

- Literacy must be the foundation of all lessons. In content areas, focusing on how to read the text is as important as mastering the content.

- Strategies and skills must be taught directly and indirectly, in small and large groups, as well as in individualized settings.

- Reading instruction must include word recognition, phonics, comprehension, fluency, vocabulary instruction, small-group instruction, large-group instruction, and independent work.

- Writing instruction must include an understanding of the *process* of writing, which students can apply to all types of pieces (such as narrative, expository, descriptive, poetry, journal writing, letter writing, etc.) as well as instruction in grammar, punctuation, and spelling.

- Reading and writing opportunities must extend into all content areas (math, art, music, social studies, science, etc.).

- The same strategies used to teach reading and writing should be applied in the same way to teach the content areas.

What Are the Components of a Balanced Literacy Program?

To maximize effectiveness, a balanced literacy program should include all areas of literacy presented in context, informed by assessment, and designed to meet the needs of all students, as outlined on page 109 and discussed later in this chapter.

What We Want Our Students to Know and Be Able to Do

Teachers at all levels of K–12 instruction must plan lessons with a clear understanding of exactly what they want their students to know and be able to do by the end of the lesson. School and district curriculum guides, based on state and

Strategies Teachers Can Use to Guide Students' Reading

Major Components	Strategy	Targeted Skills
Read-Aloud	Interactive reading in which students listen to the teacher reading, often joining in on familiar refrains or repetitious words.	Story conventions, comprehension, fluency, word sounds, function of punctuation, vocabulary, phonics.
Shared Reading	Together, students and teacher read aloud from a text (big book, enlarged text, poem, song, or part of a story, etc.).	Story conventions, vocabulary, fluency, word sounds, function of punctuation, phonics.
Reader's Workshop	Students self-select book to read. Teacher presents minilesson to target skill/concept for students to locate in their book during their independent reading, which follows the minilesson.	Targeted skills or concepts specific to the workshop.
Independent Reading	Students read self-selected texts alone or with partners.	Reading strategies, vocabulary development, reading appreciation, concept development.
Word Work	Teacher directly teaches letter knowledge, phonological awareness, high-frequency words, letter and word sounds and patterns.	Word-attack strategies, vocabulary, phonics, grammar, letter knowledge, letter/word sound connections.
Guided Reading	Teachers work with small groups as they read leveled texts that match student abilities and interests. The teacher helps students think, read, and talk about the text in a purposeful way that will lead them to become independent, strategic, fluent readers.	Word-attack strategies, story conventions, fluency, comprehension, vocabulary, phonics.
Write-Aloud	Teachers model what they are actually thinking as they write a piece in front of their students.	Writing conventions, concept development, writing process.
Shared/Modeled Writing	Teacher and students work together to compose messages and stories. Students provide the ideas as the teacher acts as scribe, modeling the writing process.	Writing conventions, concept development, syntax, vocabulary development, grammar, writing process.

(Continued)

continued

Major Components	Strategy	Targeted Skills
Interactive Writing	Teacher and students compose a story or message together. Students "share the pen" to record the text on the board, poster, or overhead.	Concept development, writing conventions, sounds of words and how sounds connect with letters, writing process, punctuation, grammar.
Guided Writing	Teacher works one-on-one or in small groups with students, focusing on specific skill deficiencies.	Sound/symbol connection, process writing, writing conventions, punctuation, syntax.
Independent Writing	Students self-select topics, draft, edit, revise, and either publish or record their writing in personal journals.	Writing conventions, process writing.
Writer's Workshop	All students in the class work independently on self-selected pieces at the same time.	Writing conventions, process writing.
Literacy Centers	Places for students to practice and explore skills and concepts while guided reading groups are in session.	Reinforce skills and concepts taught in class.
Ancillary Components		
Student-Teacher Conferences	Teacher meets one-on-one with students to discuss skill and concept strengths and weaknesses.	Targeted skills and concepts are specific to the needs of the individual student.
Direct Instruction	Teacher presents planned skill or concept instruction to whole class or small groups.	Targeted skills or concepts are specific to the lesson (i.e., vocabulary, phonics, writing conventions).
Literature Circles	Students meet in small groups to discuss, question, and challenge other opinions about text.	Analytical thinking and speaking skills, comprehension, discussion skills.
Minilessons	Small-group or whole-class instruction on a specific skill or set of skills with which the targeted group is having difficulty.	Targeted skill or concept is specific to the lesson.
Thematic Units	Teacher plans and presents literature-based units of instruction that include opportunities for students to read, write, speak, present, respond, and think critically.	Comprehension, connecting ideas, story and writing conventions, word-attack skills.

Major Components	Strategy	Targeted Skills
Field Trips	Class trips are planned to support student learning.	Add to student understanding and knowledge base. Help students make connections between what they are learning and life outside the classroom.
Guest Speakers	Guests (parents, teachers, administrators, support staff, community members, etc.) support student learning with personal experiences.	Add to student understanding and knowledge base. Help students make connections.
Guest Readers	Guests read favorite stories to the class.	Literature appreciation, listening skills.

national standards, typically identify the specific teaching and learning expectations for each grade. Certain basic teaching and learning goals should be part of all balanced literacy programs. For example, we want our students to know

- the conventions of print (Freeman, 2003)
- strategies for approaching text
- a wide range of vocabulary words
- strategies for decoding words
- conventions of grammar and how they are used to communicate meaning
- the process of writing
- how to speak effectively and how to organize an oral presentation

In addition, we want our students to be able to

- read with fluency and understanding
- use context clues to understand text
- make predictions and draw conclusions from information presented in texts
- express their thoughts verbally and in writing in a clear and logical way
- edit their work
- be reflective and ask questions

- be academic risk-takers

- participate meaningfully in class discussions and activities

- work collaboratively and independently and be able to monitor and pace themselves

- apply what they learn to other areas of their lives

Using the Balanced Literacy Approach to Teach Students to Read

Using a balanced literacy approach to teach students to read involves using a model of gradually reducing the amount of support we give to students. We begin by giving them extensive support by modeling and sharing new tasks, gradually lessening the amount of support we offer when we provide guided practice and then independent practice. Our goal is to help students become independent readers.

Learning to read and write is similar to learning any new skill. Consider how a child learns to ride a bicycle. At first, a child must see how a bike is ridden. This action is usually *modeled* by a parent who demonstrates how to ride a bike. Obviously, the child must know where the hands and feet are placed. After the modeling, the child *interacts* with the parent in a *practice setting* where the child has the opportunity to ride the bicycle with a parent holding it. The next step is *guided practice,* in which the child rides the bicycle and the parent runs alongside, helping if necessary and offering just the right amount of support. Ultimately, of course, the goal is for the parent to let go and for the child to ride *independently*. This teaching model works for all levels of instruction with all types of activities.

Read-Alouds at All Levels of Instruction

Learning to read can be done using a similar strategy. Begin by reading aloud to your students to model for them what the reading process looks like and sounds like and to provide them with a background knowledge about texts that will help them in their later efforts. Read-alouds are important for students in preschool through high school. Specifically, reading aloud

- actively engages students with the text

- introduces them to the fluency of a good reader

- teaches students how to read

- gives students the opportunity to hear the cadence of the language
- supports students' critical-thinking skills
- engages students' meaning-making processes throughout the reading
- fosters students' understanding that it is their responsibility to create meaning
- fosters a love of reading

Ways to Do a Read-Aloud

A read-aloud can be structured in several ways. It may be used to teach strategies and skills or it may be used simply to foster a love for reading. Read-alouds are critical for young children as well as for middle and high school students.

Step 1. Before Reading

a. Create enthusiasm for the text.

b. Introduce the students to the author and the illustrator.

c. Discuss the title and ask for predictions relating to the title.

d. Discuss the illustrations on the cover.

Step 2. During Reading

a. Ask questions that will activate prior knowledge.

b. Ask students to predict what they think will happen next.

Step 3. Reading Aloud

a. Read to students in an expressive, exciting way.

b. Read through the whole book for young children, a chapter or a piece of text for older students. Allow them to hear the fluency in your reading.

Step 4. After Reading

a. Ask questions about the characters.

b. Discuss the elements of the story (characters, plot, problem, solution).

c. Create a graphic organizer or chart to categorize the information for the students.

d. For young children, you may reread the story several times. Students love to hear stories over and over again.

e. For repetitive text or stories or poems with a refrain, ask students to read or sing along with you.

f. Ask students what they think would have been a better ending for the story.

g. Encourage students to make personal connections to the text.

Step 5. Providing Suggestions for Follow-up Activities (which may also be used as independent activities)

a. Read another book on the same topic.

b. Create a piece of artwork relating to the text in some way.
c. Search a magazine for ideas or objects discussed in the book.
d. Research a topic presented in the book.
e. Write a journal entry responding to the text.
f. Write a response or letter to the character.
g. Write a sequel to the story.

If you decide to do a read-aloud simply for the students' listening pleasure, provide a simple introduction to the book and let the students relax and begin to understand the joy of books and the value of listening.

Reading aloud models fluent reading, familiarizes students with language and conventions of books, and exposes students to different genres of literature. It also introduces vocabulary, and provides motivation to students by exposing them to topics they may otherwise not be ready to read on their own.

Shared Reading

Shared reading is another strategy for students to use to practice their reading skills. Whether in a small group or with the entire class, this is a time when students share in the process by reading along with you. This offers students the opportunity to hear fluency and expression in your reading and to hear you talk about the strategies you are using *while* you are reading. With younger students, you may want to use big books and have students join in by reading familiar words, refrains, or repeated text. For older students, you may bring in a piece of nonfiction or a text that offers a different perspective on a topic that you are studying. For example, teaching the Holocaust strictly from a textbook may not offer personal accounts of human suffering that may be found in a personal memoir or trade book that can be shared with the class. Shared reading also gives teachers the opportunity to challenge students by reading books that are too difficult for students to read on their own, but ones they can still understand and enjoy as they follow along, reading silently. This offers them a shared-reading experience while giving them an opportunity to activate their prior knowledge or to learn new information.

Reading Workshop

Because independent reading is always the ultimate goal, teachers must provide students with many opportunities to read independently. Reading workshop is an excellent strategy to use to foster a love of reading and to encourage students to participate in self-selecting books that they are interested in reading. Prior to the independent portion of the reading workshop, teachers present a five- to ten-minute minilesson, targeting a specific skill or strategy. These strategies can come from the scope and sequence of a basal reading series or a district curriculum guide or from students' work. During the minilesson, the teacher explains the skill or strategy, models what students are to do, provides examples, and conducts a think-aloud. Following the minilesson, students are directed to read independently and look for the strategy in their reading. For example, if you teach a minilesson on describing words (adjectives), you would discuss what an adjective is, provide some examples of interesting adjectives on the board or on an overhead, and read a short piece from a text that has wonderful adjectives. You then provide the students with sticky notes and ask them to look for adjectives in the book they're reading and to place sticky notes on some "excellent adjectives" that they recognize as they read. Students enjoy this activity and it provides a focus in their reading. It doesn't interfere with their reading, and it helps to keep them on track. Teachers often follow up this activity by asking students to respond to their reading in their journals or reading logs. After about 20 to 30 minutes of reading (depending on the grade level), the class gets together for a group share, at which time students are invited to share their favorite adjectives.

Minilessons may be conducted on all sorts of topics, including how to find the plot, setting, parts of speech, elements of good writing, adverbs, lead sentences, and so on. Teachers often use the independent reading portion of reading workshop to walk around the room, conferencing with students either for a few seconds or a few minutes, depending on the teacher's purpose. Reading workshop provides a purpose for reading and an opportunity for all students, including struggling readers, to participate meaningfully as valued members of a community of readers. Reading workshop for middle and high school students offers the opportunity to read a self-selected book that is on their level. The book may be read at home or after other work in the classroom has been completed.

Independent Reading

Independent reading, sometimes referred to as SSR (sustained silent reading), allows students to choose the books they want to read (Fountas & Pinnell, 2001). Students can select books from the classroom or school library, or they can bring books or magazines from home. Independent reading not only gives students private time to practice their reading skills but also sends students an important message that reading is not just an activity associated with "schoolwork." We want students to know that reading is enjoyable and valuable. Giving them time to read something that is of high interest to them quickly sends that message.

In some classrooms, independent reading is a time for unmonitored reading, a time when students self-select their texts and are not responsible for doing an activity relating to their reading. This can present a challenge for some teachers because some students spend their time changing books, flipping through books, or pretending they are reading. Independent reading can be most beneficial when teachers hold students accountable for their reading. That may mean that after the independent reading, the teacher takes three to five minutes to have students either meet with a partner or in a small group and tell each other a few interesting ideas about their book or to have students respond to their book in a journal or meet with the teacher in a conference to talk about the book.

Word Work

Word work, an important part of a balanced literacy program, should be included in every day's activities (Bear, Invernizzi, Templeton, & Johnston, 2003). It begins with a brief, focused experience intended to expand students' language and literacy skills. Although instruction varies based on the grade and ability level of the students, word work includes a variety of language and word activities:

- *Phonics and phonemic awareness strategies* are particularly important for children in grades K–2, who use these strategies to figure out how to pronounce and understand words.

- *Word wall* is a place where teachers post new words or frequently used words for the students to learn and practice. The words on the word wall are changed often and are practiced every day. They may be chanted with younger students or just repeated with older students.

- *Interactive edit* is used to teach mechanics, spelling, or grammar. Students work with the teacher to make corrections together. This is a great activity for middle and high school students because they are doing authentic work with their peers' writing.

- *Journal writing* gives students the opportunity to use their words in a fun and creative way. Journals may or may not be read by the teacher. Some teachers like to give their students a place to privately express their feelings. When pages are private, students fold over the page and the teacher agrees not to read that page.

A word wall may be used at all levels of instruction to reinforce vocabulary instruction.

■ *Creating morning messages* is a way of working with language and words in a meaningful context. Teachers write messages on the board and students respond.

■ *Vocabulary words* in a paragraph are featured and discussed either in groups or with the whole class. They should be introduced in context, in phrases or in sentences, to help students understand and be able to actually use the new words.

Note: Word work must not consist of isolated activities; rather, it should be done in context, using authentic text. Using a great piece of literature to teach letter sounds, verbs, or expressive language is the best way to teach a word lesson because it allows your students to associate their learning with something that makes sense to them.

Guided Reading

Guided reading provides students the opportunity to read and practice the strategies that good readers use, such as rereading when they don't understand or using context clues, while benefiting from the teacher's guidance (Fountas & Pinnell, 2006). The goal of guided reading is to train students to become strategic readers who use the strategies they learn to decode words and make meaning of what they are reading. Guided-reading instruction is usually done in small groups of four to six students and includes the following steps:

1. *Introduction:* The teacher introduces the book using a variety of strategies (providing background information, asking students to recall a previous book or author, asking students to make predictions based on the cover, etc.).

2. *Book Walk:* The teacher conducts a book walk with the students by going through the pictures in the book and asking students to make predictions about what they think is going to happen, what they think the book is about, and so on.

3. *Reading:* Younger students will "whisper read" while one student reads aloud in a slightly louder voice. More fluent readers read the book silently. Teachers can periodically check on an individual's reading by asking the student to read a portion of the text aloud.

4. *Discussion:* A discussion following the reading gives students an opportunity to discuss their understanding of the text and to explain how they used their "target" strategies to reach that understanding.

Note: The ultimate goal of guided reading is to have the students become silent, independent readers reading connected texts—readers who, just like you, call on the strategies that good readers use to understand what they are reading. Although guided reading has traditionally been a teaching activity for elementary students, the steps have implications for all levels of instruction. The basic format is simple. The teacher introduces the book, targeting a strategy that may help students; the students read the book and then discuss it, including how they used the target strategy.

For guided reading to be effective, students must be placed in flexible groups where they are reading on their own instructional level. If students are reading texts that are too difficult, students will become frustrated and they will give up. Placing students in appropriate groups prevents that from happening. The groupings are strategically formed by using assessment results (running records or individual reading inventories) and teacher observations. As students develop as readers, they advance to groups that are reading more difficult texts. To ensure that students are moved into groups as soon as they are ready, teachers should take a running record on one student individually after each guided-reading session. Taking a running record is a relatively simple and expedient way to ensure that all students are placed appropriately. (For more information on running records, see Chapter 4, pages 98–100.) In addition to grouping students appropriately, teachers must select texts that match the students' reading level. Most book publishers identify the instructional level of their texts. You can also go online to identify books and their levels. You may check the following websites to access information about books and their levels:

BSD: Leveled Books Database at www.beavton.k12.or.us/home/staff/library/books/leveling

Hoagies' Gifted Education Page at www.hoagiesgifted.org/reading_levels.htm

Leveled Book Lists at www.home.comcast.net/~ngiansante/

Muttnomah County Library School Corps: Reading Levels for Books at www.muttcolib.org/schoolcorps/readinglevels.html

Using Independent Activities to Support Student Learning

Whenever teachers think about organizing the classroom for guided reading, the question of what the other students will be doing while the teacher is with one small group always surfaces. This is a good question; it takes a strong plan to make this work. Students need to learn to be independent learners, responsible for completing tasks and for managing their own time. To teach these crucial skills, students work on independent activities while the teacher is working with guided-reading groups.

Independent activities may be organized in a variety of ways. For younger students, literacy centers, typically organized around the perimeter of the room, are where students go to practice the skills and concepts taught during class. The centers change frequently to accommodate the skills and concepts that need to be reinforced with practice. Independent activities may be organized so that each student in the class has several activities that must be completed within a certain time period. A Group Work Board organizes students into small groups in which each group has specific activities they must complete as individuals. Following are examples of activities you may want to include in your classroom:

- *word center,* where students can practice putting words together to make sentences or practice spelling new words
- *reading center,* where students can reread books that were read during read-alouds or shared readings or can read additional books on topics discussed in class
- *art center,* where students can create pictures to illustrate their understanding of a story read in class or to illustrate their own stories
- *listening center,* where students can listen to books on tape, while following along with the book
- *writing center,* where students can practice writing their letters or create original pieces of writing
- *math center,* where students can practice their math skills
- *science center,* where students can make observations and take notes on what they see (for example, plants growing, an ant farm, an aquarium)
- *music center,* where students can work together to write their own song about the plot or a character in a story

- *recording center,* where students can tape-record their reading of a book

- *computer center,* where students can do research or practice skills with educational games and tutorial programs

- *drama center,* where students can write and perform plays or skits

Note: Independent activities do not consist of busywork. The activities must be meaningful and authentic with real purposes. Each activity must be strategically planned with goals, objectives, specific directions, materials, and so on. Students should be required to produce something tangible in each center (e.g., a piece of artwork, a review of the book, a tape recording, a checklist). Having to produce a product at each center helps students focus and direct their time. It also gives them a clear message that this is their "work" and that what they are doing is important.

Using a Group Work Board is a highly recommended way to organize students' responsibilities and to differentiate instruction. A Group Work Board is a structure that includes all the students' names written on sticky notes in groups of five or six. Under each sticky note is a series of activities that students should be working on during independent-activities time. (See Figure 5.1.) These activities should be completed by the end of the week. Depending on the teacher's purposes, these groups can be self-selected or created by the teacher. They are typically not the same groups as the guided-reading groups. Sometimes, students are randomly grouped; other times, students who need to be working on similar assignments are grouped together. Although the types of activities vary from week to week, the Work Board always includes independent reading. Some teachers use icons for the Group Work Board to identify for students where they should go or what they should do during literacy-center time. For example, icons may be used to designate a location (e.g., the computer center, math center, writing center, reading center) or an activity or assignment (e.g., research a topic, practice a play, read independently).

During independent activities, students choose their activity, work at their own pace, and manage their own time in order to complete the assigned work by the end of the week. For independent activities to work effectively, students need to understand that they are expected to work quietly and independently, without interrupting the teacher while the teacher is working with guided-reading groups. Some teachers use a "Do Not Disturb" sign, while others wear a specific hat or necklace that signifies guided-reading group in progress. Students must respect the fact that teachers cannot be interrupted. Should students have a question or a problem, they are told to "Ask three before me." They may ask three classmates if they have a question, but if they do not get an acceptable answer to their question, they must wait until the teacher is available. Students can always choose another activity from the Group Work Board or read independently.

Figure 5.1

Group Work Board

Mrs. Gray's Classroom
Group Work Board
For Independent Activities

Jessica	Judy	Kitty	Jane	Matt
Jared	Richie	Al	Howard	Michele
Robyn	Alana	Sam	Jill	Peter
Michael	Jeremy	Jake	Jennifer	Hannah
Harry	Josh	Mo	Royce	Marvin

Reading Journal	Listening Center	Independent Reading	Partner Reading	Literature Circle
Computer	Literature Circle	Word Work	Poetry	Computer
Independent Reading	Poetry	Read Around the Room	Reading Journal	Independent Reading
Word Work	Independent Reading	Computer	Browsing Box	Word Work
Poetry	Readers Theatre	Overhead Projector	Independent Reading	Partner Reading

Use sticky notes for groupings of students. Change groups frequently.
Put reattachable tape on the back of the activity card so that you can change activities each week.

This process does not happen without effort, however. Teachers must model activities from the Group Work Board and provide opportunities for students to work while the teacher walks around the room checking on student assignments and answering questions. Using the first four to six weeks of the school year to model independent activities every day will ensure that students understand their responsibilities, learn how to work independently using the Group Work Board, and accept that this is a time when their teacher cannot be interrupted. As soon as independent activities run smoothly (usually by the beginning of October), the teacher may begin guided-reading groups.

Using the Balanced Literacy Approach to Teach Children to Write Write-Alouds

Because reading and writing are so closely related, you will find that many of the reading components of balanced literacy are aligned with the writing components. The goal in both reading and writing is to construct meaning. Students in elementary, middle, and high school write using similar strategies. During write-aloud, teachers model what they are actually thinking as they write a piece in front of their students. This should be done on the board or on a flipchart so that the students can follow along as the teacher composes. As they write, teachers express concern over word choices, asking the students to help revise and edit their work. Teachers may discuss why they began the piece with a particular opening and ask for suggestions for revision. This component is extremely helpful to students because it shows them the process writers have to go through to get to their finished product. It also helps students understand that writing is not easy and that it takes time, thought, and revision, even for the teacher.

Shared Writing

Shared writing requires that the teacher and the students take part in the writing process together (Freeman, 2005). They choose a topic together and decide how it will be written. In addition, they consider the voice, the audience, the form, and the purpose of the piece. During shared writing, the students provide the ideas, while the teacher acts as a scribe, modeling the process of putting the ideas into written language on the board, on a flipchart, or on an overhead projector. This strategy works with all levels of writers because it provides an opportunity for students to practice thinking and writing like a writer while having the support and guidance of the teacher.

Interactive Writing

Interactive writing is a fun activity in which the students and the teacher compose a story or message together and then "share the pen" to record the story or message on the board, a flipchart, or an overhead. The teacher uses this time to focus instruction on the conventions of writing, word sounds, cadence, spelling, and vocabulary (Fountas & Pinnell, 2006).

Guided Writing

Guided writing allows teachers to provide guided practice as they write their own pieces (Freeman, 2005). This strategy is often used by teachers when working one-on-one with students to help clarify the writing process as they are engaged in the actual process and to address individual problems as they present themselves. This strategy is also used as a whole-class activity. For whole-class guided writing, the teacher divides the class into small groups of students who share similar problems with their writing. As students meet in their groups to discuss aspects of their writing or writer's craft, teachers are free to move about the room and conference with them in small groups. This is particularly successful when students have similar needs at the same time. It allows teachers to focus on the needed skills and strategies without including students who do not have the same needs. An additional benefit of guided-writing groups is that they are short-term groupings, which prevents students from using the groups to identify themselves or their classmates as poor or struggling writers. This is another strategy that can be used for elementary, middle, and high school students.

Independent Writing

Like independent reading, independent writing is a major focus of the balanced literacy program. There are many ways to structure independent writing; however, all of them involve using the writing process, which consists of a series of stages that ask students to think as writers think and to write as writers write. Students need to understand that writers do not just sit down and write a piece without planning, drafting, revising, and editing. Having students engage in writing as process helps to bring them to this understanding in a very pragmatic and meaningful way. The writing process involves five stages: prewriting, creating the first draft, revising, editing, and publishing.

Stage 1: Prewriting   All writing, regardless of the genre, requires a prewriting stage when students strategically choose topics, consider their purpose for writing, identify their audience, select the form the piece should take, determine the information they would like to express, and decide on an organizational pattern for their piece. This stage, which is often omitted by students, is a critical piece of the writing process.

Students can approach this stage in the writing process in various ways. For some students, creating an outline works best; for others, a list seems more appropriate; and for still others, a web or graphic organizer is most useful. For students in the last group, many types of graphic organizers are available that can help them organize their thoughts during the prewriting stage. Teachers should introduce students to all of these strategies and then let students decide which works best for them.

Stage 2: Creating the First Draft   Once the prewriting stage has been completed, the student is ready to write a first draft. This drafting stage is the time for students to write without concern for spelling, punctuation, or other mechanics, knowing that this is the first draft and that this writing will be revised and edited several times before the piece is finished. Instruct the students to skip every other line so that there is room for added words and sentences, arrows, cross-outs, and other revisions. This is important because this is what "real" writers do—they revise and edit—and you want to encourage your students to be authentic thinkers and writers.

Stage 3: Revising   During the revising stage, students refine their ideas and make changes to their work to make their pieces more interesting and more complete and to reflect their purposes in a more meaningful way. Revision is often accomplished with the help of others, either a writing buddy or a writing group, who offer constructive suggestions for revisions. It is important when students share their writing during the revising stage in an author's chair (a special, decorated chair) or in a small group, that students be taught acceptable ways to comment on their classmate's writing. During this stage, appropriate comments must be modeled frequently by the teacher so that students understand exactly how to comment sensitively and effectively. A strategy for students to use to guide their comments is "P.Q.S.: Praise, Questions, and Suggestions." This strategy requires that students begin by finding something about the writing that they can compliment, even if it is as simple as "I like the topic you chose" or "I liked your opening" or "I liked your use of interesting details." Then students must think of questions related to their classmate's writing. For example, if the piece is about a dog, the student might want to know more about the dog (e.g., its name, age, or breed). Finally, students must make suggestions to improve the piece, perhaps adding more details or changing the opening, for example. Making this a procedure that all students must follow lessens the probability that students will find the criticisms hurtful. An added bonus of this strategy is that it teaches students very important life skills: (1) how to make appropriate comments, (2) how to find the good in people, (3) how to be sensitive to other people's feelings, and (4) how to help others.

Stage 4: Editing   Students should understand that revising is all about the content, and editing is all about the mechanics and the final form. Editing consists of checking for punctuation, capitalization, spelling, usage, sentence structure, and form. Students should first edit their own work. Then they should submit it for your review. Your review should identify errors, not correct the errors. Begin by putting a dot at the end of a sentence where there is an error so students can find it, identify it, and fix it. If they cannot find the error, they should come back to you for additional help. At this time, you assist them by limiting their search by putting a dot on top of the incorrect word or phrase so that they can go back and make the correction. If they cannot correct their own errors, show them the corrections and then consider a series of minilessons on editing. While this process may take a great deal of time at first, it is most important that you include it in your practice. Students will never learn to edit unless they have continued practice editing their own work.

Stage 5: Publishing   Publishing is the opportunity to present students' writing to an audience of classmates, parents, or the community. There is a tremendous feeling of pride at this stage of the writing process, regardless of the age or grade level of the students. One way for students to publish their work is to take their writing and make books that they can share with the class. Sometimes, the books are simple, stapled booklets; other times, the books are a bit more fancy and are made of cardboard and covered with wallpaper or cloth. Often, students illustrate their stories with personal drawings or pictures from magazines. Regardless, an important part of this process is to share writing with members of the class. Using an author's chair, students can read their published writings to the class. After reading, students may take turns asking questions and complimenting the author's writing. To ensure that students are treated sensitively, make sure that students are taught how to act appropriately before you begin this activity.

Writer's Workshop

Using the concept of writing as a process is also the way to approach writer's workshop. Writer's workshop, like reader's workshop, begins with a minilesson, includes independent reading and writing, and ends with a group share. Writer's workshop provides students with opportunities for authentic reading and writing. In writer's workshop, students have writing folders for their works in progress. In addition, they keep writing notebooks for jotting down ideas, thoughts, and future writing topics as ideas come to them. The teacher begins with a minilesson, focused on a strategy or skill in writing; and students are asked to consider that particular strategy as they proceed in their writing. These minilessons most often come from weaknesses noted in students' writing.

During writer's workshop, teachers may circulate through the room, conference with students, and offer assistance when needed. Students work at their own pace as they go through the stages of the writing process individually. Because students may be at different stages of their writing at any given time, teachers should do a status check at the beginning of each writer's workshop to see where everyone in the class is in terms of the stages of the writing process.

During the last ten to fifteen minutes of writer's workshop, students gather to share their pieces in the author's chair. This is a time for celebration and praise for the authors. The beauty of writer's workshop is that it allows students in elementary, middle, and high school to write at their own pace in a comfortable environment and to enjoy the applause for their creations, just as real writers do.

Literacy Activities in the Classroom

A program rich in literacy should have a wide range of activities that support student learning. In addition to the major components, a variety of activities should be incorporated into your program to add clarity and interest to your teaching. These activities might include the following:

- *Student-teacher conferences* at all grade levels should be held frequently to help you stay connected to your students as learners and as individuals. These conferences do not always have to be scheduled, nor do they have to be long. Conferencing can easily happen while the class is involved in small-group or individual activities. It is important that students have individual access to your time and attention, especially those students who have difficulty speaking in class and those who have difficulty identifying or verbalizing their problems.

- *Direct instruction* is an effective strategy to teach basic skills and concepts. However, for students to understand these skills and concepts, they must be given opportunities to apply them, practice them, and see them being modeled by their teacher. For example, in a high school history class, teaching students to outline a chapter may be an important skill. However, the process of writing an outline first needs to be modeled by the teacher, showing students how to determine the important details and information, and then practiced by the students. The teacher may provide a partially completed outline and then lead the students to completing it on their own. This will help students to understand the content material better as well.

- *Literature circles* (Daniels, 2002) are opportunities for students to meet in small groups to discuss a piece of literature. These circles are usually no larger than five or six students so that everyone has an opportunity to talk, ask questions, and challenge each other's opinions. For these groups to be effective, students need instruction on how to talk about literature. In the beginning, give groups roles to help them get started. For example, one student may be the discussion leader while another may serve as the group's great vocabulary leader. There can be a group artist or a student in charge of making connections to the text. In elementary classrooms, these roles help to focus students and provide an easier way to maintain a grand conversation. However, in middle and high school, students are better able to function in a group with limited roles. A facilitator is important to keep students on task. The teacher's role is simply to move around the room as the groups are meeting to lend them support, if needed.

- *Minilessons* are great for addressing issues as they present themselves. For example, if you see that students are having difficulty understanding how to use commas appropriately, stopping the class for a quick minilesson on commas, while they are having the problem, will have more meaning for students than waiting and learning comma usage out of context. In a high school science classroom, a minilesson on the differences between vertebrates and nonvertebrates using a semantic map may help students better understand the lesson on the animal kingdom.

- *Critic's Corner* provides students with the opportunity to view films and to think about and talk about what they are viewing in a critical way. For this to be effective, students need to be given the conventions of film and initial guidance about the kinds of things they should be looking for while watching a film. As always, students should be encouraged to make connections between what they are viewing and other areas of their academic and personal lives.

- *Thematic units* provide students the opportunity to explore a specific topic over a period of time (generally one to two weeks), using a variety of activities, texts, and tools. Organizing difficult concepts in thematic units helps students understand those concepts and issues by giving them multiple opportunities to explore them in a variety of different ways.

- *Field trips* help students see how what they are learning is applied in real-life situations. They also help students build a knowledge base that students can call on to help them understand what they are reading. For example, for students who have never seen a live animal, visiting a zoo or farm makes stories about animals come to life.

- *Guest speakers,* like field trips, help students make connections between what they are learning in class and the world outside of the classroom.

- *Guest readers* are fun and inspirational to young readers. Having a parent, the principal, a nurse, a custodian, the librarian, a crossing guard, another teacher, a police officer, a firefighter, or the mayor come in and read their favorite story quickly sends the message that reading is something that is a part of everyone's life and, more important, something that should be an integral part of their lives as well.

- *Oral presentations* are wonderful ways for students to practice their organizational and presentation skills. These presentations need not be long and can be about anything—sharing of personal experiences or possessions, book talks, projects, plans, and so on. Students must have a clear understanding in advance of the expectations of the presentation. For example, you may require students to have a beginning, a middle with three descriptive or supportive ideas, and an ending to their presentations.

These activities provide students with a variety of interesting formats that can be used to teach the skills necessary for literacy development. Teaching with a repertoire of strategies offers students opportunities to learn content while improving literacy with motivating, thoughtful activities.

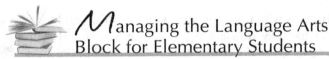

Managing the Language Arts Block for Elementary Students

A balanced literacy program provides a wide range of activities for teachers to use to teach and develop literacy skills. In many elementary schools, literacy is delivered in 90-minute daily blocks of time. Because there are too many activities to fit into a single 90-minute slot, it becomes necessary for teachers to develop weekly agendas that are comprehensive yet varied. When developing their teaching agendas, teachers should select the activities that best support the goals and objectives of the lessons with the understanding that all of the activities should be a part of their overall academic program. Because the program is intended to be flexible enough to accommodate the specific needs of the students at a given time, there is no one correct model. When making activity selections, keep in mind that students must be given opportunities to read and write every day. See Figure 5.2 for a sample 90-minute language arts block.

This 90-minute model can easily be modified to accommodate your teaching needs and teaching style. For example, you may choose to do guided reading four

Figure 5.2

Language Arts Block (90-Minute Block)

Monday	Tuesday	Wednesday	Thursday	Friday
Shared Reading (15 minutes)	Read-Aloud (15 minutes)	Shared Reading (15 minutes)	Read-Aloud (15 minutes)	Read-Aloud (15 minutes)
Guided Reading and Independent Activities (50 minutes)	Guided Reading and Independent Activities (50 minutes)	Guided Reading and Independent Activities (50 minutes)	Guided Reading and Independent Activities (50 minutes)	Guided Reading and Independent Activities (50 minutes)
Reading or Writing Workshop (25 minutes)	Reading or Writing Workshop (25 minutes)	Word Work (25 minutes)	Reading or Writing Workshop (25 minutes)	Word Work (25 minutes)

days a week and reserve one day for literature circles or another activity. Strategies such as independent reading, independent writing, and word work can easily be incorporated into independent activities. You need to be creative and strategic in your thinking and planning.

Many elementary schools have a separate, designated writing period. During that time, writer's workshop should be an ongoing process. Teachers who have the luxury of a separate writing period should set aside one day a week for writing as a test-taking genre to familiarize students with the type of writing that is required for student success on standardized tests (e.g., writing in response to a written or an oral prompt, poem, picture, graph, or chart). This is also true for middle and high school teachers. Teachers may focus their students' writing by scheduling minilessons on different writing genres (narrative, expository, descriptive) or by asking students to write in those genres during a scheduled writer's workshop.

The schedule in Figures 5.2 does not show time for a basal reading series, which many districts are using as part of their total elementary literacy program. Basal readers are comprehensive, commercial reading programs that have been around for many years. One problem with using basal readers exclusively is that they are written for a specific reading level, which is most often equated with a grade level and works for the students reading at that particular level. However, many students read either below or above grade level. The question then is how do you use the stories in the anthologies provided with each basal reading series and still have a balanced literacy program? Although they may seem at first incongruous, with a little creativity, you can blend the two programs. First, take a running record or reading inventory to determine the students' instructional reading level. When you know each child's reading level, you can make decisions about how to best teach students who are on different levels, using the basal materials. You might use the stories with small groups of students whose instructional level matches the stories and provide alternate leveled books for the rest of the students until all of the students' reading levels are in line with the basal readers. You might use the stories in the anthology as whole-group activities to expand students' background knowledge, to improve listening skills, and to provide a common text to teach literacy skills and strategies. This will require that you give added support to students whose reading is below the level of the text. You will also need to supplement the reading of students who are reading above the level of the basal text. If you do not do so, they will quickly become bored or distracted—behaviors that can easily turn into discipline problems if not addressed. Keep in mind that students need a wide variety of reading and writing experiences in their literacy program. To give your students a more appropriate, balanced program, basal programs can easily be supplemented with balanced literacy strategies (such as read-alouds, write-alouds, shared reading, guided reading, reader's workshop, writer's workshop, independent reading and writing, word work, literacy centers, etc.).

Managing Literacy Instruction in Middle and High School

Because teachers are often faced with 40-minute periods in middle and high school, it can be more challenging to manage literacy instruction for students. Teachers recognize that older students need literacy instruction as much as elementary students. Although elementary teachers are charged with teaching literacy, middle and high school teachers also must teach literacy; for some students, high school is their last chance to learn to read and write well enough to function in the world. For other students, it is a chance to build on what they learned in elementary school. For the more successful students, it is a chance to perfect and practice their skills in order to be prepared for the rigors of college.

The section on literacy activities highlights learning situations that are adaptable for all levels of instruction. High school teachers must begin to think in terms of literacy development. Generally, the expertise in a particular content area is what guides and informs secondary instruction. However, learning to read a textbook efficiently and learning to write clearly in the content area will help students in all areas. After all, doesn't all of the material you ask students to study in your classes utilize literacy skills? For example, there are many ways that teachers naturally incorporate literacy into a secondary classroom. Math teachers ask their students to explain in a journal exactly how they came up with their answers. Chemistry teachers use lab reports as a way to help students incorporate science vocabulary into their writing. American history teachers teach students how to read their textbook most efficiently. They teach outlining skills, note-taking systems and the use of graphic organizers to provide students with the skills that will help their proficiency in the content class while improving their overall literacy skills. Literacy is part of almost everything we do; we must keep highlighting it to students so that they can see the relationship between what they are learning and how they are learning.

There are a number of instructional strategies that secondary teachers can use to help students see how to best understand those relationships, including working with challenging text, comprehending text and learning to study for tests. Although this chapter focuses on ways of introducing literacy strategies to students, the next chapter addresses many more strategies to use in your specific content area.

Research supports the use of instructional strategies to promote literacy learning and reading in content-area classrooms (Greenleaf, Schlenbach, Cziko, & Mueller, 2001). By teaching students how to study, how to read the textbook, and how to study for tests, teachers are providing a tremendous advantage that will stay with students forever. One question that comes up frequently is why secondary teachers need to teach students "how" to read since they are in high school. Shouldn't they already know "how" to read? Of course they should; however, many secondary students don't know how to read strategically and would greatly benefit from the use of instructional strategies.

The key to teaching strategies lies in the development of a framework for teaching students. The teacher must model all of the strategies and provide adequate practice in order for students to truly understand and use the strategies in a productive way.

Instructional strategies should first be presented to the whole class in the form of a think-aloud. The teacher explains the value of the strategy, how she uses it in her reading of difficult or unfamiliar text, and then walks the students through the procedures. It is best to use content classroom material in the explanation to the whole class in order to elicit discussion from students to help them to better understand the process. From there, small-group work can offer students the opportunity to practice the strategy, support each other, and add to each others' learning. The teacher can walk around the room, making sure that all students understand the processes and are able to soon work independently. Ultimately, all students work independently to implement the strategies learned.

Just as the balanced literacy model suggests, in any appropriate learning environment, we begin with modeling, interactive work with a large group, guided practice and then individual practice, while always working toward independent learning. Although we consider this to be an elementary process, it clearly is the optimum way that people learn, regardless of their ages.

Independent learning always involves students thinking about their own learning, being aware of what they have to do, and then addressing their own needs. Teaching students instructional strategies helps to give students the tools they need to monitor their own learning.

The following are examples of instructional strategies that can provide support and benefits to secondary learners:

- *Think–Pair–Share:* The teacher poses a question to the students and provides time for the students to "think" about possible answers. Next, the student pairs with another student to discuss their thinking. Finally, students share their responses with a larger group or the whole class. This strategy teaches students the value of "thinking" about the reading and learning to collaborate with others. This may sound quite basic; however, most students do not really "think" while reading.

- *Discussion Journals:* After a reading and a discussion, students will be asked to write within the following categories:

  ____ An idea or two that they found interesting

  ____ Two things they would like to know more about

  ____ An idea they want to write about in their journal

  This strategy helps to organize students' thoughts and ideas while reading since they will be told what they will have to do before they begin the reading. It also helps them to "think" while reading.

- *Sorting:* Students generate words or short phrases based on a chapter and write them on index cards. Working individually, they sort their cards into categories and then "think" about the words or phrases and how and why they are important to remember. As a group activity, students meet with others in a group and discuss the words and phrases they chose. This activity gives students the opportunity to select important information from the chapter, think about it, and then discuss their choices with others.

- *Chunk and Jot:* Content material is often dense and difficult so we teach students to read for ten minutes and then stop for two minutes, think about what they have just read, and jot down a note or two or write in the margins of the book (if they can). This helps them to process the information and recognize when they may have to reread or stop to think or look something up in the dictionary.

- *Error Analysis:* Allow students to go back to their tests and analyze their errors to get back one-half of the credit. The must first identify the error, write the correct answer and where it was found, analyze why the incorrect answer was originally written, and then write a sentence or two about how this mistake can be prevented in the future. The beauty of this strategy is in the thinking that a student has to do in order to complete this task appropriately.

- *Charting Content Information:* Based upon a particular topic, have students as a group create key questions along the top of the chart. Under each question, students write what they already know about that question. As they progress with charting, students can list the sources that helped them answer the questions. They also consider if there is further research needed to provide more information about the answers to the questions. The last part of the chart is where students summarize the information they have learned about the questions. The chart looks something like this:

Topic: The Civil War	What were the major causes of the Civil War?	What was the abolitionist movement?	What were some of the major battles of the Civil War?	How did the election of Abraham Lincoln affect the war?	Interesting Facts & Details
What We Already Know					
Data Source					
Data Source					
Data Source					
Further Research Needed					
Summary					

In general, you can help your students create study skills and strategies that will serve them well in their thinking and learning by:

- Making real world connections to what they are learning.

- Breaking complex tasks into simpler parts.

- Modeling thinking aloud.

- Modeling note-taking with lectures and textbook reading.

- Presenting important information in the form of graphic organizers. Encourage students to create their own in order to organize information.

- Presenting vocabulary words in context so that students can have a way of associating words in order to remember them.

- Offering a variety of ways to outline text so that students can find the way that works for them.

- Teaching time management skills by creating schedules for students. Encourage them to create their own after they see the sample.

- Teaching them to monitor their own comprehension and provide them with information on how you comprehend difficult material. Offer opportunities for students to try your methods to see if they are compatible.

Advice from the Field

- Give students daily opportunities to read and write independently.

- Give students time to read connected text at their instructional level.

- Teach students a wide range of literacy skills that will empower them as readers and writers.

- Provide multiple forms of assessments so that students can express their learning in ways that fit their learning styles and abilities.

- Create a chart containing all of the literacy components you need to include in your literacy program to make scheduling easier.

- Be prepared to model all of the activities that you want students to do. Sometimes modeling takes a long time, but it is always worth doing. It helps students understand how to complete a task.

- Be sensitive in your approach to students who have difficulty learning to read or to read well. Treat all students with respect and understanding. Problems in reading have a significant impact on a student's life.

Differentiating Instruction for English Language Learners

For ELLs, teachers must consider the types of activities that will provide the greatest benefit. Although some may need to be adapted, many of the activities you assign and teach to your English-speaking students can be acceptable for ELLs. For example, shared reading works well because it doesn't place the entire responsibility of reading on the English learner; rather, it gives the ELL an opportunity to hear language modeled and still participate in the process.

The language experience approach also works very well in a group or as an individual activity. In a group, ELLs benefit from listening to others create a story and may be able to participate; as an individual activity, the teacher helps the student verbalize what he or she can in order to write a piece in English. The teacher is the scribe and the student retains a copy of the piece to use as practice reading.

Oral language activities such as discussions, debates, conversations, and literature circles expose ELLs to language and encourage them to become involved in whatever way they can. Other ways to help oral language fluency is to use readers theater, role-playing, skits, and rehearsed readings.

Teach literacy to ELLs in the same way that you would teach it to any student who is not functioning on grade level. Modify assignments to make them understandable and to make it possible for students to find success. Differentiating instruction must be done for all students, not only ELLs. When a student's needs are not being met by the general instruction in the classroom, further action must be taken. That action should allow the student to find success.

 ## Additional Resources

Calkins, L. M. (1983). *Lessons from a child: On the teaching and learning of writing.* Portsmouth, NH: Heinemann.

Goodman, K. S. (1996). *Reading strategies: Focus on comprehension.* Katonah, NY: Richard C. Owen.

Morrow, L. M. (2002). *Organizing and managing the language arts block: A professional development guide.* New York: Guilford.

Strickland, D. S. (1998). *Teaching phonics today: A primer for educators.* Newark, DE: International Reading Association.

 ## Online Resources

Vocabulary.com— www.vocabulary.com/wordcity.html
Annenberg Learner— www.learner.org/workshops/readingk2/support/Sound WritingProgram.1.pdf
Essay Punch— www.essaypunch.com
Paragraph Punch— www.paragraphpunch.com
Story-It— www.storyit.com
Kids' Space— www.kids-space.org

References

Applegate, M. D., Quinn, K. B., & Applegate, A. J. (2006). Profiles in comprehension. *The Reading Teacher, 60*, 48–57.

Bear, D., Invernizzi, M., Templeton, S., & Johnston, F. (2003). *Words their way.* New York: Prentice Hall.

Blachowicz, C. L., & Fisher, P. (2004). Vocabulary lessons. *Educational Leadership, 61*(6), 66–69.

Caulkins, L. (2006). *A guide to the writing workshop.* Portsmouth, NH: Heinemann.

Cooper, J. D., & Kiger, N. D. (2003). *Literacy: Helping children construct meaning.* New York: Houghton Mifflin.

Daniels, H. (2002). *Literature circles: Voice and choice in book clubs and reading groups.* Portland, ME: Stenhouse.

Fountas, I. C., & Pinnell, G. S. (2006). *Teaching for comprehending and fluency.* Portsmouth, NH: Heinemann.

Fountas, I. C., & Pinnell, G. S. (2001). *Guiding readers and writers (grades 3–6): Teaching comprehension, genre, and content literacy.* Portsmouth, NH: Heinemann.

Freeman, M. S. (2003). *Building a writing community: A practical guide.* Gainesville, FL: Maupin House.

Freeman, M. S. (2005). *Models for teaching writing-craft target skills.* Gainesville, FL: Maupin House.

Greenleaf, C. L., Schlenbach, R., Cziko, C., & Mueller, F. L. (2001). Apprenticing adolescent readers to academic literacy. *Harvard Educational Review, 71*(1), 79–127.

Mazzoni, S. A., & Gambrell, L. B. (2003). Principles of best practice: Finding the common ground. In L. Morrow, L. B. Gambrell, & M. Pressley (Eds.), *Best practices in literacy instruction.* New York: Guilford.

National Institute of Child Health and Human Development. (2000). *Report of the National Reading Panel: An evidence-based assessment of the scientific research literature on reading and its implications for reading instruction* (NIH Publication No. 00-4769). Washington, DC: U.S. Government Printing Office.

Paterson, W. A., Henry, J. J., O'Quinn, K., Ceprano, M. A., & Blue, E. V. (2003). Investigating the effectiveness of an integrated learning system on early emergent readers. *Reading Research Quarterly, 38*, 172–177.

Pinnell, G. S. (2006). Every child a reader. What one teacher can do. *The Reading Teacher, 60,* 8–83.

Routman, R. (2003). *Reading essentials: The specifics you need to teach reading well.* Portsmouth, NH: Heinemann.

Slavin, R. E., Cheung, A., Groff, C., & Lake, C. (2008). Effective reading programs for middle and high schools: A best-evidence synthesis. *Review of Education Research, 57,* 293–336.

6

Literacy across the Curriculum

Teachers are often asked how it is possible that students can get to high school with inadequate literacy skills. Year after year, we teach students and many get to high school without the skills necessary to read high school textbooks. What happens to these students? Why haven't they mastered the art of reading in elementary school?

We know that young children are generally excited about the prospect of learning to read and write. They love to be read to. They understand most stories, fairy tales, and nursery rhymes. The elements of the stories are usually clear. Each story has a beginning, a middle, and an end. Each story has characters, a plot, and a solution.

Every elementary teacher stresses the importance of introducing books into the classroom and can attest to the level of interest that students have about reading and writing. At this level, reading is enjoyable and books are available in all genres: mystery, fairy tales, funny stories, adventures, tall tales, and so on.

What happens in fourth grade that dampens the children's enthusiasm for reading? Reading becomes a serious matter. Students are no longer reading just for fun; they are now expected to read informational text from textbooks for content. Students go from reading fairy tales to reading about the American Revolution, and it's a difficult transition partly because of students' lack of exposure to expository writing. Traditionally, elementary teachers have focused on reading narrative pieces and the omission of expository text has left students with inadequate practice in reading and understanding informational text. Recently, authors have been writing more informational, illustrated trade books geared to young children, which has helped to ease the transition to serious reading.

There are other, more complex reasons why students have difficulty with reading. In some classrooms, students are not given the opportunity to read at their instructional level. Many students experience frustration because of developmental difficulties, reading disabilities, or motivational issues. One of the simplest situations to correct, however, is the transition to informational text.

This transition is difficult for both students and teachers. Many teachers do not recognize that different techniques must be implemented when teaching early childhood reading and upper elementary school reading. Teachers must use different strategies when instructing students to read content material. Content literacy, as it is sometimes referred to, addresses the question of how to teach students to read informational text, including textbooks, encyclopedias, content websites, newspapers, magazines, and journals. Content literacy is teaching students how to read informational text, comprehend it, think about it, and write about it.

Experts in the field of literacy are unanimous in their belief that authentic reading and writing prepares students to take on the challenges of content literacy. This authentic reading and writing must begin in early elementary grades.

What Elementary Teachers Can Do to Support Content Literacy

Elementary teachers have a responsibility to prepare students for success beyond their own classrooms. Knowing that students have difficulty transitioning into the content areas, teachers should incorporate strategies, such as the following, into their curriculum, which will help make the transition easier.

- Include content area (e.g., math, science, social studies) assignments and activities in learning centers and independent activities.

- Have students read nonfiction pieces from an early age and provide reading guides to help direct their reading.

- Include stories about content area subjects in the student's assigned reading and writing.

- Have content area books available in the classroom library.

- Introduce students to content area skills (e.g., reading headlines, skimming, note-taking, summarizing, sequencing, distinguishing between facts and opinions, identifying cause and effect).

- Provide students with opportunities to read a variety of texts and have students identify the authors' purposes in writing.

- Require students to defend their opinions about characters, characters' actions, and events in the story with specific examples from the story.

Keep in mind that students, to be successful, need concept and skill teaching and support *before and after* they enter the content area classes. Content area teachers must recognize the importance of literacy in their classrooms and must work to ensure that the skills and concepts students need to have in place to understand complex texts are introduced early and reinforced often with interesting, grade-appropriate materials.

Content Literacy in Middle and High School

Teachers must teach students ways of handling situations when they come across unfamiliar words or concepts in content material. We look to the strategies that good readers use—the strategies that teachers use when they don't understand a text. For example, they use context clues to try to figure out the meaning of the word, or they reread the piece that doesn't make sense. They may continue on in their reading to see if the word is explained later, or they may use a dictionary or put a sticky note on the word and check it later. These strategies must be passed along to the students.

All content area learning is grounded in reading and writing. Regardless of the subject, students have to be able to read, comprehend, interpret, and relate information with a high degree of accuracy to be successful. It is virtually impossible, for example, for students in math and science classes to solve problems and do experiments without reading a text to garner information and without reading instructions to guide their work. When students come to the content areas trained to read and write effectively, content area teachers capitalize on the training these students have had and use the reading and writing strategies the students already have in place. Content area teachers should do the following:

- Teach vocabulary in context instead of from disconnected lists.
- Provide students with multiple texts in addition to the textbook (e.g., magazines, Internet searches, short stories, videos, interviews, newspaper articles).
- Model difficult skills.
- Teach the skills needed to read and understand textbooks.
- Give students opportunities to meet in small groups to discuss, question, and challenge each other's opinions.
- Provide students with reading guides to focus their reading.
- Make sure all student writing is done using the writing process.
- Read aloud to students so that they can hear the language. (This is particularly helpful for students who have limited experience reading textbooks.)
- Think aloud for students so that they can hear what and how they should be thinking about a problem or process.
- Conference with students frequently to ensure they understand the material.
- Require students to keep journals (even in math and science classes). Student entries will help you identify how and what students are thinking so that misconceptions can be addressed before they become problems.
- Assess student progress frequently using multiple forms of assessment.
- Do guided and shared readings and writings with students, particularly at the beginning of the class to help them navigate and understand difficult texts.
- *Always* help students make connections between what they are learning and their own personal lives.

Challenges in Content Literacy

Content material can sometimes present challenges to students. The following suggestions will help teachers work with content text:

- Although textbooks are a source of content information, many other sources are available. Newspapers, magazines, trade books, and videos are just a few examples of ways to provide content information to students.

- Content learning involves all areas of language arts and literacy, not just reading. Use writing, thinking, speaking, and viewing to help students understand and learn content.

- Learn the prior knowledge and experiences of your students so that you can create lesson plans that will meet their needs.

- Expose students to and have them practice using many different types of informational text, such as trade books in various content areas.

- Provide experiences that will help students become strategic readers. Use a model of gradually released support so that you are scaffolding, or providing support to, students until they are ready to work independently.

- Model the strategies that you use as a good reader and help students to develop those strategies using authentic informational text.

- Teachers of all levels and content areas must understand that all teachers teach reading. A chemistry teacher or a history teacher has to teach content using some kind of reading text or material. Help students to learn to read that information more carefully so that you can help the student understand the content more effectively.

- Use thematic units to teach content material because the topics can easily integrate literacy skills and content areas.

- Provide students with direct instruction on how to navigate the text.

Some teachers of content areas ask, "Why do we have to think about teaching reading? The elementary teachers already taught students to read and, besides, we are physics teachers!" Although there is some truth in that statement, elementary school is not the end of the line for the reading train. Students' reading techniques are further refined and they become better as they learn and practice new strategies. Some students do not fully learn to read efficiently until they are older and others have had language barriers that prevented them from reading English well. For these reasons, many students come to a high school class unable to independently read the text. Although some teachers may advocate failing students who don't have the necessary skills, the more compassionate method is to teach these students strategies that will help them grow into better content readers. As teachers, we are responsible for teaching the students who are in our classes.

Elements of a Strong Lesson

If we approach content area literacy in the same way that we approach planning any lesson, we begin with a look at the prior knowledge our students bring to the lesson. If we are working on a social studies lesson with a textbook section on the Vietnam War, we must know if our students have any background knowledge that will help them to understand the text. The first element in any good lesson is always *prior knowledge*. We consider what we can do to stimulate a greater understanding of the background of our content area. In some cases, it may simply be a discussion that will bring the time line to the forefront of the students' minds. Or there may be the need for a film to explain the time period to provide a frame of reference. Or the teacher may bring in newspaper articles or magazines to build enthusiasm and interest in the subject. These prelesson activities would yield a very different discussion and level of understanding than the more traditional approach of "Open your book to page 200 and we will read about the Vietnam War."

The next element in building a strong lesson is *purpose setting* for the reading of the text. Setting a purpose helps the reader stay focused while reading and gives him or her something to look for while reading. For example, if I ask you to read a paragraph and then ask you why Mr. Smith went to the store, you may or may not have that answer. However, if I ask you to read a paragraph with a purpose and that is to know why Mr. Smith went to the store, chances are quite good that you will know that answer after you finish the paragraph. Setting purposes for reading a text can sometimes be done by using the subheadings and turning them into questions.

Next, we consider what happens while the student is reading. As the student reads, is he or she looking for important information; looking at charts, graphs, or maps; thinking about what he or she knows; or thinking about what is going to happen? Make students aware of their thought processes while they are reading so that they can self-question, monitor their understanding as they go along, and summarize what they have read. This is called *strategic reading* and it is the cornerstone of building comprehension in content area material. Strategic reading consists of strategies that teachers can model for their students. Teachers must model proper reading strategies for their students in order for the students to learn.

After teacher modeling, students should do a *guided practice.* Remember that the student is attempting each strategy with your guidance and you must provide feedback to help the student achieve his or her goals. At the end of the lesson, the student is asked to summarize what he or she has learned and reflect on the circumstances under which the student might use this strategy again. The follow-up activity is an *independent practice* with a student using the strategy in an authentic situation.

The use of a content area textbook has traditionally been the main tool for learning. Although this has been the time-honored technique, there are problems associated with this way of teaching. First, textbooks are often quite unappealing to students. They are also often too difficult for students to read and understand (Wade & Moje, 2001). Although they have improved considerably in recent years, a book written on a ninth-grade level is still distributed to students who are reading on the ninth-grade level but also given to students in the same class who are reading on sixth-, seventh-, and eighth-grade levels as well. This places tremendous pressure on the teacher, who often winds up reading the book to the class. This is not a great way to teach because students need the opportunity to practice reading and comprehending text. Students need to read materials that they are able to read. There may be magazines, newspapers, and trade books on topics that would be on a more appropriate level for students. These sources would provide the background knowledge students need to maximize their reading comprehension. They can also get a more in-depth view of the topic with outside sources because textbooks often give a cursory look at various subjects of importance.

How students read the content is the next part of designing a strong content lesson. If the textbook is too difficult for your students, you have several options, including reading aloud, reading silently, doing rehearsed readings for oral readings, dramatic readings (rehearsed), partner reading, independent reading, and small-group reading. If you read the text to the students, your purpose will be to provide background information on the topic. That is fine as long as you understand that your students will require other material to read. Students need opportunities to read content materials to develop the skills necessary to understand dense material and informational text. Therefore, you must find other content material suitable for your students' level of instruction. It's important to do what works for your students. Content reading is followed by discussion, activities, projects, group work, and so on. In general, literacy strategies can be used as a guide to help your students maximize their reading ability.

Literacy Strategies

The purpose of using literacy strategies is to provide help and guided practice to students. Often, teachers unknowingly assign work that students have not been shown how to do. Think about note-taking. How many people have actually been taught how to take notes? Did a teacher at one point assume you knew how to do it and say, "Take notes on this chapter"? When you teach note-taking, provide students with a few different systems so that they can choose the one that works best for them. For example, the Cornell System of Note-taking suggests that students divide their paper into two columns, one two-thirds of the page, called *Notes,* and the other one-third column of the page called *Highlights.* Students learn to determine important details in the Notes section and cues to learning in the Highlights section. They practice using a text and then compare their note-taking systems to see what works for them. Instruction that offers an explanation, modeling, and guided practice helps students learn how to be independent learners. Literacy strategies reinforce appropriate skills and understanding.

Study Guides

In addition to using a variety of sources for reading in content areas, the strategies taught to students will help them to become better readers and, in turn, help them to better understand the various content areas. For example, using a study guide is an effective strategy to help students set purposes as they read and helps to direct students through the reading of informational text. Struggling readers would benefit from a study guide that helped them construct meaning because the study guide would be designed to follow the flow of the chapter and provide hints along the way. For a struggling reader, the first study guide given could be modeled by the teacher. The teacher would go over each area, fill in the study guide, and talk about how she or he was able to complete the study guide by reading the content. The study guide provides opportunities for students to reflect, preview, predict, and write their thoughts. As students progress, less and less information would be provided by the teacher with the hope that the student could eventually create his or her own study guide. Many variations of study guides exist; some are questions and sentence completions that follow the chapter's order, others provide hints for studying for tests and for categorizing information.

K-W-L Plus

K-W-L Plus is another strategy that is effective in teaching content material (Ogle, Klemp, & McBride, 2007). This strategy works so well because the process contains all of the elements of a good lesson (What I **K**now, What I **W**ant to Know, What I Have **L**earned). To activate prior knowledge, the teacher asks the students what they know about a particular topic. The students respond and the teacher records all of the statements on the board or on an overhead under the column labeled *K*. When all of those comments have been noted, the teacher asks the students what they want to know or expect to learn about the topic. The teacher records their questions under the column labeled *W*. The students are then asked to read a selection or the teacher reads the selection to the class or the students may watch a film or listen to a tape. After the literacy experience, ask students what they have learned and then record their comments in the *L* column. At this point, the students can discuss their understanding prior to the reading and compare that to what they learned. Were their questions answered in the text, or do they now need to go one step further and find information? Ask students to use that information to write a short

Figure 6.1

K-W-L Chart

Eskimos		
K **What we know**	*W* **What we want to know**	*L* **What we learned**
Eskimos eat fish. They live in igloos. They hunt for food. They live in Alaska. They live in modern homes.	What do they eat? What kinds of schools do they go to? What do they do for fun? How do they like the cold weather? How do they protect themselves from the cold?	They live in houses. They go to schools like we do. They dress very warmly. They eat all kinds of food. Their families are like ours.

Summary paragraph of what you learned:
I learned that Eskimos are just like we are. This was surprising to me because I thought that they were always in big parkas, eating fish, and hunting. I found that they eat similar foods, live in modern homes, and do the same kinds of things that we do for fun. It is much colder in their climate, but they learn to dress warmly.

paragraph about what they learned. Some teachers use this strategy as a way of helping students gather information from a text as a prereading activity to activate schema and set a purpose for reading, others as a way of confirming predictions or as a graphic organizer. Figure 6.1 shows a sample K-W-L Plus activity for the book *Eskimo Boy: Life in an Inupiac Eskimo Village* by R. Kendall (New York: Scholastic Books, 1992).

Today's Class ...

A recap of the class is often what students need to help them recall information in the forefront of their minds. Today's Class ... is a strategy that offers students the opportunity to take a few minutes at the end of each class to reflect on what they learned. This strategy teaches students the value of reflection and the importance of thinking about the topic and what they learned. Model 24: Today's Class provides an example of the questions a student would reflect on at the end of the class period.

Graphic Organizers

Graphic organizers help students categorize information in a clear, concise way. Because most people respond and remember information that is categorized, graphic organizers provide an excellent format for helping students to recall main ideas and concepts in a text. Visual examples can help students recall and understand information from a text. Model 25: Graphic Organizer is a sample of a simple graphic organizer that can be used in a social studies class.

Story Map

A story map may be used in K–12 to illustrate the common elements of a story. As with all strategies, before you ask students to complete this activity, model the story map so that students know what is expected. A story map can help students organize ideas because students have to think about each of the elements of a story and record them. A story map is a very helpful study aid for a test. Model 26 is a sample story map for a middle school language arts/literacy class.

The G.R.E.A.T. Club

The G.R.E.A.T. Club strategy, which fosters learning in a social context, has worked well in classrooms at many different levels. The G.R.E.A.T. Club, which stands for Groups Reading, Evaluating, Analyzing Text, is a way to involve all students in cooperative learning where each student has a particular role and responsibility to the group. It began as a way to ensure that students were reading and thinking about the text and has grown into a way of teaching (Levin, 2005).

The class is divided into groups of four to six students, with one student from each group assigned to be a facilitator. All students are responsible for reading the assigned text and coming to class prepared to have a group discussion. The facilitator creates and brings to class a Discussion Guide that highlights major points and lists at least five questions for the group to discuss. Each of those questions is answered by the facilitator in her or his Book Discussion Guide. The facilitator gives a copy of the guide to each participant in the group. Each participant comes to the discussion with a double-entry journal that has a response on the left side of the paper and room for the facilitator to respond to the comments on the right side of the paper. Each group has its own discussion, with the teacher acting as an observer or participant, participating only when questions arise or issues need to be addressed. It works well because all students must be prepared; if they are not, the group cannot proceed, so there is a level of peer pressure at work. Another interesting outcome of this strategy is that many students who are normally very quiet in group discussions are able to contribute in their small group with ease. After the groups have met and completed their discussions, there is a large-group discussion in which each facilitator offers insight into the discussions of the small group. Often when students who are usually quiet in a group speak in their small group and are validated by the members, they feel more comfortable sharing their comments in a large group. The whole class participates in this large-group discussion of the topic (See Figure 6.2).

Students need to understand their roles and responsibilities in all of their activities (See Figure 6.3). For G.R.E.A.T. Clubs, keep in mind the following tips (Asbury, 2004):

- Everyone must read the text before they come to class.
- Everyone must bring the book.
- Everyone makes notes beforehand so that they are ready to share, highlight, and write notes in the book.
- Students provide page numbers when bringing out points in the text.
- Students must be willing to share and to listen.
- Students must discuss the practical application of text material.
- Everyone must be allowed an equal opportunity to participate (go around the circle) and to feel comfortable in the group.

Figure 6.2

Rubric for G.R.E.A.T. Club

Criteria for G.R.E.A.T. Club	Excellent (3)	Acceptable (2)	Unacceptable (1)
Facilitator's Discussion Guide	Thorough guide that covers all topics, with stimulating questions and personal commentary	Guide that covers most topics with a mix of short answers and thought-provoking questions with minimal personal commentary	Guide that covers a few topics, with minimal questions
Facilitator's Reflection	An accurate report on the performance of the group, what was discussed with specific comments by participants; a thoughtful reflection on the role of the facilitator; and a numeric assessment of each group member's contribution with an explanation	An accurate report on the performance of the group, with a few specific comments from some of the participants; the role of the facilitator is described, but not discussed critically; group members are assessed but not thoughtfully explained	Report of performance of the group in an incomplete manner with no participant comments and minimal personal reflection. Not all group members are assessed
Facilitator's Scoring Rubric to Grade Individual Participants	The participant has prepared materials and participatess actively and contributes fully, expanding the efforts of the facilitator	The participant prepared materials and participated cooperatively with the group	The participant was minimally prepared, contributed minimally, and was inattentive

Scoring: A = 9–7; B = 6–5; C = 4–3

- Facilitator is responsible for taking notes before coming to the group.
- Everyone must be allowed to share personal examples or experiences as well as opinions.
- Students must be able to relate text to real-life examples.
- Students must focus and stay on topic.
- Facilitator must give a quick summary of the chapter before sharing.
- Participants must discuss common points of interest.
- Facilitator asks open-ended questions to discuss key points such as "Do you agree/disagree? Why?"

Figure 6.3

G.R.E.A.T. CLUB Format: Roles of the Facilitator, Participant, and Teacher

PREPARATION

Facilitator	Participant	Teacher
Creates discussion guide	Comes prepared to discuss	Creates master schedule
Use a sticky note to mark pages in own text for easy reference	Brings double-entry journal for assigned reading	

DURING G.R.E.A.T. CLUB MEETING

Leads discussion	Demonstrates active listening	Circulates and observes
Makes sure everyone is heard	Participates in discussion	May take notes
Wraps up discussion		May join in the discussion Acts as timekeeper

AFTER G.R.E.A.T. CLUB MEETING

Responds to participants' journal entries and assigns rating	Hands in journal entry to facilitator	
Writes brief reflection about how the discussion went		
Hands in packet with discussion guide, reflections, and participant ratings		Reads information in the packet and responds to the facilitator

- Facilitator distributes copies of the discussion guide to each participant.
- Facilitator asks if everyone understood what was covered in the chapter.

Response Journals

Response journals help students incorporate literacy across the curriculum. A response journal is a notebook that students use for thinking and writing about what they have read. In their journals, they share their reactions, ask questions, and sometimes respond to prompts from the teacher. Response journals provide students with an opportunity to think about a particular topic and respond appropriately. The student does not have to agree or disagree with the subject matter; he or she simply has to voice an opinion and react to the content area material. Response journals can be a very effective way to assess students' comprehension.

Some teachers use response journals as a way to let students write in streams of consciousness without concern for spelling, grammar, and mechanics of writing. Other teachers see response journals as an opportunity for students to write, think, and respond to text in a way that reflects their knowledge of content and to show their ability to write a cohesive paragraph (See Figure 6.4).

Self-Questioning

Asking questions throughout the reading process is critical for successful content literacy. Good readers constantly ask themselves question after question as they read content. Some of the questions are simplistic, such as "What is going on here?" or "Why did they say that?" and some are more in-depth and specific, but they all lead the reader to thinking about the content and making decisions about its meaning. Struggling readers do not normally think about the content as they read. In an informal survey of college students in a remedial reading course, students were asked if they asked themselves questions and thought about the text as they read. In general, they said that they hardly ever asked questions while they were reading; most of the time, they were wondering how many more pages they had left to read or they were thinking of something entirely unrelated.

Self-questioning focuses the reader and helps to guide his or her thinking about the content. Readers should ask questions before, during, and after reading. With practice, it becomes a natural part of the reading process. For example, when you read a newspaper and the headline says "Out of Jail," you automatically ask yourself, "Who is out of jail?" As you read the article, new questions come to mind. "What was his crime? Why did he do it?" These questions help the reader develop and practice reading-comprehension skills. The handout in Model 27 helps students recognize the importance of self-questioning skills.

Anticipation Guide

Anticipation guides are an excellent way to ask students to think about a specific topic that they will be reading about (Herber, 1978). This strategy incorporates content with prior knowledge, as students are asked to agree or disagree with statements that have no right or wrong answer. Teachers create statements that challenge or support students' preconceived notions about the ideas and concepts in the text. These statements generally enhance class or small-group discussions and can be controversial. Model 28 is an example of an anticipation guide for a passage on the rights of eighteen-year-old students.

Figure 6.4

Rubric for Assessing Response Journals

Name: _____ Date: _____

Criteria	Excellent (3)	Acceptable (2)	Unacceptable (2)	Score
Format	Entry is correctly formatted with identification of response, page in text where it can be found, and the response	N/A	Entry is missing the page number or identification of the response	
Quality of Response Selection	Response selection is relevant and significant to the meaning of the text; response deals with key issues rather than a single strategy.	Response selection is relevant but has little significance to the understanding of the text; response may deal with a strategy rather than a key issue discussed in the text	Response selection is superficial or does not contribute significantly to the understanding of the major concepts developed in the test	
Quality of Response	Response evidences thinking that is literal, is analytical, and makes connections between the text and the reader's experiences and teaching practices	Response attempts to analyze the text and makes connections between the text and the reader's experiences and teaching practices	Response is literal or fails to make connections between the text and the reader's experiences and teaching practices.	
Length of Response	The ideas evidenced are fully developed	Most of the ideas are fully developed	Most of the ideas need to be developed with more information	
Grammar, Punctuation, and Word Choice	Entry is written in complete sentences and is nearly free of grammar and punctuation errors; all of the words are used correctly	Entry is written in complete sentences; there are some errors in grammar and punctuation, but they do not appear to be in a pattern or do not inhibit the understanding of the response	Entry may not be written in complete sentences or have excessive errors in grammar or punctuation. Errors in word choice inhibit the understanding of the response	
Total				

A = 14–15; B = 12–13; C = 10–11; D = 8–9; N/A = not applicable

Knowledge Rating

Vocabulary in content areas can be very challenging for students. Knowledge rating was designed as an alternative to the use of a vocabulary notebook (Blachowicz & Ogle, 2001). Although notebooks can be helpful, knowledge rating keeps the vocabulary a bit more interesting. The teacher chooses several words from the content lesson. Those words are written on a knowledge rating sheet that asks students to rate their knowledge of each word according to one of the following categories: 1—Know It Well, 2—Think I Know It, 3—Have Heard It or Seen It, 4—No Clue. The class is generally broken into groups and students are asked to discuss their knowledge of each word. The teacher acts as an observer or a participant, responding to students' questions or concerns. Use these words as a starting point for a content lesson, either predicting what the lesson will be about or predicting how these words will be used. Model 29 is a sample of this format.

Save the Last Word for Me

Save the Last Word for Me is a thought-provoking and engaging strategy (Short, Harste, & Burke, 1996). Students are given several index cards and are asked to read a content selection to identify two to three sentences, paragraphs, or sections of the text that they find interesting or provocative or that they had a reaction to while they were reading. After reading, the students use the index cards to record their information. They write the quote on the front of an index card and then they write their comments and thoughts about each of the statements on the back of the card.

Students are divided into groups of four or five and each group works independently. One student begins by reading his or her quote to the group. Each member of the group is asked to comment on the student's quote; after they have all commented, the student who wrote the quote shares his or her comments with the group.

This strategy for gaining greater understanding of the text ends with a whole-class discussion comparing the quotes chosen and the reactions of the groups. The teacher should ask whether all of the conversation related to the content helped students toward a better understanding of the text.

Save the Last Word for Me provides practice with the content in an authentic situation. Students express their reactions and opinions and learn to listen to other perspectives, with the final outcome resulting in greater understanding of the content material.

The literacy strategies discussed in this chapter are just a sample of the many ways of teaching your students to monitor their comprehension during reading and to think about the content while they are reading. The strategies provide opportunities for independent learning and for large- and small-group interactions. They show students the value of preparation and the use of graphic organizers to categorize information. In essence, they offer a variety of ways that students can learn to be successful in content areas.

The way you implement these strategies is a critical component leading to the success of your students. Take the time to teach and model each of the strategies you choose to incorporate into your content program. Explain to students the ways in which these strategies can make a difference in their academic lives. Ask students to think about and reflect on how the strategies helped them in each of the activities in which they participated. The progress that you hope to see in your students' literacy across the curriculum develops over time. Vary the strategies that you teach and make sure that you bring them back again, giving your students continued guided practice. In time, your students will be able to create their own strategies and tools, which will help them navigate difficult content material.

*A*dvice from the Field

- Remember that all teachers are reading teachers. If you want your students to understand the content, they must be able to comprehend the text. To comprehend the text, students must be strategic readers who can call on the necessary skills to better understand content area study.

- Use a variety of strategies in your classes. Students respond well to some strategies and not to others. Vary the activities that you choose and help students determine which strategies work best for them.

- Encourage students to become strategic readers by modeling what you do when you read text and write essays, science lab reports, or narrative pieces. They learn by seeing the process and trying it in a risk-free environment.

- Recognize that many of your students will not be reading on the grade level of the text being used in your content area, so you must use strategies that will help students understand the text.

- Make available a variety of reading materials (such as newspapers, magazines, books on many different levels) that will help struggling readers gain perspective and information relating to the topic they are studying.

Differentiating Instructions for English Language Learners

One of the great difficulties for ELLs is that they have to learn academic English as well as master conversational English. Academic subject matter is often dense and diffi cult to understand. Helping students to gain further competence can be enhanced by increasing the amount of oral language in your classroom. In an elementary classroom, this may be accomplished through conversations during circle time, talking about hobbies, weather, families, sports, and other topics that arise within the context of your classroom, and by cooperative learning and part- ner work. In middle and high school classrooms, it is important to allow suffi cient time for discussions, cooperative learning, and peer or partner work.

Use the following tips to help you teach and differentiate instruction for ELLs in academic content areas:

- Consider the language abilities of your students and recognize the difficulty of the tasks assigned.

- Develop your own materials that follow the subject curriculum. Rewrite con- tent in a simpler fashion or write short summaries for them.

- Tape-record directions or hints for successfully completing tasks.

- Use graphic organizers and visual aids as much as possible. Discuss with stu- dents how they relate to the text.

- Write study guides to help students understand the chapters. Gradually, leave out information so that students learn to complete the study guides and even- tually learn to write study guides by themselves.

- Teach students several methods of note-taking and provide think-alouds and examples of how you would take notes on a particular chapter.

- Provide experiences that activate prior knowledge and schemata for students, including films, read-alouds, discussions, speakers, charts, and maps.

- Break assignments into smaller, more manageable tasks. Provide alternatives if other assignments allow students to work from positions of strength.

- Construct assignments and projects using a specific routine that can be fol- lowed throughout the year. Students react more favorably if they know exactly what they have to do.

Students should be able to choose appropriate materials on their instructional levels in a comfortable environment.

- Be aware of the amount of talking you do in class. Allow sufficient wait time after you ask a question; rephrase the question, if necessary.

- Provide ample opportunities for students to speak to one another. English language learners need considerable practice speaking to other students.

- Use strategies that will help simplify the topic for your students. Use K-W-L charts, vocabulary charts, study techniques, and so on, to help them understand the text and the topic.

- Try to relate what you are teaching to students' cultural backgrounds, if possible.

- Provide hands-on materials and experiences for students.

- Review key vocabulary and concepts in chapters on a regular basis.

Additional Resources

Blachowicz, C. L. Z., & Ogle, D. (2001). *Reading comprehension: Strategies for independent learners.* New York: Guilford.

Harvey, S., & Goudvis, A. (2000). *Strategies that work: Teaching comprehension to enhance understanding.* Portland, ME: Stenhouse.

Tovani, C. (2000). *I read it, but I don't get it.* Portland, ME: Stenhouse.

Zwiers, J. (2004). *Building reading comprehension habits in grade 6–12: A toolkit of classroom activities.* Newark, DE: International Reading Association.

References

Asbury, E. (2004). Handout created for the Institute for Teacher Development (I.T.D.).

Blachowicz, C. L. Z., & Obrochta, C. (2005). Vocabulary visits: Virtual field trips for content vocabulary development. *The Reading Teacher, 59,* 262–268.

Fisher, P. (2004). Vocabulary lessons. *Educational Leadership, 61*(6), 66–69.

Levin, F. (2005). Using the G.R.E.A.T. Club strategy. *New Jersey Reading Association Newsletter, 2,* Spring issue.

Herber, H. L. (1978). *Teaching reading in the content areas* (2nd ed.). Upper Saddle River, NJ: Prentice Hall.

Ogle, D., Klemp, R., & McBride, B. (2007). *Building literacy in social studies: Strategies for improving comprehension and critical thinking.* Alexandria, VA: Association for School Curriculum and Development.

Short, K. G., Harste, J. C., & Burke, C. (1996). *Creating classrooms for authors and inquirers* (2nd ed). Portsmouth, NH: Heinemann.

Wade, S. E., & Moje, E. B. (2001). The role of text in classroom learning: Beginning an online dialogue. *Reading Online, 5*(4). www.readingonline.org/articles/art_index.asp?HREF=/articles/handbook/wade/index.html

Online Resources

www.tea.state.tx.us/reading/practices/redbk4.pdf
www.teacher.scholastic.co/reading/bestpractices/comprehension/ strategies
www.madison.k12.wi.us/tnl/langarts/mosaic.htm
www.literacymatters.org/content/readandwrite/reading.htm
www.sarasota.k12.fl.us/sarasota/interdiscrdg.htm

Model 25

Today's Class

Three things I learned today . . .
_____
_____

I have a question about . . .
_____
_____

One important fact that I never knew . . .
_____
_____

I wonder about . . .
_____
_____

I need a little more help with . . .
_____
_____

Model 26

Graphic Organizer

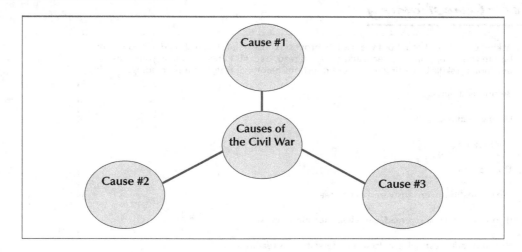

Model 27

Story Map for Middle School Language Arts/ Literacy Class

Title	
Story	
Characters	
Problem	
Events	
Solution	

Model 28

Self-Questioning

Asking questions throughout the reading process is very helpful. You should ask questions before you read, while you read, and after you read. Use this handout to help your self-questioning skills by writing down your questions before, during, and after reading.

Before reading:

During reading:

After reading:

Think about:

What questions were answered as you read?

If you went back and reread, were your questions answered?

How did self-questioning help you understand this reading?

Model 29

Anticipation Guide

Directions: Before you read this selection, read the statements below and make a check in the appropriate column, indicating those with which you agree or disagree.

Agree	Disagree	
_____	_____	1. Eighteen-year-olds are too young to join the military.
_____	_____	2. Eighteen-year-olds should be allowed to vote.
_____	_____	3. Because of the accident rate, the driving age should be twenty-five.
_____	_____	4. Eighteen-year-olds should be allowed to drink, with parents' permission.

Read the selection and then discuss your answers with your small group.

Model 30

Knowledge Rating Chart

Word	Know It Well (1)	Think I Know It (2)	Have Heard It or Seen It (3)	No Clue (4)
tropical storm				
radiometer				
storm surge				
meteorologist				
oceanic				

7

Helping All Students Find Success

Working with English Language Learners, Struggling Readers, Gifted Readers, and Students with Special Needs

Teachers have tremendous responsibilities in the classroom. Competence in a content area and an understanding of pedagogy are only part of the preparation for teaching. The major task that teachers must accept is to help each and every student in their classes find success—not always an easy task, even though teachers want all students to do their very best. There can be many impediments for students

to achieve success in their work. These impediments often include cultural differences, learning to speak English as English Language Learners, experiencing failure as struggling readers, or feeling different as gifted learners.

In just about every school district in this country, students from all over the world are entering classrooms. Diversity is a fact of life throughout the United States. Effective teachers understand students' diverse cultural and educational experiences and address their varied learning styles by using appropriate teaching techniques. As a new teacher, you should expect that all of your classes will consist of a diverse group of students in terms of family history, customs, culture, native language, special needs, reading ability, and intelligence levels. Teachers must acknowledge and honor the differences in students and respect their understanding of the world. Each classroom has students on varying academic levels as well as students of different cultures, and this will affect how they perform, how they interpret, and how they understand.

Approximately one in seven school-age children in the United States speaks a language at home that is not English. Almost five million students have been classified as limited English proficient (LEP) (National Center for Education Statistics, 2004). Although most of those students (75 percent) speak Spanish, many other languages are represented, including Vietnamese, Hmong, Korean, Arabic, Chinese, Russian, Portuguese, Navajo, and others (Smallwood, 2002). With those facts in mind, we begin our discussion.

Understanding Cultural Differences

Ironically, as school populations are becoming more ethnically diverse, the teaching force in the United States remains homogeneous. Research tells us that most teachers are middle-class, middle-aged, white women (National Center for Education Statistics, 2004). There is a significant need to heighten teachers' awareness and understanding of diversity in the classroom. Teachers must have a clear understanding of the impact that culture has on a person's life and consider that information in the planning and implementation of lessons.

In your role as teacher, you must be willing to learn and accommodate the various cultures represented in your class. In addition to reading and discussing multicultural literature throughout the year, you must be aware of specific features of your students' cultures that may be different from yours. Many cultures have different codes of behavior that must be respected. Teachers must be well-informed and sensitive to culture.

In certain cultures, for example, children are taught not to look at adults while they are being spoken to. If you are speaking to a student who is looking down, you may think the child is being disrespectful, but he actually may be showing you great respect. In some cultures, children are taught to be passive and not show off what they know. That may lead to a student's silence even when she comprehends what you are teaching. Understanding students' cultural backgrounds can lead to more effective teaching. Recommendations to promote cultural understanding include the following:

- Learn about students' cultures by researching cultural information. Learn about their basic culture, including food, dress, music, and so on, as well as the more meaningful aspects of the culture (child-rearing, gender roles, family values, etc.).
- Try to incorporate multicultural viewpoints into your discussions.
- Be empathetic and open-minded about cultural differences.
- Show an interest in the family and try to attend neighborhood or cultural events. This show of support will be greatly appreciated.
- Send newsletters home on a consistent basis. If the majority of your students' families speak Spanish, try to have the newsletter translated so that more parents can feel involved and understand what is going on in the classroom.
- Remain aware of your own attitudes toward various cultures.
- Demonstrate an interest and a caring attitude about your students' cultures.

 ## What Is Cultural Diversity?

At one time, the United States was referred to as a "melting pot" because a great number of cultural groups came to the United States wanting to assimilate and become "Americanized." For many, it was important to "lose the accent" and become just like everyone else. Immigrant adults took classes in English and their halting English was their first step, their way of beginning to integrate into American society. They wanted their children to speak English, the language of "success," and often that meant not speaking their native language at home but rather practicing English. Because their children no longer had the opportunity to speak their native language, many of them lost their first language. The children who learned English quickly became their parents' teachers, helping them to construct meaningful sentences and write and correct their mispronunciations. English became the language of the home.

Today, instead of the "melting pot," we could call the United States a "salad bowl" because this country is presently made up of people from many different cultures who are tossed together, yet who want to maintain and preserve their own individual identities. In some communities, speaking English is not necessary; immigrants are surrounded by friends and neighbors who all speak their native language. Stores and businesses in their communities cater to their native language and culture, so the need or desire to learn English is not great. That becomes an issue for you as a teacher who wants to communicate regularly with your students' families. It also becomes an issue when parents are asked to become involved in their children's education. Asking parents to read to their children or review multiplication tables becomes more difficult when there is a language barrier. It is also more difficult for students whose parents cannot help them with their schoolwork.

Given the sheer numbers, it is conceivable that you have students who have just arrived in this country who speak little or no English, students who speak limited English, or students who speak several different languages. Chances are good that at least some of your students are learning English as a second language (ESL).

Teachers' views on education and students may impact student performance and student achievement. An understanding of a multicultural perspective must begin with self-inquiry. You must examine your own fundamental values and attitudes to identify your beliefs to be certain they are consistent with your classroom practices. Use Model 30 as a starting point for assessing your cultural beliefs. When you stop to think about the importance of your own cultural background, family history, and native language, you can begin to understand how important all of those issues are to your students as well.

Sometimes, unintentionally, teachers can disregard their students' cultures. In the children's book *My Name Is Maria Isabel,* by Alma Flor Ada, the main character, Maria Isabel, moves and goes to a new school. Maria Isabel had always been very proud of her names because she was named after various members of her family. Her teacher, on learning her name, says in an off-handed way, "We have other students whose names are Maria. We will call you Mary." By altering Maria Isabel's name, that teacher was very insensitive to her cultural heritage. It is important to be sensitive to the needs and understandings of your students and to carefully consider their cultural backgrounds. It is also very important to think of all students with the same high expectations. Figure 7.1 provides a suggested lesson plan for *My Name Is Maria Isabel.*

One of the first topics in psychology that preservice teachers learn is "self-fulfilling prophecy." This relates to the expectations we have for our students. If you expect excellence from students, you will likely find excellence in their work.

You must maintain high expectations for all students, being careful not to fall prey to common stereotypes. If we maintain high expectations, students will live up to those standards. If we think they cannot succeed, they will not succeed. Therefore, any preconceived notions that you may have because of your own exposure to some cultures should be carefully considered and discarded.

In a research study of teacher book clubs (Levin, 2003), twelve teachers read and discussed a variety of multicultural literature. Some of the teachers had preconceived notions about certain ethnicities and cultures. These beliefs clearly colored their judgment and expectations relating to their students' performance in their classes. This finding suggests that teachers have to carefully examine their own upbringing and belief systems before they can begin to understand their students' needs. It also suggests that teachers cannot make judgments about their students' success based on their own experiences with various cultures. Teachers must attempt to understand students' cultures and the uniqueness and similarities they have to others. Students must be made to feel comfortable in your classroom because they recognize that you respect them and their heritage. The literature that you read aloud and the books in your classroom library must reflect the backgrounds and interests of all of the students in your class. Students need to see themselves in the literature of the classroom to feel a part of the classroom and the society as a whole. Students must read books that focus on authentic stories about people of different cultures, books that focus on topics that are universal to all people. Literature that presents a positive look at a particular culture without preaching provides students with the opportunity to see the universality of all people. Reading a text about a sibling rivalry or a coming-of-age story about characters who belong to a specific cultural group helps students see that certain experiences are universal, regardless of the specific culture. Students can take pride in their backgrounds but not feel so different and so far removed from their peers. Search online for suggestions for multicultural literature.

In some schools, the focus on diversity occurs at events or certain times of the year. Cultural information should be a natural part of the curriculum. In certain districts, multiculturalism consists of an evening called "Culture Night" where parents are invited to share their culture's food, display cultural items, and wear native dress to exhibit cultural pride to the school community. Although an evening of culture is a positive step, this should be just one small piece of a multicultural plan for a school. February is known as Black History Month; however, black history should be taught as part of the regular curriculum throughout the year. Multiculturalism is best represented if it is incorporated into the curriculum

Figure 7.1

Lesson Plan for *My Name Is Maria Isabel* by Alma Flor Ada (third-grade class)

Objective	Students will be able to identify and discuss cultural references in this story. Students will identify the feelings of the main character as they participate in a book club using *My Name Is Maria Isabel*.
Materials Needed	A copy of *My Name Is Maria Isabel* for each student Reading Response Journal Chart paper
Standards Used	3.1, 3.2, 3.3 Language Arts/Literacy
Prior Knowledge	Class will discuss what it feels like to move into a new neighborhood and go to a new school. We will record on a chart feelings and concerns that a student might have on the first day of school. Would it matter that the child is of a different culture than the other children in the class?
Strategy Used	Reading Response Journals and Book Clubs Students will write in their response journals. Class will be divided into groups of five or six students. Each group will have a facilitator who will lead the discussion. Each member must participate in this group activity. Reading response journals will be used to stimulate discussion within each group.
Purpose Setting	Teacher will read the first chapter of this book aloud. Students will be looking for the feelings and concerns that were mentioned earlier and will discuss what they thought about it. Class will also discuss the cultural references made in the book and talk about whether they are important in the story (i.e., a little girl drinking coffee for breakfast).
Reading	Students will read this book silently. Each chapter will have questions to look for while reading the text. As students read, they will be writing in their double-entry response journals. They may respond to the following questions or they may consider the feelings and concerns that Maria Isabel has in each chapter: • In this chapter, how does Maria feel about her new school? • What did you notice about Maria's culture that may be the same or different from yours? • What would you have done if you were Maria?
After Reading	Students will meet in their groups and discuss *My Name Is Maria Isabel*. The facilitator will lead the discussion and be sure to include all members. The teacher will circulate and monitor the students' understanding of the book.
After Book Club	Students will create a graphic organizer that will identify the cultural references made in the text. Each group will present its graphic organizer and discuss the impact on Maria.

in a variety of natural ways, such as through read-alouds, class library materials, discussions, use of appropriate content materials, and research. Students will gain significantly greater understanding of a multicultural text if reading the text is followed by rich discussion. Students should have time to reflect, talk to their peers, write their thoughts and questions, and participate in important discussions in the classroom.

English Language Learners

How do you teach children who do not speak English when you do not speak their native language? Traditionally, bilingual programs have addressed the needs of these students, but because so many languages are now represented in the United States, it has become impossible for even multilingual teachers to be able to speak so many different languages. Therefore, it has become the responsibility of all classroom teachers to know how to teach ELLs. Even though an ELL may be pulled out of your classroom for a period or two for additional support in English, the student will be with you for the remainder of the day. An English-speaking class greatly benefits ELLs by giving them opportunities to hear and use the language in context.

Teachers must find a way to effectively address the needs of ELLs. Using a balanced literacy approach is an appropriate way to begin this discussion. Balanced literacy addresses listening, speaking, viewing, reading, and writing. Balanced literacy involves integrated lessons that emphasize reading and writing across content areas, building vocabulary, overall fluency, engagement with text matched to the reader, and extensive use of strategies. These methodologies are used for all learners; however, the unique challenges to ELLs who are also beginning readers include the following (Whalen Ariza, 2006):

- sound/symbol dissimilarity or interference

- oral language constraints

- limitations caused by lack of background knowledge

- difficulties with the structures of the text and cultural mismatches

Becoming aware of these challenges is the first step to helping the ELLs in your classroom. Your task will be to try to fill in necessary information using films, pictures, gestures, videos, peer tutoring, and help from the ESL teacher in the school.

When students in your class are beginning to learn English, there are many activities that will help them transition into speaking English, such as shared reading, language experience approach, writing, projects, and such oral language activities as discussions, literature circles, and so on. Shared reading offers students the opportunity to listen to text read aloud and to participate when possible. Other ways to help oral language fluency is to use readers theater, role-playing, skits, and rehearsed readings.

The language experience approach provides students with the time to work closely with the teacher to dictate a story in their own words and then to have that story typed and read over and over again. This strategy teaches students that you value their words, gives them practice in oral language, and provides text that they can read. Although traditionally used in elementary grades, it is a great strategy for middle and high school students and can be done with individual students or small groups. For example, students may dictate a language experience story about a field trip or film and then use that dictated text as reading material. Flash cards can be made for practice and students begin to use their own created text to help improve their reading.

English language learners need to develop an understanding of English by using English as much as possible. Teach students by modeling appropriate greetings to other students, by asking questions, by making conversation, and by using gestures. Use print to expand your students' knowledge of English by labeling items in the classroom and by carefully writing directions, schedules, and information that students must know. Use this print as you would a word wall and go over these items with your second language learners daily or until you think they understand.

English language learners must have the opportunity to practice asking and answering questions related to content, from simple yes/no questions and answers to more challenging short responses and longer, extended responses. It is important to model clear and understandable language for students while using gestures and facial expressions to help them make meaning.

English language learners must be given many opportunities for writing and reading. Providing students with a monitored sustained silent reading period offers time for ELLs to practice reading without pressure or difficult assignments. It is a way to monitor what they are reading and how they are doing with their self-selected text. Independent reading is an excellent way for students to feel like they are a part of the class, exploring books at their own pace and reading what they like. Using learning logs and journals offers valuable experience for students. For example, writing in a journal provides an excellent opportunity for teachers to respond appropriately to students' writing, suggesting word choices or rephrasing students' words to help them see how their writing can be improved easily.

Cooperative learning is an excellent strategy to use for ELLs because students may be more likely to speak to each other and learn from one another in small groups. Peer tutoring or partner work is helpful because it provides another context where English is spoken and it is student centered. Students who are paired with other students often form bonds with one another and can provide help that reaches beyond the scope of the teacher. The key is to provide a student-centered environment that offers hands-on, active learning. Direct experiences, field trips, role-playing, group projects, photographs, charts, and concrete materials help the ELL to better understand his or her surroundings.

Using technology with ELLs is often another effective way to help students learn English. Many software programs and websites are available that can make time spent on a computer very productive for ELLs. Some websites translate most languages to English, offering dictionaries in many languages. For example, www .enchantedlearning.com/dictionary.html provides definitions with the words used in meaningful sentences.

Adapting your instruction is a way to provide additional help for ELLs. Be mindful of areas in your lessons that may be challenging for your students. Vocabulary, background knowledge, and syntax are often areas that require greater practice for ELLs.

Let's look at the way you would teach a typical lesson. Normally, you begin a lesson by activating prior knowledge and discussing the topic. You may discuss the new vocabulary words within the context of a sentence or the piece you are about to assign to your students. These are elements of a good lesson that will help all students. Next, you give students a purpose for reading and then ask them to read silently for the first read. Oral reading at that point would be inappropriate because students may have pronunciation problems and would not want to read any text aloud. Being aware of specific challenges for ELLs will help to guide your teaching. After students read silently, you begin the discussion. You may ask students questions and require them to go back to the text to find the correct answer. You may do small-group discussions or a project to help students understand of the text. These are good teaching techniques for all students, but especially for those students who are ELLs.

Many educators have been taught that teaching second language learners requires just plain good teaching. However, it is far more than just good teaching. It involves understanding that ELLs need explicit opportunities to practice using their new language, believing that all children can learn, and having high expectations for all of the students in your classroom. Therefore, in addition to appropriate teaching, the following suggestions may help guide and inform your teaching of English Language Learners:

- Give students more time to complete an assignment.
- Offer challenging work, but allow extra time for practice. Always model what you want your students to do.
- Underline important directions and focus words.
- Tape-record stories so that students can listen to them several times.
- Write directions clearly and simply.
- Allow students to work with a partner or in small groups as well as individually in a nonthreatening classroom environment.
- Permit students to use computers to complete assignments.
- Allow students to tape-record their answers if writing is a more difficult process.
- Provide many opportunities for discussion.
- Use technology to help students find success.
- Teach using thematic units or inquiry-based teaching, relating the theme to real life, authentic interests and issues.
- Always build on students' strengths.

Differentiating Instruction for English Language Learners

One of the great difficulties for ELLs is that they have to learn academic English as well as master conversational English. Academic subject matter is often dense and difficult to understand. Helping students to gain further competence can be enhanced by increasing the amount of oral language in your classroom. In an elementary classroom, this may be accomplished through conversations during circle time, talking about hobbies, weather, families, sports, and other topics that arise within the context of your classroom, and by cooperative learning and partner work. In middle and high school classrooms, it is important to allow sufficient time for discussions, cooperative learning, and peer or partner work.

Use the following tips to help you teach and differentiate instruction for ELLs in academic content areas:

- Consider the language abilities of your students and recognize the difficulty of the tasks assigned.

- Develop your own materials that follow the subject curriculum. Rewrite content in a simpler fashion or write short summaries for them.

- Tape-record directions or hints for successfully completing tasks.

- Use graphic organizers and visual aids as much as possible. Discuss with students how they relate to the text.

- Write study guides to help students understand the chapters. Gradually leave out information so that students learn to complete the study guides and eventually learn to write study guides by themselves.

- Teach students several methods of note-taking and provide think-alouds and examples of how you would take notes on a particular chapter.

- Provide experiences that activate prior knowledge and schemata for students, including films, read-alouds, discussions, speakers, charts, and maps.

- Break assignments into smaller, more manageable tasks. Provide alternatives if other assignments allow students to work from positions of strength.

- Construct assignments and projects using a specific routine that can be followed throughout the year. Students react more favorably if they know exactly what they have to do.

- Be aware of the amount of talking you do in class. Allow sufficient wait time after you ask a question; rephrase the question, if necessary.

- Provide ample opportunities for students to speak to one another. English language learners need considerable practice speaking to other students.

- Use strategies that will help simplify the topic for your students. Use K-W-L charts, vocabulary charts, study techniques, and so on, to help them understand the text and the topic.

- Try to relate what you are teaching to students' cultural backgrounds, if possible.

- Provide hands-on materials and experiences for students.

- Review key vocabulary and concepts in chapters on a regular basis.

Struggling Readers

What makes some students struggling readers while others who seem to be of similar intelligence good readers? Some students may have a disability that makes reading difficult to learn. Some students may not have been read to at home or given enough literacy experiences as young children that would help them to become better readers. Still others may have not had appropriate reading instruction in school. Regardless of the reasons, teachers must recognize that many students who are considered struggling readers, who are reading several years below their grade level, have already experienced failure and feelings of inadequacy. Many believe that they are unable to learn while others have shut down. What can teachers do to help struggling readers find success?

First of all, teachers must find out about their students, their interests and their difficulties in reading. Classroom assessments may provide some important information as would the help of the Reading Specialist or the Child Study Team. You must figure out the problems so you can address them. Student needs may be in phonemic awareness, phonics, comprehension, fluency, or vocabulary. Strategies and skill development for each of those areas will help students progress in literacy. If you don't know enough about teaching reading, seek out professional development or take a graduate course. In the meantime, think about what it must be like to struggle and create situations where struggling readers can succeed and feel good about their learning.

Differentiating instruction is very important for struggling readers. All students, including those who have had consistent difficulties with literacy, must be able to complete the work assigned in your classroom. Therefore, activities and assignments must be appropriately modified so that all students will be able to find success and feel comfortable in the process.

Readers need to know how to apply reading strategies and how these strategies fit into the big picture of reading. To teach appropriately, you need to know evidence-based reading strategies to help the struggling readers in your class. It is important to teach scaffolded lessons, lessons that offer the gradual release of responsibility to students. For example, teaching a lesson on previewing as a strategy for understanding a text might begin by looking at a specific book or chapter title and saying to the students (modeling), "When I look at this title, I think of . . ." The teacher then begins to formulate opinions about what the text might discuss. Look at illustrations in the text and talk to the students as you are thinking aloud about the text. Tell them you are thinking because that is what good readers do—they think about a text and try to make predictions and then read to see if they were right. Offer students the opportunity to do the same thing you just did. Encourage students to think aloud, describing their reactions and predictions.

Using effective strategies in the classroom can be a tremendous help to struggling readers. Considering the five components of reading as identified by the National Reading Panel's Report (NICHD, 2000) as a foundation, phonemic awareness, phonics, fluency, vocabulary, and comprehension should be embedded in your instruction.

Applying strategies in your classroom helps students achieve a level of success as readers and writers. Following are some modifications for struggling readers:

- Use both auditory and visual directions. Because some students are better able to process information when it is presented orally and others respond better when it is presented visually, using both modalities ensures that you will be supporting your students' strengths.

- Write directions to assignments on the chalkboard or on an overhead projector so that students who need visual cues can look at the board and read the directions as many times as they need to in order to complete the assignment. Leave the directions on the board so that students can refer to them at any time.

- Demonstrate concepts by using visual examples. After teaching or giving directions, provide your students with models or examples so that they know exactly what is expected of them.

- Allow students to choose activities when they can. If several assignments would meet the same objective, offer a choice. Students may be better able to do the assignment if they understand the format.

- Understand that students will be working at different rates. Provide enough time for all students to complete tasks. Provide additional time if needed.

- Provide additional assistance—whether with a paraprofessional, teacher, or student partner—for those students who need it.

- Offer direct, systematic instruction to struggling readers. Use strategies that will simplify the tasks and build strength in reading and writing.

Struggling readers benefit from both large- and small-group instruction, guided reading, interactive discussions, and lots of opportunities to practice strategies in authentic reading situations. Struggling readers need time and extra attention. They also require a great deal of support and understanding to help them overcome their feelings of inadequacy about school. Young children find it extremely difficult to have the sense that the other students are able to read and comprehend text when they cannot. Older students who have harbored negative feelings about reading and school for many years often give up and stop trying to learn. Their frustrations tend to lead them toward disciplinary problems. This puts the teacher in a difficult position. How do you provide support and praise to students who are so far behind the other students and may be acting out in class? You treat them with respect and you find something positive that they can do to find success. Perhaps you offer a student an audio version of a story that is being read in class before you read it to the class so that the struggling reader has a background of knowledge and can answer questions that will make him or her feel successful. You encourage his or her writing or send a note home praising something small that he or she has accomplished academically. You find a task or desirable job that would boost the student's self-esteem. You make assignments doable, you find something positive in the student's work and compliment the student and encourage him or her to succeed.

Some new teachers, especially those who have never struggled with literacy, are faced with students who, despite their teachers' best efforts, have a very difficult time reading and writing. Their weaknesses in literacy present a challenge to teachers, who must provide strategies and experiences that help students improve comprehension and find success in reading and writing. Struggling readers have a variety of issues that prevent them from being successful in literacy. Often, they have little prior knowledge that will help them to comprehend text. It is important to help those students set purposes for their reading. For example, asking a student prior to reading text to look for the reason Mr. Jones went to the farm can help focus the reader and offset the fact that he may have no prior knowledge of what a "farm" is all about. Targeting struggling readers with purpose-setting helps them to focus and to think while reading.

It is also helpful to ask students to predict and speculate about what the purpose might be. An inability to make predictions or create hypotheses based on the reading often prevents a student from thinking about the content. Teaching them to "think" while reading helps them frame their thinking around their predictions or hypotheses.

Struggling readers benefit greatly from the use of strategies in their reading. Instructional strategies provide a way for readers to recognize and paraphrase the most important concepts in the text. They are a way for readers to understand and organize information. Strategies are actually beneficial for all readers since, at times, all readers are faced with challenging text that is confusing or complex.

Students with Special Needs

Your students may not only be diverse culturally and linguistically, they may also be diverse educationally. How do you reach all of the students in your class, even those who have special needs?

First, you plan lessons that will serve students with a wide range of abilities and then recognize that you still may have to make adjustments to help those students who require additional attention. Students may have a variety of special needs. They may have learning disabilities, poor motor coordination, visual perception problems, emotional difficulties, lack of language experiences, poor reading skills, and other issues. Your task will be to teach these students, not to diagnose their problems. Of course, if you notice issues that have not been previously recognized, you should certainly contact the Child Study Team to initiate further testing for the student.

As special and general educators work together to plan collaboratively for their students, it is important to understand the need for accommodations for students with special needs. An accommodation is an adaptation or change in the way instruction is presented or in the way an assessment tool (i.e., individual and group measurement and evaluation) is administered. Instruction and assessment can be adapted or changed to help students meet the established standards, goals, objectives, and outcomes. This modification means that the standard has not been reduced or minimized in any way, but that students have been able to take an "alternate route" in meeting the standard (Mastropieri & Scruggs, 2005). This is an important feature of an accommodation—and one that needs to be consistently communicated to all who are involved: parents, teachers and students.

For students with disabilities, specific accommodations are highlighted in their individualized education plans (IEPs). Documenting the accommodations made in the classroom is essential, especially since statewide testing is now being used in many states as an exit requirement for graduation. Many states are now mandating that any accommodations requested for a student with disabilities on statewide assessments must be documented on the student's IEP and implemented during instruction prior to the statewide testing. The thinking is that the accommodation should not be a last-minute attempt to give the student strategies that will make the testing easier, but rather it should be a meaningful, purposeful strategy that the student learned and practiced in order to accomplish the same goals as other students.

Students with special needs are a very diverse group. It is not possible to approach all diversity with the same plan and strategies. However, since teachers adapt the curriculum to make it appropriate for all of the learners in their classes, there are general strategies and accommodations that can be considered for students with special needs:

- Build from your students' strengths.
- Increase the time that your students spend reading and writing.
- Model everything you want your students to do.
- Create a routine that students can depend on. They will work better if they know the routine and have had extensive experience with a task.
- Set short-term and reachable goals. Break assignments down into smaller parts.
- Make high-interest, lower-level texts available to your students.
- Offer your students choices in assignments, when possible.
- Use technology to support students. If students find writing difficult, allow them to type their papers on computers. If they don't understand a text, provide an audio copy for them to review.
- Provide explicit instruction in your classroom. Don't assume students understand. Teach using models, guided practice, and independent work.
- Use cooperative learning strategies in your class. Sometimes groups of students with varying abilities can work well together to accomplish a task or project.
- Keep directions simple and clear. Provide them visually and orally.
- Spend the first four to six weeks of school establishing a comfortable routine that students can learn. Model everything you want students to do.
- Provide written notes and outlines for chapters and texts you think may present problems for students.
- Use graphic organizers to organize information.
- Highlight important information in margins or with markers.
- Break lessons down into smaller segments. Begin with the concrete and move to the abstract.
- Allow the use of tape recorders or other assistive technology to simplify assignments.
- Repeat directions several times and in several different ways (board, notes, orally, etc.).
- Think of alternatives for written assignments.
- Test students orally when appropriate.
- Provide additional time to complete an assignment or test, when needed.
- Provide students with a model of the finished product they are to produce. This can be a critical element in the success of students.

- Offer one-minute and five-minute reminders to students who have difficulty transitioning to the next lesson or activity.

- Provide daily or weekly reporting to parents.

- Be aware of the visual distractions in the classroom.

- Be sure that you ask students to do a few tasks each day that they can do without your support. Help them to feel good about themselves.

- Encourage the use of technology like iPods, iPads, or podcasts to assist students.

 ## Advice from the Field

- Think of your classroom as an opportunity to experience a microcosm of society. There are many differences among us; yet there are some universal ties that bind us together.

- Learn about the cultures of your students. Research cultural values, family structures, and the role of education in the culture. It will help you to better understand your students.

- Respect students' native language and encourage them to become bilingual. Proficiency in more than one language should be valued in the classroom.

- Vary the ways in which you group students. Some groups may consist of students on similar reading levels, while other groups can be formed randomly. Students can feel stigmatized by ability grouping.

- An environment that allows students to take risks and to make mistakes will foster significant learning.

- Don't give up on any student because you're not seeing improvement. Sometimes it takes time and patience as well as creativity and flexibility for changes to be visible.

 ## Additional Resources

Armstrong, T. (2003). *The multiple intelligences of reading and writing.* Alexandria, VA: Association for Supervision and Curriculum Development.

Norton, D. E. (2005). *Multicultural children's literature: Through the eyes of many children.* Upper Saddle River, NJ: Pearson Education.

References

Ada, A. F. (1995). *My name is Maria Isabel.* Illustrated by K. D. Thompson. New York: Aladdin Paperbacks.

Henry, L. (2006). Searching for an answer: The critical role of new literacies while reading on the Internet. *The Reading Teacher, 59*(7).

Levin, F. (2003). Pitfalls and potential: Multicultural literature and study groups. In A. I. Willis, G. E. Garcia, R. Barrera, & V. J. Harris (Eds.), *Multicultural issues in literacy: Research and practice.* Mahwah, NJ: Lawrence Erlbaum.

Mastropieri, M., & Scruggs, T. E. (2005). *The inclusive classroom: Strategies for effective instruction.* Upper Saddle River: Pearson Education.

National Center for Education Statistics. (2004). *Mini-digest of education statistics 2003.* Washington, DC: U.S. Department of Education.

National Institute of Child Health and Human Development. (2000). Report of the National Reading Panel. *Teaching children to read: An evidence-based assessment of the scientific research literature on reading and its implications for reading instruction.* (NIH Publication No. 00-4769). Washington, DC: Government Printing Office.

Smallwood, B. (2002). *Thematic literature and curriculum for English language learners in early childhood education.* Washington, DC: ERIC Clearinghouse on Languages and Linguistics. (ERIC Digest EDO-FL-02-08).

Snow, C. E., Burns, S. E., & Griffin, P. (Eds.). (1998). *Preventing reading difficulties in young children.* Washington, DC: National Academy Press.

Whalen Ariza, E. (2006). *Not for ESOL teachers: What every classroom teacher needs to know about the linguistically, culturally, and ethnically diverse student.* Boston: Pearson Education.

Online Resources

www.lib.msu.edu/corby/education/multicultural
www.ed.gov/offices/OBSERS/IDEA/updates.html
www.nichey.org/index.html
www.ourkids.org/
www.multiculturalchildrenslit.com

Cultural Beliefs Assessment

Teachers must look at their own cultural beliefs in order to gain a broader understanding of the other cultures represented in their classes. Consider the following questions related to your culture and family:

1. What is your family's nationality?

2. Why did your ancestors come to the United States?

3. What would you say are the most important beliefs in your cultural community?

4. Does your family have special traditions? Are they consistent with your cultural traditions?

5. How important is receiving an education—high school? college? graduate school?—in your culture?

6. Who are the decision makers in your family? Is this traditional for your cultural community?

7. Do you believe that respect is an important part of your cultural traditions? If so, in what way?

8. Are there traditions in your culture that are different from those of what you see as the average American family?

9. Does your family have values or beliefs that are consistent with your cultural community?

10. How important are names in your culture?

11. How would you characterize the treatment of children in your cultural community?

12. Is there anything you would need to explain to a teacher about your culture to make her or him sensitive to the traditions of your culture?

Students with Special Needs in an Inclusive Classroom

 ## What is Inclusion?

As a new teacher, meeting the challenge of teaching students must include a study in best practices for inclusion. Perhaps the most important belief to embrace is the idea that all students possess the ability to learn. Implicit in that statement is the notion that teachers similiarly possess the ability to teach all types of learners. However, strong teaching skills require reflection, thought and an understanding of inclusion and effective practices in your classroom.

Inclusive education is the practice of educating all or the vast majority of children in the same classroom. This includes children with physical, mental, and developmental disabilities. Inclusion classrooms often require either a special assistant to the classroom teacher or a special education teacher who comes to the classroom for a portion or all of the school day.

The 1975 Education for All Handicapped Children Act (P.L. 94—142) mandated free and appropriate education (with related services) for each child in the least restrictive environment possible as well as an Individualized Education Program (IEP) for each qualifying child. In 1991, the bill was renamed the Individuals with Disabilities Education Act (IDEA). This revision broadened the definition of disabilities and added services.

In 1997, the regulations corresponding to the Individuals with Disabilities Education Act (IDEA , 1997), stipulated that:

> "to the extent appropriate, children with disabilities… are educated with children who are not disabled, and that special classes, separate schooling, or other removal of children with disabilities from the regular environment occurs only when the nature or severity of the disability is such that education in regular classes with the use of supplementary aids and services cannot be attained satisfactorily." (IDEA Sec. 612 (5) (B)).

By definition, inclusion proposes that students who have disabilities must be instructed in the general education classroom with the necessary special accommodations. As a new teacher, it is important to approach this with an understanding of the fact that all classes are made up of unique individuals. Students with disabilities are but one element in the greater concept of diversity. Students may differ with regard to ethnic backgrounds, culture, language development, reading ability, intelligence and ability levels. A significant step towards a positive, effective classroom involves learning to look a class in terms of specific students and their distinct needs.

At its core, inclusive education is nothing more than good teaching for all students. Accepting this basic tenet, a teacher committed to teaching all students will examine the classroom in terms of the needs of all types of learners with the understanding that the special needs students do have an additional consideration in the Individual Education Plan. The teacher must use the IEP as a guide, in conjunction with the Special Education Teacher, to determine the specific goals for the student as well as the necessary services, if any.

An IEP is a written statement that is developed for a student with special needs. It acts as a legal agreement between the school and the parents, with respect to the students' specific needs and the steps that must be taken to address those needs. The IEP is developed by the educational team with the help of the Special Education teacher and must be strictly adhered to by the classroom teacher.

While this may sound like a daunting task, working closely with the Special Education Teacher will help to create a classroom situation that works well for all of the learners. Students with disabilities are not the only ones who benefit from the accommodations that are required by law. Their non-disabled classmates are often able to receive support from the additional resources present, including attention from another teacher, knowledge of a new strategy or assistance from some type of equipment or technology. Such tools provide a wide reaching effect for both students with and without disabilities.

Models for Teaching in an Inclusion Classroom

The law requires that Special Education teachers be present in an inclusion class. In some cases, the special educator works only for short periods of time in the regular classroom while in other classrooms such special educators spend half-days or full days in one regular class before moving to another class. Regardless of the particular schedule, the Special Education teacher should generally be available to help while in the classroom. Students' learning is optimized when there is a team of teachers reviewing their IEPs, considering their abilities, their needs, and the ways in which the classroom can function most effectively. Collaboration with another teacher within the classroom is an excellent tool to help students, providing different perspectives, expertise, and personalities to access the best from students. Collaborative teaching or co-teaching includes a variety of options such as parallel teaching, supportive teaching, and team teaching, etc. to help create an effective environment for all students.

Furthermore, collaborative teaching increases instructional options, improves educational programs, reduces stigmatization for students and provides support to both teachers and parents (Cook & Friend, 1995). It provides the structure which offers effective teaching that meets the specific needs of all students.

Co-Teaching is an additional way that teachers can jointly meet the needs of students in an inclusion class. Co-Teachers coordinate to plan and conduct instruction to ensure the success of all students. This method works in elementary, middle school and secondary settings. In an elementary classroom, one general education and one special education teacher work together to plan lessons utilizing both of their talents and expertise. In a middle school and secondary classroom, students with disabilities as well as general education students benefit from the content area specialist. The content area specialist works with and supports the special education teacher who focuses on struggling learners. These teachers provide support and instructional advice, ultimately benefiting all of the students in the class.

In order to forge a successful relationship, both teachers commit the necessary time in order to co-teach in the most effective way. At times, some teachers may be territorial both with their classrooms and their specific content expertise; however, such territoriality can stifle the collaborative effort and ultimately harm the students. Teachers must collaborate with others, debate logistical questions, subject matter, disciplinary matters, and how teaching impacts students in terms of grading, testing, and standards. There are questions that co-teachers should ask themselves and then discuss with each other. For example,

- What is our vision for co-teaching?
- Will I be teaching a lesson alone or co-teaching it with you?
- In what specific areas could I be helpful to you?
- How do we best use our experience and expertise in subject matter and instruction of students with disabilities to create the right environment in our classroom?
- How do we make sure that we are both equally involved in the classroom?
- How do we make certain that neither one of us feels like an Classroom Aide?
- How can we maintain honest, open lines of communication?
- What will our schedule be? Will we be teaching together daily, weekly, or just for certain units?
- What will our schedule look like?
- How often can we meet to talk and plan together?

Another way of approaching this arrangement is to use a questionnaire to determine each co-teacher's expectations and needs. This should be an honest appraisal of beliefs, and hopes for success in the classroom. These questionnaires should be shared, discussed and then re-visited as needed.

Topics for Discussion Survey

The following topics should be reflected upon and discussed by Co-Teachers. These topics impact the effectiveness of the classroom and should be determined together.

What are the expectations for our classroom? How will we determine the following?

a) teaching responsibilities

b) planning time

c) communication time for us

d) modifications made for our students

e) homework policies

f) materials we need

g) content teaching

h) conferences (frequency, classroom, student-led, parents)

i) grading policies

j) discipline policies

k) teaching test taking skills

l) standards-based outcomes

Both Co-Teachers should write their feelings about these topics, and use this as a basis for discussion, feedback and compromise.

In order to engender better collaboration, a common planning period is very important. If this is not practical, it may be a good idea to ask an administrator if a substitute may be able to cover a class period for both co-teachers or if a spare room is available before or after school hours. When planning, be sure to come to the session armed with information. The classroom teacher should provide an overview of the content and standards to be addressed. The special educator should focus on information regarding the IEPs of the students, including goals, modifications and special services that might be necessary. In the secondary classroom, this conversation is particularly helpful since the content area teacher is focused more on the general curriculum.

In discussions with special education teachers, content area teachers should try to create a roadmap for the class to improve learning for all students. For regular meetings, teachers should focus on the units of instruction, how the teaching will be divided and specific students and issues, necessary accommodations and the most effective ways of differentiating instruction.

It is of great benefit to the co-teachers if they can truly share in the teaching, planning and implementation of the lessons so that students understand that they have two teachers and both of them are equal. Students should feel able to connect with either of the teachers for help, discussion, or information. This is quite important so that students are not stigmatized by the "Special Ed" teacher.

A discussion of learning styles is a necessary component of the conversation. This is a time for teachers to be introspective. What are the teaching styles of both teachers and how does that match up with the learning styles of the students? Are the students' auditory learners? Are they visual learners? Do they require hands-on tasks? This is the time to consider the various ways in which the co-teachers can best present material so that teaching styles can be appropriate to the students' learning styles. (See Chapter 4, pages 106–107 for more information on Learning Style Assessment.) This way of thinking ultimately helps all of the students in the class to recognize their own learning styles and provides some equality in terms of instructional modalities.

*I*nclusion Issues to Consider

There are many issues that will arise in the course of a day that will need to be addressed by co-teachers. It is critical that both teachers agree on classroom procedures for consistency's sake. For example, talking in class, lavatory breaks, headings on papers, formats for assignments, transitioning from one subject to another, gaining the attention of the students, noise levels, etc are constantly occurring issues that should have clear, consistent procedures that both teachers agree are appropriate.

Agreement is a key ingredient in a successful co-teaching situation. Co-Teachers should discuss their responsibilities and possible activities that each can do while the other is teaching. For example, if a teacher is distributing papers, the other teacher can be reviewing the directions or providing a model for one of the questions. If one of the teachers is giving oral directions, the other teacher can be writing the directions on the board. While one of the teachers is lecturing, the other teacher can be modeling notetaking on the board. While planning a lesson, one teacher may create the lesson plan while the other teacher provides suggestions for making modifications for struggling learners. There are a number of options available to Co-Teachers. However, the constant must be the attitude of helping each other and a commitment to working together. Both teachers should carry equal responsibility to the students and therefore, should be sharing in the many roles of teacher.

One of the most important areas for consideration is Assessment. Teachers need to come to agreement regarding assessment since it determines what and how units or topics should be taught. This is an opportunity to determine how effective the instruction is and what parts of the curriculum need revision or adjustment. Co-Teachers should be talking about specific student progress, accommodations that have been successful, those that have not worked quite as well, and agree on a future course of action. Assessment must be used to inform future instruction and to determine if learning has occurred.(See Chapter 4 for additional information on assessment.) Both teachers must be committed to the idea that if the material is presented appropriately, all children can learn at their own rate. The special educator should be focused on the IEPs and the ways in which work can be documented to fulfill those responsibilities.

Co-Teachers must be willing to carefully look at their teaching and be flexible; to make changes in classroom management, room arrangements, methods of teaching, etc. in order to create a better environment for their students. They must be open to suggestions and use criticism as a method to improve their own instruction and classroom.

Ways of Working Together To Benefit Students

There are a variety of ways in which Co-Teachers can work together effectively. Parallel teaching is an option whereby both teachers are working in separate groups in the classroom. This system works best when all of the groups work with both teachers and the Special Education teacher is not just reserved for those students who have disabilities. In this way, students have the benefit of two perspectives, smaller groups, and more individualized attention with two teachers instead of just one.

Another option, called Supportive Teaching is a situation in which one teacher presents content and the other teacher provides enrichment. This is particularly useful when one of the teachers has expertise in a content area. However, the content teacher must never believe she is the "real" teacher, while the special education teacher is her helper. It should be explicitly clear that the teacher providing enhancement for content offers students practical strategies that will help them understand the material. Both teachers have credibility and very clear and specific purposes in the classroom.

Team Teaching is an ideal way to approach the inclusive classroom. In this model, both teachers share the whole class instruction. They plan together, dividing lessons and providing instruction in a variety of different ways. The students assume they have two teachers and it's difficult to recognize who is the classroom teacher and who is the special education teacher.

Successful co-teaching requires a strong commitment to reflect from both teachers. Co-teachers must understand themselves as well as understanding each other. They must understand that there are often preconceived notions that can get in the way of their teaching. Sometimes, preexisting opinions about students' capabilities or lack thereof prevent teachers from seeing students as capable learners. Honesty and a willingness to acknowledge that there are challenging students and tough situations in a co-teaching situation helps to overcome difficulties.

Self-analysis and awareness are often a struggle as teachers may face questions they may not want to answer. However, these are questions that will help to create a positive relationship with each co-teacher. Some of them may include:

- How much am I willing to let the other teacher do? What do I want her to do? Can she create a unit or a lesson, or just make accommodations for students?

- Will I be resentful or intimidated if my co-teacher offers suggestions or ideas that I have not considered?

- Am I willing to share the special bond that I want to have with my students with another teacher?

- Am I willing to support my co-teacher in her teaching of a lesson that I have not created?

- Can I accept that I am not the only one responsible for creating procedures like classroom management, assessments, grading, etc. Can I share this control and be supportive in our mutual decision-making?

These are difficult questions; difficult for an experienced teacher, but perhaps even more difficult for a new teacher struggling to create a positive environment, complete with procedures, and systems that function effectively. These questions should guide reflective thinking and frame a discussion with the co-teacher.

Co-Teachers must be reflective practitioners who consider the personal benefits of this teaching arrangement as well as the benefits to the students in their classes. Both teachers must recognize that if there are criticisms or negative results in the classroom, they must approach finding a solution in a non-threatening way, without assigning blame. It is so important to communicate often and to share in the workload equally so that both teachers feel equally invested in the classroom and the student's needs.

Co-Teachers must also consider differentiation of instruction for their students. For example, offering a variety of activities that can be chosen by students as a culminating task for a unit study would be an appropriate way to differentiate instruction. Those activities may represent work that corresponds to the learning styles and talents of the students. A strong, working relationship with another teacher results in consistency and excellence in the classroom.

Competencies for the Classroom Teacher

In some schools, teachers must deal with students who have special needs almost by themselves. There are Special Education teachers who may only come in for a period or two or not at all and that places great responsibility for following the IEP and working toward success for all students on the classroom teacher. For a classroom teacher, it is often appropriate to think about the changes a student may have to make to fit into the classroom. However, in an inclusive classroom, the teacher needs to think about how to change the classroom in order to meet the needs of all of the students in the class. The competencies needed by classroom teachers to succeed in an inclusive environment are:

- the ability to informally assess students (observation, conferences, running record, etc).

- the recognition that it is important to use students' individual interests for motivational purposes.

- setting high expectations for all students, and offering alternative assessments for students with special needs.

- the understanding that modifying assignments for some students is important so that all students can learn appropriate information in the ways that best suit their learning needs.

- the notion that an environment must exist where students can find success each day.

- the realization that every child in the class is their responsibility.

- working as a team with parents and special education teachers to learn what skills each child needs and to provide the best possible teaching approach.

- knowing a variety of instructional strategies and how to use them effectively.

What Instructional Strategies Can Be Implemented in an Inclusion Classroom?

There are many teaching/learning approaches that can be implemented in an inclusion classroom. Some general teaching tips for helping students in an inclusive classroom include:

- Set a purpose for each reading assignment. Emphasize that students read in different ways for different purposes. Teach students to skim to get a general overview or to read carefully to locate specific information.

- Teach the book "format" to the students. Help them understand how books are organized.

- Review the table of contents, index, glossary, etc. to ensure that students know how to use various parts of the book.

- Write key points on the board for students to copy for studying during a lecture or oral presentation.

- Show models of class assignments on the board or in a handout for students' reference.

- Provide ample "wait time" for students having difficulty answering questions.

- Encourage the use of index cards for a variety of purposes, such as memorization, test taking, focus on important facts, etc.

- Provide a glossary in content areas. Make sure the words are listed in a meaningful context.

- Develop reading guides for the texts you read in class so students can keep track and gain greater comprehension.

- Use graphic organizers to help students organize information.

- Provide a written and oral overview of the topic before you teach a lesson.

- Provide books-on-tape or record text on tape for students to listen to as a way of reinforcing material.

Providing all students with the opportunity to succeed in the classroom is the ultimate goal for all teachers. Figuring out a way to make that happen for students with special needs, including gifted students and students with disabilities offers teachers the opportunity to think creatively about designing assignments and projects that offer students the kind of assessments and tasks that they can accomplish without any stigma.

There are many strategies that help students with special needs that also help all students in the classroom. One example of a strategy that accommodates differences is the *Olympic Medals*. It provides students with a choice of activities, specifically chosen by the teacher using information about students' needs and abilities. The first thing to do in establishing this and any other strategy is to help students understand the procedures. One of the first procedures in this strategy is the setting of goals for the week. The goals include working toward a Gold medal, a Silver medal or a Bronze medal. A list of the assignment options offered to students for Independent Activities should be provided. These assignment choices are designed to meet the needs and objectives of the students and are designed in 3 categories, Gold, Silver and Bronze. Each category has assignments that have various point values based on the difficulty of the assignment and the time required to complete it. Each category represents the various needs of the students and puts them in charge of their own grades because they can choose to do the assignments from any category.

This system works well because it differentiates instruction and provides lots of alternatives for students. The teacher conferences with students and provides assistance, as needed and always makes sure that there are activities in each category that can be modified and completed by all of the students in the class.

Other effective strategies that work well for students with special needs are various forms of tutoring such as peer tutoring, cross–age tutoring and small groupings. Research has shown that students with disabilities can perform effectively either as tutors or tutees, as well as in a reciprocal tutoring role. Reciprocal-role tutoring may offer an additional benefit of boosting students' self-esteem through the teaching role. In order to use this technique, teachers must plan effectively, train the tutors, and monitor them carefully (Swanson, H.L., Hoskyn, M., & Lee, C 1999).

Dynamic grouping provides an important opportunity for all students, especially students with special needs. Dynamic grouping includes various ways in which groupings occur and are recreated in the classroom. Groups change frequently so as to maximize instruction and eliminate the stigma of being in a "slow" group. Whole group instruction provides a way to introduce topics, units, and new information and can provide students with a foundation of background knowledge. Small group instruction is appropriate for students with similar interests, students who have similar skill needs or instructional levels. In small groups, teachers can address the specific needs of a particular group. Teachers can also create random groups to help students learn from one another. Often, stronger students motivate struggling learners by providing a model for what is appropriate behavior in the group. For example, the types of questions that strong students ask may show struggling learners how to ask questions that will help them do the assignment. Flexible grouping allows students to see themselves in a variety of contexts and not just in a group for special needs students. (Tomlinson, 1999).

*T*he Use of Technology in an Inclusive Classroom

Using technology as a strategy is an excellent way to help all students in an inclusive classroom. Teachers can help students become more proficient in technology by providing many opportunities for students to search for information using the Internet as a tool. Helping students organize information found on the Internet with software such as Inspiration (www.inspiration.com) or EDGE Diagrammer (www.pacestar.com/edge/index/html). provides graphic organizers that students may use as Study Guides or to develop a greater understanding of the topic. Teaching students to use Google (www.google.com) as a search engine can enable them to access information on any topic they choose. Use of the internet is a very effective tool to help students, especially those with special needs to be able to learn new information in a very user friendly way. Searching for information using a Web-based activity can develop skills and strategies. There are many Internet Workshops that offer students unlimited possibilities for searching the Web (Henry, 2006). These websites, in conjunction with assignments provided by the teacher have the potential to unleash skills that will provide practical proficiencies for all students. For example:

The Internet

- (http://www.rtsd26.org/trails/parent_workshop/parent_inservice.htm)
- Finding Information on the Internet: A Tutorial (www.lib.berkeley.edu/TeachingLib/Guides/Internet?FindInfo.htm)
- Untangle the Web! (http://library.ucf.edu/Reference/Instruction/Internet)

Aside from teaching students to access information from the Internet, teachers can also use technology to teach across the curriculum. For example, teachers can teach literature by bringing the Internet into the classroom by having students visit various sites online related to many genres in literature. For students with special needs, these sites can offer the opportunity to listen to books that are found in the classroom and to participate in interactive reading experiences. There are a variety of sites that offer interactive read-along stories such as:

- BookPALS Storyline (www.storylineonline.net) which is a wonderful site where students can hear online readalouds.

- TumbleBook Library (www.tumblebooks.com) interactive, electronic texts available in English, Spanish and Chinese.

- Mythic Journeys (http://mythicjourneys.org/bigmyth/index.htm) intermediate adventure stories

- RIF Reading Planet (www.rif.org/readingplanet/content/read_aloud_stories.mspx.) read along songs and stories, games, author's writing process

- The International Children's Digital Library (www.icdlbooks.org)digital collection of multicultural books

- E-encyclopedia (www.dke-encyc.com) may be used for informational searches

Using the Internet to access not only informational formats, but also stories of all types offers students a tremendous opportunity to read materials that they may not have had access to or the ability to read on their own. Using this strategy as a way to help students with special needs is very effective; however, its success with all students cannot be underestimated.

How to Make Accommodations for Students with Special Needs

As special and general educators work together to plan collaboratively for their students, it is important to focus on both the individual and the group needs of their students. An accommodation is an adaptation or change in the way instruction is presented or in the way an assessment tool (i.e., individual and group measurement and evaluation) is administered. Instruction and assessment can be adapted or changed to help students meet the established standards – goals, objectives, and outcomes. This modification means that the standard has not been reduced or minimized in any way, but that students have been able to take an "alternate route" in meeting the standard (Mastropieri & Scruggs, 2005). This is an important feature of an accommodation – one that needs to be consistently communicated to all who are involved: parents, teachers and students.

For students with disabilities, specific accommodations are highlighted in their individualized education plans (IEPs). Documenting the accommodations made in the classroom is essential, especially since statewide testing is now being used in many states as an exit requirement for graduation. Many states are now mandating that any accommodation requested for a student with disabilities on statewide assessments must be documented on that student's IEP and implemented during instruction prior to the statewide testing. The thinking is that the accommodation should not be a last minute attempt to give the student strategies that will make the testing easier, but rather it should be a meaningful, purposeful, strategy that the student learned and practiced in order to accomplish the same goals as all other students.

Since teachers adapt the curriculum to make it appropriate for all of the learners in their classes, there must be a variety of accommodations easily at hand in order to meet the varied needs of students with disabilities. In particular, general education teachers may not feel as confident in their ability to identify the areas in which they need to consider the use of accommodations. Therefore, the following are accommodations that will provide students with additional help and the ability to learn new concepts and complete reinforcement activities:

- Spend the first four to six weeks of school establishing a comfortable routine that students can learn. Model everything you want the students to do.

- Provide written notes and outlines for chapters and texts that you think may present problems for students.

- Use graphic organizers to organize information

- Highlight important information in margins or with markers

- Use mnemonic devices to help students remember formulas or facts.

- Break lessons down into smaller segments. Go from the concrete to the abstract.

- Allow the use of tape recorders or other technology to simplify assignments.

- Repeat directions several times and in several different ways (board, notes, orally, etc).

- Think of alternatives for written assignments.

- Test students orally, when appropriate.

- Use assistive technology, when needed.

- Provide additional time to complete an assignment or test, when needed.

- Divide worksheets into segments to lessen the difficulty of following varying directions.

- Provide Partner Tutoring to help students understand assignments or readings more easily.

- Work in small groups or one—to—one when possible.

- Develop clear and sometimes alternate classroom management procedures.

- Provide additional individual assistance on assignments.

- Provide daily or weekly reporting to parents.

- Rewrite directions to a more appropriate reading level.

- Limit the number of problems or questions on a page so it is not overwhelming to a student.

- Provide students with a model of the finished product they are to produce. This is a critical element in the success of students.

- Summarize key points of the lesson to ensure that students have recorded important information.

- Offer 5 minute and 1 minute reminders with students who have difficulty with transition to the next lesson or activity.

- Have students who require special attention sit in the front of the room or in a preferred seat.

- Be aware of the visual distractions in the classroom.

- Make sure the students' work areas are clear of material or artifacts that may serve as distractions.

- Be sure that you ask students to do a few tasks each day that they can do without your support. For example, they can be classroom monitors, they can deliver notes, etc. Help them to feel good about themselves.

There are many accommodations that can be made which will benefit all learners. These are procedures that make sense because they encourage students to think about the text, to explore vocabulary, and to gain greater comprehension. For example,

Before the lesson:

- pre-teach difficult vocabulary and concepts in context so students can make associations while they read.

- talk about the lesson's objective so students are clear about what they are supposed to do.

- provide study guides so students can learn how to study appropriately.
- provide outlines of chapters or texts. Begin with a model and then slowly leave parts out and have students complete the outline. The goal is for them to do it independently.

During the lesson:

- provide visuals using the board or overhead projector.
- use flash cards to help students practice vocabulary or concept development.
- ask students to close their eyes and try to visualize the information
- have students take notes and use colored markers to highlight
- provide written as well as oral directions
- have the student repeat directions
- when giving directions to the class, leave a pause between each step so students have the opportunity to think about what you're asking them to do.
- provide both written and manipulative tasks to accommodate different modalities.

These accommodations offer struggling students a way to succeed; a way to understand the lessons, to complete assignments and to learn how to manage their work. The students who require certain accommodations may not only be students who have a learning disability. They may be students who are struggling for a variety of reasons, such as cultural and language limitations, reading difficulties, developmental issues, etc. Once you learn to make accommodations for special needs, you become sensitive to individual needs and consequently, your classroom will be improved for all students.

*I*nvolving Families in an Inclusion Class

Building partnerships with families is important in all classrooms. In an inclusion class, often parents have specific questions that must be addressed. Parents of students with disabilities want to understand how the teacher will be working to compensate for some of the difficulties associated with the disability. Teachers should make every effort to stay in contact with families as often as possible to keep them apprised of all issues, including the IEP, classroom performance, accommodations that have been made, affective concerns, etc. It is sometimes easy to forget how hard it is for parents of children with disabilities. Information and a kind word are always appreciated.

Families of students who do not have disabilities are also entitled to access to information about their children and the way the class is run. They may have questions about inclusion and what the implications are for their child. Their concerns are legitimate and should be addressed in a respectful, confidential manner.

Definitions Associated with Inclusion

It is very important for a classroom teacher to understand the terminology inherent in the discussion of inclusion. Therefore, the following list represents vocabulary relating to inclusive classrooms:

Accommodations – services provided to help a student perform in a general education classroom while demonstrating learning.

Adaptations – a modification intended to meet the needs of a student with respect to individual differences.

Annual Goal – a statement in a student's Individual Education Program (IEP) that describes what a child with a disability can reasonably be expected to accomplish within a 12-month period.

Full Inclusion – Full inclusion means that all students, regardless of disability or the severity of the disability, will be in a regular classroom full time. In this situation, all services must be taken to the child in that setting.

Individualized Education Program (IEP) – Individualized Education Program (IEP) is a written agreement between the parents and the school detailing what the child needs and what will be done to address those needs. In accordance with the Individuals with Disabilities Education Act (IDEA, formerly PL 94—142), IEPs must be drawn up by the educational team and must include the following:

1. The student's present level of academic performance.
2. The annual goals for the student.
3. Short-term instructional objectives related to the annual goals.
4. The special education and related services that will be provided and the extent to which the child will participate in regular education programs.
5. Plans for starting the services and the anticipated duration of services.
6. Plans for evaluating whether the goals and objectives are being achieved.
7. Transition planning for older students.

IDEA – Individuals with Disabilities Education Act

Least Restrictive Environment – to the maximum extent appropriate, children with disabilities are educated with children who are not disabled.

Progress Monitoring – monitoring a student's progress to help the IEP team determine if changes need to be made in the IEP.

Review & Revision of IEP – An annual meeting to review each student's IEP and revise it, if necessary.

Section 504 – Section 504 of the Rehabilitation Act of 1973 is a statute which provides that: "No otherwise qualified individual with disabilities in the United States . . . shall, solely by reason of his/her disability, be excluded from the participation in, be denied the benefits of, or be subjected to discrimination under any program or activity receiving federal financial assistance or activity conducted by any executive agency or by the United States Postal Service." 29 U.S.C. 794.

Additional Resources

Alper, S. & Ryndak, D. L. (1996). Curriculum Content for Students with Moderate and Severe Disabilities in Inclusive Settings. Needham, MA: Allyn & Bacon.

Berres, Michael S. (1996). Creating tomorrow's schools today: Stories of inclusion, change, and renewal. New York: Teachers College Press.

Cohen, J. J., & Fish, M. C. (1993). Handbook of school-based interventions. San Francisco: Jossey-Bass Publishers.

McIntyre, T. (1989). A resource book for remediating common behavior and learning problems. Allyn and Bacon Publishing.

Metcalf, L. (1999). Teaching towards solutions. West Nyack, NY: The Center for Applied Research in Education

Shore, K. (1998). Special kids: Problem solver. Paramus, NJ: Prentice Hall.

Watson, G. (1998). Classroom discipline problem solver. West Nyack, NY: The Center for Applied Research in Education.

Web Sites

Our kids – http://www.our-kids.org/
Inclusion Press home page – http://www.inclusion.com/
IDEA – http://www.ed.gov/offices/OSERS/IDEA/updates.html
The Special Ed Advocate – Special Education Law -- http://www.wrightslaw.com/

*O*rganizations

National Information Center for Children and Youth with Disabilities (NICHCY)
P.O. Box 1492
Washington D.C. 20013-1492
1-800-695-0285
http://www.nichcy.org/index.html
National Parent Network on Disabilities
1600 Prince St., Suite 115
Alexandria, VA 22314
703/684-6763
http://www.npdn.org/
Council for Exceptional Children
1920 Association Dr.,
Reston, VA 20191-1589
1-888-CEC-SPED
http://www.cec.sped.org/index.html

*R*eferences

Cook & Friend. (1995). *Focus on Exceptional Children.* Vol. 28 (3) Denver: Love Publishing Co.

Deschenes, C., Ebeling, D.& Sprague, J. (1994). *Adapting Curriculum and Instruction in Inclusive Classrooms: A Teacher's Desk Reference.*

Henry, L. (2006). *Searching for an answer: The critical role of new literacies while reading on the Internet. The Reading Teacher* Vol. 59, No. 7. International Reading Association.

Mastropieri, M. & Scruggs, T.E. (2005). *The inclusive classroom: Strategies for effective instruction.* Upper Saddle River: Pearson Education, Inc.

Swanson, H.L., Hoskyn, M., & Lee, C (1999). *Interventions for students with learning disabilities: A meta-analysis of treatment outcomes.* New York: Guilford Press.

Tomlinson, C.A. (2000). *Differentiation of Instuction in the Elementary Grades.* ERIC Digest. ERIC Clearinghouse on Elementary and Early Childhood Education.

9

Using Technology to Support Literacy Instruction: Getting Started

 ## Why Integrate Literacy Teaching and Technology?

There are multiple reasons why it is important for technology to be integrated into the literacy curriculum, starting in the early grades. The most compelling reason is the connection between literacy and our mission as educators. It is the primary

job of teachers in today's schools to empower their students with the skills and concepts they will need to meet success in their classes and in their professional and personal lives once their formal schooling is completed. Because today's world is increasingly becoming computer dependent, it is incumbent upon teachers to prepare their students with an academic program that integrates technology and literacy in a meaningful way. Other than state mandates, a more immediate reason for incorporating technology in the literacy curriculum is that it allows teachers to efficiently differentiate instruction by strategically aligning tutorials and programs to individual student interests and needs as opposed to whole-class lessons that rarely meet the needs and/or interests of *all* of the students in the class at the same time. A final argument for integrating technology is that it engages students with interesting and motivating activities that require their active participation in their own learning.

Unfortunately, a problem that many new teachers face is that their technological expertise is limited to emails and basic Web searches. For them, the idea of incorporating technology into their curriculum is seen as a daunting and quite often debilitating task. If you find yourself in this group, the place to begin is by meeting with your subject supervisor and/or the technology specialist in your building to see what equipment and technical support is available to you. You also need to get copies of any software, already purchased for your grade level, for you to review. It is also a good idea to set up a regularly scheduled meeting time with the technology specialist so you can begin to expand your own awareness, knowledge, and technological capabilities.

However, while you are becoming more techno-savvy, there are activities that you can immediately incorporate into your lesson plans. For example, there is a wide range of interactive CD-Rom tutorials in all the content areas that give students an opportunity to practice thinking and responding, while reinforcing the skills and concepts being taught in your class. Also available are instructional games and simulations that require students to deal critically with real-life situations without having to suffer the consequences of their choices. Your students will find these games and simulations fun as well as academically challenging. Your supervisor and/or technology specialist should be able to provide you with catalogs and assistance in selecting appropriate software. *It is important that before you use any software in your classes that you get it approved in writing.*

Something else you could immediately do is take advantage of the Internet. There are hundreds of free sites that you can go to to support both your teaching and your students' learning. However, before doing so, you should make yourself aware of policies concerning Internet use as well as effective measures you need to take to ensure the safety of your students while on the Internet.

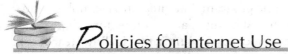

Policies for Internet Use

Copyright and Fair Use Guidelines

Fair Use Guidelines for Educational Multimedia clarify for educators, scholars, and students the conditions under which copyrighted works may be used without securing permission. The fair use of educational multimedia is a legal principle that has been amended to the Copyright Act of 1976 and codified at 17 U.S.C. Simply put, educators and students may incorporate portions of copyrighted works in their projects and presentations without securing permission as long as the products are nonprofit-making, have educational purposes, and adhere to the following limitations:

motion media: 10% or 3 minutes

text material: up to 10% or 1,000 words

music lyrics and music video: up to 10% but no more than 30 seconds

illustrations and photographs: may be used in their entirety but no more than five images by an artist or photographer

Students should be made aware of these limitations before they begin their first media project and/or assignment. The full text of these guidelines may be downloaded at www.adec.edu/admin/papers/fair10-17.html. Students should also be advised that although it may not be indicated on the site, all work posted on the Internet is the intellectual property of the author and/or host of the site; therefore, unless otherwise stipulated, they should treat all materials downloaded from the Internet as copyrighted.

Plagiarism Policy

Because text (print and nonprint) posted on the Internet is recognized as the intellectual property of the author and/or website, the issue of plagiarism should be treated in the same way as it is treated with traditional texts. All information taken from a source, even if it is paraphrased or cut and pasted from a number of sources, must be credited to the source.

Ensuring Student Safety on the Internet

Blocking and Filtering

Blocking (preventing access based on Internet address) and filtering (preventing access based on content) are methods used by parents and educators to protect students from viewing inappropriate material on websites. It is the responsibility of the information technology specialist in your school to identify and install the appropriate blocks and filters on your classroom computers. Having said that, it is your responsibility to check to ensure they are in place *before* you give your students access to the computers. It is also your responsibility to monitor students while working on the computers to ensure they are not inadvertently exposed to harmful or inappropriate websites.

Protecting Students' Privacy

It is important that you protect the privacy of your students when they are working online. Make it clear to them that they should *never* give out personal information (last names, home addresses, email addresses, Social Security numbers, etc.) for any reason when working on a class assignment. For more detailed information regarding safety guidelines see the Children's Internet Protection Act, 20 U.S.C. at www.ntia.doc.gov and the Children's Online Privacy Act of 1998, 15 U.S.C. at www.ftc.gov/ogc/coppa1.htm.

Managing Digital Instruction

Technology, like all other aspects of teaching, needs to be strategically managed in order to maximize instructional effectiveness and maintain classroom decorum. Here are some helpful hints that will allow you to accomplish both:

1. Immediately make it clear to the students, regardless of age, that the technology they will be using is intended to support literacy instruction, not replace it.

2. Tie *all* digital activities to instructional goals and objectives. These connections should be made clear before the activity begins. Students will not value what they are doing unless they understand the value of *why* they are doing it.

3. Provide readers with printed instructions that include the goals and objectives of the activity. Having the instructions in front of them will cut down on the number of unnecessary questions that can create chaos within nanoseconds.

4. Make sure the equipment and programs are working properly *before* the activity begins.

5. Create a protocol for digital activities. The protocol should be printed and displayed so there are no misunderstandings as to how students should proceed during digital time. Your protocol should include but not be limited to:

   a. When students will be working on the computers.
   b. If there are fewer students than computers, how much time each student will be allotted, a clarification of the rotation of the work stations, and the procedure for students to exchange places. It's a good idea to have a time keeper to provide students with a five-minute warning that their time is almost up.
   c. A clarification of what students should do in the event that they were unable to complete their assignments within the allotted time.
   d. Instructions for what to do with completed work.
   e. Instructions for what to do in the event of a problem. A better alternative to panicking and calling out your name for help is to provide them with two cards, a red one, indicating a problem with the equipment, and a blue one, indicating a problem with the assignment.
   f. Behavioral expectations and consequences for not meeting expectations.

6. Model equipment and programs that are new to the students. This can be done in a variety of ways: whole-class demonstrations, teacher-led small-group demonstrations, small-group demonstrations led by students who have expertise and/or who have been trained in advance, or one-on-one demonstrations. *Note:* It is not enough to just show students how to use equipment and software. They need to be able to *show* you that they know how to navigate programs before they are allowed to work independently.

7. Include questions on an interest survey which could be administered at the beginning of the year that will inform you of student capabilities. This will help you identify students who will need assistance as well those you can call on to be your student lab assistants.

8. Have a way of assessing and evaluating student work. Students want and need feedback on their work. Assessments should include an evaluation of their lab time and the products they produce during their lab time. (See Authentic Assessments, p. 80.)

Always remember, the key to good classroom discipline is (1) having students actively engaged in work *they* see as meaningful and stimulating, and (2) providing students with a *clear* understanding of what they need to do, why they need to do it, how they need to do it, and what they need to do in the event of a problem.

Create Your Own Classroom Website

A fun and pragmatic way to integrate technology into your program is to create a website for your class. It's actually quite simple to do. Websites such as www.weebly.com and www.google.sites.com are free and provide clear step-by-step directions for setting up your site. Once established, you can use your website to communicate with parents and students, post student work (with permission), list upcoming events, post assignments, and so on. It's a wonderful vehicle for sharing information and for keeping everyone (parents, students, colleagues, administrators) informed about the exciting things happening in your classroom. *Note:* Before launching your website, it's important to have it approved in writing by your supervisor or building administrator.

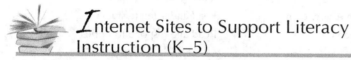

*I*nternet Sites to Support Literacy Instruction (K–5)

A sampling of the sites and activities that you can easily and immediately use to support your literacy instruction can be found in Table 9.1.

These are just a few of the hundreds of sites that are available for your use. You just need to spend some time talking to colleagues, surfing the Web, and thinking about how you can use the Internet to make your lessons more accessible, more dynamic, and ultimately more satisfying for you and your students.

Integrating Technology and Literacy Instruction (6–12)

By the time most students reach middle school, they have already spent innumerable hours on computers, playing games, emailing, and surfing the Web. This is an advantage for middle and high school teachers, who will quickly find that strategically implemented computer applications will effortlessly engage their students in meaningful work, primarily because they are being asked to use technology they already understand. Also important to note is that post-elementary literacy instruction, unlike skill instruction in the earlier years, is typically done in a more integrated way. The most effective assignments require students to critically read,

Table 9.1

Literacy Skill	Site	Activities
Reading		
Decoding	www.readingrockets.org	Reading readiness activities, letter recognitions, e-books
	www.starfall.com	
	www.abc-match.com	
Phonics	www.abcfastphonics.com	Practice word sounds
	http://pbskids.org/lions/	Play phonic skill games
	http://meddybemps.com/letterary/index.html	Interactive phonics activities
Fluency	www.voki.com	Create animated talking characters (multiple languages)
	www.bookpop.com	Read along with animated text
	www.talkingpets.org	Text-to-speech
	www.shidonni.com	Student drawings come to life (talking, dancing, playing)
Guided Reading	www.bedtime-story.com	Read and listen to stories
	www.webpop.com	Read and respond to stories, print books
Independent Reading	www.drscavanaugh.org/ebooks	Read and respond to books online
	www.storyplace.org	Read and listen to stories, interactive activities (English and Spanish)
	www.magickeys.com/books	Read books independently
Comprehension and Critical Thinking	http://interactivities.mped.org/view_interactive.aspx?id=127&tit=	Create organizational webs (cluster, cause & effect, hierarchy)
	www.eduplace.com/graphicorganizers/pdf	Create graphic organizers
	www.abcteach.com/reading/storygrammar.htm	Create story grammars
	www.palmbeachk12.fl.us	
	http://old.escambia.k12.fl.us/schscnts/brobm/te…	Create summaries of texts
	www.kizoa.com	Create slide shows
	www.voicethread.com	Talk about and share images, documents, etc.

Table 9.1, Continued

Literacy Skill	Site	Activities
Vocabulary Development	www.wordle.net	Create "word clouds"
	www.vocabulary.com/wordcity.html	Develop and practice new vocabulary words
	www.readwritethink.org/constructaword.com	Construct new words
	www.puzzlemaker.school.discovery.com	Create crossword puzzles
	www.bbc.co.uk/skillwise	Practice prefixes, suffixes, roots, letter patterns
	www.funbrain.com or www.spellingbee.com	Play spelling games
Writing	www.readwritethink.org	Create newspapers, brochures, flyers, booklets
	www.storybird.com	Create stories with text and pictures
	www.glogster.edu.com	Create interactive posters
	www.kerpoof.com	Create storybooks, paintings

analyze, and respond in some way. The computer is an ideal tool to support this type of skill integration. Just like for K–5 teachers, there are several programs that are academically effective and easily implemented by simply following the directions that accompany the program:

- The *word processing application* allows students to compose and critically edit text with relative ease. The editing features literally take the labor out of rewriting by allowing students to move, add, delete, and spell-check with a click, thus simplifying the writing process and making it more likely that students will actually spend more time thinking about and improving their writing.

- *E-notebooks* can set up as separate folders where students can store their class notes or post sample paragraphs, model essays, graphic organizers, transitions, and vocabulary lists for easy access when composing.

- *E-portfolios*, set up as separate folders, give students a place to store representative pieces of their writing so they (and you) can easily track their progress.

- *www.google.docs.com* is an application that allows students to collaborate, create, edit, and share documents, spreadsheets, and presentations from any browser, allowing groups of students to work on projects or respond to each other's writing outside the classroom at the same time from multiple locations. An added benefit to using this application is that it teaches students to work collaboratively, a skill they will need for future jobs in business and industry.

- *www.googleblogger.com* is an application that students can use in a variety of ways. For example, they could use their individual blogs (web log) as an online journal where they could respond to their readings or to a given topic, or they could allow other members in the class to have access to their blog so they could respond to each other's comments, or students could be assigned characters and be asked to respond as they think their characters would, like a threaded discussion. The possibilities are endless.

Note: To protect your students' privacy, it is important for you to limit the access to google.docs and googleblogger applications to only the students in your class and yourself. Directions for how to do this are provided at both sites.

- *www.actden.com* is a step-by-step tutorial application that literally walks students through the process of developing creative PowerPoint presentations. These presentations are a fun way for students to critically evaluate and organize, and present their ideas. For presentation and design tips, see:
  www.presentationzen.com
  http://blog.duarte.com/category/design
  www.beyondbulletpoints.com/blog/

- *Social networks like Twitter and Facebook* can be used as research tools for students. For example, students can easily access public opinion on a given topic for analysis, conduct their own public opinion poll, or communicate directly with authors, business people, politicians, or celebrities to garner information or to do a comparative analysis.

This is just a beginning. Once you see how much more interesting and engaging technology makes your teaching, you may find yourself out of control, branching out into wikis and whiteboards and making your own webcasts. If this happens, just go with it and have fun. You can be sure your students will.

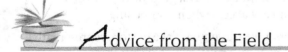

Advice from the Field

- Don't pretend to be an expert. Let students know that you are also learning. They'll appreciate the honesty and be more supportive of your efforts.

- Call on students with computer expertise to be group leaders, who can help students who are less skilled.
- *Always* check the computers and software the day before your lesson to ensure everything is working.
- If the day's lesson is computer-based, always have a Plan B.
- Have the building technical support number on your speed dial.
- Invite knowledgeable students, parents, colleagues, and/or members of the community into your class as tech guest presenters.
- Become "best friends" with the techies in the school.
- Keep building your resources. Set aside one hour every week to surf the Web for new sites.

Additional Resources

Anderson, R. S., Grant, M. M., & Speck, B. W. (2008). *Technology to teach literacy: A resource for K–8 teachers.* Upper Saddle River, NJ: Pearson/Merrill Prentice Hall.

Brozo, W. G., & Puckett, K. (2008). *Supporting content area literacy with technology: Meeting the needs of diverse learners.* Boston: Pearson/Allyn & Bacon.

Stephens, L. C., & Ballast, K. H. (2011). *Using technology to improve adolescent writing: Digital make-overs for writing lessons.* Boston: Pearson.

Tomei, L. A. (2003). *Challenges of teaching with technology across the curriculum: Issues and solutions.* London: IRM Press.

Wasburn-Moses, L. W. (September 2006). 25 best Internet sources for teaching reading. *The Reading Teacher, 60*(1), 70–75.

Online Resources

www.commonsensemedia.org
www.classroom20.com
www.google.com/apps/
www.elearnmag.org

The Home–School Connection

Research on parent involvement clearly demonstrates that students benefit greatly from adult participation in their schoolwork (Cotton & Wikelund, 1989). The more involved parents are in their children's learning, the greater the achievement in school. There are strong indications that the most effective forms of parental involvement are those in which parents work closely with their children on various activities related to learning. For example, reading to children, helping children with homework, talking to teachers about instructional practices that would help their children both at home and at school will make a difference in student achievement.

Although parents are generally more involved at the preschool and primary grade levels than at the middle and high school levels, parent participation is very beneficial in promoting positive achievement and outcomes at all levels. Parent involvement at the middle and high school levels may include monitoring homework, communicating with the school on a regular basis, attending school functions, and helping students to make postsecondary plans; involvement at the

preschool and elementary school levels is much more hands-on, including, of course, reading to children.

We know that many parents begin reading to their children at birth and continue with routines that are consistent and enjoyable for their children. They talk to their children, they engage them with questions, and they ask their opinions about a variety of topics. They provide experiences and discuss them so that their children begin to believe in their ability to communicate and learn. They are involved as their children grow and as their children's learning progresses. They take an interest in the school and ask questions, offer their help, and form a partnership with the teachers. If all parents responded to their children's learning in this way, perhaps so many students would not be failing. The need for parent involvement and a strong home–school connection is clear; the question is how we, as teachers, can achieve a positive and productive relationship with the parents of our students.

Communicating with Parents

It is very important to develop a relationship with the parents of students in your classes. As stated earlier, the greater the involvement of the parents, the higher the achievement of your students. Parents can make your job much easier if you work together for the benefit of the students. Communication is the key to success in creating an environment where parents are comfortable and able to participate in home and school activities.

Teachers and parents know the child in very different contexts, so the information shared should be respected and accepted. Many parents believe that their major role is advocacy for their child; other parents are reluctant to express concerns, some because of their past history in school and others because culturally a teacher is an authority figure who should not be questioned.

The foundation for strong home–school relationships is frequent and open communication. Teachers can consider using the following strategies to establish an environment that is conducive to opening lines of communication:

- Positive communication with parents: for example, sending a letter of introduction at the beginning of the school year (see Figure 10.1 for a sample letter to parents).
- Meeting with parents and keeping an open-door policy.
- Listening to parents' concerns and suggestions with respect.
- Building mutual trust.

As always, check with the administrators in the school on the accepted school-parent communications.

Figure 10.1

Sample Parent Letter (Elementary School)

Dear Parents:

Welcome to a new school year! I would like to take this opportunity to introduce myself to you and your family. My name is Mrs. Smith and this year I will be teaching fourth grade in Room 207. I am very excited and enthusiastic about this year because we will be working on so many wonderful projects and topics of great interest to all. Some of our learning will be focused on the history of New Jersey, multiculturalism, the study of animals, reading novels, studying informational text, computer research, and persuasive and journal writing.

I am extremely interested in getting to know Susan, her strengths, interests, learning style, and any challenges that she experiences. If you can provide any information that you believe may be helpful to me at any time this year, please either call me at 555-2222 between the hours of 4:30 p.m. and 8:30 p.m. or email me at jsmith@ael.net and we can talk about Susan and how we can work together to help her reach her potential.

I recognize how important Susan's education is to you and I will work very hard to help her in any way that I can. I believe that a strong teacher-family relationship is a key element in the success of your child. Therefore, I'd like to offer some suggestions that may help to make this an exceptional year for Susan.

- One important goal for this year will be the improvement of reading and writing skills. Please make every effort to reinforce reading at home and at school.
- Read with your child every single day. You can read to her or she can read to you.
- Be a model for your child. Let her see you reading all different types of books, newspapers, and other materials.
- Help your child develop a daily routine for homework, and check homework every night.
- Call or email me if you have any questions, concerns, or suggestions.
- Please make every effort to attend parent conferences and school functions.
- Be as active in your child's life as you can. Join us for field trips, class events, and other school activities.

Parent involvement is a critical element in school success. We know from research that the greater the parent involvement in their children's school experiences, the higher the students' achievement. We welcome your presence in our classroom. If you would like to volunteer or help at certain events, please let me know.

Best wishes for a wonderful academic year filled with positive learning and wonderful experiences. I look forward to meeting you and discussing how we both can help Susan during this school year.

Sincerely yours,
Mrs. Smith

The first communication that you have with parents should be positive, upbeat, and informative. It should provide the sense that you care about their child and are very interested in working with the student and the family. It should explain your interest in the students and offer some information on what the student will be working on during the school year. It shouldn't be a very long letter—no more than one page because we want to keep the parents' interest and give them just enough information so that they understand the goals and also the importance of becoming an involved family member.

The welcome letter may offer suggestions to parents for how they can best help their children and provide information so that they can call you or email you. Do not give parents your home phone number; however, offer them the school phone number and tell them when they might expect a phone call back. Provide them with your email address and if they email you, email them back in a timely fashion.

Some teachers get their students' addresses in the summer and send a letter of introduction to parents and a letter of introduction to students before the school year begins. This sets the tone for a partnership that can be meaningful and productive. If you are an experienced teacher, feel free to tell the parents how much teaching experience you have. If you are a new teacher, don't tell them you're brand new—tell them how excited you are to teach their child. You can also tell them where you went to school, the number of children you have, your hobbies, or any appropriate information that you would like to offer. The letter in Figure 10.1 does not have personal information because some teachers do not feel comfortable talking about their personal lives, and that is perfectly fine. Decide what your position is and augment the letter as necessary.

The purpose of sending a letter of introduction at the start of the new year is to present yourself as a teacher who is interested in promoting positive relationships with the families of your students. It is also to offer information to parents about your expectations for the year and to provide contact information should they need to get in touch with you.

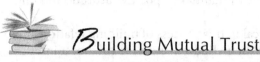

Building Mutual Trust

Building mutual trust with parents from the beginning of the school year helps to provide a foundation for learning throughout the year. Whether you send a letter to parents or arrange to meet them in person, it is important to make contact early and to follow up with them throughout the year.

Some teachers prefer to meet with parents early in the year to learn what parents think about their child's needs and goals for the year. If you schedule a conference in September, it is a good idea to provide a questionnaire for parents to complete so that they have the opportunity to discuss their child's personal, social, emotional, and physical needs, as well as any academic issues, strengths, or challenges that they see. See Model 32: Questionnaire for Parents.

If a parent does not speak English, a questionnaire will be intimidating and may make a family member feel uncomfortable. If an interpreter is available, use that person to gain information about the student and about how the parent would like you to help his or her child. Also, recognize that cultural differences may prevent you from gaining the information you would like to get from the parent; if that is the case, use the conference to gain the parent's trust and to help the family feel comfortable in the school.

Keep in mind that parents are experts on their children and possess a great deal of information that teachers do not have. This information is key in building an educational program that works for all students. It is important to ask parents about their children and then listen carefully to the parents. If, for example, a parent shares with you that her child has no friends, you may encourage some group work that will include the child with other children who may be friendly to her. The information you receive from parents may help in other ways as well. If a parent tells you that a child is spending much more time on homework than you think it requires, that offers information about the child's level of understanding in that particular subject. Find whatever information will help you to help your students.

Focus on the positive rather than the negative aspects of a child's learning. Asking questions focusing on what a child can do and how he or she learns will accent the strengths and abilities of the child rather than any weaknesses.

Even though parents know their children better than teachers do, some parents are not able to voice their concerns or suggestions in a positive way. This often makes it difficult for the teacher who does not want to support a negative discussion about the child; the teacher must maintain a positive attitude and find the pearl in the oyster.

Respect for family members is critical in this process of building relationships. Teachers must believe that parents love their children and have their best interests at heart; unfortunately, time, illness, family issues, or lack of education may be a stumbling block for parents. Discussions between parents and teachers are confidential and conversations about students are not to be shared in the faculty lounge. It is unprofessional to talk about children or their families in front of other teachers, paraprofessionals, substitute teachers, custodial staff, or office staff who may not even know the child.

Parents can become involved in their child's education in many positive ways. While some parents may read to their children every day and help with homework assignments and projects, others may be feeling the pressures of work and home lives and may need to rely on a weekly or monthly newsletter that the teacher sends home to keep informed about the classroom happenings. Whatever the situation, it is important not to become judgmental because you probably don't know what personal issues at home might be affecting parents' ability to be involved.

One way to provide information to the family is through a weekly newsletter. Preparing a newsletter may seem overwhelming at first, but it is actually quite simple once you have a format. It may be a one-page newsletter that includes what's going on in your classroom, assignments that are upcoming, items you need in your classroom, events, and information about the class. It is best to mention each student's name in the newsletter at least once a month. It may be, "Jared presented his report on Civil Rights and it was great" or "Jessica won the two-legged race during recess" or "Michele and Matt did an amazing job in reading this week." Parents like to see their child's name in print and students like to be recognized. A newsletter is a way for parents to feel connected to you and to the class. It is empowering for a parent of a student who does not volunteer any information about his or her day to be able to say, "Congratulations on your reading this week" or "Tell me about that two-legged race you had at recess." It can also bring the child into a conversation with a parent that may not have occurred without the newsletter. Here are some tips for creating an interesting newsletter.

- Highlight the students in your class. Mention as many as you can in each newsletter.

- Announce classroom, school, and community events of interest.

- Create invitations to class gatherings, parties, or other events.

- Collect newspaper or journal articles that you think may be helpful and reprint them in the newsletter.

- Write thank-you notes to families who have helped the class in some way.

- Write suggestions for ways that parents can help students at home.

- Feature children's writing or artwork in the newsletter.

- Write about classroom pets, trips, and celebrations.

- Explain state or national standards or standardized testing or a topic you think may be of interest to parents.
- Write a wish list of items that parents can collect or save for class projects.

Figure 10.2 shows a sample of a simple newsletter created on Microsoft Word.

Staying Connected

Stay connected to families in a variety of ways. Some school districts have programs in family involvement where teachers are required to send home a weekly folder of work and parents are required to sign the communication form and make comments. The folder contains graded work, notices, information about upcoming assignments, list of tests scheduled for the next week, and a two-way communication form for teachers and parents. This weekly communication fosters healthy home–school connections and keeps the parents informed. Other schools give teachers time to make phone calls called "happy calls" to report on successes and positive progress. Using email as well as school websites can greatly enhance parent communication. These ideas highlight the importance of staying connected to parents.

Phone calls help teachers maintain good home–school communication. Although we may frequently reach voice mail, it's important to try and talk to parents. Here are some important telephone tips.

- Make a habit of calling at least one parent per week to relay good news. Keep a record of those calls and make sure each family receives at least two "happy calls" during the school year.
- Before you call home, make sure that you know the parent's name. Often, parents and children have different last names.
- Keep a log of all of the phone calls you make, whether they are good-news calls or bad-news calls. Record the date, reason for the call, parent's response, and outcome.

A more traditional way of staying connected is through the use of progress reports. These notices, usually sent in the middle of a marking period, may let parents know how their child is doing in each class or that their child is in danger of failing a particular class. Progress reports are opportunities to communicate with parents and to make parents aware of their child's progress. They let students who are struggling know where they need to improve and students who are excelling or

Figure 10.2

Sample Newsletter

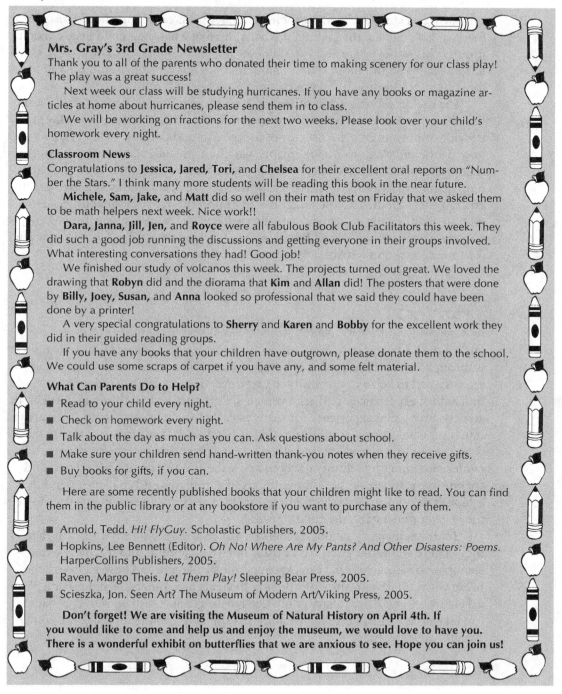

Mrs. Gray's 3rd Grade Newsletter

Thank you to all of the parents who donated their time to making scenery for our class play! The play was a great success!

Next week our class will be studying hurricanes. If you have any books or magazine articles at home about hurricanes, please send them in to class.

We will be working on fractions for the next two weeks. Please look over your child's homework every night.

Classroom News

Congratulations to **Jessica, Jared, Tori,** and **Chelsea** for their excellent oral reports on "Number the Stars." I think many more students will be reading this book in the near future.

Michele, Sam, Jake, and **Matt** did so well on their math test on Friday that we asked them to be math helpers next week. Nice work!!

Dara, Janna, Jill, Jen, and **Royce** were all fabulous Book Club Facilitators this week. They did such a good job running the discussions and getting everyone in their groups involved. What interesting conversations they had! Good job!

We finished our study of volcanos this week. The projects turned out great. We loved the drawing that **Robyn** did and the diorama that **Kim** and **Allan** did! The posters that were done by **Billy, Joey, Susan,** and **Anna** looked so professional that we said they could have been done by a printer!

A very special congratulations to **Sherry** and **Karen** and **Bobby** for the excellent work they did in their guided reading groups.

If you have any books that your children have outgrown, please donate them to the school. We could use some scraps of carpet if you have any, and some felt material.

What Can Parents Do to Help?

- Read to your child every night.
- Check on homework every night.
- Talk about the day as much as you can. Ask questions about school.
- Make sure your children send hand-written thank-you notes when they receive gifts.
- Buy books for gifts, if you can.

Here are some recently published books that your children might like to read. You can find them in the public library or at any bookstore if you want to purchase any of them.

- Arnold, Tedd. *Hi! FlyGuy*. Scholastic Publishers, 2005.
- Hopkins, Lee Bennett (Editor). *Oh No! Where Are My Pants? And Other Disasters: Poems.* HarperCollins Publishers, 2005.
- Raven, Margo Theis. *Let Them Play!* Sleeping Bear Press, 2005.
- Scieszka, Jon. Seen Art? The Museum of Modern Art/Viking Press, 2005.

Don't forget! We are visiting the Museum of Natural History on April 4th. If you would like to come and help us and enjoy the museum, we would love to have you. There is a wonderful exhibit on butterflies that we are anxious to see. Hope you can join us!

improving be congratulated for their success. A progress report should relay information that will help the parents, advising them of what their child needs to do to improve his or her grade and work. Follow up with a phone call home or an email to show support and interest in the student. Progress reports should present a way for students to improve, and not be simply a reporting tool.

The use of websites are another way to stay connected to your students' families. Many teachers now have their own websites, which are updated weekly and provide important information for both students and parents. Many teachers post homework and classroom assignments, which helps students who are absent from school complete missed work and helps parents know what their child should be doing. Some teachers post schedules for tests, reports, and classroom events. Others post extra-credit activities and links to important websites for additional information. Posting this information on a website provides an easy way for parents to stay connected with their child's classroom. Find out what your school's policy is for Internet use and websites.

 ## Parent-Teacher Conferences

One of the best ways to foster positive relationships between home and school is through informative, positive parent-teacher conferences. These conferences are designed to be an opportunity to exchange ideas about the student's activities, habits, experiences, and achievements. Recognizing that this is sometimes an anxiety-provoking experience for many parents may help teachers to structure it to be as friendly and nonintimidating as possible. Parents may not realize that this experience is as anxiety ridden for some new teachers as it is for parents. The conference is an opportunity to get to know the child's parents in a relaxed and friendly atmosphere, to hear about the child's strengths and challenges, and to establish mutual goals. It should be a time to share information in an effort to help the teacher understand the child's needs.

Many elementary school teachers try to create a specific environment that they believe will foster good relationships between parents and teachers. For example, some teachers have background music playing and have a table in the room with simple refreshments. Be sure to create a comfortable and private physical environment. Always have adult-sized seating, paper and pens so that parents can take notes, and an area large enough to spread the student's work out so that parents can examine it.

Many teachers like to give something to the parents such as an article on reading improvement or a list of suggested books to read at home. They decorate the hallway outside their classrooms with pictures of the students and/or work the students have completed. This is a great time to showcase students' portfolios so that parents can get a clear idea of the work their child is doing in the classroom. The conference then becomes a celebration of accomplishments. Specific areas you may wish to discuss with your child's parents relating to school performance include the following:

- classroom activities
- assessment
- social relationships
- classroom behavior
- homework assignments
- work habits
- attitudes about school
- strengths and challenges
- samples of work
- books and class materials

Provide parents with information about your curriculum and classroom procedures. Include a list of broad academic goals for the year and a copy of your classroom rules and procedures. Prepare a folder with samples of student work and current grades. Talk about and show examples of student work.

The topics you choose to discuss are the heart of the conference, but there are other areas to consider when preparing for a parent-teacher conference. The positive impression you make on parents can help you develop and nurture the partnership. Here are some tips to consider.

- Welcome parents at the door and thank them for coming.
- Always dress professionally.
- Start every conference on time.
- Prepare positive comments about the child so that it is clear that you enjoy having the child in your class.
- Listen to what the parents are saying about the child.

- Be clear that you believe in cooperation and success for their child.
- Talk about the child's strengths first.
- Discuss the student's progress in each subject area and show samples of the child's work to support your statements.
- Ask parents to share their thoughts and suggestions about the student.
- Prepare a few goals for the student, create a plan for meeting those goals, and provide any materials parents might need to implement the plan.
- Make sure parents know how to reach you if problems arise.
- Discuss the highlights of the conference and always end on a positive note.
- Walk the parents to the door and thank them for coming.
- Be sure that parents leave with ideas and a plan for the child.
- Take a few minutes to make personal notes about the conference. If you agreed to follow up on a particular issue, note it on your calendar.

Teachers find it frustrating to prepare for parent-teacher conferences and have very poor attendance by parents. Send home personal letters to notify parents of conference dates and available times. Some teachers ask parents to sign up for a conference by a certain date. Some teachers call parents who do not respond and encourage them to attend. Calling parents and telling them that you were just checking the schedule and noticed that they were not on it, can help to make it easier for parents to put the conference on their calendar. Recognize that even with your best efforts, some parents will not attend. Some will have work or family obligations that prevent them from coming and others will just not respond. Sometimes offering a student-led conference will ensure greater participation by parents.

Student-Led Conferences

Student-led conferences have become very popular in recent years. Student-led conferences help students take responsibility for their own learning, reflect on what they have learned, and set goals for themselves. One benefit of student-led conferences is that teachers discuss with students their work, their strengths and challenges, and their goals for the future.

Student-led conferences are run in many different ways. The format and content of student-led conferences may vary from school to school, but in each case the student takes charge of the conference. The teacher acts as a discussion facilitator who responds when needed. This process creates an environment in which the student becomes an equal partner in the interaction with the parents and teacher.

The student-led conference is usually made up of three phases: the preparation, the conference, and the evaluation (Little & Allan, 1989). The most important phase is the preparation, which determines the strength of the process. At the beginning of the school year, students should set up a binder to contain a portfolio that includes graded work. Students must keep their binders neat and orderly because they use them to lead their conferences. In the invitation for the student-led conference sent home, the parents should be made aware of the fact that their child will be responsible for leading the conference. About three days before conferences, students should prepare portfolios of their work to date, including a special project, a quiz, a homework assignment, and one assignment from which they felt they had learned the most. Students may also write a reflection on their grades and study habits. They set goals for the next term and organize their graded-work section. The day before the conference, the teacher role-plays with the students, pretending to be the student with the student playing the teacher or the parent. This gives students the opportunity to explain, for example, a poor grade or an activity in class that may be in question. Offer students a checklist of what they might want to cover in the conference.

Student-led conferences have both advantages and disadvantages. Student-led conferences help students accept responsibility for their own learning. It puts them in a position of authority, able to tell their side of the story. Students are accountable for their performance. They are in control of their goals and their work and it becomes their responsibility to produce a positive conference. Teachers can get a better picture of each student by reviewing with each student his or her strengths and weaknesses than they would from conventional assessments. Parent attendance seems higher for student-led conferences than for teacher-led ones. Despite our best efforts, however, some parents will be unable to attend conferences and that can create tremendous disappointment. If that happens, the student can still hold the conference for the parent at home because that student has made all of the preparations for the conference. Ask for an evaluation from the parents if that occurs. Immediately following conferences or shortly thereafter, students, parents, and teachers should offer their feedback on the effectiveness of the student-led conference because it will provide information needed to create the best possible student-led conference.

Schools using this model report that attendance at student-led conferences has increased and that 90 percent of the parents and students prefer this type of conference (Hackmann, 1996). Although this model remains popular, some parents may prefer to speak to you alone. Respect their wishes and reserve ten minutes at the end of the conference for a private meeting with parents. Sometimes parents would like to offer information about the student that may be personal or uncomfortable when the student is not present.

It is not easy to stay connected to the parents of your students. You should communicate regularly and clearly with parents about information important to student success. You should share information using student handbooks, teacher-parent-student conferences, the Internet, email, phone calls, newsletters, and whatever other means you have at your disposal. But sometimes it just doesn't work and you can't get parental involvement. In those cases, you may be able to get help from your school.

Schools can form partnerships with community- and faith-based organizations to help people from diverse cultural backgrounds who often do not feel comfortable in schools to hold meetings outside of the school environment. Schools can create an environment that welcomes participation. Signs that warmly greet families as they enter the school; resources available in the school that are linked to social services; a family lounge, where parents can come, have a cup of coffee, and talk to each other informally all contribute to a sense of collaboration in the school environment.

Schools can also offer services for parents that will help them develop their own knowledge and skills. They can offer basic adult education, English classes, job training, and parenting education courses to help make parents feel more comfortable in the school and to also make the home–school collaboration more meaningful. Parents would have greater contact with the school and would also become a stakeholder in the system.

Some schools support families and students by forming partnerships with community organizations that offer services to the families. There may be partnerships with youth organizations, local businesses, public health organizations, or community groups that provide information and help to parents and students. These partnerships can create goodwill and offer helpful services previously unavailable to families.

Regardless of how the communications occur, one of the most important advantages of a closer relationship with families is the higher achievement levels of students when their families are involved in the school environment. It must begin in your classroom, with a commitment to building trust, promoting a positive relationship, and establishing regular and meaningful communication between home and school.

Standards for Home–School Connections

In 1997, the National Parent Teacher Association (PTA) defined practices designed to improve home–school connections. Those practices include the following:

- Communicating: Regular communication between home and school is key.
- Parenting: Parenting skills are supported through classes or assistance.
- Student learning: Parents assist in student learning.
- Volunteering: Parents are encouraged to volunteer in the classroom and in the school.
- Decision making and advocacy: Parents are partners in decision making for their children.
- Collaborating with the community: Community resources are used to strengthen the home–school connection. (Cotton & Wikeland, 1989)

What is most important in the home–school connection is the mutual trust and bond that can develop between teachers and parents. Both groups have students' best interests in mind, yet it is sometimes a challenge to make the communication a reality. Teachers must try to find the best way to accomplish this task. If you maintain a positive attitude, provide updated information to parents, and encourage parental participation with their children, you send a strong message to your community that you care about your students, their families, and doing what is best for their children.

Advice from the Field

- Think of creative ways to communicate with the parents of your students. Use phone calls, emails, websites, invitations, letters, newsletters, and any other form of communication that may work in your situation.
- Send home positive messages as often as you can; do not contact parents only when you have bad news.
- Encourage parents to volunteer both in your classroom and outside of the classroom, collecting materials, creating materials, getting donations, and so on.

- Have students keep portfolios of their graded work, so that if parents would like to see their child's work, they have easy access to it.

- Involve families in the evaluation of your home–school program to see if they have other suggestions for ways of including more parents in this process.

- Be aware of the cultural, ethnic, and linguistic needs of the families of your students and provide access and information that will help them know what is going on in the classroom.

- Reach out to the community for resources to strengthen your program.

- Try to accommodate parents' work schedules when you schedule programs and meetings.

- Avoid speaking to parents using educational jargon; many of them have limited experience in the educational world.

- Invite parents, often a great hidden resource, into your classroom to present talks or skills they may have that fit into your curriculum.

Communicating with Parents Who Are Non-English Speakers

Communicate with all parents, including those who are non-English speakers. Many parents immigrate to the United States to give their children opportunities that they might not have in their native countries. They want their children to succeed, and school is seen as a vehicle to make that happen. While the parents may not have the language skills to be able to help their children with their schoolwork, they can still be powerful partners in their children's education. Having an understanding of the teacher's academic expectations, assignments, and homework routines would give these parents the opportunity to support their children. Knowing in advance that their child will have nightly homework assignments, for example, would alert them to the need for them to establish and monitor homework routines in their home.

Don't assume that parents are the only support system your students have. Parents may also have other resources, such as tutors and translators within their community to help children with their studies. Therefore, unless parents are informed of their child's academic needs, they have no way of knowing what they can do to help their child. For that reason, the letters, invitations, and progress reports that you send to parents should be translated for the non-English speakers, if possible. At the least, parents should be given copies of reading lists of books their children will be reading throughout the year. Many books, particularly trade books, are available in translation. Giving parents this list at the beginning of the year would give them the time needed to locate the books in their native language. This will help all students, but especially middle and high school students whose classes are content oriented. Reading assigned books in their native language would allow ELLs to continue learning content and feel comfortable as they are reading their own language. If you want support from parents, you have to let them know how they can support you and that their support is needed and welcomed. The first step in creating a partnership is opening lines of communication.

Additional Resources

National Clearinghouse for Bilingual Education. (1996). *Success in educating all students: What do some schools do differently?* Washington, DC: NCELA Pathway.

Reaching out to others: Overcoming barriers to parent/family involvement. (1992). Parent Teacher Association (online). www.ncela.gwu/pathways/success

Simic, M. (1991). *Parent involvement in elementary language arts: A program model.* ERIC Digest. Bloomington, IN: ERIC Clearinghouse on Reading and Communication Skills (Online). www.ncela.gwu.edu

Snow, C. E., Burns, M. S., & Griffin, P. (Eds.). (1998). *Preventing reading differences in young children.* Washington, DC: National Academy Press.

References

Cotton, K., & Wikelund, K. (1989). *Parent involvement in education.* School Improvement Research Series. Portland, OR: Northwest Regional Educational Laboratory.

Hackmann, D. G. (1996). Student-led conferences at the middle level: Promoting student responsibility. *NASSP Bulletin, 80*(578), 31–36.

Little, A. W., & Allan, J. (1989). Student-led parent-teacher conferences. *Elementary School Guidance and Counseling, 23*(3), 210–218.

Questionnaire for Parents

- What do you see as your child's greatest strength?

- What do you see as your child's greatest challenge?

- How was your child's experience in school last year?

- Are there any subjects in particular in which you feel your child needs greater attention?

- Does your child consistently do his or her homework?

- Does your child read for pleasure?

  If so, what types of books does he or she like to read?

  If not, how can we encourage him or her to read at home?

- Does your child have any physical limitations that I should be aware of? If so, please describe them.

- Does the child have any social or emotional issues that I should be aware of? If so, please describe them.

- What do you think motivates your child?

- What are your child's favorite free-time activities?

- How do you think your child learns best?

- What are your goals for your child for this school year? How do you think I can help?

- At what time of day would it be best to contact you? At what phone number?

- May I contact you by email? At what email address?

Index

Creating America

A History of the United States

Beginnings
through
Reconstruction

McDougal Littell

Evanston, Illinois • Boston • Dallas

Contents

Chapter 9 Launching a New Republic, 1789–1800

Chapter 10 The Jefferson Era, 1800–1816

Chapter 11 National and Regional Growth, 1800–1844

Chapter 12 The Age of Jackson, 1824–1840

Chapter 13 Manifest Destiny, 1810–1853

Chapter 14 A New Spirit of Change, 1820–1860

How to Use This Reading Study Guide

The purpose of this *Reading Study Guide* is to help you read and understand your history textbook, *Creating America: Beginnings through Reconstruction*. You can use this *Reading Study Guide* in two ways.

1. Use the Reading Study Guide side-by-side with your history book.

- Turn to the section that you are going to read in the textbook. Then, next to the book, put the pages from the *Reading Study Guide* that accompany that section. All of the heads in the *Reading Study Guide* match the heads in the textbook.
- Use the *Reading Study Guide* to help you read and organize the information in the textbook.

2. Use the Reading Study Guide to study for tests on the textbook.

- Reread the summary of every chapter.
- Review the definitions of the Terms & Names in the *Reading Study Guide*.
- Review the diagram of information that you filled out as you read the summaries.
- Review your answers to questions.

Strategy: Read the Terms & Names and the definition of each. The Terms & Names are in dark type in the section.
Try This: What are the definitions of "culture" and "civilization"?

Name _____

Chapter **1** Section 1 (pages 27–3_)

Societies of North America

BEFORE YOU READ

In this section, you will read about ancient peoples that came to the Americas and developed diverse cultures.

AS YOU READ

Use this chart to list the ancient cultures of North America and their locations.

Ancient North American Cultures	Locations

TERMS & NAMES

culture A way of life that is shared by a group of people

domestication Breeding plants or taming animals to meet human needs

civilization A complex culture that has cities, specialized jobs, organized government and religion, a system of record keeping, and advanced tools

Mound Builders Early Native Americans who built large mounds

technology The use of tools and knowledge to meet human needs

slash-and-burn agriculture Farming method in which farmers chop down and then burn trees on a plot of land

Iroquois League Alliance of five northern Iroquois nations

The First People in America; The Emergence of Civilizations (pages 27–28)

What are five features of civilization?

Scientists think that people first came to the Americas from Asia. There are two *theories* about how and when this happened. One theory is that they came 12,000 years ago during the last Ice Age. The cold created glaciers. These glaciers caused the water level drop. A land bridge appeared, and people crossed it into North America.

Another theory is that people came to the Americas as long as 30,000 years ago. According to this theory, people came at different times over thousands of years. They came by many routes, even by boat.

A **culture** is a way of life shared by a group of people. It includes arts, beliefs, and customs. The first Americans lived in hunting and gathering cultures. About 5,000 years ago, people began **domestication**, the breeding of plants and taming of animals to meet human needs. Agriculture spread

across the Americas. It created a stable food supply. People no longer had to travel to find food. They built villages.

These changes allowed cultures to become civilizations. A **civilization** is a complex culture that has five features: 1) cities, 2) specialized jobs, 3) organized government and religion, 4) a system of record keeping, and 5) advanced tools.

About 1200 B.C., a great civilization arose in Mesoamerica. This region stretches from central Mexico to present-day Nicaragua. A people called the Olmec lived there. They built large cities. Their culture spread along trade routes.

By A.D. 250, the Maya had a great civilization. They had cities in southern Mexico and Guatemala. They built pyramid mounds topped by temples. By 900, they had abandoned many of their cities.

1. Name the five features of civilization.

_____

_____

THE WORLD IN 1500 **5**

Strategy: Fill in the diagram as you read. The diagram will help you organize information in the section.
Try This: What is the purpose of this diagram?

Strategy: Read the summary. It contains the main ideas and the key information under the head.
Try This: What do you think this section will be about?

Societies of North America *continued*

Early Native American Civilizations
Peoples of the North and West
(pages 28–29)

How *did early American civilizations differ?*
The Hohokam lived in what is now Arizona. They lived from about 300 B.C. to A.D. 1400. They dug canals to *irrigate* crops. They also traded with other groups. Beginning about A.D. 100, the Anasazi lived in what is now the American Southwest. They were farmers and traders. Around A.D. 1300, *drought* or warfare caused them to leave.

The **Mound Builders** lived in the eastern part of what is now the United States. They built large earthen mounds for burial or as temples. Mound Builder cultures included the Mississippians, who lived from A.D. 800 to 1700. They built some of the first cities in North America.

By 1500, North America was home to many diverse cultural groups. *Environment* shaped each group's economy and technology. **Technology** is the use of tools and knowledge to meet human needs. Groups near the coast made tools from shells. Groups in the deserts used irrigation.

The Aleut lived on islands off Alaska. The Inuit lived near the coast of Alaska. Because their climate was too cold for farming, the Aleut and Inuit were hunters. Farther south were the Northwest Coast people. These included the Haida and Kwakiutl. These groups hunted and fished. They lived near forests. They used wood to build houses and boats.

The peoples of the West lived mainly by hunting and gathering. The Pueblo, the Navajo, and the Apache lived in what is now the American Southwest. The Pueblo used irrigation to farm in the desert. The Navajo and Apache were *nomadic* hunter-gatherers.

2. What did people in the North and West do for food?

_____

_____

Peoples of Mexico; Peoples of the Great Plains and East (page 30–31)

How *did the Aztecs build a strong empire?*
The Aztecs created a great civilization in what is now central Mexico. Using irrigation, they could grow plenty of food. They were warlike, and conquered most of their neighbors.

The Aztecs had a complex society. Rulers were the highest class. Priests and government workers ranked next. Slaves and servants were at the bottom.

The Great Plains of North America stretch from the Mississippi River to the Rocky Mountains. Some Native Americans who lived here were nomads. Others lived in villages by rivers, where they could farm. Many Plains tribes relied on buffalo for food, clothing, and tools.

The Southeast stretches from east Texas to the Atlantic Ocean. It has plenty of rain and a long growing season. As a result, southeastern groups became farmers.

The Northeast was called the Eastern Woodlands. The Iroquois adapted the forest for farming by using **slash-and-burn agriculture.** Farmers chopped down trees, then burned the trees on a plot of land. The ashes from the fire enriched the soil.

In the late 1500s, five northern Iroquois nations decided to stop fighting and raiding each other. They formed an alliance called the **Iroquois League.** The League brought peace to the Iroquois.

3. What helped the Aztecs build an empire?

_____

_____

How to Use This
Reading Study Guide

At the end of every chapter in the *Reading Study Guide,* you will find a Glossary and a section called After You Read. The Glossary gives definitions of all the words in italic type in the chapter summaries. After You Read is a two-page chapter review. Use After You Read to identify those parts of the chapter that you need to study more for the test on the chapter.

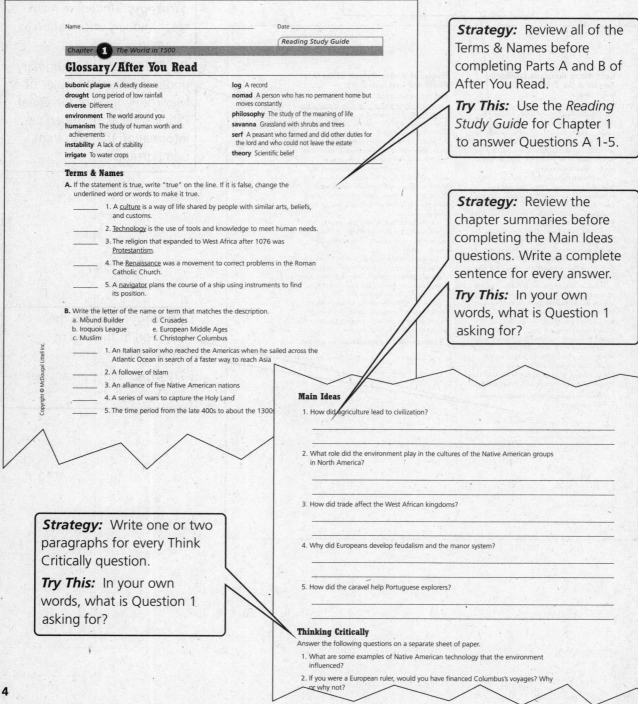

Name _____ Date _____

Reading Study Guide

Chapter 1 The World in 1500

Glossary/After You Read

bubonic plague A deadly disease
drought Long period of low rainfall
diverse Different
environment The world around you
humanism The study of human worth and achievements
instability A lack of stability
irrigate To water crops

log A record
nomad A person who has no permanent home but moves constantly
philosophy The study of the meaning of life
savanna Grassland with shrubs and trees
serf A peasant who farmed and did other duties for the lord and who could not leave the estate
theory Scientific belief

Terms & Names

A. If the statement is true, write "true" on the line. If it is false, change the underlined word or words to make it true.

_____ 1. A <u>culture</u> is a way of life shared by people with similar arts, beliefs, and customs.

_____ 2. <u>Technology</u> is the use of tools and knowledge to meet human needs.

_____ 3. The religion that expanded to West Africa after 1076 was <u>Protestantism</u>.

_____ 4. The <u>Renaissance</u> was a movement to correct problems in the Roman Catholic Church.

_____ 5. A <u>navigator</u> plans the course of a ship using instruments to find its position.

B. Write the letter of the name or term that matches the description.
a. Mound Builder   d. Crusades
b. Iroquois League   e. European Middle Ages
c. Muslim   f. Christopher Columbus

_____ 1. An Italian sailor who reached the Americas when he sailed across the Atlantic Ocean in search of a faster way to reach Asia

_____ 2. A follower of Islam

_____ 3. An alliance of five Native American nations

_____ 4. A series of wars to capture the Holy Land

_____ 5. The time period from the late 400s to about the 1300s

Main Ideas

1. How did agriculture lead to civilization?
_____
_____

2. What role did the environment play in the cultures of the Native American groups in North America?
_____
_____

3. How did trade affect the West African kingdoms?
_____
_____

4. Why did Europeans develop feudalism and the manor system?
_____
_____

5. How did the caravel help Portuguese explorers?
_____
_____

Thinking Critically
Answer the following questions on a separate sheet of paper.

1. What are some examples of Native American technology that the environment influenced?

2. If you were a European ruler, would you have financed Columbus's voyages? Why or why not?

Strategy: Review all of the Terms & Names before completing Parts A and B of After You Read.

Try This: Use the *Reading Study Guide* for Chapter 1 to answer Questions A 1-5.

Strategy: Review the chapter summaries before completing the Main Ideas questions. Write a complete sentence for every answer.

Try This: In your own words, what is Question 1 asking for?

Strategy: Write one or two paragraphs for every Think Critically question.

Try This: In your own words, what is Question 1 asking for?

Chapter **1** Section 1 (pages 27–31)

Societies of North America

BEFORE YOU READ

In this section, you will read about ancient peoples that came to the Americas and developed diverse cultures.

AS YOU READ

Use this chart to list the ancient cultures of North America and their locations.

Ancient North American Cultures	Locations

TERMS & NAMES

culture A way of life that is shared by a group of people

domestication Breeding plants or taming animals to meet human needs

civilization A complex culture that has cities, specialized jobs, organized government and religion, a system of record keeping, and advanced tools

Mound Builders Early Native Americans who built large mounds

technology The use of tools and knowledge to meet human needs

slash-and-burn agriculture Farming method in which farmers chop down and then burn trees on a plot of land

Iroquois League Alliance of five northern Iroquois nations

The First People in America; The Emergence of Civilizations (pages 27–28)

What are five features of civilization?
Scientists think that people first came to the Americas from Asia. There are two *theories* about how and when this happened. One theory is that they came 12,000 years ago during the last Ice Age. The cold created glaciers. These glaciers caused the water level drop. A land bridge appeared, and people crossed it into North America.

Another theory is that people came to the Americas as long as 30,000 years ago. According to this theory, people came at different times over thousands of years. They came by many routes, even by boat.

A **culture** is a way of life shared by a group of people. It includes arts, beliefs, and customs. The first Americans lived in hunting and gathering cultures. About 5,000 years ago, people began **domestication**, the breeding of plants and taming of animals to meet human needs. Agriculture spread

across the Americas. It created a stable food supply. People no longer had to travel to find food. They built villages.

These changes allowed cultures to become civilizations. A **civilization** is a complex culture that has five features: 1) cities, 2) specialized jobs, 3) organized government and religion, 4) a system of record keeping, and 5) advanced tools.

About 1200 B.C., a great civilization arose in Mesoamerica. This region stretches from central Mexico to present-day Nicaragua. A people called the Olmec lived there. They built large cities. Their culture spread along trade routes.

By A.D. 250, the Maya had a great civilization. They had cities in southern Mexico and Guatemala. They built pyramid mounds topped by temples. By 900, they had abandoned many of their cities.

1. Name the five features of civilization.

_____

_____

_____

Early Native American Civilizations; Peoples of the North and West
(pages 28–29)

***How** did early American civilizations differ?*
The Hohokam lived in what is now Arizona. They lived from about 300 B.C. to A.D. 1400. They dug canals to *irrigate* crops. They also traded with other groups. Beginning about A.D. 100, the Anasazi lived in what is now the American Southwest. They were farmers and traders. Around A.D. 1300, *drought* or warfare caused them to leave.

The **Mound Builders** lived in the eastern part of what is now the United States. They built large earthen mounds for burial or as temples. Mound Builder cultures included the Mississippians, who lived from A.D. 800 to 1700. They built some of the first cities in North America.

By 1500, North America was home to many diverse cultural groups. *Environment* shaped each group's economy and technology. **Technology** is the use of tools and knowledge to meet human needs. Groups near the coast made tools from shells. Groups in the deserts used irrigation.

The Aleut lived on islands off Alaska. The Inuit lived near the coast of Alaska. Because their climate was too cold for farming, the Aleut and Inuit were hunters. Farther south were the Northwest Coast people. These included the Haida and Kwakiutl. These groups hunted and fished. They lived near forests. They used wood to build houses and boats.

The peoples of the West lived mainly by hunting and gathering. The Pueblo, the Navajo, and the Apache lived in what is now the American Southwest. The Pueblo used irrigation to farm in the desert. The Navajo and Apache were *nomadic* hunter-gatherers.

2. What did people in the North and West do for food?

_____

_____

_____

Peoples of Mexico; Peoples of the Great Plains and East (page 30–31)

***How** did the Aztecs build a strong empire?*
The Aztecs created a great civilization in what is now central Mexico. Using irrigation, they could grow plenty of food. They were warlike, and conquered most of their neighbors.

The Aztecs had a complex society. Rulers were the highest class. Priests and government workers ranked next. Slaves and servants were at the bottom.

The Great Plains of North America stretch from the Mississippi River to the Rocky Mountains. Some Native Americans who lived here were nomads. Others lived in villages by rivers, where they could farm. Many Plains tribes relied on buffalo for food, clothing, and tools.

The Southeast stretches from east Texas to the Atlantic Ocean. It has plenty of rain and a long growing season. As a result, southeastern groups became farmers.

The Northeast was called the Eastern Woodlands. The Iroquois adapted the forest for farming by using **slash-and-burn agriculture.** Farmers chopped down trees, then burned the trees on a plot of land. The ashes from the fire enriched the soil.

In the late 1500s, five northern Iroquois nations decided to stop fighting and raiding each other. They formed an alliance called the **Iroquois League.** The League brought peace to the Iroquois.

3. What helped the Aztecs build an empire?

_____

_____

Societies of West Africa and Europe

BEFORE YOU READ

In the last section, you read about the Native American societies of North America.

In this section, you will learn how changes in West Africa and Europe increased interest in learning and exploration.

AS YOU READ

Use this chart to list how the changes that occurred in West African and European societies before 1500.

Changes in West Africa	Changes in Europe

TERMS & NAMES

Muslim A follower of Islam

Islam Religion founded by Muhammad that teaches that there is one god, Allah

European Middle Ages The period from the late 400s to about the 1300

feudalism A political system in which a king lets nobles use lands in return for military service

Crusades A series of wars between Christians and Muslims over control of the Holy Land

Renaissance A period in Europe of increased interest in art and learning

Reformation A movement to correct problems in the Roman Catholic Church

Africa in 1500 (page 33)

What role did Africans play in world trade?
Africa has many land forms and climates. There are rain forests and broad *savannas*. Beyond the savannas are great deserts.

By A.D. 1500, Africa had been trading with the rest of the world for centuries. Ships carried goods across the Mediterranean Sea, Red Sea, and Indian Ocean.

West Africa is bordered by the Sahara on the north. By A.D. 500, merchants regularly led caravans across the desert. Trade helped West African kingdoms become wealthy.

1. How did trade affect West African kingdoms?

_____

_____

Ghana and Islam; Mali and Songhai
(page 34–35)

Why did Ghana prosper?
Ghana was the first West African kingdom to get rich from trade. From the 700s to the mid 1000s, it became a center for salt and gold traders. Ghana's king made traders pay taxes on all gold and salt that passed through his kingdom.

Many traders who came to Ghana from North Africa were Muslims. **Muslims** are followers of Islam. The religion of **Islam** was founded by Muhammad in the 600s.

The Muslim empires of North Africa wanted to convert the people of Ghana to Islam. They also wanted to control the gold trade. In 1076, Muslim armies invaded Ghana, and the empire weakened.

By the 1200s, the kingdom of Mali took over Ghana's territory. By 1312, Mali was one of the largest empires in the world. At this time, Mali's ruler was Mansa Musa. He was a Muslim. He spread Islam throughout the empire. Mali weakened after his death.

The Songhai people lived near the Niger River. As Mali weakened, they broke away. In 1464, Sunni Ali became Mali's ruler. Sunni Ali died in 1492. Askia Muhammad rose to power. He was a devout Muslim. He expanded trade and made the government run smoothly. After his death, the empire collapsed.

Small city-states arose in other parts of West Africa. The Hausa states rose after A.D. 1000 in what is now Nigeria. The kingdom of Benin arose in the Niger River's delta region. In the late 1400s, Europeans reached Benin. The Portuguese set up a trade center near Benin's capital.

2. What caused Ghana to grow wealthy?

_____

_____

Europe Undergoes Great Changes; The Renaissance and Reformation
(pages 35–37)

What was the Renaissance?
The **European Middle Ages** lasted from the late 400s to about the 1300s. It was a time of *instability* and warfare. Europeans developed feudalism.
Feudalism is a political system in which a king lets nobles, or lords, use land in return for military service. Europeans also developed the manor system. Lords divided their land into manors, or large estates. *Serfs* farmed the manors. In return, the lords promised to protect the serfs. By the 1000s, feudalism had brought stability to Europe. Trade increased. Towns grew.

The Roman Catholic Church gained power during this time. It became a strong unifying force in Europe. In 1096, European Christians launched the **Crusades.** These were a series of wars to take the Holy Land from the Muslims. The Holy Land is the region where the Bible's events took place. The Christians did not succeed, but the Crusades changed Europe. Europeans encountered many Asian goods. After the wars, they continued to want these items.

Feudalism grew weaker as serfs left the manors to live in towns. In 1347, a deadly disease known as *bubonic plague* also weakened feudalism. There were

fewer workers, so lords had to compete for laborers. As feudal lords lost power, kings grew stronger, which began the rise of nations.

The **Renaissance** was a time of increased interest in art and learning. It began in Italy and spread through Europe. It lasted from the 1300s to 1600.

Several forces led to the Renaissance. Feudalism was growing weak. The bubonic plaque brought suffering. Europeans increasingly questioned the meaning of life. They studied the classical writings of the Greeks and Romans. These studies led to new ideas. Europeans developed *humanism.* Artists made art more realistic. History, *philosophy,* and literature became more important.

In 1455, the printing press was invented. This invention helped spread Renaissance ideas. Martin Luther criticized corrupt leaders in the Church. His protest began the **Reformation.** This was a movement to correct problems in the Church. The Reformation split Christians into Catholics and Protestants.

3. Why did the Reformation occur?

_____

_____

Changes in Trade (pages 38)

Why did Europeans want a new route to Asia?
As trade grew, Italian merchants became wealthy. The Italians and Muslims controlled the trade of goods from Asia. They did not allow others to take part. Merchants in other European countries wanted a share of the Asian trade. They began to look for another water route to Asia that did not go through the Mediterranean.

4. What caused people to seek a water route to Asia?

_____

_____

Name _____ Date _____

Early European Explorers

BEFORE YOU READ

In the last section, you read about a period of changes in West African and European society. Some of these changes spurred trade.

In this section, you will read how Europeans searched for all-water routes to Asia. Europeans wanted to trade there.

AS YOU READ

Use this diagram to take notes on the causes and effects of Columbus's voyages.

TERMS & NAMES

navigator A person who plans the course of a ship using instruments to find its position

caravel A ship with triangular and square sails that improved the ability of sailing nearly into the wind

Christopher Columbus An Italian sailor who reached the Americas when he sailed across the Atlantic Ocean in search of Asia

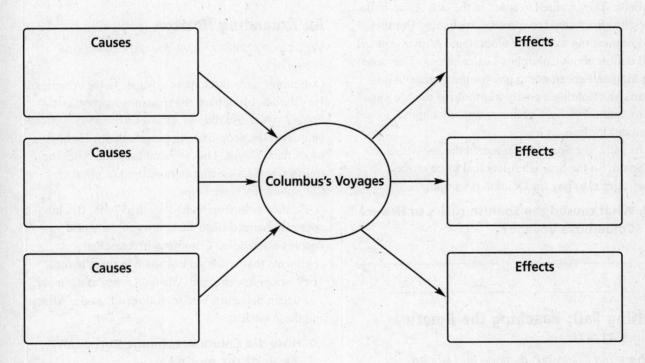

Causes → Causes → Causes → **Columbus's Voyages** → Effects / Effects / Effects

A Water Route to Asia (pages 39–40)

Why did the Portuguese merchants become rich?
Finding an all-water route to Asia required a good **navigator.** The Portuguese also developed a ship, the **caravel.** It was better than other ships at sailing into the wind. This ship had triangular sails as well as square sails. Square sails carried the ship forward when the wind was at its back. Triangular sails allowed the caravel to sail more nearly into the wind.

In 1488, the Portuguese explorer, Bartolomeu Dias, reached the southern tip of Africa. This tip is now known as the Cape of Good Hope. Ten years later, Vasco da Gama found an all-water route to Asia. This meant that the Portuguese could trade with Asia without the Italians and Muslims. Portugal took over the spice trade. Portuguese merchants grew rich.

1. Why was an all-water route to Asia important to the Portuguese?

_____

_____

Columbus's Plan; Help from Spain's Rulers (pages 40–41)

Why *did the Portuguese rulers refuse to finance Columbus's voyage?*

An Italian sailor, **Christopher Columbus,** thought he knew a faster route to Asia. He thought that sailing west across the Atlantic would be a short way to Asia. But Columbus figured the distances incorrectly. He relied on the writings of two people who were wrong about the size of Asia. He also thought the distance around the globe was smaller than it is. In 1483, Columbus asked the king of Portugal to pay for his voyage. The king refused because his advisers said that Columbus was wrong.

Spain's rulers were King Ferdinand and Queen Isabella. They wanted to share in the rich Asian trade. Isabella also wanted to spread Christianity. But they had reasons not to support Columbus. A royal council had doubts about Columbus's calculations. They told the king and queen not to pay for the voyage. Also, Spain was fighting a costly war to drive the Muslims from Spain. Finally, Columbus wanted a high payment for his services.

In 1492, the Spanish conquered the last Muslims in Spain. So the Spanish rulers had more money. They agreed to pay for Columbus's voyage.

2. What caused the Spanish rulers to finance Columbus's voyage?

_____

_____

Setting Sail; Reaching the Americas (pages 41–43)

Where *did Columbus think he had landed?*

Columbus began his voyage in August of 1492. His three ships sailed southwest toward the Canary Islands. Then Columbus relied on trade winds to speed his ships across the ocean. Columbus kept two *logs*. One was to show his men. The other he kept secret because it recorded the truth about the journey.

By October 10, the crew lost confidence in Columbus. To avoid mutiny, Columbus agreed to turn back if they did not sight land within three more days. On October 12, they sighted land.

The ships landed on a Caribbean island. Columbus thought he had reached the Indies—islands in Southeast Asia where spices grew. So he called the islanders Indians. Columbus named the island San Salvador. He set sail soon after in search of Japan. For the next three months, he visited several Caribbean islands. He found gold and precious objects on the island we call Hispaniola today. Columbus believed he had found an all-water route to Asia. So he decided to sail back to Spain.

3. Why didn't Columbus realize he had reached an unknown continent?

_____

_____

An Expanding Horizon (page 43)

What *geographic knowledge did Columbus bring back?*

Columbus made three more voyages to the Americas. He failed to bring back the treasures he promised Spain's rulers. He did not spread Christianity. Instead he treated the people of Hispaniola badly. He also made them slaves. This angered Isabella. After the fourth voyage, Spain's rulers refused to give Columbus any more help.

He died believing he had reached Asia. But his voyages changed European views of the world. People realized that Columbus had reached continents that had been unknown to them before. They stopped seeing the Atlantic Ocean as a barrier. The ocean became a bridge. It linked Europe, Africa, and the Americas.

4. How did Columbus change European views of the world?

_____

_____

Chapter **1** *The World in 1500*

Glossary/After You Read

bubonic plague A deadly disease

drought Long period of low rainfall

diverse Different

environment The world around you

humanism The study of human worth and achievements

instability A lack of stability

irrigate To water crops

log A record

nomad A person who has no permanent home but moves constantly

philosophy The study of the meaning of life

savanna Grassland with shrubs and trees

serf A peasant who farmed and did other duties for the lord and who could not leave the estate

theory Scientific belief

Terms & Names

A. If the statement is true, write "true" on the line. If it is false, change the underlined word or words to make it true.

_____ 1. A <u>culture</u> is a way of life shared by people with similar arts, beliefs, and customs.

_____ 2. <u>Technology</u> is the use of tools and knowledge to meet human needs.

_____ 3. The religion that expanded to West Africa after 1076 was <u>Protestantism</u>.

_____ 4. The <u>Renaissance</u> was a movement to correct problems in the Roman Catholic Church.

_____ 5. A <u>navigator</u> plans the course of a ship using instruments to find its position.

B. Write the letter of the name or term that matches the description.

   a. Mound Builder   d. Crusades

   b. Iroquois League   e. European Middle Ages

   c. Muslim   f. Christopher Columbus

_____ 1. An Italian sailor who reached the Americas when he sailed across the Atlantic Ocean in search of a faster way to reach Asia

_____ 2. A follower of Islam

_____ 3. An alliance of five Native American nations

_____ 4. A series of wars to capture the Holy Land

_____ 5. The time period from the late 400s to about the 1300s or 1400s

Main Ideas

1. How did agriculture lead to civilization?

   _____

   _____

2. What role did the environment play in the cultures of the Native American groups in North America?

   _____

   _____

3. How did trade affect the West African kingdoms?

   _____

   _____

4. Why did Europeans develop feudalism and the manor system?

   _____

   _____

5. How did the caravel help Portuguese explorers?

   _____

   _____

Thinking Critically

Answer the following questions on a separate sheet of paper.

1. What are some examples of Native American technology that the environment influenced?

2. If you were a European ruler, would you have financed Columbus's voyages? Why or why not?

Chapter 2 Section 1 (pages 51–54)

Spain Claims an Empire

BEFORE YOU READ

In the last chapter, you read about the European explorers' search for an all-water route to Asia.

In this section, you will read how Spanish explorers claimed land in the Americas.

AS YOU READ

Use this diagram to take notes on the empire claimed by the Spanish.

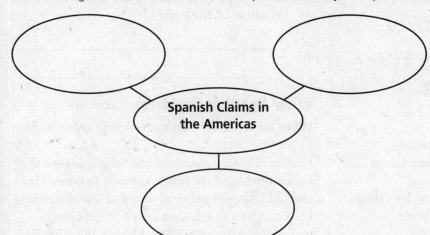

TERMS & NAMES

Treaty of Tordesillas Treaty that set the final placement for the Line of Demarcation

mercantilism An economic system that explained how to enrich treasuries

conquistador Conqueror

Hernando Cortés A Spanish *conquistador* who defeated the Aztecs

Montezuma The Aztec emperor

Francisco Pizarro A Spanish *conquistador* who defeated the Inca

Spain and Portugal Compete
(pages 51–52)

Why were colonies important to European countries?

In 1493, Pope Alexander VI drew the Line of Demarcation. This line divided the world into two parts. One would be controlled by Portugal. The other would be controlled by Spain. Portugal's king thought the pope's placement of the line favored Spain. In 1494, the rulers of Spain and Portugal met and agreed to the **Treaty of Tordesillas.** This treaty moved the Line of Demarcation more than 800 miles to the west. After this treaty, Spain and Portugal increased their exploration.

European countries had three main goals during this age of exploration. First, they wanted to spread Christianity beyond Europe. Second, they wanted to expand their empires. Third, they wanted to become rich.

By becoming richer, European countries could gain power and security. An economic system called **mercantilism** explained how Europeans could enrich their treasuries. *Colonies* helped nations do this by providing gold and silver mines, producing goods that could be traded for gold and silver. They also served as markets for the home country.

1. How did colonies help European countries enrich their treasuries?

_____

_____

Europeans Explore Foreign Lands
(pages 52)

Where did Vespucci, Balboa, and Magellan explore?

Amerigo Vespucci was an Italian sailor who, in 1501, set out to find a sea route to Asia. He realized that the land he saw on his voyage was not Asia. The continent "America" was named after him.

In 1513, the Spanish explorer Vasco Núñez de Balboa led an *expedition* that reached the Pacific Ocean. He claimed the ocean and all the land around it for Spain.

In 1519, Portuguese sailor, Ferdinand Magellan, set out to reach Asia by sailing around South America. He died on the trip. But his crew became the first people to sail around the world.

2. What did the explorations of Vespucci, Balboa, and Magellan accomplish?

_____

_____

The Invasion of the Americas
(pages 53–54)

Why did the Spanish invade Mexico?
Soldiers called **_conquistadors_**, or conquerors, explored parts of the Americas and claimed them for Spain. **Hernando Cortés** was one of these *conquistadors*. He and his men landed on the Central American coast in 1519. The Aztec emperor, **Montezuma**, warmly greeted Cortés. The friendliness ended quickly.

The Spaniards formed alliances with native peoples who hated the Aztecs. When Cortés reached the Aztec capital, Tenochtitlán, he tried to take control of the empire. The Aztecs fought back and drove the Spanish out. The Spaniards regrouped and returned to Tenochtitlán about a year later. By then, many Aztecs had died from smallpox, a disease that the Europeans had carried to Central America. Cortés and his forces defeated the Aztecs.

In 1531, an expedition led by **Francisco Pizarro** landed on the coast of what is now Peru. The Inca ruled a large territory there. With an army of only 180 men, the Spanish conquered the Inca.

There were three main reasons for the Spanish success in conquering Native American empires. First, the spread of European diseases killed millions of Native Americans. Second, the Spanish were skilled soldiers and sailors and had superior weapons. Third, Spain made alliances with Native Americans who were enemies of the Aztecs and the Inca.

3. What happened during the Spanish invasion of Mexico?

_____

_____

Other Spanish Explorers (page 54)

What influenced the Spanish to send expeditions to North America?
Rumors of golden cities gave the Spaniards hope to collect treasures from North America. Between 1539 and 1542, three expeditions set out to find these cities. Francisco Vàzquez de Coronado traveled through present-day Arizona and New Mexico. Hernando de Soto set out from Florida to explore the southeast. Juan Rodríguez Cabrillo sailed up the California coast. They all failed to find the fabled cities.

5. What were Coronado, De Soto, and Cabrillo searching for?

_____

_____

Chapter **2** Section 2 (pages 55–58)

European Competition in North America

BEFORE YOU READ

In the last section, you read about the land claimed by Spain in the Americas.

In this section, you will learn how other European counties competed with Spain for control over territory in the Americas.

AS YOU READ

Use this diagram to take notes on the competition among European countries for control over territory in the Americas.

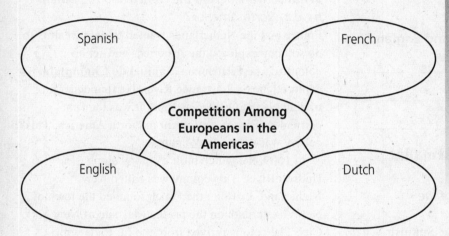

TERMS & NAMES

Henry Hudson An Englishman who made two voyages in search of the Northwest Passage to Asia

John Cabot An Italian explorer who searched for the Northwest Passage on behalf of England

Giovanni da Verrazzano An Italian explorer who sailed for the French in search of the Northwest Passage

Jacques Cartier A French explorer who explored the St. Lawrence River in search of the Northwest Passage

Spanish Armada The great Spanish fleet that was destroyed in 1588

Samuel de Champlain A French explorer who founded the first permanent French settlement in North America at Quebec

New France The French colony in North America

The Search for the Northwest Passage
(pages 55–56)

What was the Northwest Passage?
In 1609 and 1610, **Henry Hudson,** an Englishman, made two voyages from Europe to find a westward *passage* to China. His attempts failed. His voyages were among the last European attempts to find the Northwest Passage, a water route to Asia through North America.

One of the first explorers to search for a Northwest Passage to Asia was the Italian sailor **John Cabot**. In 1497, Cabot, exploring for the English, crossed the Atlantic and landed in present-day Newfoundland, Canada. He claimed the area for England. Cabot's expedition set up the basis for future English colonies along North America's Atlantic shore.

In 1524, the Italian explorer, **Giovanni da Verrazzano,** searched for the Northwest Passage on

behalf of France. He explored the Atlantic coastline but found no passage. Between 1524 and 1536, the French explorer **Jacques Cartier** also explored the St. Lawrence River but found no passage.

1. Why did explorers search for a Northwest Passage?

_____

_____

Spain Responds to Competition; Spain and England Clash (pages 56–57)

What caused fighting among European countries in the Americas?
The French and English claims to North America angered Spain. Tensions among Spain, France, and England also grew from religious conflicts and the

quest for national power. These conflicts led to fighting in the Americas. The Spanish attacked a French fort in Florida. The fort contained French Protestants.

Religious differences also led to conflict between England and Spain. In 1558, Queen Elizabeth I, a Protestant, challenged Spain's power at sea. England's navy was less powerful than Spain's. But the English fleet had many speedy ships with skillful sailors. Daring sailors, known as *sea dogs,* used these ships to attack the large, bulky Spanish ships that brought gold and silver from the Americas. One famous sea dog was Sir Francis Drake. He raided Spanish ports and ships in South America. He stole great amounts of treasure from them. He was also the first Englishman to sail around the world.

2. Why did Spain fight France and England?

_____

_____

_____

The Defeat of the Spanish Armada
(pages 57–58)

***What** was the result of the defeat of the Spanish Armada?*

In 1588, Spain's King Philip II sent the **Spanish Armada** to conquer England and restore Catholicism to that nation. The armada included 130 warships. It fought the English navy in the English Channel. Half of Spain's ships were destroyed. Spain was still a strong nation. But it was never again as powerful as it was in 1588.

The English victory over Spain had several important effects. England remained independent and

Protestant. England showed it could defend itself. Spain's image suffered because the world saw that it could be beaten. Other countries challenged Spain.

3. What were the effects of England's defeat of the Spanish Armada?

_____

_____

_____

The French and the Dutch Search for Trade (page 58)

***What** settlements did the French and the Dutch have in North America?*

France and the Netherlands wanted to gain wealth. To do so, they explored the Americas and set up colonies. The Frenchman, **Samuel de Champlain,** explored the St. Lawrence River. He founded a fur-trading post at Quebec in 1608. It was the first permanent French settlement in North America. This colony was called **New France**.

In 1609, the Dutch built a colony along the Hudson River. This colony was called New Netherland. In 1626, the Dutch founded the town of New Amsterdam on the present-day site of New York City. The colony thrived from the fur trade with Native Americans.

4. Where did the French and the Dutch set up their first colonies in North America?

_____

_____

_____

Chapter **2** Section 3 (pages 59–63)

The Impact of Colonization

BEFORE YOU READ

In this section, you will read about the consequences of contact between Africans, Native Americans, and Europeans in the Americas.

AS YOU READ

Use this diagram to compare the experiences of Native Americans and Africans under slavery

Native Americans	Africans

TERMS & NAMES

encomienda A grant of Native American labor

plantation Large farm that raises cash crops

slavery The practice of holding a person in bondage for labor

African Diaspora Forced removal of Africans to the Americas for slavery

middle passage The voyage of slave ships from Africa to the Americas

racism The belief that some people are inferior because of their race

Columbian Exchange The movement of plants, animals, and diseases between the Eastern and Western hemispheres

Life in Spanish America (pages 59–60)

What *did Spain do to establish control over the Americas?*

Spain's empire grew rapidly. By 1700, Spain controlled much of the Americas. It divided its American empire into two *provinces*. These provinces were named New Spain and Peru. Each province was ruled in the king's name by a *viceroy*. Spain also built roads. These roads helped them control the colonies and transport goods.

Spanish-born colonists had the most power in the colonies. They were the top of society. Just below them were the Creoles. Creoles were people of Spanish descent who were born in the colonies. Next were the *mestizos*, or people of mixed Spanish and Native American ancestry. The people with the least power were the Native Americans and African slaves.

The Catholic Church played an important role in the Spanish colonies. In places like New Mexico and California, the Church built missions. Missions were settlements that included a church, a town, and

farmlands. The goal of the missions was to convert Native Americans to Christianity. The missions also increased Spanish control over the land.

Some Spanish colonists received ***encomiendas,*** or *grants* of Native American labor, to help make the colonies productive. The Spanish created large estates, called *haciendas*. The estates provided food for the colony. Some *haciendas* became plantations. **Plantations** are large farms that raise *cash crops*, such as sugar or coffee.

Most Spaniards treated Native Americans badly. They forced the Native Americans to work in the fields and mines. Not all Spaniards approved of this situation. For example, Bartolomé de Las Casas, a Catholic priest, fought for better treatment of Native Americans. Because of his work, laws were passed to provide greater protection for Native Americans. But many Spanish colonists ignored these laws.

In 1680, a mane named Popé led the Pueblo Indians in rebellion against the Spanish. His forces surrounded the Spanish settlement of Santa Fe. This place is in present-day New Mexico. The Spaniards were temporarily forced to leave the region.

1. How did Spain establish control of this region?

_____

_____

The Emergence of American Slavery
(pages 60–62)

Why did Spain turn to Africa for slaves?
Many Native Americans died from overwork and European diseases. The Spanish and Portuguese needed workers. They turned to Africa for slaves. **Slavery** is the practice of holding a person in *bondage* for labor.

The Europeans enslaved Africans for four basic reasons. First, Africans were *immune* to most European diseases. Second, Africans had no friends or family in the Americas to help them resist or escape. Third, enslaved Africans offered a permanent source of labor. Even their children could be held as slaves. Fourth, many Africans had worked on farms in their native lands.

In the early 1500s, traders began bringing Africans to the Americas as slaves. This forced removal of Africans has become known as the **African Diaspora.** Before the slave trade ended in the late 1800s, about 12 million Africans had been shipped to the Americas. The voyage of the slave ships from Africa to the Americas was called the **middle passage.** It got this name because it was the middle of the triangular trade. Ships moved in a triangle between Europe, Africa, and the Americas. It is estimated that two million Africans died during the middle passage. Those who survived faced a hard life in the Americas. Some worked as servants in large homes. Most worked in the fields or in mines.

Many slaves ran away or rebelled. To prevent rebellion, the Spanish government passed slave codes. These were laws that *regulated* the treatment of slaves. Some laws tried to improve the conditions of slavery. Others were designed to punish slaves who ran away.

Over time, Europeans came to associate slavery with black Africans. To many people, dark skin color became a sign of inferiority. Slavery led to racism.

Racism is the belief that some people are inferior to others because of their race.

Africans survived in part by clinging to their cultures. This included their traditions of dance, music, and storytelling. The slave trade brought together people from different parts of Africa. These people had different cultural traditions. However, the experience of slavery helped create a common culture among African Americans.

2. Name four reasons European colonists enslaved Africans.

_____

_____

_____

_____

The Columbian Exchange (pages 62–63)

What was the Columbian Exchange?
The arrival of Europeans in the Americas brought a movement of plants, animals, and diseases between the Eastern Hemisphere and the Western Hemisphere. This movement of living things across the Atlantic Ocean is called the **Columbian Exchange.**

One result of the Columbian Exchange was the movement of germs. When Europeans came to the Americas, germs came with them. These germs caused diseases such as smallpox, measles, and influenza. Native Americans had no immunity to these diseases, and millions died.

Other effects of the Columbian Exchange were more positive. The Spanish brought many plants and animals to the Americas. Cows, pigs, sheep, and horses did will in the Americas. Grapes, onions, wheat, and many other plants also thrived in the Americas. Many American crops became part of the European diet. Potatoes and corn were particularly important. They helped feed European populations that might have gone hungry.

3. What effects did the Columbian Exchange have?

_____

_____

Chapter 2 European Exploration of the Americas

Glossary/After You Read

auction A public sale of property to the highest bidder

bondage Held by force

cash crop A crop grown to be sold

colony A settlement started by people who keep ties with their home country

debt Money owed to another

expedition A journey with a specific purpose

grant Something given for a specific purpose

heritage Things passed down to children from parents and ancestors

immune Not affected

inferior Of a lower rank

passage A course by which something passes

province A division of a country

mestizo Person of mixed Spanish and Native American ancestry

regulate To control or adjust

sea dog English sailor who attacked other nations' ships

triangular trade Movement of trade ships between Europe, Africa, and the Americas

viceroy A ruler of a viceroyalty

Terms & Names

A. Write the letter of the best description or definition of the term.

_____ 1. Hernando Cortés
   a. conquered the Aztecs.
   b. ended the Spanish Empire.
   c. stopped the enslavement of Africans.
   d. established New Amsterdam.

_____ 2. New France was the French colony in
   a. Africa.
   b. South America.
   c. North America.
   d. Europe.

_____ 3. *Encomiendas* were
   a. provinces in the Americas.
   b. grants of Native American labor.
   c. large estates for farming.
   d. alliances with native people.

_____ 4. Missions were settlements set up by
   a. the king of France.
   b. Native Americans.
   c. enslaved Africans.
   d. the Catholic Church.

_____ 5. The African Diaspora was
   a. the forced removal of Africans from Africa.
   b. laws to regulate the treatment of slaves.
   c. the artistic heritage of enslaved Africans.
   d. auctions held to sell enslaved Africans.

B. Write the letter of the name or term that matches the description.

a. mercantilism   f. plantation
b. Montezuma   g. Jacques Cartier
c. Francisco Pizarro   h. Columbian Exchange
d. John Cabot   i. middle passage
e. Samuel de Champlain   j. racism

_____ 1. A movement of living things between the Eastern and Western hemispheres

_____ 2. An economic system that aimed at enriching national treasuries

_____ 3. The belief that some people are inferior because of their race

_____ 4. French explorer who founded the first permanent French settlement in North America

_____ 5. Spanish *conquistador* who defeated the Inca

_____ 6. Italian sailor who claimed the area of Newfoundland for England

_____ 7. Large farms that raised cash crops

_____ 8. The voyage that brought enslaved Africans from Africa to the Americas

_____ 9. Aztec emperor

_____ 10. French explorer who traveled up the St. Laurence River

Main Ideas

1. What were the three main goals of European countries during the age of exploration?

_____

2. Why were the Spanish able to defeat the Aztec and Incan empires?

_____

3. Why did European nations compete for control over territory in the Americas?

_____

4. How did Spanish rule in the Americas affect the Native Americans?

_____

5. Why did slavery develop in the Americas?

_____

Thinking Critically

Answer the following questions on a separate sheet of paper.

1. Do you think the effects of the Columbian Exchange were mostly harmful or beneficial? Explain your answer.

2. What were the effects of the slave trade on the Americas and on Africa?

Chapter **3** Section 1 (pages 69–73)

Early Colonies Have Mixed Success

BEFORE YOU READ

In the last chapter, you read about slavery in the Americas.

In this section, you will read how the English established the first permanent colony in the Americas.

AS YOU READ

Use this diagram to take notes on the early English colonies. Fill it in with information about each of the colonies.

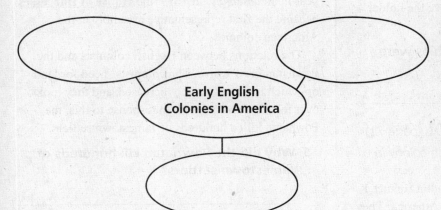

Early English Colonies in America

TERMS & NAMES

joint-stock company Company backed by people who put money into a project to earn profits

charter A written contract, issued by a government, giving the holder the right to establish a colony

Jamestown The first permanent English settlement in North America

John Smith The leader of Jamestown

indentured servant Worker who exchanged labor for help getting started in America

House of Burgesses The first representative assembly in the American colonies

Bacon's Rebellion A rebellion by poor, landless settlers against wealthy Virginia landowners

---

The English Plan Colonies (pages 69–70)

Why did England want to start a colony in the late 1500s?

England defeated the Spanish Armada in 1588. Then it decided to use its resources to establish colonies in the Americas. Colonies would provide the country with *raw materials*. They would also increase the country's trade.

Many English colonists wanted to come to the Americas to gain greater economic opportunity. Some wanted to come to the Americas to escape religious persecution.

1. What were two reasons that some English colonists had for coming to America?

_____

_____

_____

Two Early Colonies Fail (page 70)

What was England's first colony in America?

England's first colony, Virginia, was started by Sir Walter Raleigh in 1585 on Roanoke Island. The colonists who settled the colony counted on the Native Americans for food. However, the Native Americans realized that the colonists wanted their land. They cut off the colonists' food supply. The colonists who survived returned to England in 1586.

John White tried again to establish the colony in 1587. He returned to the colony in 1590, after being away for two years. He found no trace of the colonists. No one knows for sure what happened to the Roanoke colony.

The Plymouth Company financed the Sagadahoc colony, in what is now Maine. Problems in the colony, however, forced most of the colonists to return to England within a year.

2. What were the first two early colonies established by the English in America?

_____

_____

Financing a Colony (pages 70–76)

Why *did the English turn to joint-stock companies to finance colonies?*

Sir Walter Raleigh lost his *investment* in the Roanoke colony. The English realized that one person could not finance a colony. Instead they turned to the **joint-stock company,** a company backed by people who invested money. Each investor had part ownership of the company. The investors split *profits* and divided losses.

In 1601, King James I gave a **charter** to the Virginia Company of London and the Virginia Company of Plymouth. A charter was a written contract issued by a government. It gave the holder the right to establish a colony.

3. What two joint-stock companies were established in 1601?

Jamestown Is Founded in 1607 (page 71)

What *was the first permanent English colony in America?*

In 1607, the Virginia Company of London financed an expedition of over 100 colonists to America. They named the first permanent English settlement **Jamestown,** in honor of King James.

Many Jamestown colonists became sick from *malaria* and from the drinking water. They incorrectly believed that the colony was rich in gold. So they spent much of their time searching for it rather than building homes and growing food. The climate was also difficult for the colonists.

4. What hardships did the Jamestown colonists face?

Jamestown Grows; Conflicts with the Powhatan (pages 71–72)

What *helped Jamestown grow?*

Many of the first Jamestown settlers died within the first year. In 1608, **John Smith,** a soldier and adventurer, took control. He established strict rules that forced the colonists to work.

In 1612, John Rolfe introduced tobacco. The crop became very popular in England. It soon brought profits for the Virginia company. When the settlers

wanted part of the profits, the company responded by letting them own land. By 1621, there were more than 2,000 settlers in Jamestown.

To get even more laborers to work on the tobacco plantations, settlers were encouraged to come as **indentured servants.** These men and women sold their labor to the person who paid for their passage. Then after working for a number of years, they were free to farm or take up a trade of their own.

The colonists soon wanted more control of their own interests. So the Virginia Company allowed for burgesses, or elected representatives, to meet once a year in an *assembly*. In 1619, the **House of Burgesses** became the first representative assembly in the American colonies.

The relations between English colonists and the Powhatan grew worse. The colonists' need for land on which to grow tobacco increased, and they took over more Powhatan land. In response to this, the Powhatan killed hundreds of Jamestown settlers.

5. Why did the Powhatan kill hundreds of Jamestown settlers?

Bacon's Rebellion in 1676 (page 73)

What *was Bacon's Rebellion?*

By the 1670s, about one-fourth of the free white men living in Jamestown were former indentured servants. Most of these landless settlers lived on Virginia's western frontier. There, they fought the Native Americans for land.

In 1676, Nathaniel Bacon and a group of landless servants demanded that the governor of the colony approve a war against the Native Americans. The purpose of the war was to get land to grow tobacco. The governor's refusal resulted in **Bacon's Rebellion**. Bacon and his followers burned Jamestown to the ground. The rebellion ended when Bacon suddenly died. The king recalled the governor to England. The House of Burgesses passed laws to limit the governor's power.

6. Why did Nathaniel Bacon and others rebel against the governor of Jamestown?

New England Colonies

BEFORE YOU READ

In the last section, you read about the first English colonies.
In this section, you will learn about other English colonies.

AS YOU READ

Use the time line below to take notes on the important dates in the development of the Massachusetts Bay Colony and Rhode Island.

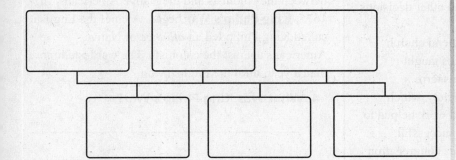

TERMS & NAMES
Pilgrims Members of a religious group who wanted to separate from the Church of England
Mayflower Compact An agreement signed by Pilgrims to obey colony laws
Puritans Religious group that wanted to "purify" the Church of England
Great Migration Movement of Puritans from England to America
Fundamental Orders of Connecticut Laws adopted by Puritans in Connecticut in 1636
Roger Williams Minister who founded colony of Rhode Island
Anne Hutchinson Woman forced to leave Massachusetts Bay Colony
King Philip's War Conflict between settlers and Native Americans

The Voyage of the Mayflower; The Pilgrims Found Plymouth (pages 76–78)

Why did the Pilgrims sail for America?
King Henry VIII started the Church of England in the early 1500s. In the early 1600s, the **Pilgrims,** a Separatist group, called for a total break with the Church of England. They thought it was too much like the Catholic Church. King James attacked them for their beliefs. To escape his harsh treatment, the Pilgrims asked the Virginia Company if they could settle in America. The company arranged for them to settle on its land on the eastern coast of North America.

In November 1620, the Pilgrims, sailing on the *Mayflower,* were blown north off their course. They landed in a place they called Plymouth. Because they landed outside the limits of the Virginia Company, their charter did not apply. To keep order, the men on the ship signed the **Mayflower Compact.** They promised to obey the laws they agreed upon.

After the first winter, many of the Pilgrims suffered from illness and starvation. About half of

them died by spring. Then Squanto, a Native American, helped the Pilgrims negotiate a treaty with the Native Americans. He showed them how to plant, hunt, and fish. The Pilgrims also traded with the Native Americans for furs and lumber. These goods were shipped back to England for a profit.

In the fall the Pilgrims and the Native Americans celebrated a good harvest with a feast. This was the first Thanksgiving.

1. How did the Native Americans help the Pilgrims survive?

_____

_____

The Puritans Come to Massachusetts Bay; The New England Way (pages 78–79)

What was the Great Migration?
Another religious group, the **Puritans,** also left England to escape religious persecution. The Puritans wanted to *reform* the Church of England by

"purifying" some of its practices. Thousands of
Puritans left for America. Their leaving was known
as the **Great Migration.**

The Massachusetts Bay Company arranged for the
Puritans to receive a charter to settle land in New
England. In 1630, about 1,000 Puritans settled the
Massachusetts Bay Colony. They were well prepared
and did not endure the hardships the Pilgrims did.

The *congregation* was the basic unit of the Puritan
community. Each Puritan congregation set up its own
town. The meetinghouse was the most important
building. People gathered there for town meetings. At
these meetings, people made laws and other decisions
for the community.

By law, everyone in town had to attend church
services. The sermons at these services taught
Puritans the "New England Way." This term
described Puritan beliefs and their society, which
stressed hard work. The belief in hard work helped to
make their colony grow and become successful.

In 1636, Thomas Hooker moved his congregation
to the Connecticut Valley. There they wrote the
Fundamental Orders of Connecticut, which was a
kind of *constitution.* These laws expanded the idea of
representative government.

**2. How did the New England Way contribute
to the success of the Massachusetts Bay
Colony?**

_____

_____

Challenges to Puritan Leaders
(pages 79–80)

Why did many people leave the Massachusetts Bay
Colony for Rhode Island?
Some people, such as minister **Roger Williams,** did
not support the New England Way. He opposed
forced church attendance. Because of his beliefs, he
was forced to leave the Massachusetts Bay Colony.
He fled southward and founded the colony of Rhode
Island in 1636. **Anne Hutchinson** believed that
people did not have to attend church services to
worship God. She was also forced to leave the colony.
She fled to Rhode Island in 1638.

The Quakers also disagreed with the New England

Way. They were persecuted for their beliefs, and
many left for Rhode Island.

3. Why was Rhode Island founded?

_____

_____

King Philip's War (page 80)

Who was King Philip?
As the Massachusetts colony grew, settlers began to
take Native American land. This led to conflict
between the colonists and the Native Americans. In
1675, **King Philip's War** began. A chief the English
called King Philip led an *alliance* of Native
Americans against the colonists. The war lasted more
than a year, until the English won.

4. What was King Philip's War?

_____

_____

The Salem Witchcraft Trials
(pages 80–81)

What events led to the Salem witchcraft trials?
By the late 1600s, the younger generation of Puritans
did not share their parents' strict religious views. In
Salem, several young girls were told frightening
stories about witches. Pretending to be bewitched, the
girls accused others of witchcraft. This started a
panic in which those accused were forced to name
others as witches. More than 100 people were
arrested and tried. Twenty were found guilty and put
to death. The religious leaders viewed the trials as a
sign from God to return to a strict Puritan lifestyle.
The panic did not last long. However, it showed how
easily a community can assign blame for its
problems.

**5. What did the religious leaders in Salem
believe was the reason for the trials?**

_____

_____

Chapter **3** Section 3 (pages 84–87)

Founding the Middle and Southern Colonies

BEFORE YOU READ

In the last section, you read about the founding of the New England colonies.

In this section, you will read how the Middle and Southern Colonies were started.

AS YOU READ

Use this diagram to take notes on the Middle and Southern colonies. Fill it in with information about each of the colonies.

MIDDLE	New York	
	New Jersey	
	Pennsylvania	
	Delaware	
SOUTHERN	Maryland	
	Carolinas	
	Georgia	

TERMS & NAMES

patroon A person who brought 50 settlers to New Netherland

Peter Stuyvesant The governor of New Netherland

Duke of York The owner of the colony of New York

proprietary colony A colony run by a proprietor, or owner

William Penn The founder of Pennsylvania

Quaker A religious group who was persecuted for its beliefs

royal colony A colony ruled by a governor appointed by the king

James Oglethorpe The founder of Georgia

The Middle Colonies (page 84)

Why did people settle in the Middle Colonies?
The Middle Colonies were New York, New Jersey, Pennsylvania, and Delaware. Settlers to these colonies came for religious freedom. They also came to take advantage of the economic opportunities. The rich soil made farming and raising livestock favorable in these colonies. The rivers supported shipping and trade.

1. What were the Middle Colonies?

_____

_____

New Netherland Becomes New York
(page 85)

Who started the colony of New Netherland?
The colony of New Netherland was founded by Dutch settlers in 1624. To attract more settlers, the Dutch set up a patroon system. A **patroon** was a

person who brought 50 settlers to New Netherland. As a reward a patroon received a large piece of land. Many different kinds of people settled in New Netherland.

Peter Stuyvesant, the governor of the colony, wanted to add more land to New Netherland. So in 1655 he attacked the nearby colony of New Sweden. The Swedes surrendered the settlement to the Dutch.

The brother of England's King Charles II, the **Duke of York,** drove the Dutch out of New Netherland. New Netherland became the **proprietary colony** of New York. The Duke became the proprietor, or owner, of the colony.

2. How did the colony of New York get started?

_____

_____

New Jersey, Pennsylvania, and Delaware
(pages 85–86)

How were New Jersey, Pennsylvania, and Delaware colonized?

The Duke of York gave part of his land to his friends. The colony of New Jersey encouraged settlers by promising freedom of religion.

William Penn was another large landowner in America. Penn joined the **Quakers,** a religious group, who were persecuted for their beliefs. Penn was given a large piece of land. He decided to use it to create a colony where Quakers could live according to their beliefs. The Pennsylvania colony gave religious freedom and equality to everyone who lived there.

Pennsylvania attracted a variety of people. It became one of the wealthiest of the American colonies. Eventually, some of the *counties* of Pennsylvania broke away to form the colony of Delaware.

3. Why did William Penn start the colony of Pennsylvania?

_____

_____

_____

The Southern Colonies; Maryland and the Carolinas (pages 86–87)

What were the Southern Colonies?

The new Southern Colonies were Maryland, the Carolinas, and Georgia. The soil and climate of these colonies made them suitable for warm-weather crops such as tobacco, rice, and indigo.

Lord Baltimore started the colony of Maryland in 1632. It was a place for Roman Catholics fleeing religious persecution in England. To attract other settlers to the colony, he promised religious freedom. Tobacco growing was an important part of Maryland's economy.

The colony of Carolina was founded in 1663. English settlers from Barbados built Charles Town, later called Charleston, in 1670. Carolina's colonists needed many laborers to grow rice and indigo. The English settlers from Barbados encouraged the use of enslaved Africans. They also sold local Native Americans into slavery. This led to wars between the colonists and the Native Americans.

Carolina became a **royal colony** in 1729. Then it was ruled by governors appointed by the king. The colony was divided into North Carolina and South Carolina.

4. What crops were an important part of the economy in the Southern Colonies?

_____

_____

_____

Georgia (page 87)

Who was James Oglethorpe?

In 1732, **James Oglethorpe** founded Georgia as a *refuge* for *debtors*. The English government wanted to use Georgia as an outpost against the Spanish in Florida and the French in Louisiana. The Spanish tried unsuccessfully to force the English out of Georgia. Oglethorpe set up strict rules that upset the colonists. The unrest caused the king to make Georgia a royal colony in 1752.

5. Why did James Oglethorpe start the Georgia colony?

_____

_____

_____

Glossary/After You Read

alliance An agreement between groups to act together for a common purpose

assembly A lawmaking body

congregation A group of people who belong to the same church

constitution A set of laws

county A unit into which a colony was divided for the purpose of government

debtor A person who owes a debt

investment Money that is invested

malaria A disease that is spread by the bite of a certain mosquito

profit The money people receive above the amount they invested

raw material Unprocessed natural resource such as timber or wool

reform To make better by getting rid of faults

refuge Protection or shelter from trouble

Terms & Names

A. Fill in the blanks with the letter of the term that best completes the sentence.

   a. joint-stock company   d. King Philip's War

   b. Mayflower Compact   e. Quakers

   c. Great Migration   f. Puritans

1. The leaving of thousands of Puritans for America was known as the _____.

2. The colony of Pennsylvania was founded to provide a place for _____ to freely practice their beliefs.

3. The Virginia Company of London was a _____ that financed the expedition to Jamestown.

4. In the _____, the Pilgrims promised to obey the laws agreed upon for everyone's good.

5. In 1675, conflict between the Puritans in Massachusetts and the Native Americans led to _____.

B. Write the letter of the name or term next to the statement that describes it best.

   a. John Smith   d. Anne Hutchinson

   b. House of Burgesses   e. William Penn

   c. Roger Williams   f. James Oglethorpe

_____ 1. I disagreed with the New England Way and started the Rhode Island colony.

_____ 2. I took control of Jamestown in 1608.

_____ 3. I started Georgia, a colony for debtors.

_____ 4. I started the Pennsylvania colony.

_____ 5. I was the first representative assembly in the American colonies.

Main Ideas

1. Why did England turn to joint-stock companies to finance colonies?

_____

_____

2. Why did the Jamestown settlers have conflicts with the Native Americans there?

_____

_____

3. Why did Roger Williams and Anne Hutchinson flee the Massachusetts Bay Colony to Rhode Island?

_____

_____

4. Why did the Dutch set up a patroon system?

_____

_____

5. Why did some English settlers bring enslaved Africans to the Southern Colonies in the 1600s?

_____

_____

Thinking Critically

Answer the following questions on a separate sheet of paper.

1. Do you think using indentured servants was helpful or harmful to the Virginia colony? Why do you think so?

2. What were some similarities and differences between the founding of the New England Colonies and the Middle Colonies?

Chapter **4** Section 1 (pages 93–97)

New England: Commerce and Religion

BEFORE YOU READ

In the last chapter, you learned how the Middle and Southern Colonies started.

In this section, you will learn what helped the New England Colonies to grow and to prosper.

AS YOU READ

Use this chart to take notes on the factors and events that influenced the lifestyle of people living in the New England Colonies.

Factors and Events	Influence on Lifestyle
Short growing season and poor soil	Practiced subsistence farming
The way land was sold	
Nearness to the Atlantic Ocean	
Royal Charter of 1691	

TERMS & NAMES

Backcountry Region running along the Appalachian Mountains through the far western part of the other regions

subsistence farming Producing just enough food for family use and sometimes a little extra to trade in town

triangular trade Name given to a trading route with three stops

Navigation Acts Laws passed by the English government to make sure that it made money from its colonies' trade

smuggling Importing or exporting goods illegally

Distinct Colonial Regions Develop
(pages 93–94)

How *were the colonies organized into regions by the 1700s?*

By the 1700s, the population of England's colonies in North America had settled in three different regions. These regions were the New England Colonies, the Middle Colonies, and the Southern Colonies. A fourth region was the **Backcountry**. It ran along the Appalachian Mountains through the far western part of the other regions.

Agriculture was the way most colonists made a living. The type of agriculture colonists practiced depended on the climate and resources of the region in which they settled.

1. What were the four different colonial regions in the 1700s?

_____

_____

The Farms and Towns of New England
(pages 94–95)

Why *did most New Englanders live near a town?*

New England officials did not usually sell scattered plots of land to individuals. Instead, they sold large plots of land to groups. The buying group was often the *congregation* of a Puritan church. After buying the land, the church divided the land among its members. Colonists usually built their farmhouses and a *meetinghouse* near a green—a central square for public activities.

Most New England farmers practiced **subsistence farming.** That is, they produced just enough food for themselves and sometimes a little extra to trade in town.

2. What did a typical New England town look like?

_____

_____

Harvesting the Sea (page 95)

What *were New England's most valuable articles of trade?*

New England had poor, rocky soil that made farming difficult. But the Atlantic Ocean offered many economic opportunities. Some of the world's best fishing grounds were not far off New England's coast. The forests of New England provided all the wood needed to build ships for fishing.

Fish and wood were among New England's most valuable articles of trade. Boston, New Haven, and other coastal cities grew rich as a result of shipbuilding, fishing, and trade.

3. Name three economic activities that helped coastal cities in New England grow rich.

_____

_____

Atlantic Trade (pages 95–96)

What *was the triangular trade?*

One kind of trade that New England settlers participated in was **triangular trade**—the name given to a trading route with three stops. For example, a ship might leave New England with a cargo of rum and iron. In Africa, the traders exchanged their cargo for slaves. The slaves then suffered through a trip to the West Indies. There, they were traded for sugar and *molasses*. The traders took this cargo back to New England. Colonists there used the molasses to make more rum to trade.

New England made huge profits from trade. England wanted a share of those profits. In 1651, England began to pass the **Navigation Acts.** The English government designed the acts to make sure that it made money from its colonies' trade. Many colonists ignored the Navigation Acts. **Smuggling,** which is the *importing* or *exporting* of goods illegally, was common.

4. Why did the English government pass the Navigation Acts?

_____

_____

African Americans in New England (pages 96–97)

Why *were there few enslaved workers in New England?*

Slavery was not economical in New England. The owners of the region's small farms did not require a large number of workers. Also, farmers could not afford to house and feed slaves during the long winters when there was little work to do.

Even so, some New Englanders in the larger towns did own slaves. Many slave owners hired out their slaves to work on the docks or in shops or warehouses. Some slaves were allowed to keep part of their wages. A number of slaves saved enough money to buy their freedom. New England became home to more free blacks than any other region.

5. How did many of New England's enslaved persons obtain their freedom?

_____

_____

Changes in Puritan Society (page 97)

Why *did the Puritan religion decline in the early 1700s?*

The Puritan religion slowly declined in the 1700s. There were many reasons for the decline. One reason was that the drive for economic gain competed with Puritan ideas. A second reason was that other religious groups established congregations in the region. These groups competed with Puritans for new members. Also, England had given Massachusetts a new royal charter in 1691. The charter took away some of the Puritans' political privileges. It gave religious freedom to other groups besides the Puritans. It also granted the right to vote based on property ownership instead of church membership.

6. What political change weakened the Puritan community?

_____

_____

Name _____ Date _____

The Middle Colonies: Farms and Cities

BEFORE YOU READ

In the last section, you read about the factors that shaped the New England Colonies.

In this section, you will learn how the people who settled in the Middle Colonies made a society of great diversity.

AS YOU READ

Use this diagram to take notes on the factors that supported the growth of large coastal cities in the Middle Colonies.

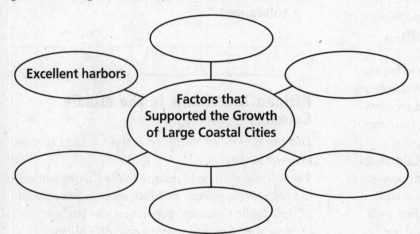

Excellent harbors

Factors that Supported the Growth of Large Coastal Cities

A Wealth of Resources; The Importance of Mills (pages 98–99)

How was farming in the Middle Colonies different from farming in New England?

The soil of the Middle Colonies was better for farming than the soil in New England. Also, the climate was milder, and the growing season was longer. These good conditions attracted *immigrants* from all over Europe. Among them were Dutch and German farmers who brought advanced farming methods from their home countries. Their skills, knowledge, and hard work soon resulted in large harvests. The Middle Colonies began to produce **cash crops**—crops raised to be sold for money.

After harvesting their crops of corn, wheat, rye, or other grains, farmers took them to a **gristmill.** At the gristmill, millers used large stones to grind grains into flour. Colonists built gristmills along the region's many rivers. The force of the flowing water was used to power the mills.

1. How did the crops grown by farmers in the Middle Colonies differ from those grown in New England?

_____

_____

The Cities Prosper (page 100)

What geographic features in the Middle Colonies made good locations for cities?

The excellent harbors along the coasts of the Middle Colonies were perfect sites for cities. Many *merchants* lived in New York City, on the Hudson River, and Philadelphia, on the Delaware River. They exported cash crops and imported manufactured goods. The valuable trade of the port cities helped them to grow. Philadelphia was the fastest growing city. Its prosperity was due mostly to its trade in wheat and other cash crops. The busy port of New York owed its growth to its trade in flour, bread, furs, and whale oil.

The wealth of Philadelphia and New York City also brought many public improvements. The cities' graceful buildings, paved roads, and streetlights made them *rival* cities in England.

2. What economic activity helped New York City and Philadelphia to grow?

_____

_____

A Diverse Region (pages 100–101)

Who *settled in the Middle Colonies?*

Many different groups of people arrived in the port cities of the Middle Colonies. Soon, the population of the Middle Colonies showed great **diversity,** or variety, in its people.

After the English, the Germans were the largest group in the region. Many Germans arrived between 1710 and 1740. Most came as indentured servants fleeing religious intolerance. Among the Germans were many skillful farmers and **artisans,** or craftspeople. German craftspeople built **Conestoga wagons,** which farmers used to carry their produce to town. These wagons had canvas covers and wide wheels suitable for dirt roads. Many of the people who later settled the American West would use wagons of this design.

The Middle Colonies became home to many people besides the Germans. There were also Dutch, Scots-Irish, African, Irish, Scottish, Welsh, Swedish, and French people among the region's inhabitants.

3. How were the Conestoga wagons built by the Germans used?

_____

_____

A Climate of Tolerance (pages 101–102)

What *factors helped to promote tolerance in the Middle Colonies?*

While the English Puritans shaped life in the New England Colonies, many different groups contributed to the culture of the Middle Colonies. There were so many groups in the region that it was hard for one group to dominate the others. Diversity helped to promote tolerance.

The Middle Colonies' earliest settlers also helped to promote tolerance. The Dutch in New York and the Quakers in Pennsylvania both practiced religious tolerance. Quakers also insisted on the equality of men and women and were the first to raise their voices against slavery. Quaker ideals influenced immigrants in the Middle Colonies—and eventually the whole nation.

4. In what ways did the Quakers promote tolerance?

_____

_____

African Americans in the Middle Colonies (page 102)

Did *the climate of tolerance in the Middle Colonies prevent slavery?*

The tolerant attitude of many Middle Colony settlers did not prevent slavery. In 1750, about seven percent of the Middle Colonies' population was enslaved.

New York City had more people of African descent than any other city in the Northern colonies. Tensions existed between the races in New York City. Sometimes the tensions led to violence. In 1712, a group of about 24 rebellious slaves set fire to a building. They then killed nine whites and wounded several others who came to put out the fire. Armed colonists caught the suspects and punished them horribly. The harsh punishments showed that whites would use force and violence to control slaves. Even so, slave *rebellions* continued to occur.

5. What was one way that white people kept control of their slaves?

_____

_____

Chapter **4** Section 3 *(pages 103–107)*

The Southern Colonies: Plantations and Slavery

BEFORE YOU READ

In the last section, you learned how the Middle Colonies became a society of great diversity.

In this section, you will learn how the economy of the Southern Colonies began to depend on slave labor.

AS YOU READ

Use the diagram to take notes on the causes and effects of the use of enslaved Africans in the Southern Colonies.

TERMS & NAMES

indigo Plant that yields a rich blue dye

Eliza Lucas Woman who introduced indigo as a successful plantation crop after her father sent her to supervise his South Carolina plantations

William Byrd II Wealthy Virginia planter best known for his writing

overseer Person hired by planters to watch over and direct the work of slaves

Stono Rebellion Bloody slave rebellion that took place at the Stono River just south of Charles Town in September of 1739

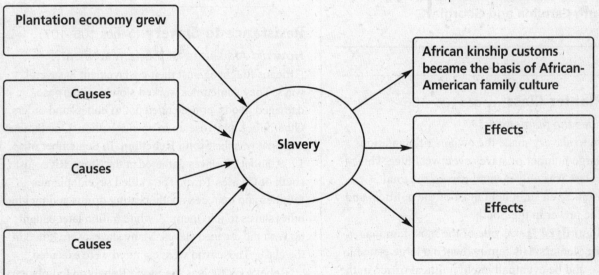

Plantation economy grew → Slavery
Causes → Slavery
Causes → Slavery
Causes → Slavery
Slavery → African kinship customs became the basis of African-American family culture
Slavery → Effects
Slavery → Effects

The Plantation Economy; The Turn to Slavery *(pages 103–105)*

Why *was the South a good place to grow plantation crops?*

The South's soil and almost year-round growing season were ideal for plantation crops such as rice and tobacco. These crops required much labor to produce. However, with enough labor, planters could grow them as cash crops.

Starting in the 1660s, planters began using more enslaved Africans on their plantations. There were several reasons for this change. One reason was that indentured servants were leaving plantations to start their own farms. Another reason was that planters were not successful when they tried to force Native Americans to work on the plantations.

As a result of the turn to slavery, the population of enslaved Africans grew rapidly. By 1750, enslaved Africans made up about 40 percent of the South's population.

1. What factors led planters to use the labor of enslaved Africans?

_____

_____

Plantations Expand (page 105)

How *did slavery affect the plantation economy?*
The increased use of slavery allowed plantations to expand in South Carolina and Georgia. The growing of rice in the lowlands of these colonies required much labor and skill. Planters bought slaves from West Africa who had those skills.

On higher ground, planters grew **indigo,** a plant that yields a deep blue dye. **Eliza Lucas** introduced indigo as a successful plantation crop. Lucas's father had sent her to run his South Carolina plantation when she was 17 years old.

2. What were two plantation crops grown in South Carolina and Georgia?

_____

_____

The Planter Class (pages 105–106)

What *was the planter class?*
The turn to slavery made the owners of plantations with a large number of slaves even wealthier. This planter class was only a small part of the total population. Even so, it held most of the political and economic power in the South.

William Byrd II was one of the most famous Southern planters. His family owned a large estate in Virginia, and he eventually held political office in the colony. But Byrd was also a great writer. His account of a trip to create a dividing line between North Carolina and Virginia is his best known work.

3. Who held most of the political and economic power in the South?

_____

_____

Life Under Slavery (page 106)

How *did slaves live?*
On large Southern plantations, slaves worked in groups of about 20 to 25. Planters hired **overseers** to watch over and direct the work of slaves. The overseer often whipped slaves who he thought were not doing their full share of work.

Slaves usually lived in small, one-room cabins furnished only with sleeping cots. Typical food for a week might be a small basket of corn and a pound of pork. In spite of these brutal conditions, Africans kept many customs and beliefs from their homelands. These customs and beliefs became the basis of African-American culture.

4. On what was African-American culture based?

_____

_____

Resistance to Slavery (pages 106–107)

How *did Africans resist their enslavement?*
Africans fought against their enslavement in several ways. They sometimes worked slowly on purpose, damaged goods, or pretended not to understand orders. Other times they rose up in open rebellion. One famous example was the **Stono Rebellion.** In September of 1739, about 20 slaves gathered at the Stono River just south of Charles Town. They killed several planter families and marched south, beating drums and inviting other slaves to join them. A white militia later caught up with the escaped slaves. Many slaves were killed in the clash. Those who were captured were executed.

Rebellions such as the Stono Rebellion led planters to make slave laws even stricter. Slaves were forbidden to leave a plantation without permission, and slaves were not allowed to meet with free blacks.

5. How did the Stono Rebellion affect slave laws?

_____

_____

Name _____   Date _____

The Backcountry

BEFORE YOU READ

In the last section, you learned how the Southern economy began to rely on slave labor and how this affected Southern society.

In this section, you will read about the people who settled the Backcountry.

AS YOU READ

Use this diagram to take notes on the skills and tasks that were typical for women in the Backcountry.

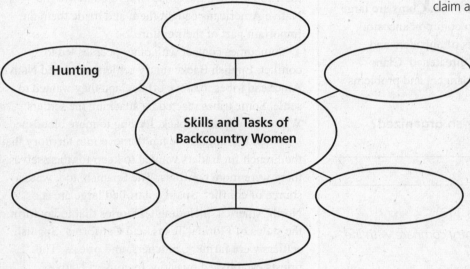

TERMS & NAMES

Appalachian Mountains The mountain range that stretches from eastern Canada south to Alabama

fall line The point at which waterfalls prevent large boats from moving farther upriver

piedmont An area of land at the foot of a mountain or mountain range

clan Large groups of families that claim a common ancestor

Geography of the Backcountry (page 110)

What was the Backcountry?

The Backcountry was a region of dense forests and rushing streams. It was located in or near the **Appalachian Mountains**—a mountain range that stretches from eastern Canada south to Alabama. The Backcountry's resources made it easy for a family to start a small farm. Springs and streams provided water. Forests furnished wood for building log cabins and fences.

In the South, the Backcountry began at the **fall line,** which is where waterfalls prevent large boats from moving farther upriver. Beyond the fall line lay the **piedmont**—an area of land at the foot of a mountain or mountain range.

1. What resources did settlers find in the Backcountry?

_____

_____

Backcountry Settlers; The Scots-Irish

(page 111)

Who settled the Backcountry?

The first European settlers in the Backcountry made a living trading with Native Americans. Backcountry settlers paid for goods with deerskins. A unit of value was one buckskin, or a "buck."

Farmers were next to move into the region. They built log cabins to shelter their families. As the number of settlements grew, settlers began to clash with the

Native Americans whose land they were taking.

Life in the Backcountry was harsh. But by the late 1600s, many families had chosen it as a place to live. In the 1700s, a new group of immigrants—the Scots-Irish—began to move into the Backcountry.

The Scots-Irish came from the border between Scotland and England. Most of them had lived for a time in northern Ireland. When England and Scotland merged in 1707 to form Great Britain, the Scots-Irish suffered many hardships. Poverty and crop failure made their situation even worse.

Hoping to better their lives, the Scots-Irish headed to America by the thousands. Once there, they quickly moved into the Backcountry. The Scots-Irish brought their clan system with them. **Clans** are large groups of families that claim a common ancestor. Clan members were suspicious of outsiders and banded together when danger threatened. Clans helped families deal with the dangers and problems of life in the Backcountry.

2. How were the Scots-Irish organized?

_____

_____

Backcountry Life (page 112)

How did life in the Backcountry compare with life along the seaboard?

Settlers along the coast carried on a lively trade with England. In the Backcountry, rough roads and rivers made it hard to move goods. Backcountry farmers had to learn to depend on themselves. They built cabins and made rough furniture from the logs they cut in the forest. They fed their families with the hogs and cattle they raised and with the fish and game they killed. Backcountry settlers grew yellow corn for their livestock and white corn to eat. Popcorn was probably their only snack.

Backcountry women were *hardy.* They worked in the fields, as well as the cabins. Women also quickly learned to use guns and axes.

3. What were common foods in the Backcountry?

_____

_____

Other Peoples in North America
(pages 112–113)

What other peoples lived in North America?

The desire for land led many Backcountry settlers to move westward. The push to the West brought settlers into contact with other peoples in North America. Among these peoples were Native Americans, who had made their homes there for thousands of years. They also encountered the French and Spanish, who claimed a great deal of land in North America.

Sometimes the contact led to changes in people's cultures. For example, North America had no horses until the Spanish colonists brought them to Mexico in the 1500s. When the horses migrated north, the Native Americans caught them and made them an important part of their culture.

Sometimes contact with other peoples led to conflict. English Backcountry settlers pressured Native American tribes to move off the land they wanted to settle. Some tribes reacted by attacking the settlers. White settlers struck back, leading to more bloodshed.

When the English began to move into territory that the French fur traders wanted to keep for themselves, there were more conflicts. The Spanish, too, were a source of conflict. Spain controlled large areas of North America, including territories that today form the states of Florida, Texas, and California. Spanish settlers were farmers, ranchers, and priests. The priests established missions to convert Native Americans. The Spanish then built forts near the missions for protection. In 1718, Spaniards built Fort San Antonio de Bexar to guard the mission of San Antonio de Valero—later renamed the Alamo.

4. With whom did the Backcountry settlers have conflicts?

_____

_____

Name _____ Date _____

Glossary/After You Read

congregation A group of people who gather to worship

exporting Sending goods or products to other countries

hardy Strong and healthy

immigrants People coming to live in a country in which they were not born

importing Bringing in goods or products from other countries

meetinghouse A building for public meetings

merchants Persons whose work is buying and selling goods

molasses A thick, sweet syrup made from sugar cane and used to make rum

rebellions Open, armed, and organized resistance

rival To be the equal of

Terms & Names

A. Write the letter of the name or term next to the description that explains it best.

a. Eliza Lucas   d. Stono Rebellion
b. William Byrd ll   e. Navigation Acts
c. Conestoga wagon

_____ 1. Introduced indigo as a successful plantation crop

_____ 2. Laws passed by England because it wanted a share in its colonies' trading profits

_____ 3. Wrote an account of an expedition to create a dividing line between Virginia and North Carolina

_____ 4. Would be important in settling the West

_____ 5. One example of Africans' resistance to their enslavement

B. Write the name or term that best completes each sentence.

Backcountry   gristmill   Appalachian Mountains
subsistence farming diversity   fall line
triangular trade   artisans   clan
smuggling   indigo
cash crop   overseers

1. The term used to describe a trade route with three stops is _____.

2. The _____ ran along the Appalachian Mountains through the far western part of the other colonial regions.

3. _____ directed the work of slaves.

4. The _____ stretch from eastern Canada south to Alabama.

5. The Middle Colonies showed more _____ in its people than the other colonies.

Main Ideas

1. Into what four different regions were the colonies divided by the 1700s?

   _____

   _____

2. How did England respond to the success that colonists had trading?

   _____

   _____

3. What attracted settlers to the Middle Colonies?

   _____

   _____

4. Why did Southern planters begin to use enslaved workers?

   _____

   _____

5. Why did the colonists' decision to push westward cause conflicts?

   _____

   _____

Thinking Critically

Answer the following questions on a separate sheet of paper.

1. How did the climate and resources of each colonial region influence the way its people made a living?

2. If you were a colonist in the 1750s, in which of the colonial regions would you choose to live? Why?

Name _____   Date _____

Early American Culture

BEFORE YOU READ

In the last chapter, you read about the various groups of people who settled the four colonial regions.

In this section, you will learn about the forces that began to draw the British colonies together.

AS YOU READ

Use this chart to note examples that show what colonists valued.

Valued by Colonists	Examples That Show It Was Valued
Land	Owning land was tied to the right to vote.
Wealth	
Hard Work	
Education	

TERMS & NAMES

apprentice Someone who learns a trade from an experienced craftsman

Great Awakening A religious movement that swept through the colonies in the 1730s and 1740s

Jonathan Edwards Well-known minister of the Great Awakening

George Whitefield Popular minister of the Great Awakening, who drew crowds of thousands

Enlightenment Intellectual movement stressing reason and science as the paths to knowledge

Benjamin Franklin American Enlightenment figure who was a scientist and inventor

John Locke English philosopher who argued that people have natural rights

Land, Rights, and Wealth *(pages 119–120)*

Why was land ownership a goal of most colonial Americans?

The cheap land and plentiful natural resources of the colonies gave colonists a chance to prosper. Colonial landowners were free to use or to sell all that their land produced. Also, owning land gave men the right to vote.

Because land ownership was the means to wealth and political power, it also helped determine *social standing*. In the colonies, people divided themselves into *ranks* based on wealth. Most colonists were in the middle rank. People were expected to show respect to those in a higher rank. The wealthy were expected to aid the poor.

1. How did land ownership affect a colonist's political, economic, and social standing?

_____

_____

Women and the Economy; Young People at Work *(pages 120–121)*

What part did women and children play in the colonial economy?

Enslaved black women helped raise cash crops. Most colonial white women were farm wives. Their duties included making household goods, such as clothing. They also tended gardens and farm animals. Farm wives bartered, or traded, with their neighbors for things they needed. Some urban women ran businesses or practiced trades.

Although women played a role in the economy, they did not have equal rights. Women could not vote. A married woman could not own property. She could not keep the money she earned unless her husband agreed.

Children also worked. Large families were common because more children meant more workers. Children did chores by age three or four. Around age 11, many boys became apprentices. An **apprentice** learned a trade by working with an experienced craftsman.

2. What were some duties of colonial farm wives?

_____

_____

Colonial Schooling (pages 121–122)

What *was education like in the colonies?*
Colonists taught children to read mainly so that they could understand the Bible. Textbooks stressed religion. Wealthy children learned from private tutors or in private schools. Poorer children learned from their mothers or in "dame schools" run by women.

Colonial America had a high literacy rate, as measured by the number of people who could sign their names. Between 50 percent and 85 percent of white men were *literate*. About half as many white women as men were literate. Most African Americans could not read. Slaves were not allowed to learn. Free African Americans often were kept out of schools.

3. How widespread was literacy?

_____

_____

Newspapers and Books (pages 122–123)

What *was published in the colonies?*
Colonists published almost 80 different newspapers. Some lasted for many years. Almanacs were popular as well. They usually had a calendar, weather predictions, and farming advice inside. Colonists also published poetry, histories, and life stories. The captivity narrative was a form of writing found only in the Americas. In it, a colonist captured by Native Americans told of living among them. Mary Rowlandson published such a book in 1682. It was a bestseller.

4. What form of writing was found only in the Americas?

_____

_____

The Great Awakening (pages 123–124)

What *was the Great Awakening?*
The **Great Awakening** was a religious movement. It swept through the colonies in the 1730s and 1740s. Its ministers preached that inner religious feelings were more important than outward religious behavior.

Jonathan Edwards was one of the best-known preachers. **George Whitefield** was another. Whitefield drew thousands of people to his sermons. He raised funds to build a home for orphans.

The movement split churches. It also stirred up ideas of individual worth, equality, and the right to challenge authority. These ideas prepared the colonists to break away from England.

5. How did the Great Awakening help prepare colonists to break away from England?

_____

_____

The Enlightenment (page 124)

What *was the Enlightenment?*
The **Enlightenment** was a movement of ideas. It valued reason and science as the paths to knowledge. **Benjamin Franklin** was a famous American Enlightenment figure.

The Enlightenment began in Europe, as scientists found out natural laws that controlled the universe. An example is the law of gravity. Other Enlightenment thinkers applied the idea of natural law to human societies. The English philosopher **John Locke** argued that people have natural rights. They create governments to protect these rights, he said. He also argued that people could change their government if it did not protect their rights. These ideas later led colonists to break away from England.

6. What Enlightenment ideas led colonists to break away from England?

_____

_____

Name _____ Date _____

Roots of Representative Government

BEFORE YOU READ

In the last section, you read about the forces that helped people in the British colonies begin to think of themselves as Americans.

In this section, you will learn about the events that shaped English people's expectations of certain rights.

AS YOU READ

Use the time line below to take notes of events that led to the colonists' expectation and claim of rights.

1215 The Magna Carta limited the powers of the English king and gave rights to noblemen and freemen.

↓

1689

↓

1735

TERMS & NAMES

Magna Carta A 1215 document granting rights to English people

Parliament England's chief lawmaking body

Edmund Andros Royal governor who limited colonists' rights

Glorious Revolution The takeover of the English throne by William and Mary during 1688 and 1689

English Bill of Rights A 1689 royal agreement to respect the rights of English citizens and of Parliament

salutary neglect Leaving alone in a helpful way

John Peter Zenger A colonial publisher whose trial in 1735 led to freedom of the press

The Rights of Englishmen
(pages 125–126)

What were "the rights of Englishmen"?
Long before the colonies were founded, English people expected certain rights. The first step toward guaranteeing these rights came in 1215. That year, English noblemen made King John sign the **Magna Carta.** This paper took away some powers of the English king. It gave certain rights to English noblemen and freemen. The Magna Carta prevented the king from taking property. He could not tax people unless a council of men agreed. People could not be put on trial without witnesses. They could be punished only by a jury of their peers.

1. What were four rights granted by the Magna Carta?

_____

_____

_____

Parliament and Colonial Government
(pages 126–127)

What was the colonists' model for representative government ?
Parliament is England's chief lawmaking body. It was the colonists' model for representative government. Parliament is made up of two houses. Members of the House of Commons are elected by the people. Members of the House of Lords are non-elected nobles, judges, and church officials. In America, colonists elected their own *assemblies*. These were similar to the House of Commons. The colonists governed themselves in some ways. However, the English king and Parliament still had power over them.

2. How was representative government limited in the colonies?

_____

_____

A Royal Governor's Rule (page 127)

Who *was Edmund Andros?*

James II became king of England in 1685. He combined Massachusetts and other northern colonies into one Dominion of New England. He named **Edmund Andros** governor. Andros ended the colonists' representative assemblies. He allowed town meetings only once a year. The colonists got angry.

3. How did Andros anger colonists?

_____

England's Glorious Revolution
(pages 127–128)

What *was the Glorious Revolution?*

Leaders of Parliament feared King James's Catholicism. Because of this, in 1688 they offered the throne to the king's Protestant daughter, Mary, and her husband, William of Orange. King James fled the country. Parliament named William and Mary the new *monarchs* of England. This change in leadership was called the **Glorious Revolution**.

In 1689, after accepting the throne, William and Mary signed the **English Bill of Rights**. This document showed that the government was to be based on laws made by Parliament, not on the wishes of a monarch. The rights of English people were strengthened. The colonists quickly claimed these rights. They jailed Governor Andros and asked Parliament to bring back their old government.

4. What did William and Mary sign after accepting the throne of England?

_____

Shared Power in the Colonies; The Zenger Trial (pages 128–129)

How *were the colonies governed in the 1700s?*

After the Glorious Revolution, Massachusetts colonists had more self-government. They could again elect representatives to an assembly. However, the crown still chose their governor. In most colonies, the assembly and the governor shared power.

During the first half of the 1700s, England did not interfere much in colonial affairs. This hands-off policy was called **salutary neglect**.

In 1735, **John Peter Zenger** went to trial. Zenger was publisher of the *New-York Weekly Journal*. His crime was printing criticism of New York's governor. At the time, criticizing the government in print was illegal. Zenger's lawyer argued that people had the right to speak the truth. The jury set Zenger free. Colonists had moved toward freedom of the press.

5. What right grew from the Zenger trial?

_____

Skillbuilder

Colonial Government

BRITISH CROWN

ROYAL GOVERNOR
- appointed by the crown
- oversaw colonial trade
- had final approval on laws
- could dismiss colonial assembly

COUNCIL
- appointed by governor
- advisory board to governor
- acted as highest court in each colony

COLONIAL ASSEMBLY
- elected by eligible colonists
- made laws
- had authority to tax
- paid governor's salary

Use the chart to answer the questions.

1. Would members of the council or of the colonial assembly be more likely to support the royal governor? Why?

_____

_____

2. In what two ways could the royal governor stop the colonial assembly from making laws he disliked?

_____

_____

The French and Indian War

BEFORE YOU READ

In the last section, you read about the events that led British colonists to expect certain rights.

In this section, you will learn about the war that gave Britain control over the northern and eastern parts of North America.

AS YOU READ

Use this diagram to take notes on the actions and reactions of the French and British and their allies during the French and Indian War.

Action	Reaction
British fur trading and land companies begin moving into the Ohio River valley.	French build forts to protect the area.
French seize and complete an unfinished British fort and name it Fort Duquesne.	
General Edward Braddock and 2,100 soldiers march toward Fort Duquesne in hopes of recapturing it.	
The British attack Quebec.	

TERMS & NAMES

French and Indian War A war (1754–1763) between Britain and France for control of North America. Each side had Native American allies

Albany Plan of Union First formal proposal to unite British colonies

Battle of Quebec British victory in 1759 that was the turning point of the French and Indian War

Treaty of Paris (1763) Treaty ending the French and Indian War and French power in North America

Pontiac's Rebellion Native American revolt against the British in 1763

Proclamation of 1763 British order forbidding colonists to settle west of the Appalachians

France Claims Western Lands; Native American Alliances (pages 130–131)

How did the fur trade help cause war?

While English colonists settled the eastern coast of North America, the French explored the *interior*. By the late 1600s, the French claimed the Ohio River valley, the Mississippi River valley, and the whole Great Lakes region. The main French settlements were Quebec and Montreal. They sat along the St. Lawrence River in Canada.

Both the English and French wanted furs. Different Native American groups traded furs for European goods. The fur trade created *alliances* between Europeans and their Native American trading partners.

Each time France and England went to war in Europe, French and English colonists and armies in America fought each other. Both sides had Native American allies. The **French and Indian War** (1754–1763) gave the English control over much of North America.

1. What was decided by the French and Indian War?

_____

_____

Conflict in the Ohio River Valley; War Begins and Spreads (pages 131–133)

What caused conflict in the Ohio River valley?
By the 1750s, British traders had moved into the Ohio River valley. British settlers also planned to move there. The British threatened the French fur trade, so the French built forts to protect the area.

The Virginia colony also claimed the area. It sent soldiers led by George Washington to tell the French to leave. The French refused. Virginia's lieutenant governor then sent men to build a fort at the head of the Ohio River. The French and their Native American allies took over the fort and completed it for themselves. They named it Fort Duquesne.

After Fort Duquesne was lost, Washington's forces built another small fort. They called it Fort Necessity. The French and their allies attacked it on July 3, 1754. Washington surrendered. The French and Indian War had begun. This war became part of the Seven Years' War—a worldwide struggle between France and Britain.

Meanwhile, at a meeting in Albany, New York, Benjamin Franklin suggested that the British colonies band together for defense. His **Albany Plan of Union** was the first formal proposal to unite the colonies. The colonial legislatures said no to the plan.

2. What actions did the French take to keep the British out of the Ohio River valley?

_____

_____

Braddock's Defeat; The British Take Quebec (pages 133–134)

***What** was the turning point in the French and Indian War?*
In 1755, the British sent General Edward Braddock and 2,100 men to fight the French at Fort Duquesne. The British were surprised and defeated by fewer than 900 French and Native American troops. This defeat was the first of many for the British.

In 1757, Britain had a new secretary of state, William Pitt. He sent the nation's best generals to America. He borrowed money to pay colonial troops for fighting. The British began to win. In late summer of 1759, they captured Quebec—the capital of New France. The **Battle of Quebec** was the turning point of the French and Indian War.

3. Why was the Battle of Quebec an important victory for the British?

_____

_____

The Treaty of Paris (1763) (page 134)

***What** were the results of the Seven Years' War?*
The **Treaty of Paris** ended the Seven Years' War in 1763. By the treaty, France had to give up most of its land in North America. Britain claimed almost all of North America east of the Mississippi. France gave New Orleans and Louisiana to Spain as a reward for siding with France. Spain also took back Cuba and the Philippines from Britain in exchange for Florida.

4. How did the Treaty of Paris divide land in North America?

_____

_____

Pontiac's Rebellion (page 135)

***Why** did Native American groups attack the British after the French withdrew?*
In the spring of 1763, Native American groups attacked British forts and settlers. They were angry because British soldiers would not give them supplies, as the French had. Also, British settlers had moved onto their land. The revolt was called **Pontiac's Rebellion** because one of its leaders was the Ottawa war leader Pontiac.

The rebellion showed the British government that defending Western lands would be costly. Therefore, it issued the **Proclamation of 1763.** This order forbade colonists to settle west of the Appalachians. The colonists were furious.

5. How was the Proclamation of 1763 related to Pontiac's Rebellion?

_____

_____

Chapter **5** *Beginnings of an American Identity*

Glossary/After You Read

alliances Partnerships formed to protect the common interests of the partners

assemblies Groups of people who meet to make laws

interior Land well away from the coastline

literate Able to read and write

monarchs Kings or queens

ranks Levels within a group

social standing Position in society

Terms & Names

A. Write the letter of the name next to the statement that best describes the person.

a. Jonathan Edwards   d. John Locke
b. George Whitefield   e. Edmund Andros
c. Benjamin Franklin   f. John Peter Zenger

_____ 1. I am the English philosopher who argued that people have natural rights.

_____ 2. I stood trial for printing criticism of New York's governor.

_____ 3. I am a minister of the Great Awakening who preached before thousands and raised funds to start a home for orphans.

_____ 4. I am a royal governor of the northern colonies who outlawed colonists' representative assemblies.

_____ 5. I am a scientist, inventor, and famous American Enlightenment figure.

B. Circle the name or term that best completes each sentence.

1. The English document of 1215 that granted certain rights to noblemen and freemen was the _____.

   Parliament   Magna Carta   English Bill of Rights

2. The _____ was a religious movement that swept through the colonies in the 1730s and 1740s.

   Great Awakening   Albany Plan of Union   Enlightenment

3. William and Mary signed the _____ , which guaranteed the rights of English citizens.

   Proclamation of 1763   Magna Carta   English Bill of Rights

4. _____ was the name given to the battle that was the turning point in the French and Indian War.

   Battle of Quebec   Pontiac's Rebellion   Glorious Revolution

5. The intellectual movement known as the _____ emphasized reason and science as the paths to knowledge.

   Enlightenment   Great Awakening   Glorious Revolution

6. The _____ forbade colonists to settle west of the Appalachians.

   Proclamation of 1763   French and Indian War   Treaty of Paris (1763)

7. King James' flight from England and the crowning of William and Mary was known as the _____.

   Albany Plan of Union   Treaty of Paris (1763)   Glorious Revolution

8. _____ is England's chief lawmaking body.

   Magna Carta   Parliament   English Bill of Rights

9. The Native American revolt against the British in 1763 was known as _____ .

   Pontiac's Rebellion   Battle of Quebec   Albany Plan of Union

10. The English government's hands-off policy toward the colonies in the first half of the 1700s was called _____.

    salutary neglect   apprentice   Enlightenment

Main Ideas

1. What were three ideas promoted by the Great Awakening?

   _____

   _____

2. What were women's contributions to the colonial economy?

   _____

   _____

3. What were two rights granted by the Magna Carta?

   _____

   _____

4. How did the fur trade push France and Britain toward war?

   _____

   _____

5. What law resulted from Pontiac's Rebellion? Why?

   _____

   _____

Thinking Critically

Answer the following questions on a separate sheet of paper.

1. How did a high literacy rate help draw the separate colonies together?

2. What were the most likely reasons that the French and British made alliances with Native American groups in the early 1700s?

Name _____   Date _____

Tighter British Control

BEFORE YOU READ

In the last chapter, you read about how the British and their American colonists pushed the French out of North America.

In this section, you will read about British actions to gain more control over the colonies. This caused the colonies and Britain to grow apart.

AS YOU READ

Use the chart below to take notes on the conflict between Britain and the colonies.

British Action	Colonists' Reaction
Proclamation of 1763	became angry and ignored it

TERMS & NAMES

King George III King of England during the American Revolution

Quartering Act Law that required the colonies to house and supply British soldiers

revenue Government income

Sugar Act British tax on imported sugar and molasses

Stamp Act Law that taxed many printed materials in the colonies

Patrick Henry A member of the Virginia House of Burgesses who opposed British taxes

boycott Refusal to buy goods

Sons of Liberty A secret society organized to oppose British policies

The Colonies and Britain Grow Apart
(pages 143–144)

Why did the British pass the Proclamation of 1763? Problems arose between Britain and the colonies after the French and Indian War. Before the war, the American colonies had been allowed to grow largely on their own. But after the war, Parliament passed new laws. These laws were passed to help Britain govern its new territories as well as the original 13 colonies. Parliament is Britain's main lawmaking body. It is similar to the American Congress.

One of these laws was the Proclamation of 1763. It said the colonists could not move west of the Appalachian Mountains. Britain wanted this land to remain with the Native Americans in order to prevent conflicts with them. The Proclamation angered many colonists. They settled the area anyway.

1. Why did the British Parliament pass the Proclamation of 1763?

_____

_____

British Troops and Taxes (page 144)

Why did Parliament pass the Sugar Act?
King George III issued the Proclamation of 1763 to keep peace with the Native Americans. As a result, he decided to keep British troops in North America. In 1764, Parliament also passed the **Quartering Act.** This law said that colonists had to supply and *quarter,* or house, British troops.

The British had spent a lot of money on the French and Indian War. Britain needed **revenue,** or income, to help pay for the war and to keep troops in the colonies. In 1764, Parliament passed the **Sugar Act**. This law placed a *tax* on sugar, molasses, and other products shipped to the colonies. Before this law, the king had always asked colonial assemblies to approve colonial taxes. But this time Parliament voted to tax the colonists directly.

Some colonists felt that Britain had no right to tax them because they had no representation in Parliament. The colonists felt that this was against their rights as British citizens.

2. Why did the Sugar Act make some colonists angry?

_____

_____

_____

Britain Passes the Stamp Act
(pages 144–145)

What was the Stamp Act?
In 1765, Parliament passed the **Stamp Act**. This law made the colonists buy and place stamps on many goods such as diplomas, contracts, and newspapers. The Sugar Act mainly affected merchants. But the Stamp Act affected all colonists.

Colonial leaders, such as **Patrick Henry,** *protested*. They believed that they were being taxed unfairly because they had no voice in Parliament.

3. How was the Stamp Act different from the Sugar Act?

_____

_____

_____

The Colonies Protest the Stamp Act
(pages 145–146)

How did the colonists protest the Stamp Act?
Colonial assemblies protested "taxation without representation." They sent *delegates* to the Stamp Act Congress in New York City. The delegates drew up a petition to the king to protest the Stamp Act. They said that only the colonial assemblies—not Parliament—could tax the colonies.

Colonial merchants protested by calling for a boycott of British goods. A **boycott** is a refusal to buy goods. Some colonists formed secret groups to protest British policies. The **Sons of Liberty** was the most famous of these groups.

Parliament finally realized that the Stamp Act was a mistake. It *repealed* the law in 1766. But then it passed the Declaratory Act. This act said that Parliament had the right to govern and tax the colonies.

4. Why did colonial assemblies send delegates to the Stamp Act Congress?

_____

_____

_____

Colonial Resistance Grows

Before You Read

In the last section, you read about the growing tension between Britain and the colonies.

In this section, you will learn how the colonists organized more protests against British policies.

As You Read

Use this diagram to take notes on the different ways that colonists protested British policies.

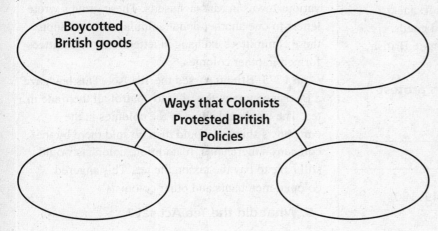

TERMS & NAMES

Townshend Acts Plan passed by Parliament in 1767 to help raise revenue in the colonies

writ of assistance Search warrant

Samuel Adams Founder of the Sons of Liberty

Crispus Attucks African American killed by British soldiers in the Boston Massacre

Boston Massacre Conflict between colonists and British soldiers in which five colonists were killed

John Adams A cousin of Samuel Adams and a lawyer who defended the British soldiers involved in the Boston Massacre

committee of correspondence A group that exchanged letters on colonial affairs with similar groups

Boston Tea Party Protest against the Tea Act in which colonists dumped British tea into Boston Harbor

The Townshend Acts Are Passed
(pages 147–148)

What were the Townshend Acts?
Parliament canceled the Stamp Act. But it still needed to raise money to pay its expenses in America. Charles Townshend, the king's finance minister, suggested the **Townshend Acts.** They were passed in 1767.

One of the Townshend Acts stopped New York's legislative assembly from meeting until the colonists agreed to house British troops. Another act placed taxes on certain goods brought into the colonies. The money raised would help to pay the salaries of British officials in the colonies. To *enforce* these laws, British officers used **writs of assistance.** These were search warrants used to enter homes or businesses to find *smuggled* goods.

1. Why were the Townshend Acts passed?

_____

_____

The Reasons for Protest (page 148)

How did colonists react to the Townshend Acts?
New Yorkers were angry that their assembly could not meet. Other colonists were upset about the new taxes. They did not think that Parliament had the right to tax the colonies directly.

The writs of assistance also angered many colonists. They felt that the Townshend Acts threatened their rights and freedoms.

2. Why were colonists against the Townshend Acts?

_____

Tools of Protest (pages 148–149)

How did colonists protest the Townshend Acts?
Colonists in Boston decided to protest the Townshend Acts. They called for another boycott of British goods. **Samuel Adams,** a leader of the Boston Sons of Liberty, led the protest.

The boycott continued to spread throughout the colonies. The Sons of Liberty asked shopkeepers not to sell goods made in Britain. The Daughters of Liberty urged colonists to weave their own cloth and to use American goods. Trade with Britain dropped.

Some colonial leaders called for peaceful protests. But riots broke out when British officials tried to search the merchant ship *Liberty*. The officials thought the ship was carrying smuggled goods. British officials reacted by calling for more British troops to be sent to Boston.

3. How did some colonial leaders protest the Townshend Acts?

_____

_____

The Boston Massacre (pages 149–150)

What was the Boston Massacre?
In 1768, about 1,000 British soldiers arrived in Boston. British soldiers were poorly paid. As a result, they hired themselves out as workers. They usually accepted less pay than American workers. The colonists disliked this because it took jobs away from Americans.

There was growing tension between British soldiers and colonists. On March 5, 1770, violence broke out between British soldiers and some colonists, including **Crispus Attucks,** an African-American sailor. The British soldiers fired at the colonists. Attucks and four other men were killed.

Colonial leaders called the shooting the **Boston Massacre.** They said that the five colonists gave their lives for freedom. The British soldiers involved in the shooting were arrested for murder. **John Adams,** a cousin of Samuel Adams and a lawyer, defended the soldiers in court. He believed that the soldiers acted in *self-defense*. The jury agreed.

4. What events led to the Boston Massacre?

_____

_____

The Tea Act (page 150)

Why were colonists angry about the Tea Act?
After the Boston Massacre, Parliament did away with all taxes except the one on tea. For most colonists, the trouble was over.

Samuel Adams, however, wanted to make sure that the colonists continued to work for freedom. He helped to form **committees of correspondence** in various towns in Massachusetts. These groups wrote letters to one another about colonial matters. Soon these committees exchanged letters with committees formed in other colonies.

In 1773, Britain passed the Tea Act. This law gave a British company the right to control all the trade in tea. The tea would come to the colonies in the company's ships. It would then be sold there by the company's merchants. In addition, colonists would still have to pay the tax on the tea. This angered colonial merchants and other colonists.

5. What did the Tea Act say?

_____

_____

The Boston Tea Party (page 151)

What was the Boston Tea Party?
Many colonists protested the Tea Act. On December 16, 1773, a group of colonists in Boston dressed as Native Americans. They boarded three tea ships. They dumped 342 chests of tea into Boston Harbor. This event became known as the **Boston Tea Party**.

Many colonists believed that Britain would now see how much they were against being taxed without representation. Some colonial leaders offered to pay for the tea if Parliament would agree to end the Tea Act. Parliament turned down the offer. It wanted the colonists to pay for the tea. It also wanted the people responsible to be brought to trial.

6. Why did several colonists dump tea into Boston Harbor?

_____

Reading Study Guide

Chapter **6** Section 3 (pages 154–157)

The Road to Lexington and Concord

Before You Read

In the last section, you learned how colonists protested British policies.

In this section, you will read about the events that led to war between the colonists and Britain.

As You Read

Use the diagram below to take notes on the events that led to the fighting at Lexington and Concord.

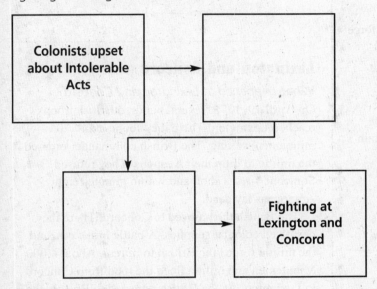

Colonists upset about Intolerable Acts

Fighting at Lexington and Concord

TERMS & NAMES

Intolerable Acts Laws passed by Parliament punishing Massachusetts for the Boston Tea Party

First Continental Congress Meeting held by the colonies in Philadelphia in 1774 to decide what to do about the problems with Britain

militia A force of armed civilians who pledge to defend their community

Minuteman A colonist who could be ready to fight at a minute's notice

Paul Revere A patriot who helped warn colonists about British movements

Lexington and Concord Sites of the first battles of the Revolutionary War

Loyalist A colonist who was loyal to Britain

Patriot A colonist who supported the colonial rebels

The Intolerable Acts (pages 154–155)

What *were the Intolerable Acts?*

The Boston Tea Party made British leaders *intolerant*. In 1774, Parliament passed a group of laws to punish the Massachusetts colony. The laws were so harsh that the colonists called them the **Intolerable Acts**.

One of the laws closed Boston Harbor until the colonists paid for the destroyed tea. Another law banned the committees of correspondence. Still another law allowed Britain to house troops wherever it wanted to.

Other colonies offered Massachusetts their support. They sent supplies to Boston. The committees of correspondence also called for a meeting of all colonies. This meeting would decide what to do about the problems with Britain.

1. Why did Britain pass the Intolerable Acts?

_____

_____

The First Continental Congress Meets (page 155)

What *was the First Continental Congress?*

In September 1774, representatives from all the colonies except Georgia met in Philadelphia. This was the **First Continental Congress.** The representatives voted to stop all trade with Britain until Parliament canceled the Intolerable Acts. They also told each colony to start training troops to prepare for possible fighting with Britain. They agreed to meet again in several months, if necessary.

2. What did representatives at the First Continental Congress agree to do?

_____

_____

Between War and Peace (pages 155–156)

***What** was the colonists' next step?*
The colonial boycott of British goods did not force Parliament to cancel the Intolerable Acts. Instead, Britain placed even more limits on colonial trade. It also sent more troops to the colonies.

By the end of 1774, some colonists formed militias to prepare for an attack. A **militia** was a force of armed civilians who pledged to defend their community. Some of the militia were **Minutemen**. They were called Minutemen because they were trained to be ready to fight at a minute's notice.

Most colonial leaders did not expect a war with Britain. They believed that any fighting with Britain would be short. They thought that Britain would change its policies when it realized that colonists were willing to use force.

3. Why did some colonists form militias?

_____

_____

The Midnight Ride (pages 156–157)

***How** were colonists warned about British movements?*
Samuel Adams had *spies* to keep track of British activities. The British also had spies. Their spies were Americans who were *loyal* to Britain. These spies learned that colonists in Massachusetts were storing guns and ammunition in Concord, about 20 miles outside of Boston.

The British also found out that Samuel Adams and John Hancock, another colonial leader, were in Lexington, a few miles east of Concord. The British ordered the two colonial leaders arrested. The British also wanted the guns and ammunition in Concord to be destroyed.

The Sons of Liberty were prepared. They had **Paul Revere,** a silversmith, and a second messenger, William Dawes, ready to spread the news about British troop movements.

On the night of April 18, 1775, Revere and Dawes galloped over the countryside warning the colonists. In Lexington they were joined by Dr. Samuel Prescott. Revere and Dawes were stopped by a British patrol. But Prescott broke away and warned the colonists in Concord.

4. What did Revere, Dawes, and Prescott do?

_____

_____

Lexington and Concord (page 157)

***What** happened at Lexington and Concord?*
On April 19, 1775, several hundred British troops reached Lexington. There they found about 70 militiamen waiting. The British commander ordered the militia to drop their weapons. They refused. Someone fired a shot, and within minutes eight Americans lay dead.

The British then moved to Concord. There they destroyed colonial supplies. A battle broke out, and the militia forced the British to *retreat*. About 4,000 Minutemen and militia lined the road from Concord to Lexington. As the British retreated to Boston, the colonial militia fired on them.

Lexington and Concord were the first battles of the Revolutionary War. Colonists were now forced to choose sides. Those who supported the British were called **Loyalists**. Those who sided with the colonial *rebels* were called **Patriots**.

5. Why were the battles at Lexington and Concord important?

_____

_____

Name _____   Date _____

Declaring Independence

Before You Read

In the last section, you read about the events that led to fighting at Lexington and Concord.

In this section, you will read about events that resulted in the Declaration of Independence.

As You Read

Use this chart to take notes on how these events led to the colonies' declaring independence from Britain.

Event	How it helped lead to independence
Continental Army captures the British Fort Ticonderoga	Artillery captured at the fort used later to force British out of Boston
Battle of Bunker Hill	
Olive Branch Petition	
Publishing of *Common Sense*	
Resolution of Richard Henry Lee	

TERMS & NAMES

Ethan Allen Leader of the Green Mountain Boys who helped to capture Fort Ticonderoga

artillery Cannon and large guns

Second Continental Congress Meeting held in Philadelphia in 1775

Continental Army The name of the American army

Benedict Arnold Colonial leader who played a part in the victory at Fort Ticonderoga and who helped in a failed invasion of Canada

Declaration of Independence Document that said the colonies were independent

Thomas Jefferson Writer of the Declaration of Independence

The Continental Army Is Formed
(pages 160–161)

***What** happened after Lexington and Concord?*
After the battles at Lexington and Concord, about 20,000 militiamen from other colonies gathered around Boston. As a result, the British moved back into the city. Boston was nearly surrounded by water, which would make it hard for the colonists to attack.

Meanwhile, colonial militia were active in other areas. On May 10, 1775, Americans attacked the British Fort Ticonderoga in New York. **Ethan Allen** and a group known as the Green Mountain Boys captured the fort and its **artillery,** or cannon.

Also on May 10, colonial leaders met in Philadelphia at the **Second Continental Congress**. At this meeting, they made George Washington the commanding general of the **Continental Army**.

1. Who was chosen to be the head of the Continental Army?

_____

_____

The Battle of Bunker Hill (page 161)

***What** happened at the Battle of Bunker Hill?*
Tensions increased around Boston. The colonial militia seized Bunker Hill and Breeds Hill in Charlestown, outside Boston.

The militia built *fortified* positions on Breed's Hill. When the British marched up the hill, the militia fired at them. The British fell back but then charged again, forcing the militia off the hill. Although the British won, they suffered huge losses.

2. What were the results of the Battle of Bunker Hill?

_____

_____

A Last Attempt at Peace (page 162)

How did the Americans try to avoid war?

Most colonists still hoped for peace. Colonial leaders sent the *Olive Branch Petition* to the king. This document asked the king to *restore* peace between Britain and the colonies. The king rejected the petition.

In the summer of 1775, Washington arrived in Boston and began to train the army. In the fall, he approved a plan to invade Canada. **Benedict Arnold** led the attack on Canada in the winter of 1775. But the attack failed, and the Americans returned home.

3. How did the British king respond to the Olive Branch Petition?

The British Retreat from Boston
(pages 162–163)

Why did British troops leave Boston?

The Continental Army surrounded British forces in Boston. Cannon and other weapons were brought in to help the Continental Army. Armed with these heavy guns, Washington moved his troops to a place overlooking Boston. The British moved out of Boston because of this threat.

More than 1,000 Loyalists left with the British. Feelings against Britain were so strong in Boston that the Loyalists did not feel safe.

4. How was the Continental Army able to force British troops out of Boston?

Common Sense Is Published
(page 163)

What was Common Sense?

In early 1776, most Americans still wanted to be a part of Britain. But Thomas Paine, an English immigrant, helped to change their minds. Paine published *Common Sense*. This was a pamphlet in which he argued for independence from Britain.

He believed that all kings and queens were dishonest. He also did not agree that staying with Britain would be better for the American economy. He said America should follow its own destiny.

Common Sense sold more than 100,000 copies in three months.

5. Why was Common Sense important?

A Time of Decision (pages 163–164)

What did the Continental Congress do?

On June 7, Richard Henry Lee of Virginia introduced an important *resolution*. It said that all political ties between the colonies and Britain were ended.

Some of the representatives in Congress were not ready to vote on the resolution. But they did set up a committee to write a **Declaration of Independence**. The committee assigned **Thomas Jefferson** the job of writing the Declaration.

On July 2, 1776, the Continental Congress considered Lee's resolution again. This time the resolution passed, and the colonies considered themselves independent.

6. What resolution did the Continental Congress pass on July 2, 1776?

The Declaration Is Adopted
(pages 164–165)

What ideas did the Declaration of Independence include?

The Second Continental Congress adopted the Declaration of Independence on July 4, 1776. The Declaration is based on the ideas of John Locke, a British *philosopher*. He said that people have certain rights that a government cannot take away.

In the Declaration, Jefferson explained that when a government doesn't protect the rights of its citizens it loses its right to govern. The people then have the right to change the government. The Declaration also listed the reasons for breaking with Britain and then declared the colonies to be independent states.

7. What did Jefferson think should happen to a government that does not protect people's rights?

Chapter **6** *The Declaration of Independence (pages 166–169)*

The Declaration of Independence

BEFORE YOU READ

In the last section, you read about events that led to the Declaration of Independence.

In this section, you will learn about the Declaration of Independence itself.

AS YOU READ

Use this informal outline to take notes on the Declaration of Independence.

I. The Preamble
  A.
  B.
II. The Right of the people to Control Their Government
  A.
  B.
  C.
  D.
III. Tyrannical Acts of the British King
  A.
  B.
  C.
  D.
  E.
  F.

IV. Efforts of the Colonies to Avoid Separation
  A.
  B.
  C.
V. The Colonies are Declared Free and Independent
  A.
  B.
  C.

TERMS & NAMES

unalienable Unable to be taken away

grievances Complaints

tyrant A ruler who uses power unjustly or cruelly

quartering Providing housing

petitioned for redress Asked for the correction of wrongs

Preamble; The Right of the People to Control Their Government (page 166)

***What** does the Preamble to the Constitution state?*
The Second Continental Congress adopted the Declaration of Independence on July 4, 1776. The Declaration voiced the reasons for separating from Britain and stated some principles of government. It was written by Thomas Jefferson.

The Preamble, or introduction, states that the American people had decided to break away from Britain and become a separate nation. It also says that the document will explain the reasons for the separation.

The Declaration then goes on to state that all people have certain **unalienable** rights. These rights include life, liberty, and the right to seek happiness.

People set up governments to protect these rights. In exchange, the people give the governments certain powers. The Declaration says that the people have a right to act when a government destroys their rights. They can do away with the government, or they can form a new one. The Declaration states that because the British government had repeatedly taken away the Americans' rights, the American colonists had the right to form a new government.

1. **Why did the Declaration of Independence state that the colonists had the right to form a new government?**

   _____

   _____

Tyrannical Acts of the British King
(pages 167–168)

What offenses did the king commit against the colonists?

The Declaration of Independence then lists 27 offenses by the British king and others against the colonies. This list of **grievances** helps to explain why it became necessary to seek independence.

The Declaration states that the king refused to approve laws that the colonists needed. The king also had demanded that colonists give up their right to representation in government—he was acting as a **tyrant.** In addition, he had tried to keep the colonies from growing and had refused to set up a system of justice.

The Declaration states that the king and others had tried to rule the colonies with laws that were completely different from their own laws. Then the Declaration goes on to say what the laws tried to do. They provided for the **quartering** of British troops by the colonists, taxation without representation, taking away the right to trial by jury, and stopping the meeting of colonial legislatures.

2. Why did the Declaration of Independence list 27 offenses by the British king?

_____

_____

_____

Efforts of the Colonies to Avoid Separation; The Colonies Are Declared Free and Independent (pages 168–169)

What happened when the colonists petitioned the British king?

The Declaration of Independence states that when the colonists **petitioned for redress,** the king rejected their petitions. The colonists also had informed the British people about the unjust way that Parliament had treated them. They had asked them to speak out against Parliament's treatment. But the British had not listened.

Finally, the Declaration of Independence states that the document had listed the facts. It then declares the colonies free and independent states, with no loyalty to Britain or the king. It says that the colonies, as free and independent states, have all the powers that such states have. The Declaration of Independence was signed by 56 representatives from the 13 original states.

3. How did the British king respond to the colonists' grievances?

_____

_____

_____

Chapter ❻ The Road to Revolution; The Declaration of Independence

Glossary/After You Read

delegate A person given power to act for others

enforce To carry out

fortify To strengthen and secure

intolerant Unwilling or unable to accept differences

loyal Faithful to

olive branch A symbol of peace

petition A request

philosopher A lover of wisdom, knowledge, and learning

protest To object to

quarter To house

rebel A person who opposes a government or ruler

repeal To cancel

resolution An opinion voted on by an official assembly

restore To bring back

retreat To withdraw

self-defense Protecting oneself from physical attack

smuggle To import or export against the law

spy A person employed by a nation to gain secret information about its enemies

tax Money paid to a government

Terms & Names

A. Fill in the blanks with the letter of the term that best completes the sentence.

a. Boston Tea Party d. Benedict Arnold
b. First Continental Congress e. committees of correspondence
c. Quartering Act

1. To enforce the Proclamation of 1763, Parliament passed the _____, which required the colonists to house British soldiers.

2. Samuel Adams helped form _____, groups throughout the colonies that exchanged letters about colonial matters.

3. The protest against the Tea Act organized by the Sons of Liberty became known as the _____.

4. Colonial delegates met at the _____ to discuss what to do about Parliament's passing of the Intolerable Acts.

5. _____ was the colonial officer who helped to launch a failed attack against the British in Canada.

B. Write the letter of the name or term next to the description that explains it best.

a. Thomas Jefferson e. Loyalists i. Sons of Liberty
b. boycott f. Declaration of Independence j. *Common Sense*
c. John Adams g. Samuel Adams
d. Stamp Act h. Intolerable Acts

_____ 1. A law passed by Parliament that placed a tax on items such as contracts and newspapers

_____ 2. A refusal to buy goods

_____ 3. Secret colonial groups organized to oppose British policies

_____ 4. A leader of Boston's Sons of Liberty

_____ 5. Lawyer who defended the British soldiers involved in the Boston Massacre

_____ 6. A group of harsh laws passed by Parliament to punish Massachusetts for the Boston Tea Party

_____ 7. Colonists who supported the British

_____ 8. Thomas Paine's pamphlet in support of independence

_____ 9. Author of the Declaration of Independence

_____ 10. Document that established America's independence

Main Ideas

1. How did colonists protest the Stamp Act?

_____

_____

2. Why were colonists angry about British officers using writs of assistance?

_____

_____

3. Who won the battles of Lexington and Concord?

_____

_____

4. What did colonial leaders decide at the Second Continental Congress?

_____

_____

5. What ideas of John Locke did Thomas Jefferson include in the Declaration of Independence?

_____

_____

Thinking Critically

Answer the following questions on a separate sheet of paper.

1. Why did many colonists believe that the British Parliament's attempts to tax them were against their rights?

2. Why do you think the colonists were able to win early battles against a more experienced, better-equipped army?

Chapter **7** Section 1 (pages 177–183)

The Early Years of the War

BEFORE YOU READ

In the last chapter, you read about the events that led the colonies to declare independence from Britain.

In this section, you will read how Americans were forced to choose whether to support the Patriots or the British.

AS YOU READ

Use this chart to take notes on the early battles in the Revolutionary War.

Battle	Date	Outcome

TERMS & NAMES

George Washington The commander of the Continental Army

mercenary A professional soldier hired to fight for a foreign country

strategy An overall plan of action

rendezvous A meeting

Battles of Saratoga The series of conflicts that led to the surrender of the British general Burgoyne and his troops at Saratoga

Americans Divided; Creating an Army

(pages 177–179)

What difficulties did George Washington face as commander of the Continental Army?

The issue of separating from Great Britain split Americans. Between 20 and 30 percent were Loyalists. About 40 to 45 percent were Patriots. The rest were *neutral*. Patriots and Loyalists came from all walks of life. Both sides came from all parts of America. New England and Virginia had many Patriots. Northern cities and the South had many Loyalists. The war also divided Native Americans and African Americans.

In 1775, **George Washington** took command of the Continental Army. It was hard for him to raise an army. At first, the Continental Army was formed from state *militias*. These were made up of untrained

volunteers. Later, men enlisted in the army. At first, their terms of service were short. Congress did not give the army enough supplies.

Martha Washington and other women helped the army. They cooked, did laundry, and nursed sick or wounded soldiers. Some women, like Mary Hays—called "Molly Pitcher"—helped fight. Washington's main goal for his army was to survive. He needed to win some battles and avoid a big defeat.

1. **Why was George Washington's job as commander of the Continental Army difficult?**

_____

_____

Struggle for the Middle States
(pages 179–180)

How *did the Continental Army attract new recruits?*
One British goal was to conquer cities on the coast.
That way, their navy could bring them troops and
supplies. Then they would march inland.

In July 1776, Britain's General William Howe
arrived in New York with a large army. It included
Hessian **mercenaries**, or soldiers hired to fight for a
foreign country. The two armies fought to take New
York. By December, the American army had to retreat.
It crossed the Delaware River into Pennsylvania. The
winter weather was hard on the badly supplied
Americans. The soldiers' spirits were low. Thomas
Paine wrote pamphlets urging them to keep fighting.

George Washington wanted a quick victory. On
December 25, he led his troops back across the
Delaware River. They surprised and defeated the
Hessians at Trenton. The Americans gained needed
supplies. They won again at Princeton a few days
later. This showed that Washington was a good
general. His army began to attract new *recruits*.

**2. What was the result of the Continental
Army's early victories?**

_____

_____

Britain's Strategy; Battles Along the Mohawk (pages 180–182)

What *was the British army's overall plan of action
in the Revolutionary War?*
The British had a **strategy**, an overall plan of action.
It was to seize the Hudson River valley so they could
cut off New England from other states. The plan
called for three British armies to meet at Albany,
New York. Burgoyne and his troops would come from
Canada. St. Leger and his troops would come from
Lake Ontario. Howe and his troops would come from
New York City.

Burgoyne had problems that slowed his journey to
Albany. Yet, he still looked forward to the **rendezvous,**
or meeting, with the others. But Howe decided to try to
capture Philadelphia and George Washington. He
defeated Washington and took Philadelphia. But he did
not capture Washington. Nor did he go to Albany.

St. Leger's troops included Iroquois led by the
Mohawk chief Joseph Brant. On their way to Albany,
St. Leger's army tried to capture Fort Stanwix. It was
in the Mohawk River valley in New York. In August
1777, American general Benedict Arnold led a small
army up the Mohawk River. To scare the British,
Arnold spread a rumor that he had a large army. St.
Leger believed the rumor and fled quickly. He left
behind cannon and supplies. He did not go to Albany.

**3. What was the British strategy in the
Revolutionary War?**

_____

_____

Saratoga: A Turning Point
(pages 182–183)

Why *did Benedict Arnold betray the Americans?*
Burgoyne's army was running out of supplies. A
raiding party went to see what it could find. New
England troops beat the raiders at the Battle of
Bennington. It took place in August of 1777. Even
so, Burgoyne's army headed toward Albany. On the
way, it met an American army led by General Gates.
They met near Saratoga, New York. There, the
Americans had built *fortifications*. Burgoyne's army
tried to break through so it could go on to Albany. At
the same time, General Arnold led an attack on the
British at a nearby farm. But he didn't defeat them.

A few weeks later, Arnold led more charges
against the British. The Americans forced Burgoyne's
forces to retreat. The British went to a former camp at
Saratoga. The Americans surrounded them and fired
on them day and night. Burgoyne surrendered. This
series of conflicts is called the **Battles of Saratoga**.

Saratoga had two results. Arnold felt that Congress
had not given him enough reward for his actions. He
grew bitter. He also married a Loyalist wife. In time,
he became a *traitor* to the American army. Also, the
victory at Saratoga was a turning point in the war. It
caused European nations to think that the Americans
might win. Several nations decided to help America.

4. Why did Benedict Arnold turn traitor?

_____

_____

Name _____   Date _____

The War Expands

BEFORE YOU READ

In the last section, you read about early battles in the Revolutionary War.

In this section, you will learn why and how the Revolutionary War spread to the sea and the frontier.

AS YOU READ

Use this diagram to take notes on how European allies helped the Americans during the Revolutionary War.

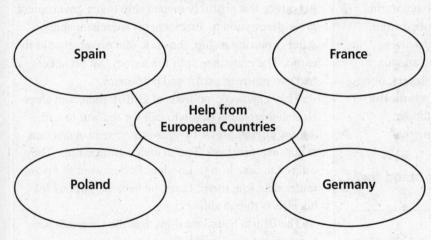

	TERMS & NAMES

ally A country that agrees to help another country achieve a common goal

Marquis de Lafayette A French nobleman who volunteered to serve in Washington's army

bayonet A long steel knife attached to the end of a gun

desert To leave military duty without intending to return

privateer Privately owned ship that a wartime government gives permission to attack an enemy's merchant ships

James Forten A 14-year-old African-American sailor who later became famous for his efforts to end slavery

John Paul Jones Continental officer and commander of the *Bonhomme Richard* who won the most famous sea battle of the war

Help from Abroad; Europeans Help Washington (pages 184–186)

How did the Europeans help the American army?
In the fall of 1776, Congress sent Benjamin Franklin to Paris. His job was to ask France to become an **ally** of the United States. An ally is a country that agrees to help another country achieve a common goal. France was bitter over losing the French and Indian War. The French wanted *revenge* against Britain. So they decided to help the American colonies gain their freedom.

News of the victory at Saratoga reached France. Then France agreed to become America's ally. The French king recognized U.S. independence. He signed two treaties of alliance with the United States. France sent funds, supplies, and troops to America.

In 1779, France persuaded its ally, Spain, to help the Americans, too. The Spanish governor of Louisiana captured Natchez and Baton Rouge. These were British forts in the Mississippi Valley. Then his army took

Mobile. In 1781, it took Pensacola in West Florida.

By entering the war, France and Spain forced the British to fight several enemies on land and sea. The British had to station troops in many places. Spain gained new land for its empire in North America.

Several army officers from Europe helped America. The **Marquis de Lafayette** was a French nobleman who served in Washington's army. He commanded an army division. He fought many battles. His men loved him because he shared their hardships and bought them warm clothes. He also persuaded the French king to send French troops to help the United States.

The Germans Baron de Kalb and Baron von Steuben also helped the American army. Kalb died fighting for the Americans. Steuben taught American soldiers how to march. He also taught the use of weapons, such as the **bayonet**, a long knife attached to the end of a gun.

1. In what ways did the Europeans help Washington's army?

_____

_____

Winter at Valley Forge (pages 186–187)

Why *was Valley Forge important?*

In late 1777, Britain's General Howe forced Washington to retreat from Philadelphia. That winter, Washington and his army camped at Valley Forge. They were short on supplies. The men suffered very much. Because of that, Valley Forge stands for the great hardships the Americans lived through during the war. At Valley Forge, many soldiers died from *malnutrition*, exposure to the cold, and diseases.

In spite of the hard times, Washington and his soldiers did not quit. Some soldiers did **desert,** or leave military duty without planning to return. But most of the army stayed together. They did so because they loved their country and Genereal Washington.

2. What did Valley Forge come to stand for?

_____

_____

War on the Frontier (pages 187–188)

What *did George Rogers Clark do in the Revolutionary War?*

In 1777, a 24-year-old man named George Rogers Clark wanted to defend the Western *frontier* from the British. He persuaded the governor of Virginia that he was right. Clark raised an army. He and his men captured British posts in the West. They captured Kaskaskia on the Mississippi River. Then they took a fort at Vincennes in present-day Indiana. Clark's victories gave Americans a hold on a large region. It stretched between the Great Lakes and the Ohio River.

3. How did George Rogers Clark defend the Western frontier?

_____

_____

War at Sea; A Naval Hero (pages 188–189)

What *role did privateers play in the Revolutionary War?*

By 1777, there was war at sea. Britain had about 100 warships off the American coast. This let Britain control the Atlantic trade routes. But American privateers attacked British merchant ships. A **privateer** is a privately owned ship that a government gives permission to attack enemy merchant ships. After capturing a ship, the crew of a privateer sold its cargo. The crew then split the money. So privateers had two motives, profit and patriotism.

They captured hundreds of British merchant ships. British merchants began to call for the war to end. **James Forten** was a 14-year-old African-American sailor on a privateer. The British captured him. They offered to take him to London. Forten went to prison rather than join them. Later, he became famous for his efforts to end slavery.

The British had more ships than the United States. Even so, the Continental Navy scored many victories against Britain. **John Paul Jones** was a U.S. officer who commanded the *Bonhomme Richard*. He won the most famous sea battle of the war. He defeated a larger British warship. Jones's success against the best navy in the world made the British angry. But it inspired Americans.

4. How did privateers help the Americans in the Revolutionary War?

_____

_____

Chapter **7** Section 3 (pages 190–194)

The Path to Victory

BEFORE YOU READ

In the last section, you read about how the Revolutionary War expanded to the frontier and the sea.

In this section, you will read how the Americans won the Revolutionary War.

AS YOU READ

Use this time line to take notes on the Revolutionary War in the South.

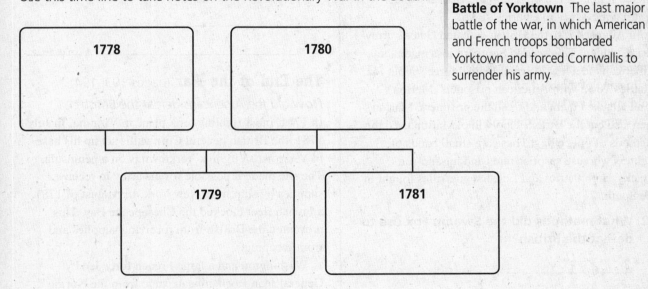

1778

1780

1779

1781

TERMS & NAMES

Lord Cornwallis British general who led an army in Camden, South Carolina

guerrillas Small bands of fighters who weaken the enemy with surprise raids and hit-and-run attacks

pacifist Opposed to war

Battle of Yorktown The last major battle of the war, in which American and French troops bombarded Yorktown and forced Cornwallis to surrender his army.

Savannah and Charles Town
(pages 190–191)

What caused the British to invade the South?

The British believed that most Southerners were Loyalists. So in 1778, the British decided to invade the South. After three years of fighting, the British had not won the war. They had captured many Northern cities. But they could not control the countryside. The British thought that if they gained territory in the South, Southern Loyalists would hold it for them.

There were two other reasons the British moved the war to the South. They expected large numbers of Southern slaves to join them because the British promised slaves their freedom. Also, Britain's West Indian colonies were close to Southern seaports. British troops were stationed in the West Indies. If the

British captured Southern ports, they could move troops between the two regions.

In 1778, the British captured Savannah, Georgia. From there, they conquered most of Georgia. In 1780, a British army trapped American forces in Charles Town. Five thousand Americans had to surrender. This was most of the Southern army. It was the worst disaster of the war for the Americans.

1. Why did the British move the war to the South?

_____

_____

_____

The Swamp Fox and Guerrilla Fighting
(page 191)

How did the Swamp Fox help the American army?

After the loss at Charles Town, General Gates formed a new Southern army. It headed for Camden, South Carolina. Its job was to fight the British forces led by **Lord Cornwallis.**

The American army met a band of Patriots. Their leader was Francis Marion, the "Swamp Fox." He told Gates about the swamplands along the coast of South Carolina. Gates sent Marion to destroy boats on the Santee River. This would stop the British from sending messages to Charles Town.

In August 1780, the British defeated Gates's army near Camden. This second Southern loss made the Americans feel low. A small British force set out for Charles Town with American prisoners. Marion's band attacked them and freed the prisoners. Marion's men also cut the British supply line. Marion used the methods of **guerrillas.** These are small bands of fighters who use surprise raids and hit-and-run attacks. Both Patriot and Loyalist guerrillas fought in the South.

2. What methods did the Swamp Fox use to defeat the British?

_____

_____

_____

The Tide Turns (page 193)

Why did the tide turn against the British?

In the South, some battles were brutal. One such battle was Kings Mountain. In it, the Americans killed almost 1,000 Loyalist and British soldiers. Many were killed after they gave up. The killings were in revenge for earlier British cruelty.

After Gates's defeat at Camden, Washington put General Nathanael Greene in charge of the Southern

army. Greene had been a Quaker. Most Quakers are **pacifist,** or opposed to war. Greene's church cast him out because he believed in the war against Britain.

The British had the edge because of superior firepower. So Greene avoided full-scale battles. Instead, American forces let the British chase them around the countryside to wear them out. Fighting dragged into its sixth year. Opposition to the war grew in Britain.

3. What caused the tide to turn in favor of the Americans?

_____

_____

_____

The End of the War (pages 193–194)

How did the Americans defeat the British?

In 1781, most fighting took place in Virginia. In July 1781, the British general Cornwallis set up his base in Yorktown, Virginia. Yorktown is on a peninsula. The site made it possible for his army to receive supplies by ship from New York. In August of 1781, a French fleet blocked the Chesapeake Bay. This prevented the British from receiving supplies and from escaping.

Washington and a large French force led by General Jean Rochambeau came from the North. They trapped Cornwallis on the peninsula. In the **Battle of Yorktown,** the American and French troops bombarded Yorktown. Cornwallis surrendered his 8,000 men. Yorktown was the last big battle of the war. British leaders had to resign.

4. How did the Revolutionary War end?

_____

_____

_____

The Legacy of the War

BEFORE YOU READ

In the last section, you read about the end of the Revolutionary War.
In this section, you will read how the new nation faced issues and an uncertain future.

AS YOU READ

Use this diagram to take notes on the effects of the Revolutionary War.

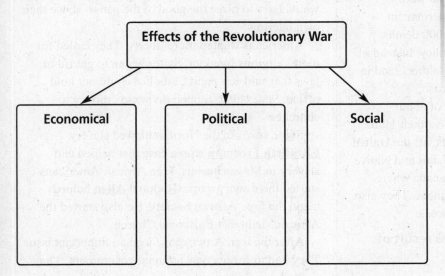

TERMS & NAMES

Treaty of Paris of 1783 Peace treaty that ended the Revolutionary War

republicanism Government in which the people rule

Elizabeth Freeman An African-American woman who sued for her freedom in a Massachusetts court and won

Richard Allen An African-American preacher who helped start the Free African Society and the African Methodist Episcopal Church

Why the Americans Won *(pages 195–196)*

What *were America's strengths during the war?*
The Americans won independence even though they faced many obstacles. They lacked training, experience, supplies, and weapons. The British forces ranked among the best trained in the world. They had experience and supplies. Yet, the Americans had four advantages over the British. 1) They had better leadership. 2) They received foreign aid. 3) They knew the land better than the British did. 4) They were more motivated.

1. Name four advantages the Americans had in the war against Britain.

_____

_____

_____

The Treaty of Paris *(pages 196–197)*

What *was the Treaty of Paris of 1783?*
The **Treaty of Paris of 1783** was the peace treaty that ended the Revolutionary War. It included the following six conditions. 1) The United States was an independent nation. 2) Its western boundary was the Mississippi River. Canada was the northern boundary. Spanish Florida was the southern boundary. 3) The United States would receive the right to fish in the Atlantic Ocean off Canada's coast. 4) Each side would pay its debts to the other. 5) The British would return any slaves they had captured. 6) Congress would tell the states to return property they had seized from Loyalists.

Neither country lived up to the treaty. Americans did not repay prewar debts to British merchants. They did not return Loyalist property. The British did not return slaves. The British did not give up forts in the Great Lakes area.

2. What were the conditions of the Treaty of Paris?

_____

_____

_____

Costs of the War (page 197)

What were America's costs of the war?

An estimated 25,700 Americans died in the war. About 1,400 were missing. About 8,200 were wounded. Many of the wounded had permanent disabilities. The British had about 10,000 deaths.

Many surviving soldiers had no money. Instead of back pay, the government gave some soldiers land in the west. Many sold their land to get cash.

The war left the nation with a debt of about $27 million. Thousands of Loyalists lost their land. Between 60,000 and 100,000 Loyalists left the United States. These included African Americans and Native Americans. Most Loyalists went to Canada where they created new towns and new provinces. They also brought English traditions to French areas.

3. What had Americans lost as a result of the war?

_____

_____

_____

Issues After the War (pages 198–199)

How did the war change Americans' ideas about government?

The American Revolution was not just a war. It was also a change in ideas. Before the war, Americans had wanted their rights as English citizens. But after declaring independence, Americans gave up that goal. They adopted the idea of **republicanism**. This idea stated that instead of a king, the people would rule. The government would gain its authority from the citizens. It would be responsible to them. People would have to place the good of the nation above their own interests.

Americans wanted more liberty. They called for more religious freedom. States began to get rid of laws that said Jews and Catholics could not hold office. States also stopped giving tax money to churches.

Some states in the North outlawed slavery. **Elizabeth Freeman** won a case that helped end slavery in Massachusetts. Free African Americans started their own groups. **Richard Allen** helped begin the Free African Society. He also started the African Methodist Episcopal Church.

After the war, Americans faced an important issue. They had to form a new national government. They needed one that would protect citizens' rights and economic freedoms.

4. How did Americans' goals for government change after declaring independence?

_____

_____

_____

Glossary/After You Read

fortification Built-up earthen wall

frontier A region that is not settled

malnutrition Lack of enough healthful food

militia A group of citizens trained to be soldiers

neutral Not favoring either side in a conflict

recruit A newly enlisted member of the armed forces

revenge To get back at someone

traitor A person who helps his or her country's enemies

Terms & Names

A. Choose the letter of the term or name that correctly fits the description or definition.

_____ 1. Professional soldiers hired to fight for a foreign country are called
   a. recruits.   c. mercenaries.
   b. militias.   d. traitors.

_____ 2. The series of conflicts that led to the surrender of the British General Burgoyne are known as the
   a. Battles of Saratoga.   c. winter at Valley Forge.
   b. war on the frontier.   d. Battle of Bennington.

_____ 3. A French nobleman who volunteered to serve in Washington's army was
   a. Joseph Brant.   c. Baron von Steuben.
   b. Benjamin Franklin.   d. Marquis de Lafayette.

_____ 4. The Continental officer and commander of the *Bonhomme Richard* who won the most famous sea battle of the Revolutionary War was
   a. George Washington.   c. William Howe.
   b. John Paul Jones.   d. George Rogers Clark.

_____ 5. Francis Marion, the "Swamp Fox," weakened the British with surprise raids and hit-and-run attacks with small bands of fighters known as
   a. guerrillas.   c. allies.
   b. pacifists.   d. frontiersmen.

B. Write the letter of the name or term that matches the description.

a. James Forten   f. republicanism
b. bayonets   g. rendezvous
c. desert   h. pacifist
d. Treaty of Paris of 1783 i. ally
e. strategy   j. Lord Cornwallis

_____ 1. An overall plan of action

_____ 2. A meeting

_____ 3. A country that agrees to help another country achieve a common goal

_____ 4. Long steel knives attached to the ends of guns

_____ 5. To leave military duty without intending to return

_____ 6. A 14-year-old African-American sailor who later became famous for his efforts to end slavery

_____ 7. British general who led the armies in the South and surrendered at Yorktown

_____ 8. Person opposed to war

_____ 9. Peace treaty that ended the Revolutionary War

_____ 10. The idea that the people, not a king, should rule government

Main Ideas

1. Why was Saratoga a turning point in the Revolutionary War?

_____

_____

2. Why were France and Spain willing to help the United States fight the British in the Revolutionary War?

_____

_____

3. How did the Revolutionary War expand to the Western frontier and the sea?

_____

_____

4. What were three reasons that the Americans defeated the British in the South?

_____

_____

5. What were four issues facing the United States after the war?

_____

_____

Thinking Critically

Answer the following questions on a separate sheet of paper.

1. Would the Revolutionary War have had a different outcome if European countries had remained neutral? Explain your answer.

2. Do you think the costs of the war were worth the outcome of the war? Why or why not?

Name _____ Date _____

The Confederation Era

BEFORE YOU READ

In the last chapter, you read about the issues that faced the United States after winning the Revolutionary War.

In this section, you will learn about the early years of the United States.

AS YOU READ

Use this diagram to take notes on the powers the national government had under the Articles of Confederation.

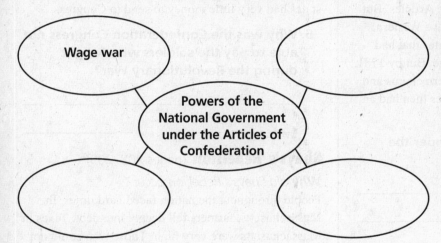

- Wage war
- Powers of the National Government under the Articles of Confederation

TERMS & NAMES
Wilderness Road A road that traveled westward over the Appalachian Mountains into Kentucky
republic A government in which the people elect representatives to govern
Articles of Confederation The first government of the United States
Land Ordinance of 1785 Law that set up townships in the Western lands, which became known as the Northwest Territory
Northwest Territory Land that formed the modern states of Ohio, Indiana, Michigan, Illinois, Wisconsin, and part of Minnesota
Northwest Ordinance Law that organized the Northwest Territory
Shays's Rebellion Anti-tax protest by farmers

Moving West (page 205)

What *was the Wilderness Road?*

In 1775, Daniel Boone and 30 others helped to build the **Wilderness Road.** This road ran westward over the Appalachian Mountains into Kentucky. Settlers traveled the road on foot and on horseback.

Some Native Americans hunted, fished, and lived in the Kentucky region. The movement of the settlers there led to violence between the Native Americans and the settlers. But the settlers continued coming. By 1790, about 100,000 Americans lived there.

1. How did settlers use the Wilderness Road?

_____

_____

New State Governments (page 206)

What *kind of governments did the independent colonies set up?*

After the colonies became independent, each state set out to create its own government. Some states created governments with separate branches. Some included a bill of rights as part of the constitution. All the states set up republican forms of government. In a **republic,** people choose representatives to govern them.

2. What form of government did all the new states set up?

_____

_____

The Articles of Confederation
(pages 206–207)

What *were the Articles of Confederation?*

In 1776, the Continental Congress met to set up a national government. They agreed on a plan called the **Articles of Confederation**. It gave much power to the states and little power to the national government. The government was run by a Confederation Congress. Each state had one vote in the Congress.

Under the Articles, most important powers were left to the states. For example, the states had the power to tax. The states were also left in control of the Western lands.

In 1778, eight states had *ratified* the Articles. But some of the small states that did not have Western lands refused to sign. They felt that states that had Western lands would have an advantage. But by 1781, all of the states had given up the Western claims and accepted the Articles. The United States then had an official government.

3. Who had the most powers under the Articles of Confederation?

_____

_____

The Northwest Ordinance (page 207)

What *was the Northwest Ordinance?*

One of the most important questions facing the Confederation Congress was what to do with the Western lands. So Congress passed laws on how to divide and govern these lands. The **Land Ordinance of 1785** staked out six-mile square plots, called townships. These lands later became the **Northwest Territory**. It included land that formed the states of Ohio, Indiana, Michigan, Illinois, Wisconsin, and part of Minnesota.

The **Northwest Ordinance** described how the Northwest Territory was to be governed. It outlined when the territories could govern themselves. It also established settlers' rights. This law was important because it set a pattern for the orderly growth of the United States.

4. What did the Northwest Ordinance do?

_____

_____

Weaknesses of the Articles (page 208)

What *major problems did the Confederation Congress face?*

The Confederation Congress had few successes other than the Northwest Ordinance. The new nation faced problems that the Congress did not have the power to solve.

One problem was *debt*. The Congress had borrowed large amounts of money during the Revolutionary War. Much of the money was owed to soldiers of its own army. Even if the Congress wanted to pay the soldiers, it did not have power to *levy* taxes. It depended on the states to send money. But the states had very little money to send to Congress.

5. Why was the Confederation Congress not able to pay the soldiers who fought during the Revolutionary War?

_____

_____

Shays's Rebellion (pages 208–209)

Why *did Shays's Rebellion occur?*

People throughout the nation faced hard times. In Massachusetts, farmers fell deeply into debt. Taxes in Massachusetts were very high. Those who could not pay their debts lost their land and were jailed.

In 1787, farmers in Massachusetts held a tax protest. They asked the state legislature for relief from their debts. The legislature refused. The farmers rebelled, led by Daniel Shays. This rebellion became known as **Shays's Rebellion**. The Massachusetts *militia* killed four protesters. Although the protesters were defeated, the protest won the sympathy of many Americans. Many people felt that the nation needed to have a stronger national government to help solve its problems.

6. What caused Shays's Rebellion?

_____

_____

Name _____   Date _____

Creating the Constitution

BEFORE YOU READ

In the last section, you read about the problems the nation faced under the Articles of Confederation.

In this section, you will learn how these problems led to the creation of the Constitution.

AS YOU READ

Use this chart to take notes on how the following plans and compromises helped to form a new plan of government.

PLAN/COMPROMISE	WHAT IT CALLED FOR
Virginia Plan	
New Jersey Plan	
Great Compromise	
Three-Fifths Compromise	

TERMS & NAMES

Constitutional Convention Meeting in Philadelphia called to change the Articles of Confederation

James Madison One of the leaders of the Constitutional Convention

Virginia Plan Plan that called for representation in the legislature to be based on states' population or wealth

New Jersey Plan Plan that called for each state to have equal representation in the legislature

Great Compromise Called for a two-house legislature with representation based on population in one house and equal representation in the other house

Three-Fifths Compromise Called for counting three-fifths of the slave population for representation and taxation

A Constitutional Convention Is Called
(pages 212–213)

Why did Alexander Hamilton want the states to send representatives to Philadelphia?
In September 1786, *delegates* from five states met in Annapolis, Maryland. They wanted to help promote trade among the states by creating national trade laws. But creating such changes would require *amending* the Articles of Confederation. Under the Articles, the national government had no power to regulate trade among the states.

The Annapolis delegates called for the states to send representatives to Philadelphia the following May to discuss such changes. In the meantime, Shays's Rebellion broke out. Fearing the rebellion might spread, 12 states sent delegates to Philadelphia in 1787.

1. Why did 12 states send delegates to Philadelphia in 1787?

_____

_____

The Convention's Delegates (page 213)

What were the delegates at the Constitutional Convention like?
Fifty-five delegates came to the **Constitutional Convention** in Philadelphia. They were an impressive group. About three-fourths had been representatives to the Continental Congress.

Most of the nation's leaders were there, including George Washington, Benjamin Franklin, and **James Madison.**

But not every American leader was there. Thomas Jefferson and John Adams were not at the meeting because they were overseas. Patrick Henry refused to go because he opposed the Convention.

In addition, there were no women, blacks, or Native Americans invited to participate in the Convention.

2. Who were some of the famous men at the Constitutional Convention?

_____

_____

The Delegates Assemble; The Convention Begins
(pages 213–214)

How did the delegates want to change the Articles of Confederation?

At first, the delegates did not have a clear idea about what they wanted to do. Some thought they would amend the Articles. Others thought they would set up a whole new government. They all agreed that the plan should protect people's rights. They all believed that the government needed to be strong enough to protect people's rights. But it should not be too strong to be controlled by the people.

The first order of business at the Convention was to elect a president. Every single delegate voted for George Washington. Next, the delegates had to decide on the rules for the Convention. The delegates decided that in order for everyone to speak freely and not be pressured by the politics of the time, the discussions would remain secret.

3. What kind of government did the delegates want to set up?

_____

_____

The Virginia Plan; The Great Compromise (pages 214–216)

What was the Great Compromise?

The first speaker at the Convention, Virginia's Edmund Randolph, proposed a whole new plan of government. The plan is known as the **Virginia Plan**. It called for three branches of government. The legislature would be made up of two houses and representatives from each state would be based on the state's population.

The larger states supported the plan. The smaller states opposed the plan because they believed that the larger states would have the most power.

New Jersey delegate William Paterson presented a different plan. It was called the **New Jersey Plan**. This plan called for a one-house legislature in which each state would have one vote. After some debate, the Virginia Plan won. The **Great Compromise** solved the problem of representation in the legislature. According to the compromise, the House of Representatives would

be based on state populations. But each state would have an equal number of votes in the Senate.

4. How did the Great Compromise settle the issue of representation in the legislature?

_____

_____

Slavery and the Constitution
(pages 216–217)

How did the Convention address the issue of slavery?

Next, the Convention had to decide who would be counted in the population of each state. The Southern states wanted slaves to be counted for representation but not taxation. The Northern states, who had fewer slaves than the Southern states, wanted slaves to be counted for taxation but not for representation. After some debate, the delegates reached the **Three-Fifths Compromise.** It said that three-fifths of the slave population would be counted to determine representation in the legislature and taxation. The Convention also agreed that Congress could not ban the slave trade until 1808.

5. What issue did the Three-Fifths Compromise settle?

_____

_____

Regulating Trade (page 217)

Who would control trade?

The delegates gave the national government the power to regulate trade. The national government could pass laws on how goods could be *exported*.

On September 15, 1787, all but three of the delegates voted to support the Constitution in its final form. Washington sent it to the Confederation Congress, and Congress sent it to the states to be ratified.

6. According to the new Constitution, who had the power to regulate trade?

_____

_____

Name _____ Date _____

Ratifying the Constitution

BEFORE YOU READ

In the last section, you read how the Constitution was created. In this section, you will learn how the Constitution was ratified.

AS YOU READ

Use this time line to take notes on the events that led to the ratification of the Constitution.

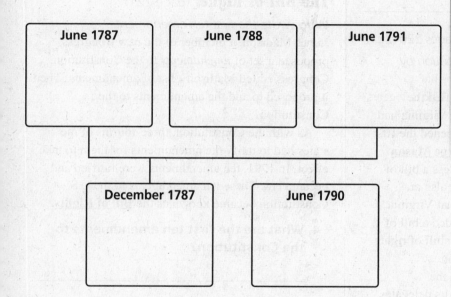

June 1787	June 1788	June 1791

December 1787	June 1790

TERMS & NAMES

federalism A system of government in which power is shared among the federal government and the states

Federalists People who supported ratification of the Constitution

Antifederalists People who opposed ratification of the Constitution

The Federalist **papers** Essays that explained and defended the Constitution

George Mason Influential Virginian who opposed ratification of the Constitution

Bill of Rights Set of amendments to the Constitution passed to protect individual rights

Federalists and Antifederalists

(pages 218–219)

Who were the Federalists and Antifederalists?
The framers of the Constitution knew that the Constitution would cause *controversy*. They began to work for its *ratification*.

The framers knew that people feared that the Constitution might give the national government too much power. The framers explained that the new Constitution was based on **federalism**. In a federal system, the national government and state governments share power.

The people who supported ratification were known as **Federalists**. People who opposed the Constitution were known as **Antifederalists**. They thought that the Constitution took too much power

away from the states. They also thought it did not guarantee people's rights. Both sides published their arguments in newspapers and pamphlets.

1. What side did the Federalists and Antifederalists take on the Constitution?

_____

_____

The Federalist Papers (pages 219–220)

Who wrote The Federalist *papers?*
The Federalists wrote and published essays in support of the Constitution. The best known essays are ***The Federalist* papers.** They were later published as a book called *The Federalist.*

The authors of *The Federalist* papers were Alexander Hamilton, James Madison, and John Jay. Jay had been the secretary of foreign affairs for the Confederation Congress.

Most of the newspapers supported the Constitution. As a result, they gave more publicity to the Federalists than the Antifederalists. Even so, opposition to ratification was strong in many areas.

2. What were *The Federalist* papers?

_____

_____

The Battle for Ratification (pages 220–221)

How many states ratified the Constitution by June 1788?

By late June 1788, nine states had ratified the Constitution. However, New York and Virginia had not yet voted. Virginia's convention opened the first week in June. Patrick Henry and **George Mason** refused to sign the final document unless a bill of rights was added. James Madison was also at Virginia's convention. He suggested that Virginia ratify the Constitution and recommended a bill of rights be added. With the addition of a bill of rights likely, Virginia ratified the Constitution.

The news that Virginia had ratified the Constitution reached New York while its delegates were still meeting. New York also ratified the

Constitution and called for a bill of rights to be added. Rhode Island became the last state to ratify the Constitution in 1790. By then, the new Congress had already written a bill of rights and submitted it to the states for approval.

3. Why were Virginia and New York reluctant to ratify the Constitution?

_____

_____

The Bill of Rights (page 221)

Who wrote the first ten amendments?

James Madison, a member of the new Congress, proposed a set of *amendments* to the Constitution. Congress edited Madison's list of amendments. Then it proposed to add the amendments to the Constitution.

As with the Constitution, three-fourths of the states had to ratify the amendments for them to take effect. In 1791, ten amendments were ratified and became law. These ten amendments to the U.S. Constitution became known as the **Bill of Rights**.

4. What are the first ten amendments to the Constitution?

_____

_____

Skillbuilder

Federalists	Antifederalists
• Supported removing some powers from the states and giving more powers to the national government	• Wanted important political powers to remain with the states
• Favored dividing powers among different branches of government	• Wanted the legislative branch to have more power than the executive
• Proposed a single person to lead the executive branch	• Feared that a strong executive might become a king or tyrant
	• Believed a bill of rights needed to be added to the Constitution to protect people's rights

1. Which group wanted the national government to have more power?

2. Which group was more in favor of adding a bill of rights to the Constitution?

Glossary/After You Read

amending Changing

amendments Formal changes to the Constitution

controversy A dispute between sides holding opposing views

debt Money owed

delegates People given power to act for others; representatives to a convention

exported Sent to another country for trade

levy To order to be paid

militia A group of citizens who receive military training but are only called in emergencies

ratification Approval

ratified Approved

Terms & Names

A. If the statement is true, write "true" on the line. If it is false, change the underlined word or words to make the statement true.

_____ 1. The Articles of Confederation gave little power to the national government and much power to the states.

_____ 2. The Land Ordinance of 1785 described how the Northwest Territory was to be governed.

_____ 3. The disagreement over the Virginia Plan and the New Jersey Plan was settled by the Three-Fifths Compromise.

_____ 4. Essays supporting the Constitution were published as *The Federalist papers*.

_____ 5. The first ten amendments to the Constitution are known as the Bill of Rights.

B. Write the letter of the name or term that matches the description.

a. Wilderness Road
b. Shays's Rebellion
c. Constitutional Convention
d. Virginia Plan

e. New Jersey Plan
f. federalism
g. Federalists
h. Antifederalists

_____ 1. People who wanted to ratify the Constitution

_____ 2. Plan that called for representation in the legislature to be based on population or wealth

_____ 3. An anti-tax protest by farmers

_____ 4. Road that ran across the Appalachian Mountains into Kentucky

_____ 5. Meeting held to discuss changes to the Articles of Confederation

Main Ideas

1. What was the purpose of the Northwest Ordinance?

_____

_____

2. What weakness of the Articles of Confederation led to money problems for the new nation?

_____

_____

3. Why did the smaller states oppose the Virginia Plan?

_____

_____

4. Why did the framers of the Constitution base the new plan of government on federalism?

_____

_____

5. Why did the Antifederalists want a bill of rights to be added to the Constitution?

_____

_____

Thinking Critically

Answer the following questions on a separate sheet of paper.

1. What were the main arguments for and against the Constitution?

2. Do you think the writers of the Constitution were right to compromise over the issue of slavery? Explain.

Name _____ Date _____

The Constitution Handbook (pages 232–239)

The Preamble and Article 1: The Legislature

BEFORE YOU READ

In Chapter 8, you saw how the Constitution was created.

In the Preamble and Article I, you will learn how the Preamble introduces the Constitution and how Congress is set up.

AS YOU READ

Use the chart below to take notes on the Preamble and on the powers of Congress.

Preamble	

Article 1: The Legislature
  House of Representatives
  Senate	

Preamble. Purpose of the Constitution

(page 232)

What does the Preamble do?

The **Preamble** is the introduction to the Constitution. It sets out to do two things. The first is to show the authority, or right to rule, of the new government. The Preamble states that this government is based on the approval of those who are to be governed. It is the people themselves who have the power to create a government. That is why the Constitution begins with the words, "We the people of the United States. . . . "

The second purpose of the Preamble is to state that this new government is being formed to:
- create a nation in which states work together
- set up and enforce fair laws
- keep peace within the country
- protect the country against attack
- ensure the well-being of the people, and
- make sure future citizens remain free.

1. What are the two purposes of the Preamble?

Article 1, Sections 1–6. The Organization of Congress (pages 233–235)

How are the House of Representatives and Senate different?

Article 1 of the Constitution sets up **Congress.** It is the legislative, or law-making, branch of government.

Congress is made up of two houses. Article 1, Section 2 sets up the **House of Representatives.** It is the lower house of Congress. Its members are elected every two years. The number of representatives each state has in the House is based on population. To be a member of the House, a person must be:
- 25 years old
- a U.S. citizen for seven years, and
- an inhabitant of the state where he or she was elected.

Section 2 also states that the representatives shall choose a Speaker of the House. The Speaker is the leader of the House.

This section also gives the House of Representatives the power of *impeachment*. It can bring official charges of wrongdoing against officials in other branches of government, including the president. The Senate has the power to hold trials in impeachment cases. It takes a two-thirds vote of the Senate to convict the impeached person. If convicted, the person is removed from office.

Article 1, Section 3 sets up the **Senate.** This is the upper house of Congress. Each state is represented by two senators. At the Constitutional Convention, the framers decided to have the state legislatures choose the senators for their own state. (Senators are now elected directly by the voters in each state because of the 17th Amendment.) Senators serve six-year terms. Every two years, one-third of the Senate seats are up for election. To be a senator, a person must be:

- 30 years old
- a U.S. citizen for nine years, and
- an inhabitant of the state that elected him or her.

Article 1, Section 4 states that Congress shall meet at least once every year. Article 1, Section 5 establishes how Congress shall conduct business, including:

- the quorum, or minimum number of representatives that need to be present for an official meeting to be held
- the power to set rules for meetings
- the keeping of records of meetings, and
- rules for adjournment, or ending meetings.

Article 1, Section 6 establishes how senators and representatives shall be paid. It also states that no senator or representative can be arrested while attending meetings in Congress. Nor can they be punished for anything said during debate. In addition, senators and representatives cannot hold any other office in the U.S. government while serving in Congress.

2. What are two important differences between the House of Representatives and the Senate?

Article 1, Sections 7–10. Powers of Congress (pages 236–239)

What powers does Congress have?

Article 1, Section 7 explains how new laws are passed. A *bill* may be introduced in either the House or the Senate. (Bills regarding revenue, or raising money, are an exception. They can only be introduced in the House of Representatives.) But it must be approved by a majority vote in both houses.

To become a law, a bill needs the approval of the president. Presidential approval is part of the system of **checks and balances.** It gives the president, the head of the executive branch, a say in legislation. If the president does not approve the bill, he or she can *veto,* or reject, it. The bill can still become law if two-thirds of both houses vote to *override* the veto. This procedure ensures that neither the president nor Congress has too much power.

Section 8 lists specific powers of Congress. These powers are often called **enumerated powers.** They include the power to tax, to borrow money, and to set up courts. Clauses 11–16 give Congress control over the military. Clause 17 gives Congress legislative control over the District of Columbia, the seat of the federal government.

Clause 18 is a unique clause. It gives Congress the power to do what is "necessary and proper" to carry out its other powers. This clause is called the **elastic clause** because it can be used to expand the powers of Congress. This is the basis of the **implied powers** of the federal government.

Section 9 tells what powers Congress does not have. For instance, the government cannot take away a citizen's right to a fair trial.

Section 10 tells what powers the states do not have. They cannot exercise the powers given to Congress in Section 8, such as making treaties or war. In addition, they cannot tax imports or exports.

3. How does Congress limit the power of the president?

Articles 2 and 3: The Executive and the Judiciary

BEFORE YOU READ

In the Preamble and Article I, you learned about the powers of Congress.

In Articles 2 and 3, you will read about the powers of the president and the powers of the judiciary.

AS YOU READ

Continue to use the chart you began in the last section to take notes on the powers of the executive and the judicial branches of government.

Article 2: The Executive	
Article 3: The Judiciary	

TERMS & NAMES

Electoral College Electors chosen by the states to elect the president and vice-president

succession Order in which the office of president is filled if it becomes vacant before an election

State of the Union Address Message delivered by the president each year

Supreme Court Highest federal court in the United States

Article 2. The Executive (pages 240–243)

What are the powers of the president?

Article 2 sets up the executive branch. Section 1.1 creates the offices of the president and the vice-president. It also sets their terms at four years. The president is the leader of the executive branch. The president's chief responsibility is to execute, or carry out, the laws of the nation.

Section 1.2 sets up the **Electoral College** to elect the president. The president and vice-president are elected by electors chosen by the states.

Section 1.3 created the original rules for the election of the president. In this system, the electors used only one ballot to elect both the president and the vice-president. The candidate that received the most votes became president. The candidate with the second most votes became vice-president.

This system did not work well. The election of 1796 resulted in a vice-president from a different political party than the president. The election of 1800 resulted in a tie between two candidates of the

same party. The House of Representatives went through many votes before settling the issue. (To prevent such problems from happening again, the 12th Amendment was passed in 1804. It called for separate ballots for president and vice–president.)

The Electoral College is still important. Each state has as many electors as it has senators and representatives in Congress. The candidate that gets the most votes in a state almost always gets all the electoral votes of that state.

Section 1.5 sets the qualifications for the president. To be president, a person must be:
- a natural-born citizen
- 35 years old, and
- a resident of the United States for 14 years.

Section 1.6 explains **succession,** or what happens if a president cannot complete his or her term. The vice-president takes the president's office if the president is unable to finish the term. The Congress has the power to decide who should become president if neither the president nor vice-president can finish the term.

Section 1.7 sets the president's salary. The salary cannot be changed during his or her term of office. In this way, the president cannot be punished or rewarded by payment for certain political or official acts. Section 1.8 establishes the oath of office.

Section 2.1 makes the president commander-in-chief of the armed forces. This authority helps ensure that *civilians* maintain control over the military. This clause also helps the executive branch balance the power of Congress to declare war.

Section 2.2 gives the president the power to appoint ambassadors, federal judges, and other officers of the U.S. government.

The Constitution states that presidential appointments to these offices are to be made "by and with the advice and consent of the Senate." In other words, the Senate must approve the president's appointments. The president can also make treaties. But these must also be approved by the Senate.

Section 3 sets out other duties for the president. These duties include the requirement to give Congress "information of the State of the Union." This requirement has led to the president's **State of the Union Address,** which is delivered each year. The subject of the address is the condition, or state, of the nation.

Section 4 explains that the president and other officers can be removed from office if they are impeached and convicted of certain crimes. These crimes include treason, bribery, and other serious offenses.

1. What is one example of checks and balances found in Article 2?

_____

_____

_____

_____

Article 3. The Judiciary (pages 244–245)

***What** are the powers of the federal courts?*
Article 3 sets up the judicial branch of the federal government. It established one **Supreme Court,** the highest court in the nation. But it allows for Congress to set up "inferior," or lower, federal courts.

Judges serve "during good behavior." In other words, they are appointed for life, unless they are found guilty of misbehavior. The salary of a judge cannot be lowered while the judge is in office.

Section 2 lists the kinds of cases that federal courts have jurisdiction, or authority, over. These cases include those that involve:

- ambassadors and other public officials
- admiralty and maritime issues, or issues related to shipping
- the U.S. government
- disagreements between two or more states, and
- disagreements between citizens of different states.

Section 2.3 again protects citizens' rights to a trial by jury. (See Article 1, Section 9.) Finally, Section 3 defines the crime of treason. It also sets limits on the punishments Congress can establish for treason.

2. What cases does the federal judiciary have jurisdiction over?

_____

_____

_____

_____

The Constitution Handbook (pages 246–249)

Articles 4–7: The States, Amendments, Federal Supremacy, and Ratification

BEFORE YOU READ

In Articles 2 and 3, you read about the powers of the executive and judicial branches.

Now you will see how Articles 4–7 grant specific powers to the national and state governments. You will also learn how the Constitution assures the supremacy of the national government.

TERMS & NAMES

extradition Procedure for returning a person charged with a crime to the state where the crime was committed

ratify To officially approve the Constitution or an Amendment to it

AS YOU READ

Continue your outline of the Constitution. Take notes on the relations among the states, how to amend the Constitution, how the Constitution was to be ratified, and the relation between the states and the national government.

Relations among states	
Amendments	
Ratification	
National government	

Article 4. Relations Among States

(pages 246–247)

How do the states relate to one another?
Article 4 sets out many principles of the federal system. It describes the relations among the states. It also describes the relations between the national government and the states.

Section 1 declares that the separate states must accept decisions, such as criminal convictions, that occur in other states. Section 2.2 allows for extradition. **Extradition** means that if a person charged with a crime in one state flees to another state, he or she must be returned to the state where the crime was committed.

Section 2 states that citizens of any of the United States are citizens of the whole nation. They have the same rights and privileges of citizenship no matter

which state they are in. However, slaves were not considered to be citizens. As a result, they did not have the rights of citizens.

Section 2.3 provides for the return of "people held to service or labor" to "the party to whom such service or labor be due." This clause was meant to ensure that runaway slaves be returned to their slaveholders. This shows that the Constitution recognized slavery as valid, even though the word "slavery" is not used. When the Thirteenth Amendment abolished slavery in 1865, it canceled this clause.

Section 3 describes the process for forming new states. It says that new states cannot be formed from any existing state without that state's approval. It also forbids the creation of a new state by joining together other states or parts of states unless the affected states and Congress approve.

Section 3.2 gives Congress the authority to regulate any territory or property that belongs to the United States.

Section 4 guarantees that the states will have a republican form of government. It also ensures that the national government will defend the states against invasion or domestic violence.

1. According to Article 4, what responsibilities do the states owe to one another?

_____

_____

Amending the Constitution; The Supremacy of the National Government; Ratification (pages 247–249)

How can the Constitution be amended?

Article 5 sets up two ways of amending, or changing, the Constitution. In both cases, it takes more votes to **ratify,** or officially approve, an amendment than to propose an amendment.

To propose an amendment, it takes two-thirds of

Congress or two-thirds of state legislatures. It takes three-fourths of state legislatures or state conventions to ratify an amendment.

Article 6, Section 1 states that the new federal government that takes power after ratification of the Constitution will pay the debts of the United States that existed while the Confederation Congress governed the nation.

Section 2 makes the laws of the federal government the supreme law of the land. If a state law is in conflict with a national law, it is the national law that must be obeyed.

Section 3 states that senators and representatives must take an oath to support the Constitution. But no religious test shall ever be required to hold public office in the United States.

Finally, Article 7 says that the Constitution was to go into effect as soon as nine states voted to accept it. Nine was more than two-thirds of the states.

2. Why is it harder to ratify an amendment than to propose it?

_____

_____

Skillbuilder

Use the chart below to answer the questions.

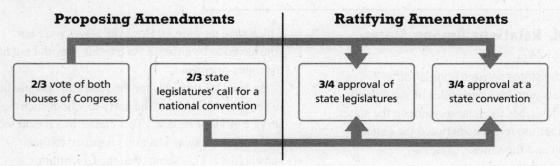

Proposing Amendments	Ratifying Amendments

2/3 vote of both houses of Congress

2/3 state legislatures' call for a national convention

3/4 approval of state legislatures

3/4 approval at a state convention

1. In what two ways can a constitutional amendment be proposed?

_____

_____

2. In what two ways can an amendment be ratified?

_____

_____

The Constitution Handbook (pages 250–261)

The Bill of Rights and Amendments 11–27

BEFORE YOU READ

In Articles 4–7, you learned about the process of amending the Constitution.

   Now you will learn about the Bill of Rights and the other amendments to the Constitution.

AS YOU READ

Continue your outline of the Constitution. Take notes on how amendments affected the government of the United States.

Amendments 1–10 (The Bill of Rights)	
Amendments 11–27	

TERMS & NAMES

Bill of Rights First ten amendments

double jeopardy Being tried more than once for the same crime

due process of law All the procedures for fair treatment that must be carried out whenever a citizen is accused of a crime

reserved powers Powers not specifically granted to the federal government or denied to the states belong to the states and the people

suffrage Right to vote

The Bill of Rights (pages 250–252)

What *liberties are protected by the Bill of Rights?*
The first ten amendments are called the **Bill of Rights.** They were added to the Constitution in 1791. The supporters of the Constitution had to promise to include these protections of citizens' rights in order to get enough of the states to ratify the Constitution.

   Amendment 1 protects basic civil liberties. It prevents Congress from passing laws limiting citizens' freedom of religion, speech, and press. It says that citizens can assemble, or gather together, freely. Citizens also have the right to ask the government to correct injustices.

   Amendment 2 says the federal government cannot prevent the people from having weapons. This amendment was meant to ensure that states and citizens could protect themselves from the military power of a cruel government—as the colonists did during the Revolution. Many people believe that this amendment was meant to protect the right of the states to have armed militias. For this reason, the right of individual citizens to carry weapons has

become controversial in modern times.

   Amendment 3 says that citizens cannot be forced to let soldiers stay in their homes during peacetime.

   Amendment 4 extends the people's right to privacy. It requires that a search warrant be issued before a citizen's home or belongings can be searched. Such a warrant can be issued only if a judge decides that it is likely that evidence of a crime will be found. The warrant must state exactly what evidence the government is looking for.

   Amendment 5 requires that an indictment, or official accusation, be issued before a citizen can be held for a serious crime. It also prevents **double jeopardy,** or being tried more than once for the same crime. In other words, if a citizen is found not guilty in a trial, the government cannot keep bringing the case to trial. (Citizens found guilty do have the right of appeal, however.) This amendment also gives citizens the right to refuse to testify when their own testimony might *incriminate* them. It also guarantees **due process of law.** Due process means that all of the procedures for fair treatment must be carried out whenever a citizen is accused of a crime.

Amendment 6 guarantees the right to a "speedy and public trial." It is intended to protect citizens from being kept in jail for long periods of time before they are brought to trial. The right to know the charges and to have a lawyer helps citizens defend themselves in court. This amendment also makes sure the people know what is going on in their courts.

Amendment 7 ensures that citizens will have a trial by jury.

Amendment 8 limits the fines and punishments that the government can impose.

Amendment 9 guarantees that rights are not denied to the people simply because they have not been mentioned in the Constitution.

Amendment 10 establishes the so-called **reserved powers**. It states that the powers that are not specifically given to the national government—as long as they are not specifically denied to the states—are reserved for the states and the people.

1. What are two ways the Bill of Rights protects citizens accused of crimes?

_____

_____

Amendments 11–27 (pages 253–261)

How have amendments changed American society?

Amendment 11 (1798) says that citizens of another state or a foreign country cannot sue a state in federal court unless the state agrees to it.

Amendment 12 (1804) changes the way presidents are elected. It kept the Electoral College from the original system. But it created one ballot for president and one for vice-president. The person to get a majority of electoral votes for president becomes president. The person who gets the majority of electoral votes for vice-president becomes vice-president.

Amendment 13 (1865) abolishes slavery.

Amendment 14 (1868) extends the rights of citizenship. It states that all persons born or *naturalized* in any of the United States are citizens of the United States. This was meant to protect African Americans by giving them the same rights as other Americans.

Amendment 15 (1870) states that citizens cannot be prevented from voting on the basis of race, color, or if the person had been a slave. This amendment was intially intended to protect the voting rights of African Americans.

Amendment 16 (1913) gives Congress the power to impose a national income tax.

Amendment 17 (1913) states that senators shall be elected directly by the people rather than by the state legislatures.

Amendment 18 (1919) is known as Prohibition. It banned the manufacture, sale, or shipment of alcoholic beverages. It was repealed by Amendment 21 (1933).

Amendment 19 (1920) grants **suffrage,** or the right to vote, to women.

Amendment 20 (1933) changes the day that a new president takes office. It moved the day from March 4 to January 20 of the year following the election. It also states that Congress shall meet on January 3, every year. Finally, this amendment sets rules for who should act as president if no one has been qualified to do so at the time of the inauguration.

Amendment 22 (1951) sets limits on the number of terms a president may serve. No person may be elected president more than twice.

Amendment 23 (1961) gives the District of Columbia the right to have electors in the Electoral College. It has the same number of electors as if it were a state. But it cannot have more electors than the state with the lowest population.

Amendment 24 (1964) makes poll taxes, charges that need to be paid in order to vote, illegal.

Amendment 25 (1967) sets rules for who should succeed, or take the place of, the president if he or she is unable to perform the duties of the office.

Amendment 26 (1971) extends the right to vote to 18-year olds.

Amendment 27 (1992) states that pay raises for senators and representatives cannot take effect until after the next election for representatives is held.

2. How did Amendments 15, 19, 24, and 26 affect American society?

_____

_____

The Constitution Handbook

Glossary/After You Read

bill Draft of a proposed law presented to the legislature for approval

civilians People who are not in the armed forces

impeachment Official accusation of wrongdoings by the House of Representatives against a government official

incriminate To cause to appear guilty of a crime

naturalized Granted full citizenship to one of foreign birth

override To declare null and void; to set aside

veto Power of a chief executive to reject a bill passed by the legislature and prevent it from becoming a law

---

Terms & Names

A. Write the letter of the name or term next to the description that explains it best.

a. Preamble   d. Congress
b. Senate   e. judicial power
c. Supreme Court   f. House of Representatives

_____ 1. The lower house of Congress

_____ 2. The introduction to the Constitution

_____ 3. The legislative branch of government

_____ 4. The upper house of Congress

_____ 5. The highest federal court

B. Write the name or term that best completes each sentence.

enumerated powers   Bill of Rights
succession   double jeopardy
elastic clause   suffrage

1. The Fifth Amendment protects citizens against _____, or being tried twice for the same crime.

2. Several amendments expanded _____, or the right to vote.

3. The first 10 amendments are known as the _____.

4. Particular powers of the Congress that are listed in Article 1 are often called the _____ of Congress.

5. The clause giving Congress power to do whatever is "necessary and proper" to govern is called the _____.

Main Ideas

1. Why are there more House members than Senate members?

_____

_____

2. How can the president lose his or her job before election time?

_____

_____

3. How are Supreme Court justices appointed?

_____

_____

4. What is the importance of the Bill of Rights?

_____

_____

5. What did the 26th Amendment do?

_____

_____

Thinking Critically

Answer the following questions on a separate sheet of paper.

1. How does the Constitution reflect the fear of making the country's leader too strong?

2. Which two amendments do you think have had the greatest effect in protecting democracy in the United States?

Chapter 9 Section 1 (pages 277–281)

Washington's Presidency

BEFORE YOU READ

In the last chapter, you read about how the Constitution was ratified.

In this section, you will learn how the first president and Congress of the United States set up the nation's new government.

AS YOU READ

Use this diagram to take notes on setting up the new government in the United States.

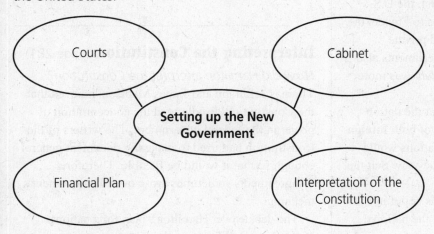

inaugurate To swear into office

Federal Judiciary Act The act that created a court system and divided authority between the state and federal courts

cabinet Heads of the departments that help the president lead the nation

tariff Tax on imported foreign goods

Washington Takes Office (pages 277–278)

What difficulty did Washington face as the first president?

George Washington was **inaugurated,** or sworn in, as the nation's first president. John Adams became vice-president. Washington faced a difficult task. He knew his actions as president would set an example. Congress agreed that Washington should be called "Mr. President" rather than by a title that would suggest he was a king. Congress also had to settle differences about how to run the new government.

1. Why was Washington's task as the nation's first president difficult?

_____

_____

Setting Up the Courts; Washington's Cabinet (pages 278–279)

Why did Congress pass the Federal Judiciary Act?

Congress had many matters to decide that were not spelled out in the Constitution. One problem was how to divide authority between the state and federal courts. Congress passed the **Federal Judiciary Act** of 1789. This act gave the Supreme Court six members: a chief justice and five associate judges. The current number is nine. The act also provided for other lower federal courts. John Jay was appointed Chief Justice.

The Constitution gave Congress the power to create departments to help the president. The president appointed the heads of these departments, which became his **cabinet.** Washington chose Henry Knox as secretary of war, Thomas Jefferson as secretary of state, and Alexander Hamilton as secretary of the treasury. To help him with matters of law, Washington picked Edmund Randolph as attorney general. These department leaders were called together to advise Washington. Since then, other presidents have followed this example.

2. What was the Federal Judiciary Act?

_____

_____

Economic Problems; Hamilton's Financial Plan (pages 279–281)

Why did Hamilton want to tax imported goods? Alexander Hamilton, secretary of the treasury, had to straighten out the nation's finances. First, the U.S. government needed to pay its war debts to France, the Netherlands, Spain, and merchants and private citizens in the United States. State governments also had war debts. By 1789, the *national debt* was more than $52 million.

Most government leaders agreed that the nation must repay its debts to win the respect of both foreign nations and its own citizens. Foreign nations would do business with the United States if they saw that the country would pay its debts.

Hamilton's financial plan showed his belief in a strong central government. He thought the national government should be stronger than the state governments. He also believed that government should encourage business and industry. Hamilton believed that the nation's economic well-being depended on them.

In 1790, Hamilton proposed his financial plan to Congress. The plan included the following steps to improve the nation's finances: 1) paying off all war debts (including state debts); 2) raising government *revenues*; 3) creating a national bank.

Sectional differences arose over repayment of state debts. Many Southern states had already repaid their debts and resented being asked to help pay Northern states' debts. Hamilton asked Thomas Jefferson to help him gain Southern support. They reached a *compromise*. In exchange for Southern support of the plan, Northerners agreed to place the nation's capital in the South. Washington, D.C., was built on the Potomac River between Virginia and Maryland.

Hamilton favored **tariffs**—taxes on imported foreign goods. Tariffs had two purposes: they raised money for the government and encouraged the

growth of American industry. The government placed the highest taxes on foreign goods that Americans used in large quantities. This ensured a steady flow of income to the government, and encouraged people to buy less expensive American-made goods.

Hamilton called for the creation of a national bank. A national bank would give the government a safe place to keep money, make loans to government and businesses, and issue *bank notes*.

3. Why did Hamilton favor tariffs?

_____

_____

Interpreting the Constitution (page 281)

How did Hamilton interpret the Constitution? Thomas Jefferson and James Madison believed that the Constitution discouraged the concentration of power in the federal government. The writers of the Constitution had tried to make the document general enough so that it would be flexible. Therefore disagreements sometimes arose over the document's meaning.

The debate over Hamilton's plan for a national bank exposed differences about how to interpret the Constitution. Madison and Jefferson argued that the Constitution did not give the government the power to set up a bank. They believed in the strict construction of the Constitution. They stated that the government has only those powers that the Constitution clearly says it has. Therefore, if the Constitution does not mention a national bank, the government cannot create one.

Hamilton disagreed. He favored a loose construction of the Constitution. He argued that the bank was necessary to carry out the government's duties. According to this view, where a power has been created by the Constitution, the "necessary and proper" clause (the elastic clause) permits it to be exercised flexibly. Hamilton won the debate, and the Bank of the United States was set up in 1791.

4. What was Hamilton's interpretation of the Constitution?

_____

_____

Chapter ⑨ Section 2 (pages 282–286)

Challenges to the New Government

BEFORE YOU READ

In the last section, you read about decisions made in setting up the new republic of the United States.

In this section, you will learn how Washington established central authority at home and avoided war with European powers.

AS YOU READ

Use this chart to take notes on the challenges facing the United States as a new nation.

BATTLE / TREATY	RESULTS

Battle of Fallen Timbers Clash between native tribes and the federal army

Treaty of Greenville Agreement between 12 Native American tribes and the U.S. government

Whiskey Rebellion Rebellion in 1794 by farmers in western Pennsylvania against the tax on whiskey

French Revolution A conflict for liberty and equality in France

neutral Not taking sides in a conflict

Jay's Treaty Agreement in which the British gave up their forts on the Northwest frontier and paid damages for American vessels they had seized

Pinckney's Treaty Agreement with Spain that gave Americans certain rights

Securing the Northwest Territory
(pages 282–283)

Why was there trouble in the land between the Appalachian Mountains and the Mississippi River?
The 1783 Treaty of Paris tried to resolve the claims to the land between the Appalachian Mountains and the Mississippi River. But a few years later, trouble arose again in this area known as the Trans-Appalachian West. Spain, Britain, the United States, and Native Americans each claimed parts of the area.

Spain claimed much of North America west of the Mississippi, Florida, and the Port of New Orleans. This port was key to trade for American settlers in the West. The settlers carried goods to market by flatboat down the Mississippi to New Orleans. The Spanish threatened to close the port. They stirred up trouble between the white settlers and Native American groups in the Southeast.

In *violation* of the Treaty of Paris, the British held forts north of the Ohio River. The strongest resistance

to white settlement came from Native Americans in the Northwest Territory. They hoped to join together to form an independent Native American nation bordered by the Ohio River to the south and Canada to the north. Britain encouraged them in order to maintain its access to the fur in these territories.

1. Who claimed land in the Trans-Appalachian West?

_____

_____

Battle of Fallen Timbers (pages 283–284)

How did the Battle of Fallen Timbers affect the Native Americans?
Washington sent troops, headed by Anthony Wayne, to the Ohio Valley in order to secure the Northwest. The Native Americans did not have strong leadership or an overall battle plan. They were defeated by Wayne's troops in the **Battle of Fallen Timbers.** The

British refused to help the Native Americans. This battle crushed Native American hope of keeping their land. They signed the **Treaty of Greenville** in 1795. They agreed to surrender much of present-day Ohio and Indiana to the U.S. government.

2. What was the result of the Battle of Fallen Timbers?

_____

_____

_____

The Whiskey Rebellion (pages 284–285)

***What** was the Whiskey Rebellion?*
A conflict arose over the government's tax on whiskey. Farmers were against the tax because whiskey—and the grain it was made from—were important products. Farmers could more easily carry whiskey to market than the grain it was made from. Whiskey was used by farmers as money to trade for other goods. In 1794, a group of farmers in western Pennsylvania rebelled against the tax. Washington sent an army to crush the **Whiskey Rebellion.** Washington showed that the government had the power and the will to enforce its laws.

3. What caused the Whiskey Rebellion?

_____

_____

_____

The French Revolution; Remaining Neutral (pages 285–286)

***What** was Jay's Treaty?*
In 1789, the French launched the **French Revolution** in search of liberty and equality. At first the United States strongly supported the struggle. The struggle turned violent, however. King Louis XVI and thousands of French citizens were killed. Also,

France declared war with Britain, Spain, and Holland. Britain led the fight against France.

The war put the United States in an awkward position. France had been America's ally against the British. Also, a 1778 treaty bound France and the United States together. And many saw France's revolution as proof that the American cause was justified. Thomas Jefferson felt that a move to crush the French Revolution was an attack on liberty everywhere. Other Americans thought that British trade was too important to the American economy to risk war. As a result, Washington decided the United States would remain **neutral.** This meant it would not side with one country or another. Congress then passed a law forbidding Americans to help either side.

In 1792, Britain began seizing the cargoes of American ships. This made it hard for the United States to remain neutral. So, Washington sent Chief Justice John Jay to England to persuade the British to end the seizures of American ships. Jay also tried to get them to give up their forts on the Northwest frontier. News of the Battle of Fallen Timbers helped Jay convince the British to give up the forts by 1796. In **Jay's Treaty,** the British also agreed to pay damages for American vessels they had seized. Jay's treaty was unpopular. This was mainly because he did not convince the British to open trade with the British West Indies to Americans.

In 1795, **Pinckney's Treaty** with Spain gave Americans the right to travel freely on the Mississippi River and to store goods at the port of New Orleans without paying custom duties. Also, Spain accepted the 31st parallel as the northern boundary of Florida and the southern boundary of the United States.

4. What did the British agree to in Jay's Treaty?

_____

_____

_____

The Federalists in Charge

BEFORE YOU READ

In the last section, you read about the challenges facing the United States in its first few years.

In this section, you will read how political divisions between Alexander Hamilton and Thomas Jefferson led to the formation of political parties.

AS YOU READ

Use this time line to take notes on the events during John Adams's presidency.

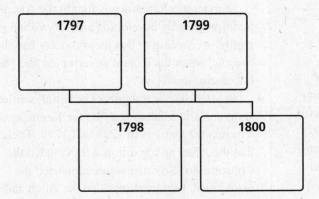

1797

1799

1798

1800

Washington Retires; Growth of Political Parties (pages 287–288)

What *kind of foreign policy did Washington favor?*
In George Washington's farewell address, he warned that political disagreements could weaken the nation. He warned against the formation of political parties.

He also gave parting advice on **foreign policy**—relations with the governments of other countries. He urged the United States to remain neutral because agreements with foreign nations might work against American interests.

Thomas Jefferson and James Madison debated with Hamilton about how to interpret the Constitution and on economic policy. Hamilton favored the British government and opposed the French Revolution. Jefferson and Madison thought the opposite. Hamilton wanted a strong central government. Jefferson and Madison thought such a government would lead to *tyranny*. Finally, Hamilton wanted an America in which trade, manufacturing, and cities grew. Jefferson and

Madison wanted an America of planters and farmers.

These differences on foreign and domestic policy led the nation to form political parties. A **political party** is a group of people who try to promote ideas and influence government. It also backs candidates for office. Jefferson and Madison founded the Democratic-Republican Party. This party reflected their belief in democracy and the republican system. Hamilton and his supporters formed the Federalist Party.

1. Why did Washington favor neutrality with other countries?

_____

_____

_____

John Adams Takes Office (page 289)

Who *became president and vice-president in 1796?*
In 1796, the Federalists chose John Adams as their

candidate for president. The Democratic-Republicans chose Jefferson. Adams won the electoral vote for president. Since the Constitution said the runner-up should become vice-president, Jefferson—Adams's chief rival—became vice-president. Therefore, the country had a Federalist president (John Adams) and a Democratic-Republican vice-president (Thomas Jefferson).

2. Why did rival candidates become president and vice-president?

_____

_____

_____

Problems with France (pages 289–290)

What *was the XYZ affair?*

When Washington left office in 1797, relations with France were tense. The French began seizing American ships to prevent them from trading with the British. Adams sent Pinckney, Elbridge Gerry, and John Marshall to Paris to meet with the French Minister of Foreign Affairs. The French ignored them until three agents—later referred to as X, Y, and Z—told the Americans that the minister was ready to hold talks if the Americans agreed to loan France ten million dollars and pay the minister a bribe.

The Americans refused. A report of this incident became known as the **XYZ Affair.** In 1798, Congress canceled its treaty with France and allowed American ships to seize French vessels. Congress also set aside money to expand the navy and army.

3. What was the result of the XYZ Affair?

_____

_____

_____

The Alien and Sedition Acts; Peace with France (pages 290–291)

Why *did Congress pass the Alien and Sedition Acts?*

The conflict with France made Adams and the Federalists popular with the public. Democratic-Republicans criticized the Federalists. To silence their critics, whom they identified as newspapers and new immigrants, the Federalist Congress passed the **Alien and Sedition Acts** in 1798. The acts targeted aliens—immigrants who were not yet citizens. One of the acts outlawed sedition—saying or writing anything false or harmful about the government. The Federalists clamped down on freedom of speech and the press.

Democratic-Republicans fought the Alien and Sedition Acts by developing a theory called **states' rights.** According to this theory, states had the right to judge when the federal government had passed an unconstitutional law.

Resolutions, or statements of belief, written by Jefferson and Madison passed the Kentucky and Virginia legislatures in 1798 and 1799. These stated that the Alien and Sedition Acts violated the Constitution. No other states supported the resolutions. Congress repealed the Alien and Sedition Acts and let them *expire* within two years when the Democratic-Republicans won control of Congress.

Adams opened talks with France, and peace was made. The treaty, called the Convention of 1800, cleared the way for American and French ships to sail the ocean in peace. Adams's actions made him many enemies, and he lost the presidential election of 1800 to Jefferson.

4. Why did Jefferson and Madison write the Kentucky and Virginia resolutions?

_____

_____

_____

Chapter **9** *Launching a New Republic*

Glossary/After you Read

bank notes Paper money that could be used as currency

compromise A dispute settled by each side's giving up some of its demands

expire To end

national debt Money owed by a country

resolutions Statements of belief

revenue Source of income

tyranny Oppressive power

violation The act of going against something or someone

Terms & Names

A. If the statement is true, write "true" on the line. If it is false, change the underlined word or words to make it true.

_____ 1. George Washington was <u>inaugurated</u> as the nation's first president.

_____ 2. President George Washington appointed the heads of the departments, which became his <u>Supreme Court</u>.

_____ 3. Alexander Hamilton favored <u>bank notes</u>, or taxes on imported foreign goods.

_____ 4. The land between the Appalachian Mountains and the Mississippi River was called the <u>Trans-Appalachian West</u>.

_____ 5. The <u>Battle of Fallen Timbers</u> was the clash over the Northwest Territory in which the Native Americans were defeated by a federal army.

_____ 6. The United States remained <u>neutral</u> in the French Revolution.

_____ 7. <u>Jay's Treaty</u> gave Americans the right to travel freely on the Mississippi River.

_____ 8. The Federalists were a <u>political party</u> that tried to promote their ideas and influence government.

_____ 9. Immigrants who are not yet citizens are known as <u>agents</u>.

_____ 10. <u>Sedition</u> is saying or writing anything false or harmful about the government.

B. Write the letter of the name or term that matches the description.

a. French Revolution   d. foreign policy
b. states' rights   e. Whiskey Rebellion
c. Federal Judiciary Act   f. Treaty of Greenville

_____ 1. The act that created a court system and divided authority between the state and federal courts

_____ 2. Agreement between 12 Native American tribes and the United States to surrender much of present-day Ohio and Indiana

_____ 3. A conflict for liberty and equality in France

_____ 4. Relations with the governments of other countries

_____ 5. Theory that says states have the right to judge when the federal government had passed an unconstitutional law

Main Ideas

1. What economic problems did the United States face after the Revolutionary War?

_____

_____

2. What three steps did Hamilton's financial plan include?

_____

_____

3. Why did Washington crush the Whiskey Rebellion?

_____

_____

4. Why was it difficult for the United States to remain neutral during the French Revolution?

_____

_____

5. How did the Democratic-Republicans react to the Alien and Sedition Acts?

_____

_____

Thinking Critically

Answer the following questions on a separate sheet of paper.

1. How would the United States be different today if Washington had agreed with Madison and Jefferson's interpretation of the Constitution?

2. Do you think Americans should have listened to Washington's warning about political parties? Why or why not?

Chapter **10** *Section 1 (pages 297–301)*

Jefferson Takes Office

BEFORE YOU READ

In the last chapter, you read about the growth of political parties in the United States.

In this section, you will learn how the Democratic-Republicans replaced Federalist programs with their own.

AS YOU READ

Use this diagram to take notes on the philosophy of Thomas Jefferson.

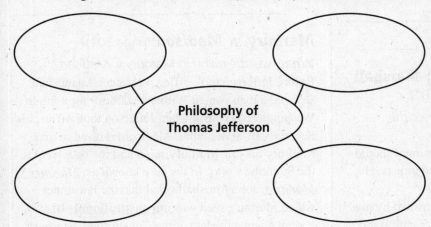

TERMS & NAMES

radicals People who take extreme political positions

Judiciary Act of 1801 Act under which President Adams appointed as many Federalist judges as he could before Thomas Jefferson took office

John Marshall A Federalist appointed by President John Adams as Chief Justice of the Supreme Court

Marbury* v. *Madison Supreme Court case in which John Marshall declared that a law passed by Congress was unconstitutional, thereby establishing the principle of judicial review

unconstitutional A contradiction of the law of the Constitution

judicial review Principle that says that the Supreme Court has the final say in interpreting the Constitution

The Election of 1800; Breaking the Tie
(pages 297–298)

Who won the election of 1800?

Two parties had candidates in the presidential election of 1800. They were the Federalists and the Democratic-Republicans. The Democratic-Republicans argued that the Federalists' Alien and Sedition Acts violated the Bill of Rights. The Federalists called the Democratic-Republicans <u>radicals</u>—people who take extreme political positions. The Federalists' candidate, President John Adams, lost the election. But there was a tie between two Democratic-Republican candidates—Thomas Jefferson and Aaron Burr.

According to the Constitution, the House of Representatives had to choose between Burr and Jefferson. The Federalists, however, still controlled the House of Representatives. It was true that the Democratic-Republicans wanted Jefferson as their president. Even so, the Federalists would decide the

winner. Members of the House of Representatives voted 36 times before finally electing Jefferson as president. Burr became vice-president.

1. How was the election of 1800 decided?

_____

_____

_____

The Talented Jefferson; Jefferson's Philosophy (pages 298–299)

What were Jefferson's thoughts about the country?

Thomas Jefferson was one of the United States most talented presidents. He was a skilled violinist, horseman, and amateur scientist. Jefferson was also an architect. He helped in the planning and design of Washington, D.C. Jefferson loved to read, too. His book collection became the core of the Library of Congress.

As president, Jefferson tried to unite Americans by promoting a common way of life. He wanted the United States to be a nation of independent farmers. He did not like the crowded city life he had seen in Europe. He believed that a nation of independent farmers would have strong morals and good democratic values. As president, Jefferson lived a simple life. He believed in a *modest* role for the central government, too.

2. What kind of nation did Jefferson want?

_____

_____

_____

Undoing Federalist Programs; Marshall and the Judiciary (pages 300–301)

Why did Jefferson have little power over the courts?

Jefferson thought that the central government should have less power than it did under the Federalists. He sought to end many Federalist programs.

Jefferson asked Congress—now controlled by his party—to let the Alien and Sedition Acts end. It did, and Jefferson released people imprisoned under the acts. Congress also ended many taxes passed by the Federalists, including the whiskey tax. The loss of tax moneys lowered the government's income. To save money, Jefferson reduced the number of government employees and the size of the military.

Jefferson also tried to replace the financial system set up by Federalist Alexander Hamilton. Hamilton's system relied on a certain amount of government debt. He thought that people who were owed money by their government would make sure that the government was run well. Jefferson, however, was against public debt. He worked hard to reduce the amount of money the government owed.

Jefferson had less power over the courts. Under the **Judiciary Act of 1801,** John Adams had appointed as many Federalist judges as he could before Jefferson took office. This meant that the new Democratic-

Republican president faced a firmly Federalist judiciary. Adams had also appointed Federalist **John Marshall** as Chief Justice of the Supreme Court. Marshall served as Chief Justice for over 30 years. During that time, the Supreme Court upheld federal authority and strengthened the federal courts.

3. How did the Judiciary Act of 1801 affect Jefferson's power over the courts?

_____

_____

_____

Marbury v. Madison (page 301)

What was the ruling in Marbury v. Madison?

Before Jefferson took office, President Adams had selected a man named William Marbury for a job in Washington, D.C. But when Jefferson took office, his Secretary of State, James Madison, refused to give Marbury his job. Marbury *sued,* and the case went to the Supreme Court. In the case known as, **Marbury v. Madison,** John Marshall ruled that the law under which Marbury sued was **unconstitutional**—that is, it went against the law of the Constitution. Marbury did not get his job.

The Supreme Court had decided against Marbury. But the Court's decision had another result. By declaring a law unconstitutional, the Court established the principle of **judicial review**. This principle says that the Supreme Court is the branch of government that has the power to say exactly what the Constitution means. If the Supreme Court says that a law goes against the Constitution, then that law cannot be put into effect.

4. How did Marshall rule in *Marbury* v. *Madison?*

_____

_____

_____

Chapter **10** Section 2 (pages 302–307)

The Louisiana Purchase and Exploration

BEFORE YOU READ

In the last section, you read about some of the changes made by Jefferson and his political party.

In this section, you will learn how the nation doubled in size.

AS YOU READ

Use this time line to take notes on the events that occurred before and after the purchase of the Louisiana Territory.

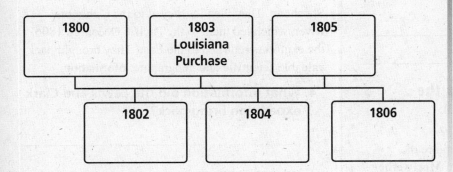

1800	1803 Louisiana Purchase	1805
	1802	1804	1806

TERMS & NAMES

Louisiana Purchase An 1803 land purchase from France, which gave the United States the port of New Orleans and doubled the size of the country

Meriwether Lewis Explorer chosen to lead an expedition into the Louisiana Territory

William Clark A skilled mapmaker and outdoorsman chosen to explore the Louisiana Territory

Lewis and Clark expedition A trip to explore the Louisiana Territory

Sacagawea A Shoshone woman whose language skills and knowledge of geography helped Lewis and Clark

Zebulon Pike An army officer who led an expedition into the southern part of the Louisiana Territory

The West in 1800 (pages 302–303)

What did westerners want in the early 1800s?
In the 1800s, thousands of settlers moved westward across the Appalachian Mountains. Many moved into areas long inhabited by Native Americans. Even so, some of these areas soon became American states. Kentucky and Tennessee had become states by 1800. Ohio became a state in 1803.

There was much activity further west, too. In 1800, France and Spain were negotiating for ownership of the Louisiana Territory—the vast region between the Mississippi River and the Rocky Mountains. Also, along the Pacific coast, Spain, Russia, Great Britain, and the United States were establishing settlements.

As the number of westerners grew, so did their political power. An important issue for many settlers was the use of the Mississippi River and the port of New Orleans. Westerners used the river and port to send their goods to east coast markets.

1. What was an important issue for many westerners in the early 1800s?

_____

_____

Napoleon and New Orleans; The Louisiana Purchase (page 303)

Which countries controlled New Orleans?
New Orleans was originally claimed by France. After losing the French and Indian War, France turned it over to Spain. Then in a secret treaty in 1800, Spain agreed to return the Louisiana Territory, including New Orleans, to France's leader, Napoleon. Now Napoleon planned to colonize the territory.

In 1802, these changes nearly resulted in war. Just before turning the colony over to France, Spain closed New Orleans to U.S. ships. Westerners called for war against Spain and France. To avoid war, Jefferson offered to buy New Orleans from France. He received a surprising offer back. France offered to sell the entire Louisiana Territory to the United States.

Jefferson wanted to accept the offer. But the Constitution said nothing about a president's right to buy land. This troubled Jefferson. He believed in the strict interpretation of the Constitution. But he also believed in a nation of independent farmers, and that required land. So, on April 30, 1803, the **Louisiana Purchase** was approved for $15 million. The purchase gave the United States the port of New Orleans and doubled the size of the country.

2. Why did Jefferson question his right to buy the Louisiana Territory?

_____

_____

Lewis and Clark Explore; Up the Missouri River (pages 304–305)

Who *explored the Louisiana country?*
Jefferson planned an expedition to explore the Louisiana Territory. He chose Captain **Meriwether Lewis** to lead the expedition. Lewis chose his old friend Lieutenant **William Clark** to put together a volunteer force for the trip. Clark was skilled as a mapmaker and outdoorsman. The trip soon became known as the **Lewis and Clark expedition**.

Lewis and Clark set out in the summer of 1803. By winter, they reached the town of St. Louis. They stayed in the town throughout the winter. In May 1804, the explorers left St. Louis and headed up the Missouri River. They had instructions from Jefferson to explore the river and find a water route across the country. In addition, they were to establish good relations with Native Americans along the way. The president also asked them to write accounts of the landscapes, plants, and animals they saw.

By the next winter, the explorers had reached what is now North Dakota. There, they stayed with the Mandan Indians. In the spring of 1805, the expedition set out again along with a French trapper and his wife, **Sacagawea.** She was a Shoshone Indian whose language skills and knowledge of geography helped Lewis and Clark.

3. Who led the expedition of the Louisiana Territory?

_____

_____

On to the Pacific Ocean (page 306)

What *was the outcome of the expedition?*
As the explorers traveled toward the Rocky Mountains, Sacagawea pointed out Shoshone lands. When they finally made contact with the chief, he recognized Sacagawea as his sister. The explorers crossed the Rocky Mountains with the help of the Shoshone. They then journeyed to the Columbia River, which led them to the Pacific Ocean. In 1806, the explorers returned to the East. They brought back valuable scientific and geographic information.

4. What information did the Lewis and Clark expedition bring back?

_____

_____

Pike's Expedition; The Effects of Exploration (pages 306–307)

What *was the purpose of Pike's expedition?*
In 1806, another expedition, led by **Zebulon Pike**, left St. Louis to explore southern areas of Louisiana. Pike's mission was to find the *headwaters* of the Arkansas and Red Rivers. The Red River was a boundary between Spanish territory and Louisiana.

Pike's party headed westward across the Great Plains. They followed the Arkansas River toward the Rocky Mountains. When they reached the Rocky Mountains, they turned south. They hoped to run into the Red River. Instead they ran into the Rio Grande, a river in Spanish territory. There, they were arrested by Spanish troops. Spanish officials released them in 1807. They returned with important descriptions of the Great Plains and the valley of the Rio Grande.

5. What information did Pike's expedition bring back?

_____

_____

Chapter 10 Section 3 (pages 310–313)

Problems with Foreign Powers

BEFORE YOU READ

In the last section, you read about the Louisiana Purchase and explorations of this area.

In this section, you will learn how Jefferson handled foreign affairs during his presidency.

AS YOU READ

Use this diagram to take notes on the causes of the declaration of war on Britain in 1812.

TERMS & NAMES

impressment Kidnapping of sailors to work on ships

Embargo Act of 1807 An act passed by Congress to stop all foreign trade with the United States

Tecumseh A Shawnee chief who tried to unite Native American tribes

War Hawks Westerners who called for war against Britain

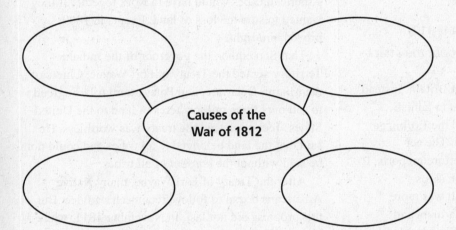

Causes of the War of 1812

Jefferson's Foreign Policy (pages 310–311)

***What** kind of foreign policy did Jefferson want?*
When Jefferson took office, he hoped to keep the United States from getting involved with other countries. He was not successful for many reasons. One reason was that American merchants were already trading with countries all over the world. Another reason was that the purchase of Louisiana opened the country to westward expansion. This also brought Americans into contact with people from other nations. Finally, the United States had little control over the actions of other countries.

1. What was Jefferson's foreign policy plan?

_____

_____

Problems with France and England (page 311)

***How** did Britain interfere with American trade?*
For years after the French Revolution, Europe was at war. For a while, the United States managed to stay out of these conflicts. At first, the country even benefited from the wars. France had sold Louisiana to the United States, partly as a result of the war. And U.S. merchants took over much of Europe's trade.

By 1805, however, the British began to clamp down on U.S. shipping. They did not want Americans to provide their enemies with food and supplies. The actions of the British angered France, which made its own laws to control foreign shipping.

These changes put American merchants in a tough position. If they obeyed the French rules, their ships could be taken by the British. If they obeyed the British rules, their ships could be taken by the French.

Britain also interfered with U.S. shipping by **impressment**—the kidnapping of American sailors to work on British ships. One of the worst incidents of impressment occurred in 1807. Off the coast of Virginia, the British ship *Leopard* attacked the American ship *Chesapeake*. The British killed three U.S. sailors in the battle. The attack angered Americans, many of whom wanted war.

2. How did the British interfere with U.S. trade?

_____

_____

Trade as a Weapon (pages 311–312)

What did Jefferson decide to do about the attack on the Chesapeake?
Jefferson did not declare war against Britain. Instead, he asked Congress to pass trade laws to punish Britain and France. Congress passed the **Embargo Act of 1807** to stop all foreign trade. The act prohibited U.S. ships from sailing to foreign ports. It also closed American ports to British ships.

Jefferson's policy was a disaster. It was more harmful to Americans—especially farmers and merchants—than to the British and French. Many shippers violated the embargo by making false claims about where they were going. Congress *repealed* the embargo in 1809. Madison became the next president in 1809. He reopened trade with all countries except France and Britain. Trade with these countries would begin again when they agreed to respect U.S. ships. Madison's policy was not effective either.

3. How did Jefferson react to the British attack on the *Chesapeake*?

_____

_____

Tecumseh and Native American Unity; War Hawks (pages 312–313)

Why were Americans angry with the British?
Americans were angry with the British for their interference with American shipping and impressment of U.S. citizens. British actions in the Northwest also angered Americans. Many thought that the British were stirring up Native American resistance to American settlements.

After the Battle of Fallen Timbers, thousands of white settlers had moved into Ohio and Indiana. **Tecumseh,** a Shawnee chief, wanted to stop the loss of Native American land. He believed that Native American tribes would have to work together if they wanted to stop the loss of land. Events in 1809 proved him right.

That September, the governor of the Indiana Territory signed the Treaty of Fort Wayne. Chiefs of the Miami, Delaware, and Potawatomi tribes agreed to sell over three million acres of land to the United States. Tecumseh said the treaty was worthless. He said that the land belonged to all tribes and could not be sold without the *consent* of all tribes.

After the Treaty of Fort Wayne, many Native Americans began to follow Tecumseh's advice. But this progress did not last. In November 1811, while Tecumseh was away recruiting tribes for his alliance, U.S. forces defeated the Shawnee at the Battle of Tippecanoe. It was a major set back for Tecumseh.

After the battle, Tecumseh and his followers fled to Canada. They received a warm welcome from the British. Americans, already upset by British interference at sea, became even angrier. Many westerners demanded war. Urged on by the **War Hawks,** as these westerners were called, Congress declared war on Britain on June 18, 1812.

4. Why did Congress declare war on Britain in 1812?

_____

_____

Chapter **10** *Section 4 (pages 314–317)*

The War of 1812

BEFORE YOU READ

In the last section, you read about the events that led up to the War of 1812.

In this section, you will learn about that war and its effects on the United States.

AS YOU READ

Use this diagram to take notes on the effects of the War of 1812.

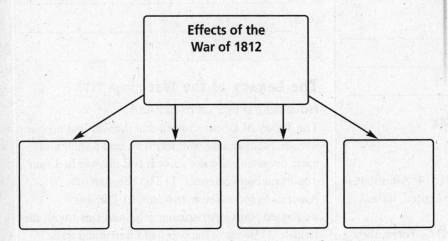

TERMS & NAMES

Oliver Hazard Perry Naval officer whose fleet defeated the British force on Lake Erie

Battle of the Thames Fight in which General Harrison defeated British forces in the Northwest

Francis Scott Key A Washington lawyer who watched the all-night battle at Fort McHenry and showed his pride by writing what became the national anthem

Treaty of Ghent Treaty that ended the War of 1812

The War Begins (pages 314–315)

What *were the strengths of America's military at the start of the War of 1812?*

Britain was already at war with France in 1812. It did not want another war with the United States. British leaders announced that they would stop interfering with U.S. shipping. But slow mail prevented this news from reaching America until it was too late.

The War of 1812 had two main phases. From 1812–1814, Britain concentrated on its war against France. After Britain defeated France in 1814, British leaders turned their attention to the United States.

When the war began, the United States military was weak. The navy had only about 16 ships. The army had fewer than 7,000 men. These men were poorly trained and equipped. They were led by officers with little experience.

1. Describe the state of the U.S. military when war was declared on Britain in 1812.

_____

_____

_____

The First Phase of the War (pages 315–316)

Why *was the Battle of the Thames important?*

Although the U.S. Navy was small, it performed well. American naval officers had gained valuable experience fighting pirates overseas. The navy's warships were the fastest afloat. Early in the war, before the British blockaded the coast, U.S. ships won battles that boosted American confidence.

The most important U.S. naval victory took place on Lake Erie. In September 1813, a British force on the lake set out to attack American ships. <u>Oliver Hazard Perry</u> led the American forces. The two sides exchanged cannon shots for two hours. After Perry's ship was demolished, he rowed to another ship and took charge. He then went on to win the battle.

After the victory, Perry sent a note to General William Henry Harrison, who then set out to attack the British on land. By the time Harrison reached Detroit, the British had fled to Canada. Harrison pursued the British forces and defeated them at the **Battle of the Thames**. This victory ended the British threat in the Northwest. The battle also claimed the life of Tecumseh, who died fighting for the British.

2. What was the importance of the Battle of the Thames?

_____

_____

_____

The Second Phase of the War
(pages 316–317)

What happened at Fort McHenry?
The war in Europe ended in April of 1814. After that, Britain concentrated on defeating the United States. They attacked on several fronts.

The British attacked Washington, D.C. There, they burned public buildings, including the White House. Then they attacked Fort McHenry at Baltimore. A Washington lawyer named **Francis Scott Key** watched the all-night battle. At dawn, Key saw the fort's flag still flying. He showed his pride by writing what became the U.S. national *anthem,* the "Star Spangled Banner."

In the North, the British sent a force from Canada across Lake Champlain. Its goal was to push south and cut off New England. The plan had failed by September 1814. At that time, an American fleet defeated the British in the Battle of Lake Champlain.

In the South, the British made the strategic port of New Orleans their target. A U.S. general, Andrew Jackson, put together an army to defend the port city. When the British launched their attack, they were quickly defeated by Jackson's soldiers. The Battle of New Orleans made Jackson a hero. Even so, it was unnecessary. Officials had signed the **Treaty of Ghent**—which ended the War of 1812—two weeks earlier. Slow mails from England had delayed the news.

3. Who led the U.S. forces at the Battle of New Orleans?

_____

_____

_____

The Legacy of the War (page 317)

How did the War of 1812 end?
The Treaty of Ghent showed that the war had no clear winner. Neither side won territory, and border and trade disputes were not solved. But the war had four important *consequences.* 1) The heroism of Americans increased patriotism. 2) The war weakened Native Americans, who had sided with the British. 3) Because the war had interrupted trade, Americans were forced to make many of their own goods. This encouraged the growth of U.S. manufacturers. 4) Finally, the United States proved it could defend itself against the mightiest military power of the time.

4. Who won the War of 1812?

_____

_____

_____

Glossary/After You Read

anthem A song in praise of something
consent Agreement
consequence An outcome or result
headwaters The source of a river

modest Limited in size
repeal To end
sue To take to court

Terms & Names

A. Write the letter of the name or term that matches the description.
   a. radicals   c. Sacagawea   e. impressment
   b. Judicial Act of 1801   d. Zebulon Pike   f. Treaty of Ghent

_____ 1. The kidnapping of sailors to work on ships

_____ 2. A Shoshone woman whose language skills and knowledge of geography helped Lewis and Clark

_____ 3. The treaty that ended the War of 1812

_____ 4. People who take extreme political positions

_____ 5. An explorer chosen to lead an expedition into the southern part of the Louisiana Territory

B. Write the name or term that best completes each sentence.
   Marbury v. *Madison*   Lewis and Clark expedition   War Hawks
   Battle of Thames   Louisiana Purchase

1. The _____ gave the United States the port of New Orleans and doubled the size of the United States.

2. The Supreme Court case _____ established the principle of judicial review.

3. The American victory at the _____ ended the British threat to the Northwest.

4. The purpose of the _____ was to explore the Louisiana Territory.

5. Westerners who called for war against Britain were known as _____.

Main Ideas

1. Why did Thomas Jefferson try to end Federalist programs?

_____

_____

2. Why was the Louisiana Purchase important to the United States?

_____

_____

3. What instructions did President Jefferson give Lewis and Clark?

_____

_____

4. Why did Jefferson have trouble avoiding involvement with foreign nations?

_____

_____

5. For the United States, what were four important consequences of the War of 1812?

_____

_____

Thinking Critically

Answer the following questions on a separate sheet of paper.

1. Explain how the ruling in *Marbury* v. *Madison* had a lasting effect on the federal government.

2. What were the long-lasting effects of exploration by the first American explorers of the West?

Chapter **11** Section 1 (pages 325–329)

Early Industry and Inventions

BEFORE YOU READ

In the last chapter, you read about the effects of the War of 1812 on the United States.

In this section, you will learn how new machines and factories changed the way people in the United States lived in the late 1700s and early 1800s.

AS YOU READ

Use this chart to take notes on the changes brought about by inventions and developments of the late 1700s and early 1800s.

Invention or Development	Changes
Textile mill	
Interchangeable parts	
Steam engine	
Telegraph	
Steel plow	
Mechanical reaper	

TERMS & NAMES

Industrial Revolution A time when factory machines replaced hand tools and large-scale manufacturing replaced farming as the main work

factory system System that brought many workers and machines together under one roof

Samuel Slater Built first spinning mill in Rhode Island

Lowell mills Early factories in Massachusetts that made cloth

interchangeable parts Parts that are exactly alike

Robert Fulton Inventor of the steamboat

Samuel F. B. Morse Inventor of the telegraph

The Industrial Revolution Begins; Factories Come to New England

(pages 325–326)

What was the Industrial Revolution?

The **Industrial Revolution** began in Britain during the late 1700s. In this revolution, factory machines replaced hand tools and large-scale *manufacturing* replaced farming as the main form of work. Before the revolution, women spun thread and wove cloth at home. However, the invention of machines such as the spinning jenny and the power loom made it possible for unskilled workers to make cloth.

The **factory system** brought many workers and machines together under one roof. Most factories were built near water to power the machines. People left farms and moved to where the factories were.

Many people did not want the United States to *industrialize*. However, during the War of 1812 the British blockade kept imported goods from reaching the United States. So Americans had to start manufacturing their own goods.

America began to build its own factories, starting in New England. This region was a good place for factories. It had many rivers to provide water power. It had ships and access to the ocean. In addition, it had many willing workers who were not able to make a living by farming. **Samuel Slater** built his first spinning mill in Rhode Island in 1790 and a larger mill later. There he hired whole families to work.

1. Where were the first U.S. factories?

_____

The Lowell Mills Hire Women
(pages 326–327)

What did the Lowell mills manufacture?
In 1813, Francis Cabot Lowell built a factory in
Waltham, Massachusetts. This factory spun cotton
into yarn and wove it into cloth on power looms. The
factory was so successful that Lowell and his partners
built a new factory town, called Lowell, near the
Merrimack and Concord rivers.

Instead of families, the **Lowell mills** employed farm
girls who lived in company-owned boardinghouses.
These girls worked long hours in deafening noise. At
first the girls received high wages. However, by the
1830s, wages dropped and working conditions
worsened.

The Lowell mills and other early factories ran on
water power. Later factories were run by powerful
steam engines.

2. Who worked in the Lowell mills?

_____

_____

A New Way to Manufacture
(pages 327–328)

What were interchangeable parts?
In 1798, the U.S. government hired the inventor
Eli Whitney to make 10,000 *muskets* for the army.
Before then, guns were made one at a time by
gunsmiths, from start to finish. Whitney wanted to
make them in a different way. In 1801, he went to
Washington with a box containing musket parts. He
took parts from different piles and put a musket
together in seconds. He had demonstrated the use of
interchangeable parts, parts that were exactly
alike.

Interchangeable parts made production faster and
made repairs easy. They also allowed the use of
lower-paid and less-skilled workers.

**3. How did using interchangeable parts
change factory work?**

_____

_____

Moving People, Goods, and Messages
(pages 328–329)

*How did inventions change transportation and
communication in the United States?*
New inventions improved transportation and
communication. **Robert Fulton** invented a steamboat
that could move against the current or strong wind. In
1807, he launched the *Clermont* on the Hudson River.

In 1816, Henry Miller Shreve, a trader on the
Mississippi River, designed a more powerful steam
engine. It ran a double-decker boat with a paddle
wheel in the back. Shreve sailed the boat up the
Mississippi and started a new era of trade and
transportation on the river.

In 1837, **Samuel F. B. Morse** demonstrated the
telegraph. This invention allowed messages to travel
between cities in seconds. By 1861, telegraph lines
spanned the country.

**4. How did the telegraph change
communication in the United States?**

_____

_____

Technology Improves Farming (page 329)
What inventions improved agriculture?
Several inventions increased farm production in the
United States. In 1836, John Deere invented a light-
weight plow with a steel cutting edge. His invention
made it easier for farmers to prepare heavy Midwestern
soil for planting. As a result, more farmers began
moving west.

In 1834, Cyrus McCormick's reaper cut ripe grain.
The threshing machine separated kernels of wheat
from husks.

New inventions helped to link regions of the United
States. New farming equipment helped Midwestern
farmers feed Northeastern factory workers.
Midwestern farmers became a market for the goods
manufactured in the Northeast. Northeastern textile
mills increased the need for Southern cotton.

**5. How did the steel plow improve
agriculture?**

_____

_____

Name _____   Date _____

Plantations and Slavery Spread

BEFORE YOU READ

In the last section, you read about how new machines and factories changed the way people lived and worked.

In this section, you will learn how the demand for cotton caused slavery to spread in the South.

AS YOU READ

Use this diagram to take notes on the ways that the cotton gin changed Southern life.

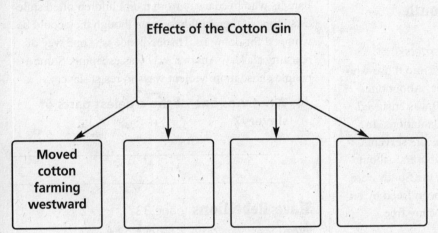

Effects of the Cotton Gin

Moved cotton farming westward

TERMS & NAMES

TERMS & NAMES

Eli Whitney Inventor of the cotton gin

cotton gin Invention that made the cotton-cleaning process easier

spirituals Religious folk songs sung by enslaved people

Nat Turner Leader of a famous slave rebellion in 1831

The Cotton Boom (pages 332–333)

Who *invented the cotton gin?*

Eli Whitney invented the **cotton gin** in 1793. This invention made the cotton-cleaning process much easier and quicker. It allowed one worker to clean as much as 50 pounds of cotton a day. The cotton gin changed Southern life in four ways:

1. Cotton farming moved westward beyond the Atlantic coastal states.
2. Because cotton was such a valuable crop, planters put most of their efforts into growing it.
3. More Native American groups were driven off Southern land as cotton *plantations* took over the land.
4. Slavery continued to be an important source of labor for growing cotton.

1. How did the cotton gin change the cotton-cleaning process?

_____

_____

Slavery Expands; Slavery Divides the South (pages 333–334)

How *did cotton production affect slavery in the South?*

Cotton production rose greatly between 1790 and 1860. So did the number of enslaved people in the South. As earnings from cotton rose, so did the price of slaves.

Slavery divided white Southerners into those who held slaves and those who did not. Only about one-third of white families in the South owned slaves in 1840. Of the slaveholding families, only about one-tenth had large plantations with 20 or more slaves. Although most white Southern farmers owned few or no slaves, many supported slavery anyway. They worked their small farms and hoped to buy slaves someday so that they could raise more cotton and make more money.

2. How did slavery divide white Southerners?

_____

_____

African Americans in the South
(pages 334–335)

How did slavery divide black Southerners?
Slavery also divided black Southerners into those who were enslaved and those who were free. About one-third of the South's population in 1840 was enslaved. About half of them worked on large plantations. In cities, enslaved people worked as *domestic* servants, craftsmen, factory workers, and day laborers. About eight percent of African Americans in the South were free. They had either been born free, been freed by an owner, or bought their own freedom. Many free African Americans lived in cities.

Free blacks, however, faced many problems. Some states forced them to leave once they gained freedom. Most states did not allow them to vote or go to school. Many employers would not hire them. Free blacks also had to worry about being captured and returned to slavery.

3. What problems did free blacks face?

_____

_____

Culture and Resistance; Families Under Slavery (pages 335–336)

Why did enslaved African Americans rely on their own culture?
By the early 1800s, African Americans on plantations had developed their own *culture*. They relied on that culture to survive the hardships on plantations. They

especially relied on their religion. Enslaved people expressed their religious beliefs in **spirituals,** or religious folk songs. The songs often contained coded messages. Spirituals later influenced blues, jazz, and other forms of American music.

One of the cruelest parts of slavery was the selling of family members away from one another. When enslaved people ran away, they often did so to find other family members. Family members that did stay together took comfort in their family lives. They married, although their marriages were not legally recognized. Most slave children lived with their mothers, who tried to protect them from punishment. Parents who lived away from their children often stole away to visit their children, even though they could be whipped for doing so. Disobedience was one way of resisting slavery. Another way was escaping. Some people chose more violent ways to resist slavery.

4. What was one of the cruelest parts of slavery?

_____

_____

Slave Rebellions (page 337)

What was Nat Turner's rebellion?
Several armed *rebellions* took place in the early 1800s. The most famous rebellion was led by **Nat Turner** in 1831. Turner and 70 followers killed 55 white men, women, and children. Most of Turner's followers were captured and 16 were killed. When Turner was caught, he was tried and hanged.

Turner's rebellion spread fear in the South. Whites killed more than 200 African Americans in revenge. States passed laws that kept free blacks and slaves from having weapons or buying liquor. They could not hold religious services unless whites were present. Tensions over slavery increased between the South and the North.

5. How did whites react to Nat Turner's rebellion?

_____

_____

Name _____   Date _____

Nationalism and Sectionalism

BEFORE YOU READ

In the last section, you read about the spread of slavery in the South.

In this section, you will learn how nationalism united the country and how tensions continued between the North and the South.

AS YOU READ

Use this diagram to take notes on the factors that contributed to feelings of nationalism in the United States in the early 1800s.

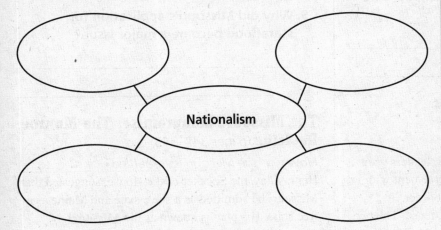

TERMS & NAMES
nationalism The feeling of pride, loyalty, and protectiveness toward a country
Henry Clay Speaker of the House of Representatives and political leader from Kentucky
American System Clay's plan for economic development
James Monroe President elected in 1816
sectionalism Loyalty to the interests of one's own region rather than to the nation as a whole
Missouri Compromise Agreement that temporarily settled the issue of slavery in the territories
Monroe Doctrine Warning to European nations not to interfere in the Americas

Nationalism Unites the Country
(pages 338–339)

What was the American System?

In the early 1800s, a sense of **nationalism** pulled people of different regions in the United States together. Nationalism is a feeling of pride, loyalty, and protectiveness toward a country. Congressman **Henry Clay**, a strong nationalist, called for strengthening the country and unifying its regions. His plan—the **American System**—included three parts.

1. Set up a protective tariff, a tax on foreign goods.
2. Set up a national bank with a single currency.
3. Improve the country's transportation systems.

1. What were three parts of the American System?

_____

_____

Roads and Canals (pages 339–340)

How was transportation improved in the 1800s?

Transportation in the United States improved in the first half of the 1800s. In 1806, Congress funded a road that eventually stretched from Cumberland, Maryland, west to Vandalia, Illinois.

The building of canals improved water transportation. The Erie Canal opened the upper Ohio River valley and the Great Lakes region to settlement and trade. It increased nationalism by uniting the regions.

Around the 1830s, steam-powered trains began to be used for transportation. By 1850, there were more than 9,000 miles of track across the United States.

2. What was the impact of the Erie Canal?

_____

_____

A Spirit of National Unity
(page 340)

What was the Era of Good Feelings?
As nationalism increased, people became more loyal to the federal government. **James Monroe** won the presidential election in 1816 by a large majority of votes. The lack of political differences led one newspaper to call the times the Era of Good Feelings. During Monroe's term, several Supreme Court decisions strengthened the powers of the federal government.

3. What was the effect of several Supreme Court decisions?

_____

_____

Settling National Boundaries
(pages 340–341)

How did U.S. borders expand?
Feelings of nationalism also made U.S. leaders want to extend the country's borders. An agreement with Britain helped to set the U.S.-Canada border.

However, relations with Spain were tense. The two nations disagreed on the boundaries of the Louisiana Purchase and the ownership of West Florida. Runaway slaves and pirates used Spanish-held East Florida as a *refuge*. Also, the Seminoles of East Florida, a Native American tribe, raided white settlements in Georgia to get back their land.

After U.S. general Andrew Jackson invaded Florida, Spain gave Florida to the United States in 1819.

4. What caused tensions with Spain?

_____

_____

Sectional Tensions Increase
(pages 341–342)

How did sectionalism help divide the country?
Although nationalism helped to unite the country, sectionalism was dividing it. **Sectionalism** is loyalty to the interests of your own region rather than to the nation as a whole. The interests of the North, South, and West were often in conflict.

Sectionalism became a major issue when Missouri applied for statehood in 1818. People in Missouri wanted slavery to be allowed there. But this would change the balance of 11 slave states and 11 free states.

5. Why did Missouri's application for statehood become a major issue?

_____

_____

The Missouri Compromise; The Monroe Doctrine (pages 342–343)

How was the Missouri issue settled?
Henry Clay, the Speaker of the House, suggested that Missouri be admitted as a slave state and Maine as a free state. His plan is known as the **Missouri Compromise.** It kept the balance of power.

The nation felt threatened for other reasons. Some European countries planned to help Spain and Portugal take back American colonies that had broken away. Also, Russian settlements reached from Alaska almost to San Francisco. In 1823, President Monroe issued the **Monroe Doctrine.** This was a warning to European countries not to set up any more colonies in the Americas.

6. What was the Missouri Compromise?

_____

Chapter **11** *National and Regional Growth*

Glossary/After You Read

culture Ways of living that belong to a group of people
domestic Relating to a home or household
industrialize To develop industries
manufacturing Making things by machine

musket A shoulder gun
plantation A large farm or estate
rebellion Open revolt
refuge A place of protection or shelter

Terms & Names

A. Write the letter of the term that best answers the question.

a. Robert Fulton
b. Samuel Slater
c. Eli Whitney

d. Samuel F. B. Morse
e. Nat Turner
f. Henry Clay

_____   1. Who suggested the Missouri Compromise?

_____   2. Who invented the telegraph?

_____   3. Who invented the cotton gin?

_____   4. Who led a slave rebellion in 1831?

_____   5. Who invented the steamboat?

B. Write the name or term that best completes each sentence.

Industrial Revolution
interchangeable parts
nationalism

American System
sectionalism
spirituals

1. In the early 1800s, a feeling of _____ brought people of different regions in the United States together.

2. _____, or loyalty to the interests of one's own region rather than to the nation as a whole, helped to divide the United States.

3. In the _____, factory machines replaced hand tools and large-scale manufacturing replaced farming as the main form of work.

4. The _____ was a plan to strengthen the United States economically.

5. The use of _____ made production faster and repairs easier.

Main Ideas

1. Why was New England a good place to set up factories?

_____

_____

2. How did new technology link different regions of the United States in the early 1800s?

_____

_____

3. How did enslaved people resist slavery?

_____

_____

4. What did several Supreme Court decisions do in the early 1800s?

_____

_____

5. What was the message of the Monroe Doctrine?

_____

_____

Thinking Critically

Answer the following questions on a separate sheet of paper.

1. How were the economies of the North and the South different? What problems did the differences cause?

2. Do you think the Missouri Compromise was a good decision? Give reasons for your opinion.

Chapter **12** Section 1 (pages 353–357)

Politics of the People

BEFORE YOU READ

In the last chapter, you read about the increase in nationalism and sectionalism in the United States.

In this section, you will learn how Andrew Jackson's election led to a popular democracy.

AS YOU READ

Use this diagram to take notes on ideas and events that described Jacksonian democracy.

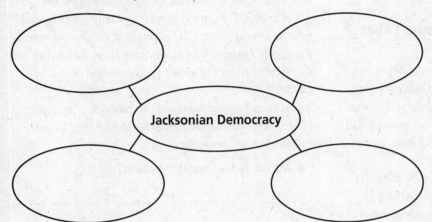

Jacksonian Democracy

The Election of 1824 (pages 353–354)

Who wanted to run for president in the 1824 election?

In the 1824 elections, regional differences led to a split in the Republican Party. Four men hoped to replace President Monroe. **John Quincy Adams,** Monroe's secretary of state, was the choice of the New England states. William Crawford of Georgia was the Southern choice. Westerners supported Henry Clay of Kentucky and **Andrew Jackson,** a military hero from Tennessee.

Jackson won the most popular votes. But he did not receive the majority of electoral votes. According to the Constitution, the House of Representatives has to choose the president if no person wins a majority of electoral votes.

Clay had come in fourth and was out of the running. In the House vote, he gave his support to Adams, who won. Because Adams made Henry Clay his secretary of state, Jackson's supporters claimed that Adams made a deal with Clay and stole the election.

1. How did regional differences affect the 1824 election?

_____

_____

_____

Jacksonian Democracy (pages 354–355)

What promise did Jackson make in the 1828 election?

The split between Jackson and Adams grew over the next four years. Jackson believed that he represented the "common poeple." He believed that Adams represented rich Easterners. This division created another two-party system. The supporters of Jackson became the Democrats. The supporters of Adams became the National Republicans.

The election of 1828 again had Adams running against Jackson. The campaign was a bitter one. Jackson promised to look out for the interests of the common people and to promote the idea of majority rule. This idea became known as **Jacksonian democracy.**

In the early 1800s, laws were passed that allowed more people to vote. The expansion of voting rights helped Jackson win the election by a *landslide*. His election was looked at as a victory for common people.

2. What two-party system was created with the 1828 election?

_____

_____

The People's President; Jackson Takes Office (pages 355–356)

What *happened at Jackson's inauguration?*
Andrew Jackson was the first president who was not from a rich Massachusetts or Virginia family. He was the first president from the West. His background and his reputation as a war hero helped make him president.

Shortly after the election, Jackson's wife died. He blamed her death on the bitter campaign. Although Jackson looked worn out and sad at his inauguration, the people at the capital were joyful and excited. People from all kinds of backgrounds came to the

inauguration and to the White House reception. Eventually the crowd at the White House became rowdy and destructive, forcing the president to leave the White House.

3. How was Andrew Jackson's background different from previous presidents?

_____

_____

A New Political Era Begins (page 357)

How *did Jackson reform the government?*
In his campaign, Jackson promised to *reform* the government. He started by giving many government jobs to his supporters. This practice became known as the **spoils system.** The term came from the saying "to the victor brings the spoils [possessions] of the enemy."

Jackson's opponents said the practice was unfair. He replied that it gave new people a chance to get involved in government.

4. What is the spoils system?

_____

_____

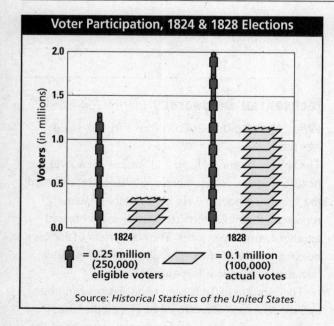

Voter Participation, 1824 & 1828 Elections

Voters (in millions)

= 0.25 million (250,000) eligible voters

= 0.1 million (100,000) actual votes

Source: *Historical Statistics of the United States*

Skillbuilder

Use the graph to answer the questions.

1. How many eligible voters were there in 1824? in 1828?

_____

_____

2. How many people actually voted in 1824? in 1828?

_____

_____

Name _____ Date _____

Chapter **12** Section 2 (pages 358–362)

Jackson's Policy Toward Native Americans

BEFORE YOU READ

In the last section, you read about Jacksonian democracy.

In this section, you will learn about Jackson's policy toward Native Americans.

AS YOU READ

Use this time line to take notes on the important events that affected Native Americans during the Age of Jackson.

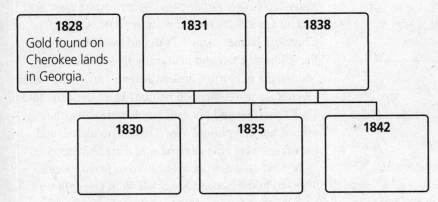

| **1828** Gold found on Cherokee lands in Georgia. | **1831** | **1838** |
| **1830** | **1835** | **1842** |

TERMS & NAMES

Sequoya A Cherokee who invented a writing system for the Cherokee Nation

Indian Removal Act Law that required Native Americans to move west

Indian Territory Area that is now Oklahoma and parts of Kansas and Nebraska to which Native Americans were moved

Trail of Tears Route the Cherokees were forced to travel from Georgia to Indian Territory

Osceola Seminole who was an important leader in Second Seminole War

Native Americans in the Southeast; The Cherokee Nation (pages 358–359)

***Who** were the Native Americans in the Southeast?*
Since the 1600s, white settlers had pushed Native Americans westward as they took more and more of their land. Some whites believed that moving Native Americans west was the only way to avoid conflict over land. In the 1820s, many Native Americans still lived east of the Mississippi River. The major tribes included the Cherokee, Chicksaw, Choctaw, Creek, and the Seminole. Whites called these tribes the Five Civilized Tribes because they had adopted many parts of the white culture.

The Cherokees, more than any other Native American people, had adopted white ways of living. They owned farms and cattle ranches. A brilliant Cherokee named **Sequoya** invented a writing system for the Cherokee language. The Cherokees also published their own newspaper. In 1827, the Cherokees drew up a constitution that was based on the U.S. Constitution and founded the Cherokee Nation.

In 1828, gold was found on Cherokee land in Georgia. Soon settlers and miners wanted the land. The federal government responded to white demands by planning to remove all Native Americans from the Southeast.

1. In what ways did the Cherokees adopt white culture?

_____

_____

_____

Jackson's Removal Policy (pages 359–360)

***What** were Jackson's policies toward Native Americans?*
President Jackson strongly supported a policy of moving Native Americans west of the Mississippi River. He believed that the government had the power to tell Native Americans where they could live. He also believed that Native Americans should accept

white culture or be moved to western territories. Jackson did not think that they could have their own governments within the borders of the United States.

After gold was discovered in the Southeast, Southern states passed laws that gave whites the right to take Native American lands. Jackson supported these laws. He asked Congress to pass a law that would force Native Americans to move west or to submit to state laws. Many Americans opposed this kind of law. But after much debate, Congress passed the **Indian Removal Act** in 1830. It said that Native Americans must *relocate* west of the Mississippi River.

2. What was the Indian Removal Act?

_____

_____

_____

The Trail of Tears (pages 360–361)

How *did the Supreme Court rule on the Indian Removal Act?*
Many Native Americans saw no other choice but to move west to the **Indian Territory.** This was an area that covered what is now Oklahoma and parts of Kansas and Nebraska. Beginning in 1831, the Choctaws and other Southeastern tribes were relocated to Indian Territory.

The Cherokees, however, fought the Indian Removal Act in court. They asked the Supreme Court to protect their land from being *seized* by Georgia. The Supreme Court struck down the Indian Removal Act. It said that the Cherokees were *wards* of the U.S. government. Only the federal government, not the states, could make laws governing the Cherokees. The ruling meant that Georgia laws did not apply to the Cherokee Nation.

Jackson refused to obey the court's ruling. In 1838, federal troops were used to force the Cherokees to move from Georgia to the Indian Territory. A

quarter of the Cherokees died in this journey, known as the **Trail of Tears.**

3. How did President Jackson react to the Supreme Court ruling on the Indian Removal Act?

_____

_____

_____

Native American Resistance (page 362)

How *did Native Americans resist moving west?*
Not all Cherokees moved west in 1838. An old Cherokee farmer named Tsali and his family fought the soldiers. Tsali and his family fled to the Smoky Mountains in North Carolina, where they found other Cherokees who remained behind. The U.S. army told Tsali that if he and his sons would surrender, the other Cherokees could stay. They surrendered, and the others were able to remain in their homeland.

In 1835, the Seminoles refused to leave Florida. This led to the Second Seminole War. **Osceola** was an important leader in the war. He and his followers defeated the U.S. army in many battles. In 1837, a *truce* was called. However, when Osceola arrived for peace talks, he was captured. He later died in prison. The Seminoles continued to fight until forced to end the war in 1842.

Other tribes also fought relocation to the Indian Territory. In 1832, a Sauk chief named Black Hawk led a band of Sauk and Fox back to lands in Illinois that they had been forced to leave. In the Black Hawk War, the U.S. army crushed the uprising.

4. What was the Second Seminole War?

_____

_____

_____

Conflicts Over States' Rights

BEFORE YOU READ

In the last section, you read about President Jackson's policy towards Native Americans.

In this section, you will learn about issues President Jackson faced regarding sectional differences.

AS YOU READ

Use this diagram to take notes on the issues that contributed to sectional differences in the 1800s.

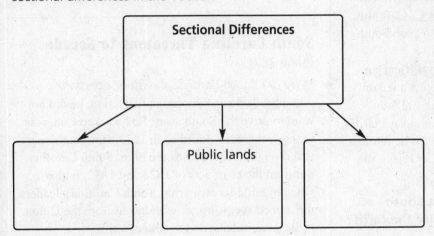

Sectional Differences

Public lands

TERMS & NAMES

"Tariff of Abominations" The tariff of 1828

John C. Calhoun Vice-president and congressional leader from South Carolina

doctrine of nullification The belief that states could ignore federal laws that they did not like

Webster-Hayne debate Debate between Senators Daniel Webster and Robert Hayne over nullification

Daniel Webster A Senate leader from Massachusetts

secession Withdrawal from the Union

Rising Sectional Differences

(pages 363–365)

What *issues caused sectional differences in the United States?*

When President Jackson took office in 1829, conflicts between the Northeast, the South, and the West were pulling the nation apart. Lawmakers from these sections were arguing about three economic issues.

The first was conflict over the large areas of land that the federal government was selling as public lands. Northeasterners did not want the lands in the West to be sold at low prices. They were concerned that the cheap land would attract workers who were needed in the Northeastern factories. Westerners wanted low prices so that more people would settle in the West.

The second conflict was about improvements in transportation. The Northeast and West wanted the

government to spend money on transportation to help transport goods. Southerners opposed this because the money to pay for the improvements would come from *tariffs*, and Southerners did not want an increase in tariffs.

The issue of tariffs was the third sectional conflict. Northerners supported high tariffs because they made imported goods more expensive to buy than American-made goods. Southerners were against higher tariffs. They sold their cotton to foreign buyers in exchange for foreign manufactured goods. Higher tariffs would make these goods more expensive.

1. How did the Northeast, West, and South feel about the government spending money on transportation improvements?

_____

_____

"Tariff of Abominations"; Crisis over Nullification (page 365)

What *was the "Tariff of Abominations"?*
In 1828, Congress raised the tariff on raw materials and manufactured goods. This tariff outraged Southerners, who called it the **"Tariff of Abominations"**. Southerners had to sell their cotton at low prices to be competitive. But tariffs forced them to pay high prices for the manufactured goods they needed. The tariff issue helped Andrew Jackson win the election in 1828.

South Carolina was especially hit hard by the tariff. Some leaders in the state began talking about leaving the Union over this issue. **John C. Calhoun,** then Jackson's vice-president, wanted to keep South Carolina from leaving the Union.

Calhoun proposed the **doctrine of nullification.** This said that a state had the right to reject a federal law that it thought was unconstitutional. Calhoun believed that Congress had no right to impose a tariff that favored one section of the country. So he felt that South Carolina had the right to nullify, or reject, the tariff.

2. Why did Calhoun believe that South Carolina had the right to nullify the tariff?

_____

_____

_____

The States' Rights Debates
(pages 366–367)

What *was the Webster-Hayne debate?*
Calhoun's ideas about nullification caused much controversy. Some people supported a strong federal government. Others defended the rights of the states. The Senate debated the issue in the **Webster-Hayne debate** in January 1830. **Daniel Webster,** a senator from Massachusetts, was opposed to the idea of nullification. Robert Hayne, a senator from South Carolina, supported it.

In April 1830, Calhoun and other supporters of nullification tried to use a Democratic party dinner to win support for their position. But at the dinner, President Jackson made it clear that he supported the power of the federal government and was opposed to nullification. From that time, Jackson and Calhoun were political enemies.

3. What was President Jackson's view of nullification?

_____

_____

_____

South Carolina Threatens to Secede
(page 367)

Why *did South Carolina threaten secession?*
Although Jackson opposed nullification, he did not want to drive the South away. So he asked Congress to lower the tariff. It did so in 1832. But Southerners still thought the tariff was too high. South Carolina nullified the tariff acts of 1828 and 1832. It also voted to build its own army. South Carolina's leaders threatened **secession,** or withdrawal from the Union, if the government tried to collect tariffs.

Jackson was angry. He ran for reelection in 1832, without Calhoun as his running mate. Jackson won the election. He then said that he would use force to make sure that federal laws were obeyed and that the Union would stay together. Henry Clay worked out a compromise tariff in 1833. The compromise kept South Carolina in the Union.

4. How was the tariff issue settled?

_____

_____

_____

Chapter **12** Section 4 (pages 368–371)

Prosperity and Panic

BEFORE YOU READ

In the last section, you read about the sectional conflicts facing President Jackson.

In this section, you will learn about the economic problems President Jackson faced.

AS YOU READ

Use this diagram to take notes on the causes of economic problems in the United States during the 1830s.

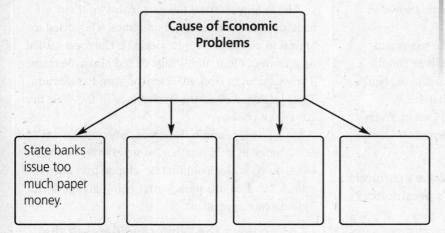

Cause of Economic Problems

State banks issue too much paper money.

TERMS & NAMES

inflation An increase in prices and a decrease in the value of money

Martin Van Buren Eighth president

Panic of 1837 Widespread concern about the state of the economy in 1837

depression A severe economic slump

Whig Party Party formed by opponents of President Jackson

William Henry Harrison Ninth president

John Tyler Tenth president

Mr. Biddle's Bank (page 368)

What was the Second Bank of the United States?
The Second Bank of the United States was the most powerful bank in the country. Its president, Nicholas Biddle, set policies that controlled the country's money supply. President Jackson disliked the bank. He thought it had too much power. He felt that the bank's policies favored wealthy people and hurt the average person.

To operate, the bank needed a *charter* from the federal government. Its charter was scheduled to expire in 1836. But Biddle asked Congress to renew it in 1832. That was an election year. Biddle thought that Jackson would agree to the renewal and not risk being defeated. But Jackson took the risk.

1. Why did President Jackson oppose the Second Bank of the United States?

_____

_____

Jackson's War on the Bank (page 369)

How did the Supreme Court rule on the national bank?
Jackson vetoed Congress's renewal of the bank's charter. He said the bank was unconstitutional. The Supreme Court had ruled that the bank was constitutional. But Jackson claimed that elected officials could judge whether a law was constitutional for themselves. They did not have to rely on the Court.

Jackson's opposition to the bank was a major issue in the 1832 election. The people agreed with Jackson. After Jackson won, he set out to destroy the bank. He took federal money out of the national bank and put it in state banks. As a result, the national bank went out of existence.

2. What did Jackson do about Congress's renewal of the national bank charter?

_____

_____

Prosperity Becomes Panic (page 370)

What was the Panic of 1837?

Most of the nation prospered during Jackson's last years in office. But many of the banks that Jackson had put money into during the bank war issued too much paper money. The increase in the supply of money made each dollar worth less. So the prices of goods rose. This resulted in **inflation,** or an increase in prices and a decrease in the value of money.

The nation seemed prosperous when Jackson left office. But it was a false prosperity. Jackson's vice-president, **Martin Van Buren,** won the 1836 presidential election. Shortly after he took office, a *panic* spread over the country. It became known as the **Panic of 1837.**

People took their paper dollars to the banks and wanted them exchanged for gold and silver. But the banks could not pay in gold or silver, and many banks failed. The nation's money system collapsed. A **depression,** or a deep economic slump, set in. Every part of the country suffered. But the depression hit the cities the hardest.

3. How did Jackson's actions cause economic problems during Van Buren's presidency?

_____

_____

The Rise of the Whig Party; The Election of 1840 (pages 370–371)

Who formed the Whig Party?

President Van Buren lost the 1840 election because many people blamed him for the depression. During that election, he faced a new political party, the **Whig Party.** This party originally was formed by Jackson's opponents. It was opposed to a president having too much power. The Whigs thought Jackson had too much power. In fact, they called him "King Andrew."

The Whigs chose **William Henry Harrison** to run for president in 1840. They picked **John Tyler** to run for vice-president.

The Whigs stressed the personality of their candidate and not his stand on issues. They tried to appeal to common people. Because Harrison settled on a farm in Ohio, the Whigs called him a Westerner. Their campaign worked. Harrison won the election. The election showed the importance of the West in American politics.

At his inauguration, Harrison, who was an old man, spoke in cold weather for nearly two hours. He came down with a cold that developed into pneumonia. He died one month after being inaugurated. Tyler became president.

4. Who were the Whig candidates in the 1840 presidential election?

_____

BORN TO COMMAND.

OF VETO MEMORY.

HAD I BEEN CONSULTED.

KING ANDREW THE FIRST.

Skillbuilder

Use the political cartoon at the left to answer the question.

How does this political cartoon support the Whigs' position that President Jackson had too much power?

_____

_____

Glossary/After You Read

charter A formal written document from an authority granting rights or privileges

landslide A large majority of votes for the winning side in an election

panic A widespread concern about the state of the economy

relocate To move

reform To make better

seize To take possession of with force

tariff Tax on imports

truce A temporary stop in fighting

ward Person put under the care or protection of someone else

Terms & Names

A. If the statement is true, write "true" on the line. If it is false, change the underlined word or words to make is true.

_____ 1. The idea of spreading political power to all the people and ensuring majority rule became known as <u>Jacksonian democracy</u>.

_____ 2. The <u>doctrine of nullification</u> is the practice of giving government jobs to political supporters.

_____ 3. <u>Sequoya</u> was an important Seminole leader in the Second Seminole War.

_____ 4. The <u>Webster-Hayne debate</u> was a congressional debate over nullification.

_____ 5. <u>Depression</u> is an economic term that refers to an increase in prices and decrease in the value of money.

B. Circle the name or term that best completes each sentence.

1. During the 1824 presidential election, the West supported _____.

   John Quincy Adams   John Calhoun   Andrew Jackson

2. President Jackson reformed the government by using the _____ to fill government positions.

   spoils system   doctrine of nullification   Indian Removal Act

3. _____ invented a writing system for the Cherokee nation.

   Osceola   Sequoya   Black Hawk

4. President Jackson supported the _____, which called for the government to negotiate treaties that would require Native Americans to relocate to the West.

   Indian Removal Act   doctrine of nullification   spoils system

5. The Panic of 1837 resulted in the nation's money system collapsing and the country's economy falling into a(n) _____.

   inflation   secession   depression

Main Ideas

1. What was Jacksonian democracy?

_____

_____

2. Why did President Jackson support a policy of moving Native Americans west of the Mississippi River?

_____

_____

3. How were Northern views towards tariffs different from Southern views?

_____

_____

4. Why did South Carolina threaten to secede from the Union in 1832?

_____

_____

5. What did President Jackson do about the national bank?

_____

_____

Thinking Critically

Answer the following questions on a separate sheet of paper.

1. Do you think the states should have had the right to nullify laws that they considered unconstitutional? Why?

2. Do you agree with the statement "President Jackson was a people's president"? Why or why not?

Trails West

BEFORE YOU READ

In the last chapter, you read about the economic problems facing the United States in the 1840s.

In this section, you will learn how Americans continued to move westward.

AS YOU READ

Use this diagram to take notes on the people who helped open the West.

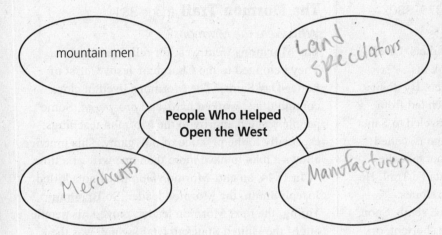

mountain men

Land speculators

People Who Helped Open the West

Merchants

Manufacturers

TERMS & NAMES
mountain man A fur trapper or explorer who discovered trails through the Rocky Mountains
Jedediah Smith Famous mountain man
Jim Beckwourth Famous mountain man
land speculator A person who buys land in the hope that it will increase in value and bring in a profit
Santa Fe Trail Trail from Missouri to Santa Fe, New Mexico
Oregon Trail Trail from Missouri to the Oregon Territory
Mormon A member of the Church of Jesus Christ of Latter-Day Saints
Brigham Young Mormon leader

Mountain Men and the Rendezvous

(pages 377–378)

Who *were mountain men?*

During the early 1800s, daring fur trappers and explorers, known as **mountain men,** helped open up the West by discovering the best trails through the Rocky Mountains. **Jedediah Smith** and **Jim Beckwourth** were two famous mountain men. These men were tough and resourceful. They spent most of the year alone, trapping small animals, such as beavers. Easterners wanted furs from these animals to make men's hats that were in fashion at that time.

The mountain men were connected to the businessmen who bought their furs. They created a trading arrangement called the *rendezvous* system. Under this system, individual trappers came to a chosen site to meet with traders from the East. The trappers bought supplies from the traders and paid them with

furs. This rendezvous took place every summer from 1825 until 1840. In that year, silk hats replaced beaver hats as the fashion, and the fur trade died out.

1. Who were the mountain men connected with in the rendezvous system?

Jedediah Smith and Jim Beckwourth

Mountain Men Open the West; The Lure of the West (page 378)

How *did mountain men open the West?*

Mountain men killed off so many beavers from some streams that they had to find new streams where beavers lived. The explorations of these men provided Americans with some of the earliest knowledge of the Far West. The trails these men *blazed* helped make it possible for later pioneers to move west.

Many people moved west to make money. **Land speculators** bought huge areas of land. They divided their land holdings into smaller sections. They made great profits by selling those sections to thousands of settlers who wanted to own their own farms. Manufacturers and merchants followed the settlers west. They hoped to make money by making and selling items that the farmers needed.

2. How did land speculators make a profit?

They ~~bot~~ bought large lots cheap, broke them into sections and sold them expensive

The Trail to Santa Fe (pages 379–380)

What *was the Santa Fe Trail?*

Traders also went west in search of markets. One Missouri trader, William Becknell, took his *merchandise* to Santa Fe in New Mexico. By doing so, he opened the **Santa Fe Trail,** which led from Missouri to Santa Fe. Becknell then traveled to Santa Fe by loading his goods in covered wagons, called prairie schooners. However, he could not take the wagons over the mountains on the Santa Fe Trail. He found a shortcut that avoided the steep slopes. Instead, it passed through a desert to the south. Soon, hundreds of prairie schooners used the shortcut, or cutoff, to make the journey from Missouri to New Mexico each year.

3. Where did the Santa Fe Trail run?

Independences Missouri to Santa Fe, NM

Oregon Fever; One Family Heads West
(pages 380–381)

What *was the Oregon Trail?*

Many settlers traveled west on the **Oregon Trail**. It ran from Independence, Missouri, to the Oregon

Territory. The first white people to cross into the Oregon Territory were missionaries. Their reports of rich land in Oregon encouraged many other American settlers to make the 2,000-mile journey.

Traveling on the Oregon Trail was dangerous. So, settlers joined wagon trains. Before setting out, the wagon train members agreed on rules and elected leaders to enforce them.

4. Where did the Oregon Trail run?

~~Missouri~~ Independence Missouri to the Oregon ~~to~~ ~~territ~~ Territory

The Mormon Trail (page 381)

Who *were the Mormons?*

The **Mormons** went west for religious reasons. They belonged to the Church of Jesus Christ of Latter-Day Saints. The Mormons lived in close communities, worked hard, and *prospered*. Some people reacted angrily to the Mormon teachings, especially to the practice of polygamy. This practice allows a man to have more than one wife at a time.

In 1844, an anti-Mormon *mob* in Illinois killed Joseph Smith, the Mormon leader. So **Brigham Young,** the next Mormon leader, moved his people out of the United States to Utah, which was then part of Mexico. In 1847, about 1,600 Mormons followed part of the Oregon Trail to Utah, where they built a new settlement by the Great Salt Lake. The Mormons built dams and canals to bring water to their farms. Through teamwork, they made their desert homeland bloom.

5. Why did the Mormons move west?

For religious reasons/there leader was killed by an anti-Mormon & Mob

The Texas Revolution

BEFORE YOU READ

In the last section, you read about how Americans continued to move westward.

In this section, you will learn how Texas gained independence from Mexico.

AS YOU READ

Use this time line to take notes on the events that resulted in the independence of Texas.

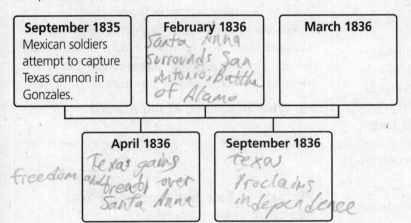

September 1835	February 1836	March 1836
Mexican soldiers attempt to capture Texas cannon in Gonzales.	*Santa Anna surrounds San Antonio, Battle of Alamo*	

April 1836	September 1836
freedom *Texas gains and treaty over Santa Anna*	*texas Proclaims independence*

Spanish Texas (pages 384–385)

Where *was* Tejas *located?*

The Spanish land called *Tejas* bordered the U.S. territory called Louisiana. Although *Tejas* was a Spanish colony, it had few Spanish settlers. In 1821, only about 4,000 *Tejanos* lived in Texas. ***Tejanos*** are people of Spanish *heritage* who consider Texas their home. The Native Americans who lived in *Tejas* fought against Spanish settlement.

The Spanish wanted more people to settle there to help defend against the Native Americans and the Americans who illegally entered Texas. The Spanish government offered huge pieces of land to *empresarios*. However, they were still not able to attract settlers. So, when Moses Austin, a bankrupt Missouri mine owner, asked for permission to start a colony in Texas, Spain agreed. When Moses Austin died, his son **Stephen Austin** took over. Spain promised Austin a large section of land. He agreed that the settlers on the land would follow Spanish laws.

1. Why did Spain give Moses Austin permission to start a colony in Texas?

To help keep others out and no one else wanted to settle there

Mexican Independence Changes Texas (page 385)

Why *did Mexico take over Texas?*

Shortly after Stephen Austin arrived in Texas in 1821, Mexico gained independence from Spain. *Tejas* was now part of Mexico. So the land grant that Austin received from Spain was worthless. He then persuaded the Mexican government to let him start his colony. The Mexican government would agree only if settlers would become Mexican citizens and Roman Catholics.

By 1827, Austin attracted 297 families to his colony. The success of the colony attracted more settlers and speculators to Texas. By 1830, Americans outnumbered *Tejanos* six to one.

2. What did American settlers have to agree to do in order to settle in Austin's colony?

_____

_____

Rising Tensions in Texas (pages 385–386)

Why *did tension increase between Americans and Tejanos?*

Conflicts arose between the Americans and *Tejanos*. Americans did not like following Mexican laws and dealing with documents that were in Spanish. Mexico also upset American slave owners by outlawing slavery in 1829. The Americans wanted slavery so they could grow cotton.

The *Tejanos* found the Americans difficult to live with. They thought the Americans believed they were superior and seemed unwilling to adapt to Mexican laws. So the Mexican government closed Texas to further settlement by Americans. It required Texans to pay taxes for the first time. To enforce these laws, the Mexican government sent more Mexican troops to Texas.

3. Why were the American settlers in Texas upset with Mexico?

_____

_____

Texans Revolt Against Mexico
(page 386)

Why *did Stephen Austin meet with the Mexican president?*

In 1833, Stephen Austin took a petition to Mexico City. The document listed changes that were supported by both Americans and *Tejanos*.

In Mexico City, Austin met the Mexican president, General **Antonio López de Santa Anna.** At first, he agreed to Austin's requests. But then Santa Anna found out that Austin had said that if Santa Anna did not approve the changes, he would support breaking away from Mexico. Santa Anna jailed Austin for a year. When they found out about Austin, the Texans wanted to rebel. Santa Anna responded by sending more troops to Texas.

4. Why did Santa Anna jail Stephen Austin?

_____

_____

The Fight for the Alamo (pages 386–388)

What *was the Alamo?*

In 1836, the Texans decided to declare Texas an independent *republic*. **Sam Houston** took command of the small Texas army. One small company was stationed at a fort in southeast Texas. The second company, headed by **William Travis,** stood at the Alamo, an old mission in San Antonio. In addition, **Juan Seguín** led a group of *Tejanos* in support of the rebellion.

Travis's force defended the Alamo for 12 days. Then the Mexicans captured it and killed all but five Texans. The **Battle of the Alamo** ended. The Mexicans executed the five survivors.

5. What happened at the Alamo?

_____

_____

Victory at San Jacinto; Lone Star Republic (pages 388–389)

How *did Texas win its independence?*

Under Sam Houston's command, the Texans captured Santa Anna near the San Jacinto River in April 1836. Houston forced Santa Anna to sign a treaty giving Texas its independence.

In September 1836, Texans proclaimed Texas an independent nation and adopted the nickname **Lone Star Republic.** Texans elected Sam Houston as president. Many Americans wanted Texas to be a part of the United States. So in 1836, the Texas government asked Congress to *annex* Texas into the Union.

Many Northerners objected because they did not want another slave state. Other people feared that annexing Texas would lead to war with Mexico. Congress voted against annexation, and Texas remained a republic for almost ten years.

6. Why were Northerners against annexing Texas?

_____

The War with Mexico

BEFORE YOU READ

In the last section, you read about how Texas gained its independence from Mexico.

In this section, you will learn how the War with Mexico extended the United States westward.

AS YOU READ

Use this diagram to take notes on the events that led to the Treaty of Guadalupe Hidalgo.

| **Event 1** Zachary Taylor stations troops on northern bank of Rio Grande. | **Event 2** | **Event 3** |

| **Event 4** | **Treaty of Guadalupe Hidalgo** |

TERMS & NAMES

manifest destiny Belief that the United States would expand across the continent

James K. Polk 11th president of the United States

Zachary Taylor U.S. General in the War with Mexico

Bear Flag Revolt Rebellion by Americans against Mexican rule in California

Winfield Scott U.S. General in the War with Mexico

Treaty of Guadalupe Hidalgo Treaty ending the War with Mexico

Mexican Cession Vast region given up by Mexico to the United States after the War with Mexico

Americans Support Manifest Destiny
(pages 390–391)

What was manifest destiny?

Many Americans believed that the United States was meant to stretch across the continent from the Atlantic Ocean to the Pacific Ocean. A journalist named this belief **manifest destiny**. The idea of manifest destiny became government policy after Americans elected **James K. Polk** as president in 1844.

The idea of manifest destiny was not a new one. By the 1840s, thousands of Americans had moved into the Oregon Territory. Both the United States and Britain occupied this area. In his campaign, Polk had talked of taking over all of Oregon. However, in 1846 the United States and Britain agreed to divide Oregon at the 49th parallel. This line determined the boundary between the United States and Canada.

1. How was Oregon divided?

_____

_____

Troubles with Mexico (pages 391–393)

Why did the United States go to war with Mexico?

In 1845, Congress admitted Texas as a slave state. However, Mexico still claimed Texas as its own. In addition, Texas and Mexico could not agree on the official border between them. Texas claimed the Rio Grande, a river south of San Antonio, as its southern boundary. Mexico insisted on the Nueces River as the border. Polk sent General **Zachary Taylor** and the U.S. army to blockade the Rio Grande. A Mexican *cavalry* unit crossed the Rio Grande and *ambushed* an American patrol, killing or wounding 16 American soldiers. Two days later, Congress declared war, and the War with Mexico began.

Not everyone favored war. Some people felt that the conflict was unjust and did not see the need to declare war. Slavery also became an issue. Southerners saw expansion into Texas as an opportunity to extend slavery. Antislavery representatives introduced a bill that would prevent slavery in any lands taken from Mexico. Despite opposition, the United States plunged into war. In May 1846, General Taylor led troops into Mexico.

2. Why did some people oppose a war with Mexico?

_____

_____

Capturing New Mexico and California
(page 393)

Who was Stephen Kearny?
Shortly after the war began, General Stephen Kearny—a U.S. army officer—and his soldiers left Kansas with orders to occupy New Mexico. Kearny took New Mexico without a fight. Part of Kearny's forces then marched to California, and part moved south toward Mexico.

In California, Americans rebelled against Mexican rule in the **Bear Flag Revolt.** The rebels declared California independent of Mexico and named it the Republic of California. The U.S. army reached California in the fall and joined forces with the rebels. Within weeks, Americans controlled all of California.

3. What happened in New Mexico and California?

_____

_____

The Invasion of Mexico (pages 393–394)

Who led the invasion of Mexico?
U.S. forces invaded Mexico from two directions. General Taylor marched south from Texas to the Mexican city of Monterrey. Near a ranch called Buena Vista, Taylor met 15,000 Mexican soldiers led by Santa Anna. After two days, Santa Anna retreated. The war in northern Mexico ended.

In southern Mexico, a second force led by General **Winfield Scott** landed at Veracruz and moved toward Mexico City. Despite fierce resistance by Mexican soldiers, Mexico City fell to Scott in September 1847.

4. How did the United States invade Mexico?

_____

_____

The Mexican Cession; "From Sea to Shining Sea" (pages 394–395)

What was the Treaty of Guadalupe Hidalgo?
The war officially ended in February 1848 with the **Treaty of Guadalupe Hidalgo.** This treaty recognized Texas as part of the United States and the Rio Grande as the border between Mexico and the United States. Mexico also *ceded* almost half of its land in the **Mexican Cession** to the United States. The United States promised to protect the 80,000 Mexicans living in Texas and the Mexican Cession and to ensure them the rights of citizens of the United States.

The United States bought more land from Mexico with the Gadsden Purchase in 1853. This strip of land crossed what is now southern New Mexico and Arizona.

5. What ended the War with Mexico?

_____

_____

_____

Name _____ Date _____

The California Gold Rush

BEFORE YOU READ

In the last section, you read how the War with Mexico extended the United States westward.

In this section, you will learn how the gold rush affected California.

AS YOU READ

Use this diagram to take notes on the effect of the California gold rush.

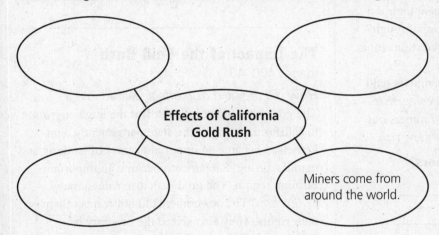

TERMS & NAMES

forty-niner A person who went to California to find gold, starting in 1849

Californio A California settler of Spanish or Mexican descent

Mariano Vallejo A *Californio* and a member of one of the oldest Spanish families in America

John Sutter A California settler on whose land gold was found

James Marshall A carpenter who found gold at Sutter's Mill

California gold rush Occurred when large numbers of people moved to California to find gold, starting in 1849

California Before the Rush

(pages 396–397)

Who were the forty-niners?

After gold was discovered in California, many people decided to become **forty-niners,** or people who went to California to find gold, starting in 1849. Before the forty-niners came, California had about 150,000 Native Americans and 6,000 *Californios*—California settlers of Spanish or Mexican descent. Most *Californios* lived on huge cattle ranches. One important *Californio* was **Mariano Vallejo.** He was a member of one of the oldest Spanish families in America and owned 250,000 acres of land.

Mexico did not give land to foreigners. But **John Sutter,** a Swiss immigrant, persuaded the Mexican governor of California to grant him 50,000 acres in the Sacramento Valley. In 1848, Sutter sent a carpenter named **James Marshall** to build a sawmill on the nearby American River. One day, as he was inspecting the canal that brought water to Sutter's Mill, Marshall found gold.

1. On whose land was gold found in California in 1848?

_____

_____

Rush for Gold (page 397)

What happened after Marshall's discovery?

Once news of Marshall's discovery spread, people raced to the American River. This started the **California gold rush.** A gold rush occurs when large numbers of people move to a site where gold has been found.

Miners soon found gold in other streams flowing out of the Sierra Nevada Mountains. Thousands of gold seekers set out to find their fortune. Forty-niners traveling from the East faced a dangerous journey on one of three routes. Some sailed around South America and up the Pacific coast. Others sailed to the Isthmus of Panama, crossed overland, and then sailed to California. Still others traveled the trails across North America.

2. How did forty-niners reach California?

_____

_____

Life in the Mining Camps (page 398)

What *was life like in the mining camps?*
Mining camps started out as rows of tents. Gradually, the tents gave way to rough wooden buildings that housed stores and saloons. Life in the mining camps was dangerous and hard. Although a few miners grew rich overnight, most did not. Miners spent their days standing knee-deep in icy streams, sifting through mud and sand to find gold. Miners faced exhaustion, poor food, and disease.

In addition to having a difficult life, miners paid high prices for supplies. Gamblers and *con artists* worked the mining camps and *swindled* miners out of their money. As a result, few miners grew rich.

3. Why was life difficult for miners?

_____

_____

Miners from Around the World; Conflicts Among Miners (pages 398–400)

Where *did miners come from?*
Most of the forty-niners were Americans. However, Native Americans, free blacks, and enslaved African Americans also worked the mines. In addition, miners came from Mexico, Europe, South America, Australia, and China. Most of the Chinese miners were farmers who left China because of several crop failures there. By the end of 1851, one of every ten immigrants was Chinese.

Often the Chinese miners took over sites that American miners had *abandoned* because the easy-to-find gold was gone. Through hard work, the Chinese yielded profits from the used sites. American miners resented the success of the Chinese, and anger toward the Chinese miners grew.

Once the easy-to-find gold was gone, Americans began to force Native Americans and foreigners out of the gold field to reduce competition. After California became a state in 1850, it passed the Foreign Miners tax. This called for miners from other countries to pay $20 a month. Most foreigners could not pay it and were forced to leave the mine fields.

4. Why did Americans resent Chinese miners?

_____

_____

The Impact of the Gold Rush (pages 400–401)

How *did the gold rush affect* Californios?
The gold rush ended in 1852. But the huge *migration* to California changed the state permanently. San Francisco became an important center of banking and manufacturing. Sacramento became an important farming region. The gold rush also ruined many *Californios*. The newcomers did not respect them or their rights. They also seized the property of *Californios*. However, Spanish heritage became an important part of California culture.

Many Native Americans died from diseases brought by newcomers. The miners hunted down and killed thousands more. As a result, by 1870 the Native American population fell from 150,000 to 58,000.

By 1849, California had enough people to apply for statehood. The United States admitted California as a free state in 1850. This upset the balance between free states and slave states, with free states outnumbering slave states.

5. What happened to Native Americans as a result of the gold rush?

_____

_____

Glossary/After You Read

abandon To leave behind

ambush To attack from a hidden place

annex To add to something else

blaze To mark new trails

cavalry Military troops that were trained to fight on horseback

cede To give up

con artist A person who cheats others out of money

empresario A person who agreed to recruit settlers for the land they were given

heritage Something handed down to later generations from earlier generations

merchandise Things that are bought and sold

migration A group moving together from one place to another

mob A large disorderly crowd

prosper To be fortunate or successful

rendezvous A meeting; from a French word meaning "present yourselves"

republic A form of government in which power lies with the voters

swindle To cheat of money or property

Terms & Names

A. Write the letter of the best description or definition of the word.

_____ 1. Mountain men were
   a. farmers.
   b. trappers and explorers.
   c. miners.
   d. ranchers.

_____ 2. Brigham Young was
   a. a Mormon leader.
   b. a mountain man.
   c. a forty-niner.
   d. a *Tejano.*

_____ 3. Antonio López de Santa Anna was
   a. the president of Mexico.
   b. a forty-niner.
   c. a Mormon leader.
   d. the president of the Lone Star Republic.

_____ 4. Sam Houston was
   a. the president of Mexico.
   b. a forty-niner.
   c. a Mormon leader.
   d. the president of the Lone Star Republic.

_____ 5. James Marshall was
   a. a soldier at the Alamo.
   b. a mountain man.
   c. a carpenter who discovered gold at Sutter's Mill.
   d. a famous *Californio.*

B. Write the letter of the name or term that matches the description.

a. land speculators   d. manifest destiny

b. Mormons   e. John Sutter

c. *Tejanos*   f. *Californios*

_____ 1. People of Spanish heritage who consider Texas their home

_____ 2. Belief that the United States would expand across the continent

_____ 3. Members of the Church of Jesus Christ of Latter-Day Saints

_____ 4. People who buy huge areas of land in hope that it will increase in value

_____ 5. Swiss immigrant who received a land grant in the Sacramento Valley on which gold was found

Main Ideas

1. What was the rendezvous system?

_____

_____

2. What caused tensions between the *Tejanos* and Americans in Texas in the late 1820s?

_____

_____

3. What happened at the Alamo?

_____

_____

4. What were some provisions of the Treaty of Guadalupe Hidalgo?

_____

_____

5. Why did California's becoming a state create conflict in the United States?

_____

_____

Thinking Critically

Answer the following questions on a separate sheet of paper.

1. What do you think would have been the most difficult hardship facing the people who moved westward on the Santa Fe and Oregon trails? Explain.

2. What were some of the causes of the War with Mexico?

The Hopes of Immigrants

BEFORE YOU READ

In the last section, you read how the gold rush affected California.

In this section, you will learn about the millions of Europeans who came to the United States in the mid-1800s.

AS YOU READ

Use this diagram to take notes on why some immigrant groups came to the United States.

Immigrant Group	Why They Came
Scandinavians	
Germans	
Irish	

Why People Migrated (pages 407–408)

Why did many people migrate to the United States?
In the mid-1800s, millions of Europeans became **emigrants,** or people who leave a country. They came to the United States. There, they were **immigrants,** or people who settle in a new country. Most immigrants made the ocean voyage in **steerage.** It is the cheapest deck on a ship. Steerage was crowded and dirty. Many passengers died or grew sick.

Even so, many people made the hard voyage. They came because of **push-pull factors.** These forces push people out of their native lands and pull them to new lands. There were five push factors. 1) The population boomed in Europe. 2) Changes in farming forced people off the land. 3) Crop failures caused hunger. 4) The Industrial Revolution made factory goods cheap. This put *artisans* out of work. 5) Some countries had religious and political conflicts.

Three pull factors drew people to the United States. 1) There was freedom of religion. 2) Americans had economic opportunity. 3) There was a lot of land.

1. What were push-pull factors?

_____

_____

Scandinavians Seek Land; Germans Pursue Economic Opportunity
(pages 408–410)

Where did various immigrants settle in the United States?
Public land sold cheaply in the United States. There was much poverty in *Scandinavia.* People left there for the United States. Many settled in the Midwest. It had forests, lakes, and cold winters like their homelands. Most Scandinavians became farmers.

Some Germans also moved to the Midwest. Many settled in Wisconsin, where the climate allowed them to grow oats. Germans also moved to Texas. Many Germans became farmers. But some settled in cities. There they opened their own businesses. Many Germans became very successful in the United States.

The Germans were the largest immigrant group to come to the United States in the 1800s. They had a strong influence on American culture.

2. Where did German immigrants settle in the United States?

_____

_____

The Irish Flee Hunger (page 410)

What was the Potato Famine?

Most Irish immigrants were Catholic. For centuries the Protestant British had ruled Ireland. The British controlled the Irish by denying them their rights. British rule caused many Irish to be poor.

In 1845, a disease attacked Ireland's main crop, the potato. This caused a **famine,** or severe food shortage. About one million people died as a result of the Potato Famine. And about two million people left Ireland.

In the United States, the Irish settled in cities. They had little education and few skills. So they had to take low-paying, backbreaking jobs. They competed with free blacks to get the jobs no one else wanted.

3. What effect did the Potato Famine have?

_____

_____

U.S. Cities Face Overcrowding

(pages 410–411)

What problems did American cities face?

Many immigrants came to live in U.S. cities. So did native-born Americans. They all hoped for a chance to make more money. The population of cities such as New York, St. Louis, and Cincinnati grew rapidly.

Urban growth caused problems. There were not enough places for everyone to live. People lived in cramped, unhealthy conditions. Crime spread. Most cities could not handle the problems. So immigrants

set up groups to help new arrivals from their home countries. Politicians gave help in return for votes.

4. What problems did immigrants face in the cities?

_____

_____

Some Americans Oppose Immigration

(pages 411–412)

Who were nativists?

Some people born in the United States thought that foreigners could not learn American ways. And they feared that immigrants might come to outnumber natives. So they treated immigrants with **prejudice.** This is a negative opinion not based on facts.

Some U.S.-born citizens wanted to end foreign influence. They were called **nativists.** Some refused to hire immigrants. Some formed secret societies. In the 1850s, nativists began a political party. If asked about their secret society, they said, "I know nothing about it." So their party was called the Know-Nothing Party. It wanted to cut immigration and to stop Catholics and foreigners from being elected to office. The party elected six governors. But it broke up over slavery.

5. Why were some U.S.-born citizens prejudiced against immigrants?

_____

_____

Immigration to the United States
(by decade)

Source: *Historical Statistics of the United States*

Skillbuilder

Use the graph at left to answer the questions.

1. About how many immigrants came to the United States between 1820 and 1830?

_____

_____

2. In which decade did the greatest number of immigrants come to the United States?

_____

_____

Chapter **14** Section 2 (pages 413–416)

American Literature and Art

BEFORE YOU READ

In the last section, you read about the immigrants who came to the United States in the mid-1800s.

In this section, you will learn about the start of truly American art and literature.

AS YOU READ

Use this diagram to take notes about important people who shaped American art and literature.

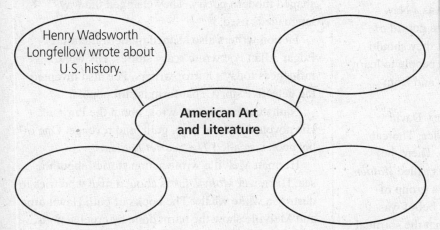

Henry Wadsworth Longfellow wrote about U.S. history.

American Art and Literature

TERMS & NAMES

romanticism A style of art that stressed the individual, imagination, creativity, and emotion

Hudson River school American painters who painted peaceful landscapes

transcendentalism A philosophy that taught that the spiritual world is more important than the physical one

civil disobedience A form of peaceful protest in which people refuse to obey laws they consider unjust

Writing About America (pages 413–414)

What was romanticism?

In the 1800s, writers began to use a new style of art. That style came from Europe. It was called **romanticism.** These writers portrayed individuals. They also wrote about imagination, creativity, and feelings. They saw nature as inspiring. Some Americans wrote about nature in the wilderness. For example, James Fenimore Cooper wrote several books about a wilderness scout.

Writers began to use a more American style. Noah Webster gave rules for that style in his new dictionary. It listed the type of English spoken in the United States. It gave American, not British, spellings. It also listed American *slang.*

Other writers retold stories from U.S. history. Henry Wadsworth Longfellow wrote poems about the past. One of his poems was about Paul Revere. For many years, students learned that poem by heart.

1. How did romanticism influence writers?

_____

_____

_____

Creating American Art (pages 414–415)

Who were the Hudson River school artists?

American painters also used nature in their work. One group of painters was called the **Hudson River school.** Those artists worked in the Hudson River valley in New York. They painted peaceful landscapes. Their paintings showed mountains, forests, and rivers.

Some artists took trips in the West. They painted the grand scenery they saw there. John James Audubon traveled across the continent. He sketched birds and animals.

Enslaved African Americans also made art. They created beautiful baskets, quilts, and pottery. Most of them did not sign their work.

2. What did American painters focus on?

_____

_____

_____

Following One's Conscience (page 415)

What *did Emerson and Thoreau believe?*
By the 1840s, Americans took pride in the growth of their *culture*. Ralph Waldo Emerson was a New England writer. He urged Americans to get rid of European influence. Emerson thought they should develop their own beliefs. He advised people to learn about life from examining themselves and from nature and books.

One of Emerson's students was Henry David Thoreau. He followed his teacher's advice. Thoreau moved to a cabin he built in the woods. There, he wrote about his simple life. The book is called *Walden*.

Emerson and Thoreau belonged to a group of thinkers with a new *philosophy*. Their belief was called **transcendentalism.** It taught that the spiritual world is more important than the physical one. It also told people to find the truth within themselves.

Thoreau believed a person's conscience was important. So he urged people not to obey laws they thought were unjust. Instead, they should peacefully refuse to obey these laws. This form of protest is called **civil disobedience.** Thoreau went to jail for practicing his belief.

3. What was civil disobedience?

_____

_____

_____

Exploring the Human Heart (page 416)

What *did writers of the 1800s write about?*
Many writers changed older styles of writing. Walt Whitman wrote poems that did not rhyme. His work praised ordinary people. Emily Dickinson wrote poems about God, nature, love, and death. Both poets shaped modern poetry. They changed the way language is used.

Fiction writers also shaped modern literature. Edgar Allan Poe wrote scary stories. His work influences today's horror writers. Poe also invented the detective story. That form is still popular.

Nathaniel Hawthorne wrote about the Puritans. His novels are about love, guilt, and revenge. One of his books is called *The Scarlet Letter*.

Herman Melville wrote action stories about the sea. His novel *Moby Dick* is about a man who tries to destroy a white whale. The books of both Hawthorne and Melville show the harm done by cruel actions.

4. How did American writers of the 1800s shape modern literature?

_____

_____

_____

Chapter **14** Section 3 (pages 417–421)

Reforming American Society

BEFORE YOU READ

In the last section, you read about the start of American art and literature.

In this section, you will learn about reform movements in the United States in the 1800s.

AS YOU READ

Use this diagram to take notes on the kinds of changes that reform movements in the United States in the mid-1800s worked for.

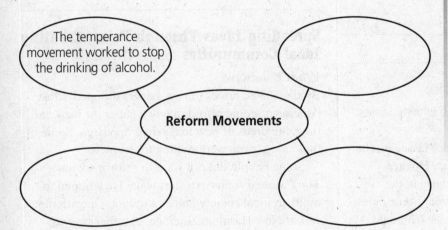

The temperance movement worked to stop the drinking of alcohol.

Reform Movements

A Spirit of Revival (page 417)

What were revivals?

In the 1800s, many Americans had a growing interest in religion. Many attended **revivals.** These are meetings to renew religious faith. There was a wide renewal of faith in the 1790s and early 1800s. It is called the **Second Great Awakening.** At revivals, preachers urged people to give up their sinful ways. Many revivals spread across the frontier. Revivals also took place in cities in the East. There, preachers taught that religious faith led people to help others.

1. What was the Second Great Awakening?

_____

_____

Temperance Societies; Fighting for Workers' Rights (pages 418–419)

What did workers demand in the early 1800s?

Some Americans began the **temperance movement.** This was a campaign to stop the drinking of alcohol. Heavy drinking was common in the early 1800s. Some workers spent most of their wages on alcohol. Because of that, their families did not have enough money. Many women joined the temperance movement. They urged people to sign a pledge to give up alcohol. By 1838, about a million people signed.

Business owners also supported the temperance movement. They needed workers who could run machines and keep schedules. Drinking made it hard to do that. Some states banned the sale of alcohol. But most of these laws were *repealed* over time.

In the 1830s, workers called for better working conditions. Young women mill workers in Lowell, Massachusetts, started a **labor union.** This is a group of workers who band together to seek better working conditions. In 1836, the mill owners raised the rent of the company-owned boarding houses. About 1,500 women went on **strike,** stopping work to demand better conditions. Other workers called for shorter hours and higher wages. Hard times made the labor movement fall apart. But in 1840, President Van Buren ordered a ten-hour workday for public workers. This met some of the goals of the labor movement.

2. How did workers seek to get better working conditions?

_____

_____

Improving Education (page 419)

How *was education improved in the United States in the mid-1800s?*

Americans also wanted better schools. Massachusetts set up the first state board of education. **Horace Mann** was its head. By 1850, many states in the North started public schools for children. Some cities in the North opened public high schools. Churches and other groups opened hundreds of new private colleges. Women could not attend most colleges. Oberlin College in Ohio was the first college to admit women as students.

African Americans faced barriers to getting an education. In the South, it was against the law to teach a slave. Even in the North, most public schools did not let African-American children go to school.

3. How did Horace Mann help reform education in the United States?

_____

_____

Caring for the Needy (pages 419–420)

Who *was Dorothea Dix?*

Some people tried to improve the way society took care of its weakest members. **Dorothea Dix** was a reformer from Boston. She learned that the mentally ill often received no treatment. Instead, they were beaten and chained. She traveled all over the United States pleading for better care for the mentally ill. As a result, 32 new hospitals were built.

Other reformers tried to make life better for people with other disabilities. New schools opened for the deaf and blind. Some reformers worked to improve prisons. They did not want children to go to the same jails as adults. They also called for adult prisoners to be *rehabilitated.*

4. What kind of reforms did Dorothea Dix work for?

_____

_____

Spreading Ideas Through Print; Creating Ideal Communities (pages 420–421)

What *is a utopia?*

By the 1830s, prices of newspapers dropped. Most Americans could afford to buy a paper. At the same time, hundreds of new magazines appeared. Some of these magazines were written for women.

Some people did not want to reform society. They wanted society to start over. They hoped to build an ideal society called a utopia. One attempt was at New Harmony, Indiana. Another was at Brook Farm, Massachusetts. In both places, residents received food and the other things they needed in exchange for work. But both places experienced conflicts and financial problems. They ended after a few years.

Some people formed utopias because of religious beliefs. One group was the Shakers. They believed that people should lead holy lives in communities. Shakers promised not to marry or have children. They shared their goods. They believed that men and women are equal. And they refused to fight for any reason. People called them *Shakers* because they shook with emotion during church services. Shakers built simple furniture in styles that are still used today. The Shakers had about 6,000 members in the 1840s. By 1999, there were only seven Shakers.

5. Why did some people build utopias?

_____

_____

Chapter **14** Section 4 (pages 424–429)

Abolition and Women's Rights

BEFORE YOU READ

In the last section, you read about reform movements in the United States in the 1800s.

In this section, you will learn about the calls for freedom for slaves and equal rights for women.

AS YOU READ

Use this diagram to take notes about the people who worked for abolition and women's rights.

Reformer	Contributions to Abolition/Women's Movements
William Lloyd Garrison	Published abolitionist newspaper Supported women's rights

TERMS & NAMES

abolition The movement to end slavery

Frederick Douglass An escaped slave who became a noted abolitionist leader

Sojourner Truth Former slave who became an abolitionist and supporter of women's rights

Underground Railroad An above-the-ground series of escape routes for runaway slaves from the South to the North

Harriet Tubman The most famous conductor on the Underground Railroad

Elizabeth Cady Stanton Leader in the abolitionist and women's rights movements

Seneca Falls Convention Convention held in 1848 to argue for women's rights

suffrage The right to vote

Abolitionists Call for Ending Slavery
(pages 424–425)

What was abolition?

<u>Abolition</u> was the movement to end slavery. It began in the late 1700s. By 1804, most states in the North had outlawed slavery. In 1807, Congress made it illegal to bring new African slaves into the United States. *Abolitionists* began to demand a law to end slavery in the South. David Walker was a free African American in Boston. He printed a pamphlet that urged slaves to revolt.

William Lloyd Garrison published a newspaper called *The Liberator.* It called for the end of slavery. Many people hated his views. Sarah and Angelina Grimké were sisters who grew up in the South. Because they thought slavery was wrong, they moved north. They became Quakers and joined an antislavery society. They spoke out for abolition.

1. How did William Lloyd Garrison work to end slavery?

_____

_____

Eyewitnesses to Slavery (page 425)

Who were Frederick Douglass and Sojourner Truth?

<u>Frederick Douglass</u> and <u>Sojourner Truth</u> were both former slaves. They became abolitionists. They spoke against slavery by telling about their lives. Douglass wrote an autobiography that described how it felt to be a slave. Douglass was a powerful speaker in favor of freeing the slaves. He also published an antislavery newspaper.

Sojourner Truth had fled her owners. She went to live with Quakers, who set her free. She spoke for abolition in the North and drew huge crowds.

2. How did Frederick Douglass and Sojourner Truth fight for abolition?

_____

_____

The Underground Railroad; Harriet Tubman (page 426)

What *was the Underground Railroad?*
Some people helped slaves escape to freedom along the **Underground Railroad.** This was an above-the-ground series of escape routes from the South to the North. Runaway slaves traveled these routes on foot, on wagons, and by boats and trains.

Runaways on the Underground Railroad usually traveled by night. They hid by day in places called stations. The people who led the runaways to freedom were called conductors. One of the most famous conductors was **Harriet Tubman.** Tubman was an escaped slave herself. She made 19 dangerous journeys to free enslaved persons. Among the people she saved were her parents.

3. How did runaway slaves escape to freedom on the Underground Railroad?

_____

_____

Women Reformers Face Barriers; The Seneca Falls Convention (pages 427–428)

What *was the Seneca Falls Convention?*
Lucretia Mott and **Elizabeth Cady Stanton** were also abolitionists. They were part of an American group that attended an antislavery convention in London in 1840. But when they tried to enter the convention, some men stopped them. The men said women should not speak in public. So the women had to sit behind a curtain.

To show his support, William Lloyd Garrison joined them. Most other people agreed that women should stay out of public life. Women in the 1800s had few legal or political rights. Many laws treated them

as children. At the end of the convention, Stanton and Mott decided to demand equal rights for women.

In July 1848, they held the **Seneca Falls Convention** in Seneca Falls, New York. It called for women's rights. The women wrote a document like the Declaration of Independence. The document listed several *resolutions*. It ended with a demand for rights. The group at the convention easily voted in favor of most of the resolutions. But they disagreed about the one for **suffrage,** or the right to vote. Stanton argued that the right to vote would give women political power. This would help them win other rights. The resolution won by a small margin. Many people made fun of the women's rights movement.

4. What did the women at the Seneca Falls Convention demand?

_____

_____

Continued Calls for Women's Rights (pages 428–429)

Who *supported women's rights in the mid-1850s?*
In the mid-1850s, three women added their support for the women's movement. In 1851, Sojourner Truth gave a speech for women's rights at a convention in Ohio. She urged men to give women their rights. Maria Mitchell was an astronomer. She helped to found the Association for the Advancement of Women.

Susan B. Anthony had worked for both temperance and abolition. She built the women's movement into a national organization. She worked to give married women the right to their own property and wages. By 1865, 29 states had such laws. Anthony also fought for women's right to vote. It was not a reality until the 1900s.

5. How did Susan B. Anthony work for women's rights?

_____

_____

Name _____ Date _____

Chapter *A New Spirit of Change*

Glossary/After You Read

abolitionist Someone working to end slavery

artisans Skilled workers who make products by hand

culture A people's customs, beliefs, laws, and ways of living

philosophy A set of opinions about life and the world

rehabilitate To prepare people to live useful lives after their release from prison

repeal cancel

resolution Pledge to do something or to keep from doing it

Scandinavia Region that includes the countries of Denmark, Norway, and Sweden

slang Special words and meanings that are used in place of standard language

urban Related to a city

Terms & Names

A. Write the letter of the name or term next to the statement that describes it best.

a. Dorothea Dix   d. nativist

b. Sojourner Truth   e. Harriet Tubman

c. Elizabeth Cady Stanton   f. Horace Mann

_____ 1. I was a person who wanted to eliminate foreign influence.

_____ 2. I was the head of the first state board of education.

_____ 3. I devoted my life to try to reform the treatment of the mentally ill.

_____ 4. I was a former slave who became an abolitionist and worked for women's rights.

_____ 5. I was a famous conductor on the Underground Railroad.

B. Write the letter of the name or term that matches the description.

a. famine   e. revivals   i. transcendentalism

b. emigrant   f. abolition   j. immigrant

c. suffrage   g. labor union   k. strike

d. prejudice   h. romanticism

_____ 1. A person who leaves a country

_____ 2. A person who settles in a new country

_____ 3. A severe food shortage

_____ 4. A negative opinion that is not based on facts

_____ 5. A style of art that stressed the individual, imagination, creativity, and emotion

_____ 6. A philosophy that taught that the spiritual world is more important than the physical one

_____ 7. Meetings to reawaken religious faith

_____ 8. A stopping of work to demand better conditions

_____ 9. The movement to end slavery

_____ 10. The right to vote

Main Ideas

1. Why did many Irish come to the United States in the mid-1800s?

_____

_____

2. Who were the Hudson River school artists?

_____

_____

3. What was the Second Great Awakening?

_____

_____

4. Why did some workers in the 1800s start labor unions?

_____

_____

5. What was the purpose of the Seneca Falls Convention?

_____

_____

Think Critically

Answer the following questions on a separate sheet of paper.

1. Some people in the 1800s set up ideal societies called utopias. Describe what you think would be a utopia.

2. Many different reform movements were started in the early 1800s. Which reform movement do you think was most important? Give reasons for your choice.

Growing Tensions Between North and South

BEFORE YOU READ

In the last chapter, you read about the movement to abolish slavery.

In this section, you will learn how differences between the North and the South threatened to tear the nation apart.

AS YOU READ

Use this diagram to take notes on how the issue of slavery contributed to the growing tensions between the North and the South.

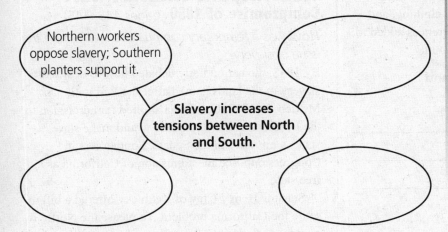

TERMS & NAMES

Wilmot Proviso A bill that proposed to ban slavery in many territories

Free-Soil Party A political party dedicated to stopping the expansion of slavery

Henry Clay U.S. senator from Kentucky who proposed the Compromise of 1850

Daniel Webster U.S. senator from Massachusetts who supported the Compromise of 1850

Stephen A. Douglas U.S. senator from Illinois who worked to pass the Compromise of 1850

Compromise of 1850 Effort by Congress to settle the issue of slavery in the territories that arose when California was admitted as a free state

North and South Take Different Paths
(pages 441–442)

How were the economies of the North and the South different?

The economies of the North and the South developed differently in the early 1800s. Farming was important in both regions. But the North began to develop more industry and trade than the South. The South continued to depend on plantation farming.

The growth of industry in the North led to the rapid growth of Northern cities. Much of this population growth came from immigration. Many immigrants and Easterners moved west. They built farms in the new states formed from the Northwest Territory. Roads and canals linked the Eastern and Midwestern states.

A few wealthy planters controlled Southern society. Their profits came from slave labor. Most slaves worked in the fields to grow crops. The most important crop was cotton. Much Southern wealth came from the export of cotton. Planters invested in slaves instead of industry. As a result, the South developed little industry.

Most Southern whites were poor farmers who owned no slaves. Poor whites accepted slavery because it kept them off the bottom of society.

1. Why did the South develop little industry?

_____

_____

_____

Antislavery and Racism
(pages 442–443)

How did the antislavery movement grow?

The issue of slavery caused tensions between the North and the South. The antislavery movement was gaining in strength in the North in the 1830s. Many Northern workers and immigrants opposed slavery. They feared that slaves, who did not work for pay, would take jobs away from them.

Although they opposed slavery, most Northerners were *racist* by today's standards. Many whites refused to go to school with, work with, or live near African Americans. In most states, African Americans could not vote.

White Southerners defended slavery by claiming that white people were superior to blacks. Slaveholders claimed that slaves benefited by being introduced to Christianity. They also argued that slaves benefited by having their food, clothing, and shelter provided for them. These differences added to tensions between the North and the South.

2. Why did Northern workers and immigrants oppose slavery?

_____

_____

_____

The Wilmot Proviso (page 443)

What was the Wilmot Proviso?
The North and the South disagreed whether slavery should be allowed in territories that were not yet states. In 1846, Congress debated the **Wilmot Proviso.** This bill proposed to ban slavery in any territory that the United States acquired from the War with Mexico. Slaveholders argued that slaves were property protected by the Constitution.

Congress divided along regional lines over the Wilmot Proviso. Northerners supported it. Southerners opposed it. Although it passed the House of Representatives, the Wilmot Proviso never passed the Senate. Southerners had more power in the Senate than in the House.

The Wilmot Proviso led to the formation of the **Free-Soil Party.** This party wanted to stop the expansion of slavery. It made slavery a key issue in national politics.

3. Why did slaveholders oppose the Wilmot Proviso?

_____

_____

_____

Controversy over Territories; The Compromise of 1850 (pages 443–445)

How was a temporary compromise reached on the issue of slavery?
By 1848, the nation hotly debated how to deal with slavery in the lands gained after the War with Mexico. In 1850, California applied for admission to the Union as a free state. This would make slave states a minority in the Senate. Southerners in Congress opposed the admission of California as a free state.

Senator **Henry Clay** of Kentucky offered a bill to settle the California problem. To please the North, it proposed to admit California as a free state. For the South, it included a strong law to help slaveholders recapture runaway slaves. The law would also let some territories decide for themselves about slavery.

Daniel Webster, senator from Massachusetts, supported the compromise. Senator **Stephen A. Douglas** of Illinois worked to pass the plan. In September, the plan became law. The plan is now known as the **Compromise of 1850.**

4. What were two features of the Compromise of 1850?

_____

_____

_____

The Crisis Deepens

BEFORE YOU READ

In the last section, you read how differences between the North and the South threatened to tear the nation apart.

In this section, you will learn how conflicts over slavery led to violence.

AS YOU READ

Use the time line below to take notes on the events that led to increasing tensions over the slavery issue.

TERMS & NAMES

Harriet Beecher Stowe Author of the antislavery novel *Uncle Tom's Cabin*

Uncle Tom's Cabin Antislavery novel written by Harriet Beecher Stowe

Fugitive Slave Act Law that helped slaveholders recapture runaway slaves

popular sovereignty A system where residents vote to decide an issue

Kansas–Nebraska Act Law that split the Nebraska Territory into Kansas and Nebraska and allowed people to vote on slavery in these territories

John Brown An extreme abolitionist

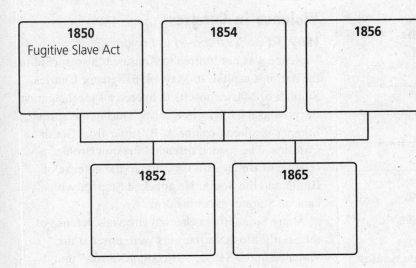

1850	1854	1856
Fugitive Slave Act		

1852	1865

The Fugitive Slave Act; Uncle Tom's Cabin (pages 446–447)

What was the Fugitive Slave Act?

The 1850 law that helped slaveholders recapture runaway slaves was called the **Fugitive Slave Act.** People accused of being *fugitives* could be arrested without a warrant.

Fugitives had no right to a jury trial. Instead, a federal official heard the case. The official was paid five dollars for releasing the fugitive. He was paid ten dollars if he turned the fugitive over to a slaveholder.

The law also required that Northerners return runaway slaves to their masters. It placed fines on people who helped runaway slaves escape.

Southern slave catchers traveled through the North. Sometimes they captured free African Americans.

The Fugitive Slave Act upset many Northerners. Northerners could no longer ignore that by supporting the Fugitive Slave Act, they played a role in supporting slavery.

In 1852, **Harriet Beecher Stowe** published the novel *Uncle Tom's Cabin.* The novel dealt with the moral issues of slavery. It described slavery as cruel and immoral. The book was popular in the North. But white Southerners believed it falsely criticized the South and slavery.

1. What did the Fugitive Slave Act call for?

_____

_____

_____

_____

The Kansas–Nebraska Act (pages 447–448)

Who *proposed the Kansas–Nebraska Act?*

In 1854, Senator Stephen A. Douglas proposed a bill that would divide the Nebraska Territory into two territories—Nebraska and Kansas. He suggested that the decision to allow slavery in these territories should be decided by **popular sovereignty**. This is a system where the *residents* vote to decide an issue.

Popular sovereignty would allow slavery in areas where it had been banned by the Missouri Compromise. Southerners supported the bill for this reason. But the bill angered opponents of slavery. Even so, the bill passed. The bill became known as the **Kansas–Nebraska Act**.

2. How was the issue of slavery to be decided in Nebraska and Kansas?

_____

_____

_____

"Bleeding Kansas" (pages 448–449)

What *happened after the Kansas–Nebraska Act was passed?*

Proslavery and antislavery people rushed into Kansas. Each side wanted to have enough people to win the vote on slavery. Five thousand Missourians came and voted in the election illegally. The Kansas legislature was packed with proslavery representatives.

Antislavery settlers *boycotted* the official government and formed one of their own. Settlers on both sides armed themselves. In May 1855, a proslavery mob attacked the town of Lawrence, Kansas. They destroyed the offices and house of the governor of the antislavery government. This attack is known as the Sack of Lawrence.

John Brown, an extreme abolitionist, entered the scene at this point. He wanted revenge for the Sack of

Lawrence. He and seven other men came into Kansas and murdered five proslavery people. This attack became known as the Pottawatomie Massacre. As news of the violence spread, a small war broke out in Kansas. It lasted for three years. The area came to be called "Bleeding Kansas."

3. Why did violence break out in Kansas in 1855?

_____

_____

_____

Violence in Congress (page 449)

Why *did violence spread to Congress?*

Violence was not limited to Kansas. It also spread to the nation's capital. In May 1856, Senator Charles Sumner of Massachusetts delivered a speech against the proslavery forces in Kansas. During the speech, Sumner insulted Senator A. P. Butler from South Carolina. The speech offended Preston Brooks, a relative of Butler. Brooks came to the defense of Butler and the South. He attacked Sumner with a cane as Sumner sat at his desk.

Many Southerners cheered Brooks's defense of the South. Most Northerners were upset at the violence in the Senate. "Bleeding Kansas" and "Bleeding Sumner" became antislavery rallying cries. They also became slogans for the new Republican Party.

4. Why did Preston Brooks attack Sumner in the Senate in 1856?

_____

_____

_____

_____

Name _____ Date _____

 Chapter **15** *Section 3 (pages 450–454)*

Slavery Dominates Politics

BEFORE YOU READ

In the last section, you read how increasing tensions over the issue of slavery led to violence.

In this section, you will learn how conflicts over slavery led to the creation of a new political party.

AS YOU READ

Use this diagram to take notes on how the slavery issue affected politics in the mid-1800s

Political Party	Views Toward Slavery	Candidates in 1856 Presidential Election
Democrats		
Republicans		
Whigs		

TERMS & NAMES

Republican Party Antislavery political party that formed in the 1850s

John C. Frémont Republican Party candidate in the 1856 presidential election

James Buchanan 15th president

Dred Scott* v. *Sandford Court case that extended the rights of slaveholders and limited legal efforts to challenge slavery

Roger B. Taney Chief Justice of the Supreme Court, who wrote the lead opinion in the *Dred Scott* case

Abraham Lincoln Illinois Republican candidate for the U.S. Senate in 1858

Harpers Ferry Location of U.S. arsenal in Virginia, which was raided by John Brown

The Republican Party Forms

(pages 450–451)

Why was the Republican Party formed?
The Whig Party split over the issue of slavery. The Southern Whigs were destroyed by the split. A few Southern Whigs joined the Democratic Party. Most searched for leaders who supported slavery and the Union.

The Northern Whigs, however, joined with other slavery opponents and formed the **Republican Party**. The Republicans quickly gained support in the North. Many Northerners blamed the Democratic Party for the violence in Kansas.

In the 1856 presidential election, the Republicans nominated **John C. Frémont**. They supported him because he was in favor of admitting California and Kansas as free states. He was also a young, handsome war hero. But the Republican position on slavery was very unpopular in the South. Frémont's name did not even appear on the ballot there.

1. Why did the Republicans nominate Frémont for the presidency in 1856?

_____

_____

The Election of 1856 (page 451)

Who ran for president in 1856?
The Democrats nominated **James Buchanan** for the presidency in 1856. He said little about slavery. He said his goal was to keep the Union together. Southerners supported him. Some Northerners also supported him because they were afraid that the nation would split apart if Frémont was elected.

The Know-Nothing Party nominated Millard Fillmore. He had been president following the death of President Zachary Taylor. The Know-Nothing Party had little strength because it was divided over slavery.

The 1856 election became two separate races. In the North, it was Buchanan against Frémont. In the

South, it was Buchanan against Fillmore. Buchanan won the election.

Although Frémont lost, he did win 11 Northern states. This showed that the Republican Party was an important force in the North. It also showed that the nation was sharply split over slavery.

2. Who were the candidates in the 1856 election and what parties did they represent?

_____

_____

_____

The Case of Dred Scott (pages 451–452)

Who *was Dred Scott?*
Dred Scott was a slave who had been taken by his master into free states. Scott claimed that being in free states had made him a free man. He sued for his freedom.

His case, ***Dred Scott* v. *Sandford*,** reached the Supreme Court in 1856. The Supreme Court, under Chief Justice **Roger B. Taney,** ruled that Dred Scott was not a U.S. citizen. As a result, he could not sue in U.S. courts.

The Court also ruled that slaves were property. As such, slaveholders' right to own slaves was protected by the Constitution. Southerners supported the decision. Northerners looked to the Republican Party to stop the growing power of Southern slaveholders.

3. What was the Supreme Court ruling in the *Dred Scott* case?

_____

_____

_____

Lincoln and Douglas Debate
(pages 452–453)

What *were the Lincoln–Douglas Debates?*
After the *Dred Scott* decision, the Republicans charged that the Democrats wanted to make slavery legal in all U.S. states and territories. Senator Stephen A. Douglas, a Democrat from Illinois, was one of their main targets.

In 1858, Stephen Douglas ran for reelection to the Senate. Republican **Abraham Lincoln** ran against him. Lincoln and Douglas held a series of debates about the expansion of slavery. Lincoln argued that slavery should not be expanded. Douglas argued that voters in each territory should decide the slavery issue for themselves.

Douglas won the election. But the Lincoln–Douglas debates made Lincoln a national figure.

4. What was the main issue in the Lincoln–Douglas debates?

_____

_____

_____

John Brown Attacks Harpers Ferry
(pages 453–454)

What *happened at Harpers Ferry?*
In 1859, John Brown wanted to inspire slaves to fight for their freedom. He planned to capture the weapons in the U.S. *arsenal* at **Harpers Ferry,** Virginia. He hoped to inspire slaves to rebel against slavery.

On October 16, 1859, Brown and his followers captured the arsenal. He sent out the word to arm local slaves. But no slaves joined to fight with Brown. Brown and his followers were captured by the U.S. Marines. They were tried, convicted, and *executed*.

Brown was praised in the North for his fight against slavery. Southerners were furious at the reaction of Northerners to Brown's execution.

5. Why did John Brown attack the arsenal at Harpers Ferry?

_____

_____

_____

Chapter 15 Section 4 (pages 455–459)

Lincoln's Election and Southern Secession

BEFORE YOU READ

In the last section, you learned how the slavery issue led to the formation of the Republican Party.

In this section, you will learn how the 1860 election led to the secession of the Southern states from the Union.

AS YOU READ

Use the diagram below to take notes on the events that occurred as a result of Lincoln's election to the presidency.

TERMS & NAMES

platform A statement of beliefs

secede To formally withdraw from the Union

Confederate States of America Confederation formed by the seceded Southern states

Jefferson Davis President of the Confederacy

Crittenden Plan Compromise plan to prevent secession

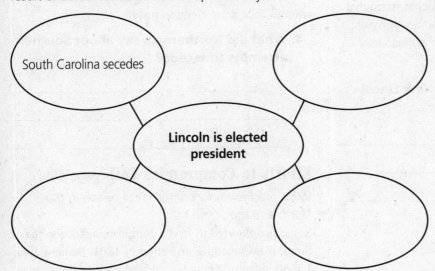

South Carolina secedes

Lincoln is elected president

Political Parties Splinter

(pages 455–456)

Who were the presidential candidates in the 1860 election?

The Republicans nominated Abraham Lincoln for president in 1860. The Democratic party split over the issue of slavery. They disagreed about what to say about slavery in the party's **platform,** or statement of beliefs.

The Southern Democrats wanted the party to defend slavery in the platform. The Northern Democrats wanted the platform to support popular sovereignty. They believed that would be the best way to decide the issue of slavery in new territories and states.

The Northern Democrats nominated Stephen A. Douglas for president. He was a supporter of popular

sovereignty. The Southern Democrats refused to support Douglas. They nominated John Breckinridge of Kentucky, a supporter of slavery. A fourth party, called the Constitutional Union Party, nominated John Bell of Tennessee. This party had one aim—to preserve the Union.

1. What parties nominated presidential candidates in 1860?

_____

_____

_____

The Election of 1860 (pages 456–457)

What were the results of the election of 1860?

The election turned into two different races for

president. Lincoln and Douglas had support in the North. Breckinridge and Bell had support in the South.

Lincoln and Breckinridge were believed to have the most extreme views on slavery. Lincoln was against expanding slavery in the territories. Breckinridge wanted the federal government to protect slavery in any territory.

Douglas and Bell were considered to be moderates. They did not want the government to pass any new laws on slavery.

The election made it clear that the nation was tired of compromise. Lincoln carried the North. Breckinridge won in the South. The North had the most people, so Lincoln won the election. Lincoln stated that he would do nothing about slavery in the South. White Southerners did not trust him. They viewed his victory as a threat to slavery and their way of life.

2. How did white Southerners view Lincoln's election as president?

_____

_____

_____

Southern States Secede
(pages 457–458)

How did the Southern states react to the election of President Lincoln?

Many Southerners warned that if Lincoln was elected, the Southern states would **secede**, or withdraw from the Union. They believed that the states had voluntarily joined the Union. As a result, they believed the states had the right to leave the Union.

In December 1860, South Carolina became the first state to secede. By February 1861, six more states seceded. They formed the **Confederate States of America**. They named **Jefferson Davis** president of the Confederacy.

3. What was the Confederacy?

_____

_____

The Union Responds to Secession
(pages 458–459)

How did the Union respond to secession?

Northerners believed that secession of the Southern states was unconstitutional. President James Buchanan argued against secession. He believed that the states did not have the right to leave the Union. He said the federal government, not the state governments, was *sovereign*.

Secession also brought up the issue of majority rule. Southerners claimed that the Northerners wanted to use their majority to abolish slavery. Northerners claimed that the Southerners did not want to accept the election results.

4. What did Northerners say about Southern attempts to secede?

_____

_____

_____

Efforts to Compromise Fail (page 459)

Who tried to find a compromise between the North and the South?

Some people tried to find a compromise to stop the South from seceding. In February 1861, Senator John J. Crittenden of Kentucky created a compromise plan. His plan, called the **Crittenden Plan,** did not pass.

In his inaugural address, President Lincoln assured the South that he would not abolish slavery there. But he spoke strongly against secession.

Lincoln did not want to press the South. He did not want to force the South to stay in the Union. Several forts in the South were still under Union control. These included Fort Sumter in South Carolina. These forts needed to be resupplied. The whole nation waited to see what would happen to the fort.

5. What issues did President Lincoln speak to in his inaugural address?

_____

_____

_____

Glossary/After You Read

arsenal A place where weapons are stored

boycot To refuse to be a part of

execute To put to death

fugitive Person who is running away

racist Having prejudice based on race

resident A person who lives in a particular place

sovereign Having supreme authority

Terms & Names

A. If the statement is true, write "true" on the line. If it is false, change the underlined word or words to make it true.

_____ 1. The <u>Wilmot Proviso</u> called for a ban on slavery in any territory that the United States acquired from the War with Mexico.

_____ 2. The <u>Compromise of 1850</u> called for popular sovereignty to decide the slavery issue in the Nebraska Territory.

_____ 3. The <u>Democratic Party</u> was formed by former Whigs and other opponents of slavery.

_____ 4. The <u>Confederate States of America</u> were formed by the seceded Southern states.

_____ 5. <u>John Brown</u> became the first President of the Confederate States of America.

B. Write the letter of the name or term next to the description that explains it best.

a. Harriet Beecher Stowe
b. Stephen A. Douglas
c. John Brown
d. Roger B. Taney
e. Abraham Lincoln
f. Jefferson Davis

_____ 1. The Republican who won the presidency in 1860

_____ 2. President of the Confederate States of America

_____ 3. Supported popular sovereignty as a way to settle the issue of slavery

_____ 4. Author of *Uncle Tom's Cabin*

_____ 5. The Chief Justice who declared in the *Dred Scott* decision that African Americans were not citizens

Main Ideas

1. What major political party was formed as a result of the Wilmot Proviso?

_____

_____

2. How did *Uncle Tom's Cabin* address slavery?

_____

_____

3. How did Abraham Lincoln and Stephen A. Douglas differ in their views on slavery?

_____

_____

4. What major event led to the secession of the Southern states from the Union?

_____

_____

5. How did Northerners and Southerners view the secession of the Southern states?

_____

_____

Thinking Critically

Answer the following questions on a separate sheet of paper.

1. What were the differences between the views of Northerners and Southerners on slavery?

2. Suppose your state wanted to secede. What arguments would you make against it?

Name _____   Date _____

War Erupts

Before You Read

In the last chapter, you read about how the nation broke apart over the divisive issue of slavery.

In this section, you will learn about the early years of the Civil War.

As You Read

Use the diagram below to take notes on the advantages of the North and South as the war began.

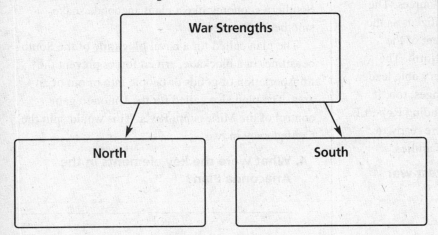

	War Strengths	
North		South

TERMS & NAMES

Fort Sumter Federal fort in harbor of Charleston, South Carolina

Robert E. Lee Confederate military leader

border state Slave state that bordered the North

King Cotton Title showing cotton's importance to the South

Anaconda Plan Union's plan to surround and defeat the South

blockade The preventing of goods or people from entering or leaving an area

First Battle of Bull Run Early battle that ended with a Confederate victory

---

First Shots at Fort Sumter; Lincoln Calls Out the Militia (pages 465–466)

Which side took the first shot?

Southern states began seceding from the Union. State officials took over most of the federal forts inside their borders. Major Robert Anderson attempted to hold on to **Fort Sumter** in the harbor of Charleston, South Carolina. However, his troops soon ran low on supplies.

President Lincoln knew that supplying the fort might lead to war. But if he withdrew the troops, he would be giving in to the rebels. He decided to send supplies. Confederate leaders responded by attacking the fort on April 12, 1861. Major Anderson soon surrendered. With this battle, the Civil War had begun.

President Lincoln called on Northerners to put down the Southern rebellion. As a result, many Northern men joined the army. States such as Kentucky, Virginia, North Carolina, Tennessee, and Arkansas reacted angrily to the president's call to

arms. They did not want to fight against their neighbors. These states seceded from the Union. They sent their men to fight for the Confederacy.

The Confederacy was happy to have Virginia on its side. Virginia was a large and wealthy state. In addition, Virginia was the home of **Robert E. Lee**. Lee was a talented and respected military leader. The Confederacy soon moved its capital to Richmond.

1. Why was Virginia important to the Confederacy?

_____

_____

Choosing Sides; Strengths and Weaknesses (pages 466–467)

What were the Union's war advantages?

Delaware, Maryland, Kentucky, and Missouri were known as **border states.** These were slave states that bordered the North. Because of their resources and location, these states could tip the scales toward one side in the war.

Keeping Maryland in the Union was especially important to the North. If Maryland seceded, then Washington, D.C., would be cut off from the Union. Pro-Union leaders quickly gained control of the Maryland legislature. As a result, the state stayed in the Union. Kentucky, Missouri, and Delaware also stayed in the Union. In the end, 24 states made up the Union. Eleven states joined the Confederacy.

The Union appeared to have a significant war advantage—in both manpower and resources. The North had more than twice as many citizens as the South. In addition, more than 80 percent of the nation's factories were located in the North. The North also had President Lincoln, a very able leader.

The Confederacy had some advantages, too. It began the war with able generals, including Robert E. Lee. In addition, Southern soldiers were ready to fight hard to defend their homes and families.

2. What were the South's greatest war advantages?

_____

_____

The Confederate Strategy (page 468)

Why was cotton king in the South?

The South did not want to conquer the North. The Confederacy only wanted to be independent. Confederate leaders hoped the North would soon tire of war and accept Southern independence.

The Confederacy hoped to win foreign support in the war. Southerners looked to **King Cotton** to win this support. Cotton was king in the South because of its importance in the world market. The South grew most of the cotton for Europe's textile mills. When war broke out, Southern planters withheld cotton from the market. They hoped that this would force France and Britain to aid the Confederate cause. However, these nations had a surplus of cotton. As a result, Europe did not get involved in the war.

3. How did the South hope to win European support?

_____

_____

The Union Strategy (page 468)

What was the Union's war goal?

The North's goal was to bring the Southern states back into the Union. To do this, the North developed an offensive strategy known as the **Anaconda Plan**. Under this plan, the North would squeeze the Southern economy like a giant anaconda snake smothering its prey.

The plan called for a naval **blockade** of the South's coastline. In a blockade, armed forces prevent the transportation of goods or people into or out of an area. The plan also called for the Union to gain control of the Mississippi River. This would split the Confederacy in two.

4. What were the key elements in the Anaconda Plan?

_____

_____

Battle of Bull Run (page 469)

Who won the Battle of Bull Run?

In the summer of 1861, Lincoln ordered an invasion of Virginia. His goal was to conquer Richmond. After marching into Virginia, Northern troops clashed with Southern soldiers near a river called Bull Run. In the North, this battle became known as the **First Battle of Bull Run**.

The Confederates won the battle. The rebel victory thrilled the South and shocked the North. The North realized it had underestimated its opponent. As a result, President Lincoln began preparing for a long war.

5. How did each side react after the Battle of Bull Run?

_____

_____

Chapter 16 Section 2 (pages 472–475)

Life in the Army

Before You Read

In the last section, you read about the first battles of the Civil War.

In this section, you will learn about the soldiers who fought the war and the hardships they endured.

As You Read

Use the diagram below to take notes on the reasons why Americans joined the Civil War.

TERMS & NAMES

hygiene Conditions and practices that promote health

rifle Barreled gun that shot a bullet long distances

minié ball A bullet with a hollow base

ironclad Warship covered with iron

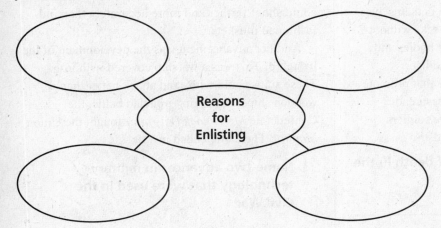

Those Who Fought; Turning Civilians into Soldiers (pages 472–474)

***Why** did Americans enlist?*

A majority of soldiers in the Civil War were between 18 and 30. About half the soldiers on both sides came from farms. Many of them had rarely left their fields. As a result, many viewed going off to war as an exciting adventure.

A majority of soldiers in the war were born in the United States. However, *immigrants* from other countries served on both sides. Irish and German immigrants made up the largest ethnic groups. Native Americans also served on both sides.

Many African Americans wanted to fight in the war. They saw the war as a way to end slavery. At first, neither side accepted African Americans into their armies. However, as the conflict wore on, the North let African Americans serve.

In all, about three million Americans fought in the war. Roughly two million soldiers served the Union. Just under a million served the Confederacy. Many of

the soldiers were volunteers. They enlisted for a variety of reasons. Some sought adventure and glory. Some wanted to escape a life of boredom. Some fought for loyalty. Others signed up for the recruitment money.

Volunteers trained in local army camps. Soldiers did hours of drills and exercises each day. They learned to stand correctly, march in *formation,* and handle their guns. Between drills, soldiers performed numerous chores. These included digging trenches, cutting firewood, and cleaning camp.

Union soldiers wore blue uniforms. Confederate troops wore gray and yellowish-brown uniforms. The uniforms often were of poor quality. Contractors took advantage of the need for uniforms and supplied shoddy goods. Some Southern states had trouble even providing full uniforms for their soldiers.

Most soldiers in army camps received plenty of food. Their rations included beef or salt pork, flour, vegetables, and coffee. On the battlefield, the soldiers' diet became more limited. Some soldiers went hungry because supply trains could not reach them.

1. What were some of the reasons that soldiers on both sides enlisted to fight in the Civil War?

_____

_____

Hardships of Army Life (page 474)

What conditions did soldiers endure?

Soldiers endured terrible conditions on the battlefield and in the camps. The fields often were wet, muddy, and cold. Many camps were unclean due to piled up garbage and outdoor toilets. The soldiers themselves often were filthy. They usually went weeks without bathing or washing their clothes. Their bodies and clothing became overrun with fleas and lice.

Hygiene—conditions and practices that promote health—was poor during the war. Widespread sickness resulted. Diseases killed more soldiers during the Civil War than battle wounds.

2. What was the main cause of death in the Civil War?

_____

_____

Changes in Military Technology (page 475)

What were some advances in military technology?

The Civil War brought about many advances in military technology. These advances led to higher death rates for both sides. One such improvement was the development of the **rifle.** A rifle is a gun with a grooved barrel that causes a bullet to spin through the air. This spin gives a bullet more distance and accuracy. A **minié ball** is a bullet with a hollow base. The bullet expands upon firing to fit the grooves in the barrel. Rifles with minié balls could shoot farther and more accurately than old-fashioned muskets.

Another advancement was the development of the **ironclad.** This was a warship covered with iron. These ships could withstand attack better than wooden ships. In the first ironclad battle, the Confederate *Merrimack (Virginia)* fought the Union *Monitor.* The battle ended in a tie.

3. Name two advances in military technology that were used in the Civil War.

_____

_____

Skillbuilder

Look at the photograph and then answer the question.

How might drill help turn recruits into soldiers?

_____

_____

No End in Sight

Before You Read

In the last section, you read about the hardships of army life during the Civil War.

In this section, you will learn about the war's early battles and how they resulted in a bloody stalemate.

As You Read

Use the diagram below to take notes on the key events of the war's early years.

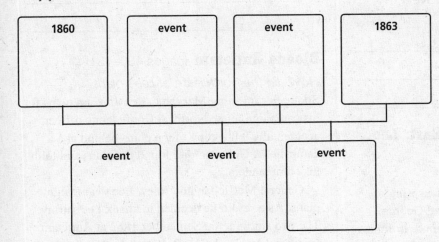

| 1860 | event | event | 1863 |

| event | event | event |

TERMS & NAMES

Ulysses S. Grant Union general

Battle of Shiloh Battle in Tennessee noted for its fierce fighting

cavalry Soldiers on horseback

Seven Days' Battles Week-long fighting in which Confederates turned back the Union effort to take Richmond

Battle of Antietam Battle in Maryland that left 25,000 soldiers dead or wounded

Union Victories in the West (page 477)

Who *was Ulysses S. Grant?*

The Union army won victories in the West. The victorious Union general was **Ulysses S. Grant.** In 1862, Grant captured two Confederate river forts in Tennessee. These were Fort Henry on the Tennessee River and Fort Donelson on the nearby Cumberland River.

The seizure of Fort Henry opened up a river highway into the heart of the South. Union gunboats could now travel on the river as far as northern Alabama. Soon after taking the forts, Union troops marched into Tennessee's capital, Nashville.

1. Why was capturing Fort Henry important?

_____

_____

_____

The Battle of Shiloh (pages 478–479)

Who *won the Battle of Shiloh?*

As a result of Grant's victories, the Confederate troops along the Western front retreated. Grant followed. The two sides met in April 1862 near Shiloh Church in Tennessee. The **Battle of Shiloh** turned out to be the bloodiest battle the Civil War had yet seen.

The North won—but at a terrible cost. The number of dead and wounded Union soldiers was more than 13,000. The Confederates lost nearly 11,000 of out 41,000 soldiers.

2. Why was the Battle of Shiloh considered a costly victory for the North?

_____

_____

_____

The Fall of New Orleans (page 479)

Why was the capture of New Orleans significant?
Another setback for the Confederacy occurred in the spring of 1862. In April, a Union fleet led by David Farragut captured New Orleans. New Orleans was the largest city in the South.

The fall of New Orleans was a heavy blow to the South. After the victories of General Grant and Admiral Farragut, the Union controlled most of the Mississippi River. The North was well on its way to cutting the Confederacy in two.

3. What goal was the North on its way to achieving with the capture of New Orleans?

_____

_____

_____

Lee Claims Victories in the East; Lee Invades the North (page 480)

Why did Lee invade the North?
Fighting increased in the East during the spring of 1862. After many delays, Union General George McClellan attempted to capture Richmond. In June, Confederate General Robert E. Lee prepared to turn McClellan's army back. Lee sent his **cavalry**—soldiers on horseback—to spy on McClellan's army and to find out its size. Lee then attacked McClellan's forces. For about a week, the two sides fought a series of clashes known as the **Seven Days' Battles.** In the end, the Confederate troops forced the Union army to retreat to Washington.

Encouraged by his victory, Lee decided to invade the Union. In September 1862, the Confederate general took his army into Maryland. Lee had several reasons for attacking the North. He hoped that a victory would force Lincoln to talk peace. In addition, the invasion would give Virginia farmers a break from the war during harvest season.

Lee also hoped that a successful invasion of the North might convince Europe to side with the South. Britain and France originally had chosen to stay out of the war. But by 1862, both countries were leaning toward supporting the Confederacy. Both nations were impressed by Lee's victories. In addition, their textile industry was suffering from a lack of Southern cotton.

4. For what reasons did Lee invade the North?

_____

_____

_____

Bloody Antietam (pages 480–481)

How did the North learn of Lee's plans?
Soon after invading Maryland, Lee drew up plans for his campaign in the North. A Confederate officer accidentally left a copy of the plans behind at a campsite. A Union soldier found the plans and told his commanders.

General McClellan now knew Lee's campaign plans. As a result, he decided to attack Lee's army. The two sides met in September 1862 at Antietam Creek in Maryland. The **Battle of Antietam** was the bloodiest day in all of American history. By the end of the one-day clash, about 25,000 soldiers lay dead or wounded.

Lee lost about one-third of his fighting force. As a result, he withdrew to Virginia. McClellan did not follow, missing a chance to finish off the wounded Southern army. President Lincoln fired McClellan.

5. Why did Lee retreat after the Battle of Antietam?

_____

_____

_____

Chapter **16** *The Civil War Begins*

Glossary/After You Read

formation A particular arrangement   **immigrant** Person arriving from another country

Terms & Names

A. Fill in the blanks with the letter of the term that best completes the sentence.

a. minié ball
b. First Battle of Bull Run
c. King Cotton
d. border states
e. Battle of Antietam

1. The _____ could sway the outcome of the war because of their location and their resources.

2. The Southerners hoped to use _____ to gain support from European textile traders.

3. The _____ is a bullet with a hollow base.

4. The Confederacy stunned the Union by winning the _____.

5. The _____ was the bloodiest day in American history.

B. Write the letter of the name or term next to the description that explains it best.

a. Robert E. Lee
b. Fort Sumter
c. Seven Days' Battles
d. Ulysses S. Grant
e. Battle of Shiloh

_____ 1. Civil War started at this fort

_____ 2. Thunderstorm made this battle a muddy one

_____ 3. Confederate military leader

_____ 4. Union general

_____ 5. Southern troops won this battle

Main Ideas

1. How did the war goals of the Union and Confederacy differ?

   _____

   _____

2. What was the significance of the First Battle of Bull Run?

   _____

   _____

3. Why were the Union victories in the West and the fall of New Orleans significant to the Union cause?

   _____

   _____

4. What factors contributed to the spread of disease among Civil War soldiers?

   _____

   _____

5. Why did General Lee go on the offensive against the North?

   _____

   _____

Thinking Critically

Answer the following questions on a separate sheet of paper.

1. Do you agree or disagree with General Lee's decision to go on the offensive against the North? Explain your answer.

2. How might both sides believe that they were fighting for a just cause in the Civil War?

The Emancipation Proclamation

Before You Read

In the last chapter, you read about the first years of the Civil War.

In this section, you will learn about the Emancipation Proclamation, which helped to change the course of the war.

As You Read

Use this diagram to take notes on the different responses to Lincoln's Emancipation Proclamation.

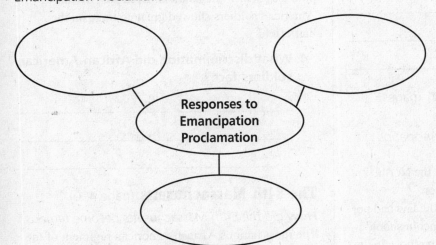

TERMS & NAMES
Emancipation Proclamation Legally freed all slaves in rebellious Confederate states
54th Massachusetts Regiment Most famous African-American regiment of the Civil War

Calls for Emancipation (pages 487–488)

Why *was Lincoln slow to end slavery?*
During the war, *abolitionists* urged President Lincoln to call for an end to slavery. Many were upset because they thought that the president was being too cautious. Some even said that Lincoln helped the Confederate cause by not acting on slavery.

Even so, Lincoln *hesitated*. He felt he did not have the power to abolish slavery. Also, he did not want to anger pro-Union groups in the South and the border states. In addition, he knew that many white Northerners opposed emancipation.

Lincoln felt that his most important task was to bring the Union back together. He did not want the issue of slavery to divide the nation further than it already had.

Even so, Lincoln realized how important slave labor was to the South. Without it, the South would grow weak and be easier to defeat. By the summer of 1862, the president had decided in favor of

emancipating, or freeing, enslaved African Americans.

1. Why did Lincoln decide in favor of emancipation?

_____

_____

_____

The Emancipation Proclamation
(page 488)

Why *was the Emancipation Proclamation important?*
On January 1, 1863, President Lincoln issued the **Emancipation Proclamation**. This proclamation freed all the slaves in rebellious Confederate states. Lincoln said the proclamation was a military action. Ending slavery in the South, he argued, would weaken the Confederacy. As Commander-in-Chief,

he was allowed to take such action. But Lincoln did not have the power to end slavery in the North. Even so, he asked Congress to gradually abolish slavery throughout the land.

There were few Union troops in the South to *enforce* the proclamation. As a result, Lincoln's act freed few slaves. But it was an important symbolic measure. For the North, the Civil War was now a war of *liberation*.

2. Why were few slaves freed by the Emancipation Proclamation?

_____

_____

_____

Response to the Proclamation (pages 488–489)

How did Americans react to the Emancipation Proclamation?

Reaction to the proclamation varied. In the North, abolitionists rejoiced at the Emancipation Proclamation. Still, many thought that the law had not gone far enough. They believed that Lincoln should have freed all enslaved persons, including those in the border states.

Many Northern Democrats opposed the president's act. They felt that the proclamation would only prolong the war by further angering the South. Even so, most Union soldiers welcomed emancipation. They believed that it would help to weaken the South.

In the South, whites reacted to the proclamation with rage. Although the proclamation had little effect in areas outside the reach of Northern armies, many slaves began to run away to Union lines.

3. How did Southerners react to the Emancipation Proclamation?

_____

_____

_____

African-American Soldiers (pages 489–490)

How many African Americans fought?

The Emancipation Proclamation allowed African Americans to join in the union army. Before the proclamation, the government had *discouraged* black enlistment. After emancipation, African Americans rushed to join the army. By the end of the war, 180,000 black soldiers had fought for the Union army.

African-American soldiers fought in all-black units. White officers usually led these units. African Americans often were assigned the worst jobs and paid less than white soldiers. Even so, African-American soldiers showed great courage on the battlefield.

4. What discrimination did African-American soldiers face?

_____

_____

_____

The 54th Massachusetts (page 490)

How did the 54th Massachusetts become famous?

The most famous African-American regiment of the Civil War was the **54th Massachusetts regiment**. The unit earned its greatest fame in July 1863, when it led a heroic attack on Fort Wagner in South Carolina. The regiment's bravery at Fort Wagner made it popular in the North. It also increased African-American enlistment.

African Americans faced greater danger than whites if captured. Southerners rarely took African Americans as prisoners. Instead, they shot black soldiers or returned them to slavery.

5. Why did African Americans face great danger if captured?

_____

_____

_____

War Affects Society

Before You Read

In the last section, you read about the Emancipation Proclamation and the effect it had on the war effort.

In this section, you will learn how the war caused social and economic changes in the North and the South.

As You Read

Use this diagram to take notes on the conditions in the North and South during the war.

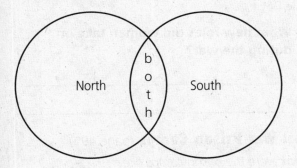

TERMS & NAMES

Copperhead Northerner who opposed the war

conscription Law that forced men to fight in the war

bounty Payment to men who volunteered for the army

income tax Tax on earnings

greenback New type of paper money

Clara Barton Woman who organized relief agencies to help soldiers

---

Disagreement About the War
(pages 491–492)

Who were Copperheads?

By 1863, people in both the North and the South had grown tired of war. Confederate soldiers began to flee the army. By the end of the year, the Confederacy had lost a large portion of its army. As the war grew more difficult, Southern states started *quarreling* among themselves.

Disagreements over the war effort also occurred in the North. Some Northerners wanted to make peace with the South. They were called **Copperheads,** after a poisonous snake. President Lincoln had many war protestors arrested. He also suspended habeas corpus, which prevents the government from holding citizens without a trial.

1. How did President Lincoln deal with war protests?

_____

_____

The Draft Laws (pages 492–493)

What was the draft?

As the war dragged on, both sides needed more soldiers. As a result, both sides passed laws of **conscription,** also known as the draft. These laws required men to serve in the military. In the South, all healthy white men between the ages of 18 and 45 had to join the army. But wealthy men could get out of the draft by hiring substitutes. Planters who owned 20 or more slaves also could avoid military service. For this reason, many Southerners complained that it was a "rich man's war but a poor man's fight."

The North offered **bounties,** or cash payments, to men who volunteered to serve. As a result, only a small percentage of men in the North were drafted. Most volunteered and received the bounty. Even so, the draft law was not popular in the North. In July 1863, anger over the draft, along with racial tensions, led to the New York City draft riots. More than 100 people were killed. Many of the victims were African Americans.

2. What led to the New York City draft riots?

_____

_____

Economic Effects of the War; Resistance by Slaves (pages 493–494)

How *did the war help the Northern economy?*
Many people had economic hardships during the war. Food shortages were common in the South. This was partly the result of farmers abandoning their farms to fight. Another problem in the South was inflation, or increasing prices. Over the course of the war, prices rose 9,000 percent in the South.

Slave resistance also hurt the Southern economy. Many slaves slowed their pace or stopped working. Some even ruined crops and *sabotaged* farm machines. A few slaves rose up in rebellion against their owners. More often, slaves simply fled their plantations to join the Union forces. With fewer slaves to provide the region's backbreaking labor, the South's economy suffered.

On the other hand, the war helped the Northern economy. War production boosted Northern industry. Also, inflation in the North was much lower than it was in the South. Even so, prices did rise faster than wages. This made life hard for working people.

During the war, the Union passed two important economic measures. In 1861, the government established the first **income tax.** This is a tax on people's earnings. The next year, the government issued a new paper currency. The bills were known as **greenbacks** because of their color. The new money helped the Union government to pay for the war.

3. How did the war affect the Northern and Southern economies differently?

_____

_____

Women Aid the War Effort (page 494)

What *did women do during the war?*
During the war, women took on new duties. With so many men away at war, women had to plow the fields and run the plantations. They also took over jobs in offices and factories.

Women also helped in the war effort. Many served on the front lines as nurses. **Clara Barton** organized a relief agency of women who washed clothes and cooked for Union soldiers. Women also played a key role as spies for both the North and the South. Harriet Tubman served as a spy for Union forces in South Carolina. The most famous Confederate spy was Belle Boyd.

4. What new roles did women take on during the war?

_____

_____

Civil War Prison Camps (page 495)

What *were the prison camps like?*
Soldiers captured during the war faced terrible conditions. One of the worst prison camps in the North was in Elmira, New York. The sanitary conditions there were awful. The harsh winters were even worse. During one year, almost one-fourth of Elmira's 12,122 prisoners died of sickness and *exposure* to severe weather.

The South had its share of horrible prison camps. The worst was at Andersonville, Georgia. Inmates held there had little shelter from the heat and cold. Many slept in holes scratched in the dirt. As many as 100 men per day died at Andersonville from starvation, disease, and exposure.

5. Name two of the nation's worst prison camps.

_____

_____

Name _____   Date _____

The North Wins

Before You Read

In the last section, you learned about the many ways the war affected society in both the North and the South.

In this section, you will learn how the Union finally won the war.

As You Read

Use this diagram to take notes on the events that led up to the Confederacy's surrender.

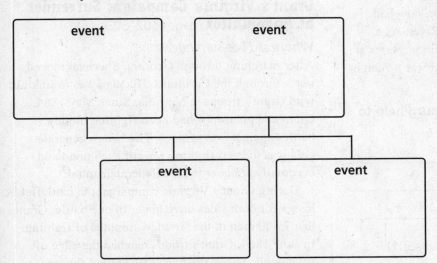

The Road to Gettysburg; The Battle of Gettysburg (pages 496–497)

Why *was the Battle of Gettysburg significant?*
Confederate forces had failed in their first attempt to invade the North. In September 1862, Union forces turned back Southern troops at the bloody Battle of Antietam. Soon, however, Confederate leaders decided to head north once again. They hoped that a Confederate victory in the North would make people in the North tired of the war. In turn, this might lead to calls for peace. Southern leaders also hoped that a victory in the North would lead to help from countries in Europe.

In June 1863, Confederate forces crossed into southern Pennsylvania. They met Union troops near the town of Gettysburg. The **Battle of Gettysburg** raged for three days. An important moment came when General George Pickett attacked the middle of the Union line. It proved to be a deadly mistake. **Pickett's Charge**, as it was called, was torn to pieces by Union troops. The Confederates retreated. As was the case after the Battle of Antietam, Union forces failed to pursue the Confederate general, **Robert E. Lee**.

Even so, the Union victory at Gettysburg was a turning point of the war. While the North had lost 23,000 men, more than 28,000 Confederate soldiers lay dead or wounded. With such losses, Lee's hopes for a Confederate victory in the North were gone.

1. Why was Gettysburg considered a turning point of the war?

_____

_____

_____

The Siege of Vicksburg (page 500)

Why was victory at Vicksburg important?
The day after Pickett's Charge, Union general
Ulysses S. Grant defeated rebel troops at the **Siege
of Vicksburg.** Grant had gained control of much of
the Mississippi River by 1863. Vicksburg was the
last Confederate stronghold on the river. Grant
began his attack on Vicksburg in May 1863. His
troops surrounded the city and prevented the
delivery of food and supplies. After a month and a
half, the starving Confederates finally surrendered.

Grant's victory at Vicksburg fulfilled a major
part of the *Anaconda Plan*. The Union now had
complete control of the Mississippi River. As a
result, the South was split in two. With victories at
Vicksburg and Gettysburg, the tide of war turned in
favor of the North.

**2. How did the victory at Vicksburg help to
fulfill the Anaconda Plan?**

_____

_____

_____

Sherman's Total War (pages 500–501)

What is total war?
Unlike other Union generals, Ulysses Grant was
willing to follow and fight General Lee. This
impressed President Lincoln. In March 1864,
Lincoln made General Grant commander of all the
Union armies. Grant quickly made a plan to defeat
the Confederacy. He would pursue Lee's army in
Virginia. Meanwhile, Union forces under **William
Tecumseh Sherman** would push through the Deep
South to Atlanta and the Atlantic Coast.

As he marched through the South, Sherman
waged total war. This was war not only against the
enemy troops. It was also against everything that
supported the enemy. His troops tore up rail lines,
destroyed crops, and burned towns.

Sherman's victories were important for Lincoln.
In 1864, Lincoln was involved in a tough reelection

campaign. Many Northerners were tired of the war.
With Sherman's successes, Northerners suddenly
could sense victory. This optimism helped Lincoln
to win reelection.

**3. Why were Sherman's successes important
for Lincoln?**

_____

_____

_____

Grant's Virginia Campaign; Surrender at Appomattox (pages 502–503)

Where did Lee surrender?
After marching through Georgia, Sherman moved
north through the Carolinas. His plan was to link up
with Grant's troops in Virginia. Since May 1864,
Grant and his troops had been fighting bloody
battles against Lee's forces. The Union general's
goal was to keep fighting toward Richmond and
eventually conquer the Confederate capital.

During Grant's Virginia campaign, the battlefield
losses for both sides were huge. In one battle, Grant
lost 7,000 men in the first few minutes of fighting.
In June 1864, Grant's troops reached the edge of
Richmond. There, the two sides battled for ten
months. In the end, Lee could not hold out. The
Union army marched into Richmond on April 3,
1865.

On April 9, 1865, Lee and Grant met at
Appomattox Court House in Virginia. There, the
two men arranged a surrender. Grant offered
generous terms. After handing over their weapons,
the Confederates were free to return home. After
four long years, the Civil War was over.

**4. Why were Grant's terms of surrender
considered generous?**

_____

_____

_____

Chapter **17** Section 4 (pages 504–507)

The Legacy of the War

Before You Read

In the last section, you read about how the Union won the war.

In this section, you will learn how the Civil War brought many changes and challenges to the United States.

As You Read

Use this diagram to take notes on the social, economic, and political legacy of the war.

Thirteenth Amendment Constitutional amendment that officially ended slavery

John Wilkes Booth Confederate who murdered President Lincoln

Legacy of the War		
Social	Economic	Political

Costs of the War (pages 504–505)

What *was the war's human cost?*

The Civil War was the deadliest war in American history. In four years of fighting, about 620,000 soldiers died. The Union lost about 360,000 soldiers, while roughly 260,000 died fighting for the Con federacy. Another 535,000 soldiers were wounded.

Altogether, about 3 million soldiers served in the armies of the North and the South. That was nearly 10 percent of the country's population. Along with the soldiers, many other Americans had their lives disrupted by the war.

The war also had great economic costs. Together, the North and the South spent more than five times the amount spent by the government in the previous 80 years. Many years after the war, the federal government was still paying interest on loans taken out during the war.

1. How many soldiers were killed on each side?

_____

_____

_____

The Thirteenth Amendment (page 505)

What *did the Thirteenth Amendment declare?*

One of the greatest effects of the war was the freeing of millions of enslaved persons through the Emancipation Proclamation. As the Union army marched through the South during and after the war, soldiers released African Americans from slavery.

The Emancipation Proclamation applied mainly to slaves in the Confederacy. However, African Americans in the border states were still enslaved. In 1864, President Lincoln had approved a constitutional amendment to end slavery throughout the nation. The measure failed to pass Congress.

In January 1865, Lincoln tried again. This time, Congress passed the **Thirteenth Amendment.** The amendment officially banned slavery in the United States. By the end of the year, the required number of states had ratified the amendment. As a result, it became part of the U.S. Constitution.

2. What was the difference between the Emancipation Proclamation and the Thirteenth Amendment?

_____

_____

_____

Lincoln's Assassination (pages 505–506)

Who *killed President Lincoln?*

President Lincoln did not live to see the end of slavery. Five days after the South surrendered, the president and his wife went to see a play at Ford's Theater in Washington, D.C. During the play, a Confederate supporter named **John Wilkes Booth** crept into the balcony where Lincoln and his wife sat. He shot the president in the back of the head. Booth managed to escape but was found several days later and killed by soldiers.

President Lincoln died the next day. He was the first American president to be assassinated. Lincoln's murder stunned the nation and caused intense grief. The loss of his experience and political skills was a terrible setback for a people faced by the challenges of rebuilding their nation.

3. Why did Booth assassinate President Lincoln?

_____

_____

_____

Consequences of the War (pages 506–507)

How *did the war affect the nation?*

The Civil War changed the nation in many ways. In the North, the conflict changed the way people thought about the country. In fighting to defend the Union, people began to think of the United States as a single nation rather than as a collection of states.

The war also caused the national government to *expand.* Before the war, the government was relatively small and had limited powers. With the demands of war, the government grew larger and more powerful. The war also *transformed* the Northern economy. New industries such as steel, petroleum, food processing, and manufacturing grew rapidly. By the late 1800s, industry was replacing farming as the basis of the national economy.

For the South, the war brought economic disaster. Farms and plantations were destroyed. About 40 percent of the South's livestock was killed. Half of its farm equipment was wrecked. Factories were destroyed, and thousands of miles of railroad tracks were torn up. In addition, slavery—the system that built the Southern economy—was gone.

The country as a whole faced other difficult challenges after the war. How would the South be brought back into the Union? Moreover, how would the nation address the needs of four million former slaves and bring them into national life? These questions would occupy the nation's energies for many years to come.

4. What challenges did the nation face after the war?

_____

_____

_____

Chapter **17** *The Tide of War Turns*

Glossary/After You Read

abolitionist Someone who called for an end to slavery

Anaconda Plan A plan that called for the control of the Mississippi River

discourage To deter from doing

enforce To compel obedience to

expand To enlarge, grow

exposure Subjected to elements, such as weather

generous Lacking meanness or pettiness

hesitate To wait before acting

liberation Freedom from oppression or slavery

quarrel To argue

sabotage To secretly damage property

transform To change appearance

Terms & Names

A. Fill in the blanks with the letter of the term that best completes the sentence.

  a. Emancipation Proclamation   d. Appomattox Court House
  b. conscription   e. Clara Barton
  c. Ulysses S. Grant

  1. Robert E. Lee surrendered to Ulysses S. Grant at _____ in Virginia.

  2. Anger over _____ helped spark riots in New York City.

  3. The _____ freed slaves living in rebellious Confederate states.

  4. _____ organized other women to help with the war effort by washing clothes and cooking for the Union soldiers.

  5. _____ led the Siege of Vicksburg.

B. Write the letter of the name or term next to the description that explains it best.

  a. General Sherman   e. John Wilkes Booth   h. Ulysses S. Grant
  b. Battle of Gettysburg   f. greenbacks   i. Robert E. Lee
  c. Copperheads   g. Pickett's Charge   j. bounties
  d. 54th Massachusetts

_____ 1. Most famous African-American regiment

_____ 2. Confederate general

_____ 3. Union commander that finally stopped Lee

_____ 4. President Lincoln delivered an important speech after this battle

_____ 5. Assassinated President Lincoln

_____ 6. Bold Confederate attack in the middle of Union lines

_____ 7. Paper currency issued in the North

_____ 8. Waged total war on the Deep South

_____ 9. Northerners who wanted to make peace with the South

_____ 10. Cash payments offered to men who volunteered to serve in the Union army

Main Ideas

1. What were Lincoln's reasons for not emancipating slaves when the war began?

   _____

   _____

2. How did the draft laws in the North and South differ?

   _____

   _____

3. How did women aid the war effort?

   _____

   _____

4. Why was the Battle of Gettysburg important?

   _____

   _____

5. What did the Thirteenth Amendment achieve?

   _____

   _____

Thinking Critically

Answer the following questions on a separate sheet of paper.

1. How did the Emancipation Proclamation change the role of African Americans in the war?

2. Do you agree with President Lincoln's methods of dealing with war protestors? Why or why not?

Chapter **18** Section 1 (pages 517–521)

Rebuilding the Union

Before You Read

In the last chapter, you read about how the North won the nation's long and bloody civil war.

In this section, you will learn about the effort to rebuild the Union— and the conflict it caused between the president and Congress.

As You Read

Use this diagram to take notes on the different plans for Reconstruction.

Person(s)	Reconstruction Plan
Lincoln	
Johnson	
Radical Republicans	

TERMS & NAMES

Reconstruction The process of readmitting Confederate states to the Union

Freedmen's Bureau Organization that helped former slaves

Andrew Johnson 17th president

black codes Laws limiting freedom of former slaves

Radical Republicans Congressmen who wanted the federal government to change Southern society

civil rights Rights granted to all citizens

Fourteenth Amendment Amendment providing equal rights for all U.S. citizens

Reconstruction Begins (pages 517–518)

What was Reconstruction?

Reconstruction was the process of bringing the Confederate states back into the Union after the Civil War. It lasted from 1865 to 1877.

President Lincoln's Reconstruction plan included pardoning Confederate officials. He wanted Southern states to quickly form new governments and send representatives to Congress.

To help former slaves, Lincoln set up the **Freedmen's Bureau.** The Bureau set up schools and hospitals for African Americans. It also gave out clothes, food, and fuel.

Lincoln was killed in 1865. Vice-President **Andrew Johnson** became president. Johnson based his Reconstruction plan on Lincoln's goals. Southern state governments had to forbid slavery. They had to accept the *supreme* power of the federal government. Johnson pardoned white Southerners who pledged loyalty.

1. What did President Johnson require of the Confederate states?

_____

_____

Rebuilding Brings Conflict (pages 518–519)

Who were the Radical Republicans?

The new state governments in the South seemed very much like the old ones. Some states refused to *ratify* the Thirteenth Amendment. This amendment had ended slavery. Southern states also passed **black codes.** These laws limited the freedom of former slaves.

When Congress met late in 1865, its members would not seat representatives from the South. Instead, Congress set up a committee to study conditions in the South.

There were more Republicans than Democrats in Congress. Most Republicans believed that the federal government should stay out of affairs of the states. The **Radical Republicans** did not agree. They wanted the federal government to be active in changing Southern politics and society. They demanded full and equal citizenship for freed African Americans. Their goal was to turn the South into a place of small farms, free schools, respect for labor, and political equality.

2. What did Radical Republicans want?

_____

_____

The Civil Rights Act; The Fourteenth Amendment (pages 519–520)

***What** did the Fourteenth Amendment state?*
Urged by the Radical Republicans, Congress passed a bill promoting **civil rights.** These are rights granted to all citizens. The Civil Rights Act of 1865 declared that all persons born in the United States were citizens. The act also stated that all citizens were entitled to equal rights regardless of their race.

President Johnson rejected, or *vetoed,* the bill. He argued that making African Americans full citizens would "operate against the white race." Congress voted to override the president's veto. This meant that two-thirds of the House and two-thirds of the Senate voted for the bill after the president's veto. As a result, the bill became law.

Republicans were not satisfied with passing laws that *ensured* equal rights. They wanted the Constitution to protect equality. As a result, Congress proposed the **Fourteenth Amendment.** It stated that all people born in the United States were citizens and had the same rights. President Johnson refused to support the amendment. So did most Southern states. This made both moderate and Radical Republicans angry.

Together, the two groups passed the Reconstruction Acts of 1867. This began the period known as Radical Reconstruction. One of the acts divided the South into five districts under Army rule. The act also set two requirements for a state to reenter the Union. First, it had to grant African-American males the right to vote. Second, it had to ratify the Fourteenth Amendment.

3. What did Southern states have to do before they could reenter the Union?

_____

_____

The New Southern Governments (page 520)

***Who** wrote the new state constitutions?*
In 1867, Southern voters chose delegates to draft their new state constitutions. About three-fourths of the delegates were Republicans. Almost half of the Republicans were poor white farmers. These delegates were called scalawags (scoundrels) for going along with Radical Reconstruction.

One-fourth of the Republican delegates were carpetbaggers. These were white Northerners who had rushed to the South after the war. African Americans made up the rest of the Republican delegates.

The new state constitutions set up public schools. They gave the vote to all adult males, including African Americans. By 1869, voters in each former Confederate state had approved their new constitutions. As a result, the states came back into the Union. They could again send representatives to Congress.

During Reconstruction, more than 600 African Americans served in Southern state legislatures. More than a dozen also served in Congress.

4. To what three groups did the Republican delegates belong?

_____

_____

Johnson Is Impeached (page 521)

***Why** was Johnson impeached?*
President Johnson fought many of Congress's efforts during Radical Reconstruction. The conflict between Johnson and Congress soon brought a showdown.

In 1867, Congress passed the Tenure of Office Act. This act said that the president could not fire Cabinet members without the Senate's approval. Johnson did not support the law. In February 1868, he fired his secretary of war. Because of this, the House of Representatives voted to impeach the president. This means that the House formally accused him of improper behavior.

The lawmakers charged Johnson with disobeying the Tenure of Office Act. But most saw Johnson's real crime as blocking their Reconstruction plans. The case went to the Senate for trial. President Johnson was *acquitted,* or cleared, by one vote.

5. What did Congress see as Johnson's "real" crime?

_____

_____

Chapter **18** *Section 2 (pages 524–528)*

Reconstruction and Daily Life

Before You Read

In the last section, you read about the conflict that arose between the president and Congress over Reconstruction.

In this section, you will learn how Southerners—in particular, freed African Americans—worked to improve their lives.

As You Read

Use this diagram to take notes on the advances and struggles African Americans experienced with their newfound freedom.

TERMS & NAMES

freedmen's school A school set up to educate former slaves

sharecropping System in which a landowner provided land to a farmer in return for a share of the crop

Ku Klux Klan Group that sought to keep former slaves powerless

lynch To punish a person by killing him or her without a trial

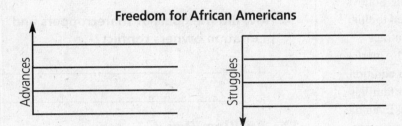

Freedom for African Americans

Advances

Struggles

Responding to Freedom; Starting Schools (pages 524–525)

Why *did freed slaves travel?*

African Americans' first reaction to freedom was to leave plantations. Some former slaves returned to where they had been born. Others traveled in search of family members separated from them during slavery. The Freedmen's Bureau helped many families to reunite.

No longer slaves, African Americans could work for themselves. However, first they had to learn to read and write. Throughout the South, African-American children and adults flocked to **freedmen's schools.** These schools were set up by the Freedmen's Bureau, Northern missionary groups, and African-American organizations.

More than 150,000 African-American students were attending 3,000 schools by 1869. Southern and Northern teachers, both white and black, taught in the schools. However, many white Southerners worked against these teachers' efforts. White racists even killed teachers and burned schools in some parts of the South.

1. Why did former slaves want an education?

_____

_____

_____

40 Acres and a Mule (page 526)

Why *did freedmen want land?*

More than anything else, freed people hoped to own land. They saw land as a key to economic freedom. As the Civil War ended, a rumor spread that all freedmen would get 40 acres and a mule. In the end, most freedmen never got land.

Radical Republican leaders pushed to make land reform part of the Reconstruction Acts of 1867. Their plan called for taking land from plantation owners and giving it to freed people.

However, many in Congress were against the plan. They believed that new civil rights and voting freedoms were enough to give African Americans a better life. Supporters of the plan disagreed. They argued that civil rights meant little without economic independence. They added that owning land could give freedmen that independence. In the end, Congress did not pass the land-reform plan.

2. Why did many in Congress oppose the land reform plan?

_____

_____

The Contract System (pages 526–527)

What was the contract system?
Without their own land, many freedmen had to return to work on the plantations. They returned not as slaves, but as wage earners. This meant that plantation owners had to pay them for their work.

After the Civil War, planters desperately needed workers to raise cotton. Cotton was still the South's main cash crop. African Americans reacted to this demand for labor by choosing the best contract offers. Under the contract system, African Americans could decide which planter to work for. In addition, planters could not abuse freedmen or split families.

The contract system had its drawbacks. Even the best contracts paid very low wages. Workers often could not leave the plantation without permission. Many owners cheated workers out of wages and other benefits. Furthermore, laws punished workers for breaking their contracts. This was true even if owners were abusing or cheating workers.

3. What were the drawbacks of the contract system?

_____

_____

Sharecropping and Debt (pages 527–528)

What was sharecropping?
The drawbacks of the contract system made many African Americans turn to **sharecropping**. Under the sharecropping system, a worker rented a plot of land to farm. The landowner provided the tools, seed, and housing. At harvest time, the sharecropper gave the landowner a share of the crop. This system gave families without land a place to farm. In return, landowners got cheap labor.

Problems soon arose with the sharecropping system. One reason was that farmers and landowners had opposite goals. Farmers wanted to grow food to feed their families. But landowners forced them to grow cash crops, such as cotton. This meant that farmers had to buy their food. Most farmers were too poor to pay for goods. As a result, they had to borrow money and thus were always in *debt*.

African Americans were not the only ones who became sharecroppers. Many white farmers also began sharecropping. Some had lost their land in the war. Others had lost it to taxes.

After the war, the value of cotton dropped. Southern planters responded by trying to grow even more of the cash crop. As a result, the price of cotton dropped even further.

4. How did the goals of sharecroppers and plantation owners conflict?

_____

_____

The Ku Klux Klan (page 528)

What was the Ku Klux Klan?
During Reconstruction, African Americans in the South faced violent racism. Many planters and former Confederate soldiers did not want African Americans to have more rights. Such feelings spurred the rise in 1866 of the **Ku Klux Klan**. The members of this secret society wanted to restore Democratic control of the South. They also wanted to keep former slaves powerless.

Klansmen dressed in white robes and hoods. They attacked African Americans and other Republicans. They beat people and burned homes. They even hanged some victims without a trial. This was known as **lynching**. Klan victims had little protection. Military authorities were sympathetic to white Southerners. They often ignored the Klan violence.

The Klan's terror tactics kept Republicans away from the polls. As a result, Democrats increased their power in the South.

5. What were the goals of the Ku Klux Klan?

_____

_____

Name _____ Date _____

Chapter **18** Section 3 (pages 529–533)

End of Reconstruction

Before You Read

In the last section, you read how African Americans in the South coped with their newfound freedom.

In this section, you will learn about how Southern Democrats regained power and Reconstruction ended.

As You Read

Use this diagram to take notes on the events contributing to the end of Reconstruction.

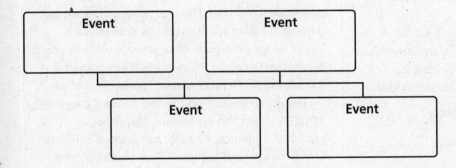

The Election of Grant; The Fifteenth Amendment (pages 529–530)

What *was African Americans' role in Grant's election?*

Republican candidate Ulysses S. Grant won the presidency in 1868. Grant got 214 electoral votes. His Democratic opponent received only 80. The popular count was much closer. Grant received a majority of only 306,000 votes.

This slim majority highlighted freedmen's role in the Republican victory. About 500,000 African Americans voted in the South. They did so despite attacks by the Ku Klux Klan. Most voted for Grant.

African Americans played an important role in the 1868 presidential election. As a result, Radical Republicans worried that Southern states might try to keep African Americans from voting in future elections. To prevent this, Radical leaders proposed the **Fifteenth Amendment**. This amendment stated that citizens could not be stopped from voting "on account of race, color, or previous condition of servitude." The amendment became law in 1870.

1. What did the Fifteenth Amendment state?

_____

_____

Grant Fights the Klan
(page 530)

How *did Grant battle the Klan?*

During President Grant's first year in office, Ku Klux Klan violence continued. As a result, Grant asked Congress to pass a tough law against the Klan. Congress approved the anti-Klan bill. Federal marshals then arrested thousands of Klansmen.

Klan violence against African Americans declined. As a result, the 1872 presidential election was both fair and peaceful in the South. Grant won the election and served a second term.

2. What was the result of the anti-Klan bill?

_____

_____

Scandal and Panic Weaken Republicans
(page 531)

What was the Panic of 1873?

Scandals hurt the Grant administration. They also weakened support for Reconstruction. Many of Grant's advisers were unqualified. Others took bribes. In 1872, some outraged Republican officials formed a new group, the Liberal Republican Party. The Republicans suddenly were split. As a result, they were less willing to *impose* tough Reconstruction plans on the South.

In 1873, an economic depression struck the nation. The depression began when several powerful Eastern banks failed. A financial panic, known as the **Panic of 1873,** followed. Banks across the land closed. The stock market temporarily collapsed.

The depression lasted about five years. Railroads failed, and many farmers were ruined. Many Americans blamed the Republicans for the crisis. During the depression, the nation lost interest in Reconstruction.

3. What hurt the Republican Party?

_____

_____

_____

Supreme Court Reversals (page 532)

How did the Supreme Court affect Reconstruction?

The Supreme Court also hurt the Republicans' Reconstruction efforts. In an 1876 case, *U.S.* v. *Cruikshank,* the Court ruled that the federal government could not punish individuals who *violated* the civil rights of African Americans. Only the states had that power, the Court ruled. Southern state officials rarely punished attackers. As a result, violence against African Americans increased.

In another 1876 case, *U.S.* v. *Reese,* the Court weakened the Fifteenth Amendment. This amendment sought to ensure the right to vote for African Americans. The Court ruled that the amendment merely listed grounds on which states could not deny the vote. As a result, states could

prevent African Americans from voting for other reasons.

4. In what ways did the Supreme Court weaken Reconstruction?

_____

_____

_____

Reconstruction Ends; Legacy of Reconstruction (pages 532–533)

What was the Compromise of 1877?

The final blow to Reconstruction came with the 1876 presidential election. The race between Democrat Samuel J. Tilden and Republican Rutherford B. Hayes ended in dispute. Congress appointed a special committee to decide the election. The committee included eight Republicans and seven Democrats.

The group made a deal known as the **Compromise of 1877.** Under this agreement, Hayes became president. In return, Republicans granted Southern Democrats several requests. They would remove federal troops from the South and provide federal funds for construction and improvement projects. After the removal of troops, Reconstruction governments in the South collapsed.

African Americans made lasting gains during Reconstruction. Protection of civil rights became part of the U.S. Constitution. Black schools and churches begun during Reconstruction *endured.*

But many African Americans still lived in poverty. Legally, they could vote and hold public office. But few took part in politics. Furthermore, African Americans continued to face widespread violence and prejudice.

5. How was the legacy of Reconstruction a mixed one for African Americans?

_____

_____

_____

Chapter 18 Reconstruction

Glossary/After You Read

acquit To clear of a charge

debt A state of owing money or goods

endure To carry on despite hardship

ensure To make certain or guarantee

impose To force or set requirements

ratify To approve or make valid

supreme Highest

veto To reject

violate To break a law or refuse to honor

Terms & Names

A. Fill in the blanks with the letter of the term that best completes the sentence.

a. black codes

b. Reconstruction

c. Fourteenth Amendment

d. Fifteenth Amendment

e. Compromise of 1877

1. Republicans and Democrats reached an agreement known as the _____, which gave Rutherford Hayes the presidency.

2. The _____ stated that all people born in the United States were citizens.

3. _____ was the process of bringing Confederate states back into the Union.

4. To ensure full voting rights for African Americans, Congress passed the _____.

5. While African Americans were no longer enslaved, _____ greatly limited their freedom.

B. Write the letter of the best description or definition of the word.

1. The Freedmen's Bureau was
   a. a group that terrorized African Americans.
   b. a new political party.
   c. a government organization that helped former slaves.
   d. a branch of the Democratic Party.

2. Radical Republicans were
   a. congressmen who wanted to change the South.
   b. a group that terrorized African Americans.
   c. ex-Confederate soldiers.
   d. supporters of President Andrew Johnson.

3. Lynching is
   a. a form of farming.
   b. the act of charging a president with wrongdoing.
   c. the act of killing someone without a trial.
   d. a type of land reform.

4. The Panic of 1873
   a. was caused by African American riots.
   b. was caused by bank failures.
   c. led to the destruction of cities.
   d. led to years of economic boom.

5. Sharecropping is
   a. a form of farming.
   b. a form of education.
   c. a form of terrorism.
   d. a form of sharing political power.

Main Ideas

1. What were some activities of the Freedmen's Bureau?

   _____

   _____

2. What did the Reconstruction Acts of 1867 do?

   _____

   _____

3. How did former slaves try to improve their lives after freedom?

   _____

   _____

4. Why was the Ku Klux Klan created?

   _____

   _____

5. What did Republicans and Democrats gain from the Compromise of 1877?

   _____

   _____

Thinking Critically

Answer the following questions on a separate sheet of paper.

1. Why were land ownership and education so important to freed African Americans?

2. Do you think Reconstruction was a success or a failure? Explain.

A Time of Growth

BEFORE YOU READ

In the last chapter, you learned about Reconstruction. In this section, you will read about Western expansion and industrial growth in the United States between the Civil War and World War I.

AS YOU READ

Use this diagram to list the factors that contributed to the industrial growth in the United States.

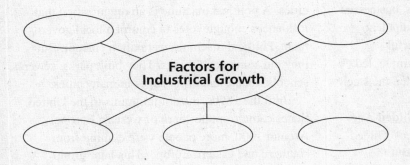

Factors for Industrial Growth

TERMS & NAMES

frontier Sparsely populated area on the western edge of the U.S. settlements

Great Plains The area from the Missouri River to the Rocky Mountains

Homestead Act Law that offered free land to settlers to encourage them to settle in the West

Dawes Act Law designed to encourage Native Americans to become farmers

Gilded Age The late 1800s, a time of great wealth but also of great poverty

urbanization Growth of cities

new immigrants Immigrants arriving from southern and eastern Europe after 1900

Westward Expansion (pages 539–540)

Why *did settlers move to the frontier?*

After the Civil War, more Americans began to settle on the **frontier.** The frontier was the *sparsely* populated area on the western edge of U.S. settlements. Only a few Native Americans lived there. The frontier included the **Great Plains,** the area from the Missouri River to the Rocky Mountains.

Some Americans went to the West to get rich. Gold had been discovered in California. Some settlers wanted to have ranches to supply beef to growing cities. Many others went to the frontier to be farmers.

The federal government encouraged western settlement. Congress passed the **Homestead Act** in 1862. This law offered 160 acres of free land to anyone who would live on the land and improve it.

Railroads played an important role in the western movement. Trains took miners, ranchers, and farmers west to work. They also brought minerals, timber, crops, and cattle from the West to the East.

White settlers who moved to the frontier often clashed with Native Americans. Most Native American tribes had been forced onto *reservations.*

Many reformers believed Native Americans should give up their traditional cultures. The **Dawes Act** was passed in 1887. This act encouraged Native Americans to give up their traditional cultures and become farmers. The U.S. government sent many Native American children to boarding schools to be "Americanized." In the end, the Dawes Act did little to help Native Americans. Not all of them wanted to be farmers. Those who did want to be farmers often lacked the tools, money, or other resources to be successful.

1. What attracted people to the West?

_____

_____

The Growth of Industry (pages 540–541)

What *helped the United States industrialize?*

While thousands of Americans started new lives in the West, the rest of the nation experienced the Industrial Revolution. A number of factors sped up industrialization in the United States:

1. **Plentiful natural resources** The country was rich in raw materials, including forests, water, coal, iron, copper, silver, and gold.
2. **Improved transportation** Steamboats, canals, and railroads made it easier to ship items.
3. **Growing population** From 1860 to 1900, the U.S. population grew from 31.5 million to 76 million. This was largely due to immigration. Immigrants provided labor for the nation's growing factories.
4. **New inventions** New inventions and technologies made industry more efficient.
5. **Investment capital** Banks and wealthy people invested in businesses. Because of this, businesses had funds to improve factories and equipment.

Industrialization led to the rise of powerful businessmen. John D. Rockefeller, for example, led the oil industry. Andrew Carnegie controlled the steel industry. Some people built great fortunes.

The late 1800s became known as the **Gilded Age.** To gild something is to coat it with gold leaf. Gilded decorations were popular during this era. But the name had another meaning. Gold leaf can disguise the object it covers. Similarly, the wealth of a few people disguised society's problems, including poverty and corrupt politics.

Many of the nation's poor worked in factories. To improve their lives, workers formed labor unions. Unions were groups of workers that negotiated with owners to get better wages and working conditions.

2. List the factors that sped up industrialization.

_____

_____

Cities Grow and Change; The New Immigrants (pages 541–543)

What are urban reformers?

The Industrial Revolution changed how and where people worked. Factories were built in cities because cities contained good transportation and many workers. As more factory jobs appeared in U.S. cities, more people moved in to take those jobs. The growth of cities that resulted is called **urbanization**.

Overcrowding in the cities became a serious problem. Many poor people lived in apartment houses that were run-down and dangerous. Many Americans were disgusted by the poverty in the cities. People known as urban reformers worked to solve such problems. Some reformers opened settlement houses. Settlement houses offered services such as education, daycare, and health care to needy people in poor neighborhoods.

Political machines also addressed problems in cities. A political machine is an organization that influences enough votes to control a local government. Political machines were often corrupt. But they did some good things. They built parks, sewers, schools, roads, and orphanages in many cities.

Until the 1890s, most immigrants to the United States came from northern or western Europe. Around 1900, more people were coming from southern and eastern Europe. This later group of immigrants came to be known as the **new immigrants**.

Immigrants settled where they could find jobs. Many immigrants found work in U.S. factories. They tried to fit into American society. At the same time, they were changing America. Immigrant languages, foods, and music became part of American culture.

New immigrants often faced *prejudice.* Many native-born Americans were afraid there would not be enough jobs for everyone. In 1882, Congress passed laws to limit immigration. Asians faced some of the worst prejudice. In 1882, Congress passed the Chinese Exclusion Act. It banned Chinese immigration for 10 years. Later, Congress made the ban permanent, but it was *repealed* in 1943.

3. What problems did reformers address?

_____

_____

Chapter **19** *Epilogue Section 2 (pages 546–550)*

Life at the Turn of the Century

BEFORE YOU READ

In the last section, you read about western expansion and industrial growth after the Civil War.

In this section, you will read about the rise of mass culture and the struggle against racism.

AS YOU READ

Use this diagram to note the factors that contributed to the rise of a mass culture in the United States.

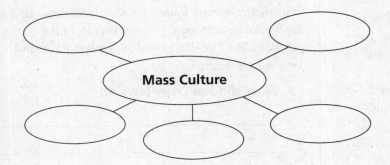

TERMS & NAMES

mass culture A common culture experienced by large numbers of people

leisure Free time

vaudeville Live stage show that featured song, dance, and comedy

ragtime Type of jazz music that blended African-American and European musical forms

Jim Crow Laws that enforced segregation

segregation Separation of white and black people in the United States

Plessy v. Ferguson Supreme Court ruling that upheld segregation

NAACP Acronym for National Association for the Advancement of Colored People, a civil rights organization

Life in the West; Women in the West
(pages 546–547)

How did farmers overcome the challenges on the Plains?

In the West, farmers faced many challenges. The Plains were nearly treeless. Farmers built their homes out of sod, or prairie soil. For fuel, they burned corncobs or "cow chips" (dried manure). In many places, water was hard to find. Some farmers had to dig wells more than 280 feet deep to reach water. Other problems included blizzards, prairie fires, hailstorms, tornadoes, grasshoppers, and drought.

New inventions helped farmers meet some of these challenges. The steel plow sliced through the tough soil. Windmills pumped water up from deep wells. Barbed wire allowed farmers to fence in land and raise livestock.

There were many cowhands in the West. They drove the cattle to cow towns. From these towns, cattle could be shipped on trains to markets in the East.

Many people moved to the West to mine for silver and gold. Cities such as Denver in the Colorado Territory and San Francisco, California, grew quickly.

Western life provided new opportunities for women. Many women were teachers or servants. Some did sewing or laundry. A few became sheriffs or gamblers. In some settlements, women ran dance halls or boarding houses.

Western lawmakers recognized women's contributions to Western communities. Women there gained more rights than in the East. In most territories, women could own property and control their own money. In 1869, the Wyoming Territory led the nation in giving women the vote.

1. What inventions made farm work more efficient?

_____

_____

_____

Society and Mass Culture; New Leisure Activities (pages 548–549)

How did leisure change during this era?

During the late 1800s, cities were changing. Urbanization and industrialization helped create an American **mass culture**—a common culture experienced by large numbers of people.

More and more Americans read newspapers. The popularity of newspapers led to the rise of modern advertising. Companies used images of celebrities in newspaper ads to encourage people to buy products. Advertisements also helped people learn about new inventions, such as the electric washing machine. These inventions promised to help people do house-hold chores more easily. Women did most of these chores. Women also did most of the shopping. For this reason, manufacturers directed their advertising toward women.

Leisure, or free time, activities also changed. New parks helped bring grass and trees into city land-scapes. Amusement parks provided a place to have fun. World's fairs were also popular. Between 1876 and 1916, several U.S. cities hosted world's fairs.

Sports such as baseball, football, and boxing drew thousands of spectators. Many people also played these sports. Other entertainments attracted people to theaters and music halls. **Vaudeville** featured a mixture of song, dance, and comedy. **Ragtime,** a type of jazz music that blended African-American and European musical forms, became important. Early in the 20th century, movies began to compete with live entertainment.

2. Name four popular leisure activities of the era.

_____

_____

Segregation and Discrimination; African Americans Organize (pages 549–550)

What were Jim Crow laws?

The nation's racial minorities often found their economic, political, and social freedoms limited. Racism that had developed over centuries led many whites to discriminate against nonwhites.

When Reconstruction ended in 1877, Southern states passed laws to restrict African-Americans' rights, such as voting. **Jim Crow** laws *enforced* segregation, or separation, of whites and blacks. In 1896, the Supreme Court upheld the practice of segregation. Its decision in ***Plessy* v. *Ferguson*** stated that "separate but equal" facilities did not violate the Constitution.

Booker T. Washington was a former slave. He urged blacks to improve their lives by learning trades and gaining economic strength. In 1881, he founded Tuskegee Institute in Alabama.

W. E. B. Du Bois (doo-BOYS) encouraged African Americans to reject segregation. In 1909, Du Bois and other reformers founded the National Association for the Advancement of Colored People, or the **NAACP.** The NAACP played an important role in fighting segregation.

3. What did Jim Crow laws do?

_____

_____

Discrimination in the West (page 550)

What problems did Chinese immigrants face?

Chinese immigrants who came to the American West in the 1800s *endured* low wages and violence. In one incident in Wyoming, white miners refused to work in the same mine as Chinese workers. White people rioted in the Chinese part of town. During the riot, 28 Chinese were killed and 15 were injured.

4. What form did discrimination take in the West?

_____

_____

Chapter 19 Epilogue Section 3 (pages 551–555)

An Era of Reform

BEFORE YOU READ

In the last section, you read about the rise of mass culture and the struggle against racism.

In this section, you will learn about the efforts of various groups to solve the nation's problems.

AS YOU READ

Use this chart to list examples of progressive reforms.

Goals	Reforms
Expanding Democracy	
Protecting Social Welfare	
Creating Economic Reform	

TERMS & NAMES

Populist Party Political party formed, mostly by farmers

William Jennings Bryan Democratic and Populist nominee in the 1896 presidential election

progressivism Name given to a group of reform movements with related goals around 1900

Theodore Roosevelt Progressive president who supported conservation and regulating business

William Howard Taft Succeeded Theodore Roosevelt as president of the United States

Woodrow Wilson Progressive president who supported regulating business

The Rise of Populism; The Election of 1896 (pages 551–553)

What was populism?

By the 1870s, many farmers faced serious economic problems. New tools helped them grow more food. But new farm machines were costly. As supplies of farm products grew, prices fell. Also, railroads charged high fees to carry crops to market.

Farmers looked for solutions to their problems. They formed the **Populist Party,** or People's Party. The Populists wanted the government to adopt policies to help farmers. Populists believed that increasing the supply of money would raise crop prices. Higher prices would help farmers pay back the money they had borrowed to improve their farms.

In 1892, the Populist candidate for president was James B. Weaver. He won more than one million votes. But he still finished a distant third. Democrat Grover Cleveland won the election.

In 1893, the country fell into a *depression* that lasted until 1897. The Populists hoped the weak economy would increase support for their candidate in the 1896 presidential election. The Democrats nominated William Jennings Bryan of Nebraska for president. The Populists also supported Bryan. The Republicans nominated Ohio governor William McKinley.

Bryan received heavy support from farmers in the South and the West. But McKinley won the election. Bryan's defeat marked the beginning of the end for the Populist Party.

1. What happened in the 1896 presidential election?

_____

_____

_____

Progressivism Emerges (pages 553–554)

***What** is progressivism?*

Several reform movements emerged to address the problems caused by industrialization and urbanization. These reform movements are commonly grouped under the label of **progressivism.** The progressive reformers shared three basic goals: 1) to reform the government and expand democracy, 2) to promote social welfare, and 3) to create economic reform.

To expand democracy, progressive leaders supported reforms to give voters more control over their government. For example, three reforms passed in Oregon were the initiative, the referendum, and the recall. The initiative and the referendum allowed voters to propose and pass laws without going through the legislature. The recall allowed people to vote an official out of office.

Progressives also wanted to promote social welfare. They tackled problems such as poverty, unemployment, and poor working conditions.

The third progressive goal was to create economic reform. Economic reform often meant limiting the power of big business. The Sherman Antitrust Act of 1890 outlawed trusts. Trusts were combinations of businesses that could control a market and squeeze out competition.

An important aspect of progressivism was the role women played. Educated, middle-class women led many social reform movements. These women worked to make other people's lives better. They also worked to improve their own status in society. Many women progressives worked for woman suffrage, or the right to vote. They finally won that right in 1920, when the states ratified the 19th Amendment to the Constitution.

2. Name the three basic goals of progressive reformers.

_____

_____

Progressive Presidents (pages 554–555)

***What** did Roosevelt think government should do?*

Many Americans supported progressive reforms. They elected presidents who also supported reform. The first progressive president was **Theodore Roosevelt.** Roosevelt thought government should ensure fairness, or a "square deal," for workers, consumers, and business.

Roosevelt thought industries should be regulated for the public's good. For example, he worked to break up trusts. He also acted to regulate the meat-packing industry. He signed the Pure Food and Drug Act. This law banned the sale of impure foods and medicines. In addition, Roosevelt fought to protect America's natural resources. He preserved more than 200 million acres of public lands. He doubled the number of national parks in the United States.

William Howard Taft followed Theodore Roosevelt as president. Taft was not a progressive. But he oversaw the passage of two progressive amendments to the Constitution. The 16th Amendment was passed in 1909 and ratified in 1913. This amendment gave Congress the power to establish income taxes. It was intended to spread the cost of government more fairly among the people. The 17th Amendment also was ratified in 1913. This amendment provided for the direct election of U.S. senators by the voters in each state.

Woodrow Wilson was elected president in 1912. At Wilson's urging, Congress passed the Clayton Antitrust Act of 1914. This law banned business practices that reduced competition. During Wilson's tenure, the U.S. financial system was reformed. The Federal Reserve Act was passed in 1913. This act improved the nation's monetary and banking system.

Despite many successes, however, few politicians during the Progressive era promoted civil rights for African Americans.

3. Name three things Theodore Roosevelt accomplished as president.

_____

_____

Chapter 19 Epilogue Section 4 (pages 556–562)

Becoming a World Power

BEFORE YOU READ

In the last section, you read about populism and progressivism. In this section, you will learn how the United States extended its influence beyond its borders.

AS YOU READ

Use this chart to record causes of U.S. expansion overseas in the late 1800s and early 1900s.

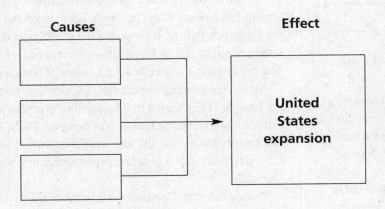

Causes	Effect
	United States expansion

TERMS & NAMES

imperialism Policy of extending economic, political, or military control over other nations

Spanish-American War 1898 war between the United States and Spain that was won by the United States

yellow journalism Sensational style of reporting the news

Platt Amendment Part of Cuba's constitution that allowed the United States to intervene in Cuban affairs

Panama Canal Canal built to create a shorter route between the Atlantic and Pacific oceans

Roosevelt Corollary U.S. policy to intervene in Latin American affairs to maintain stability

Fourteen Points Woodrow Wilson's plan for peace following World War I

Great Migration The movement of African Americans from the rural South to cities, especially in the North

Growth of U.S. Imperialism; The Spanish-American War (pages 556–558)

Why *did people want economic expansion?*
Imperialism is a policy of extending economic, political, or military control over other nations. By the 1880s, European nations were competing to expand their empires. Many Americans believed the United States should join this competition. Three factors supported American imperialism.

1. **Economic Interests** Expansion could increase U.S. financial prosperity. New colonies could supply raw materials and markets for American products.

2. **Military Interests** Foreign policy experts agreed that military interests and economic interests went together. They urged U.S. leaders to follow the Europeans and have a military presence overseas.

3. **Belief in Cultural Superiority** Many Americans believed American culture was superior to other cultures. They wanted to spread democracy and Christianity.

In 1867, the United States bought Alaska from Russia. In 1893, the U.S. Marines helped American planters in Hawaii overthrow the Hawaiian queen. The United States then *annexed* Hawaii.

The **Spanish-American War** began in 1898 after Cubans rebelled against Spain. Cuba was a colony of Spain. The United States sided with the Cuban rebels. Americans were influenced in part by newspaper stories that described Spanish cruelty. Some stories were exaggerated. This *sensational* style of reporting news became known as **yellow journalism.**

The war was fought in Spain's colonies in the Caribbean and the Philippine Islands. One of the more famous American fighting units was the Rough Riders. This unit was led by Theodore Roosevelt. The Rough Riders helped capture Santiago, a key Spanish stronghold in southern Cuba.

When Spain surrendered, the United States gained the Spanish colonies of Puerto Rico, Guam, and the Philippines. Cuba won its freedom. However, the United States had the Cubans add the **Platt Amendment** to their constitution. This gave the United States the right to *intervene* in Cuban affairs.

Some Americans opposed U.S. imperialism. They formed the Anti-Imperialist League. Most Americans, however, wanted the power and prestige that came from having an overseas empire.

1. What were the arguments in favor of U.S. imperialism?

_____

_____

U.S. Influence Expands (pages 558–560)

What was the U.S. policy on China?
The United States joined other countries in competing for access to China. In 1899, the United States supported an Open Door Policy. This policy asked nations with interests in China to open the door to other nations to trade there.

The United States also became more involved in Latin America. In 1904, the United States began to build the **Panama Canal.** This canal shortened the trade route between the Atlantic and Pacific oceans. In addition, many U.S. businesses built relationships with Latin American countries.

In 1904, President Theodore Roosevelt added the **Roosevelt Corollary** to the Monroe Doctrine. The Monroe Doctrine is a U.S. policy opposing European intervention in Latin America. The Roosevelt Corollary said the United States could intervene in Latin American affairs to maintain stability.

2. What was the Open Door Policy?

_____

_____

World War I; Postwar America
(pages 560–562)

What was the League of Nations?
World War I began in 1914. On one side were the Central Powers: Austria-Hungary, Germany, the Ottoman Empire, and Bulgaria. On the other side were the Allies: Serbia, Russia, France, Great Britain, and Italy.

When the war started, the United States said it would not take sides. As time passed, American sympathy for the Allies increased. In 1917, the United States entered the war on the side of the Allies. U.S. forces tipped the balance in favor of the Allies. In 1918, the German emperor gave up his throne. The new German government asked for peace.

World War I was the most devastating conflict the world had ever seen. About 8.5 million soldiers died. About 21 million were wounded. In addition, millions of civilians died, often due to starvation or disease.

As World War I ended, President Woodrow Wilson announced a peace plan. This plan became known as the **Fourteen Points.** It proposed the creation of an international organization to settle disputes peacefully. The organization was called the League of Nations.

Many Americans opposed the U.S. participation in the League. They feared that further involvement in Europe would lead the nation into more conflicts. For this reason, the Senate did not ratify the treaty. The United States made a separate peace agreement with Germany.

During the war, Communists had taken over Russia. Then shortly after the war ended, the United States experienced a number of labor strikes. These strikes sparked fear of Communists in the United States. This fear is known as the Red Scare.

For decades, African Americans had been leaving the rural South. This movement was known as the **Great Migration.** During the war, this movement grew as African Americans filled war-related jobs in cities, especially in the North. In cities where blacks settled in large numbers, racial tensions arose over housing, job competition, and segregation.

By 1920, Americans were tired of turmoil. Republican presidential candidate Warren G. Harding of Ohio promised a "return to normalcy." He won a landslide victory.

3. Why did Americans oppose the League of Nations?

_____

_____

Name _____ Date _____

Glossary/After You Read

annex To add territory

depression A period of low economic activity and high unemployment

discriminate To treat people differently

endure To live through something, especially hardship, without giving in

enforce To carry out

intervene To get involved in

prejudice A judgment formed without good information

repeal To revoke or take back

reservation Piece of land set aside by the U.S. government for Native Americans

sensational Arousing interest or emotional reaction through exaggerated details

sparsely Thinly

Terms & Names

A. Write the letter of the term or name next to the description that explains it best.

a. Great Migration   d. ragtime
b. new immigrants   e. Jim Crow
c. vaudeville

_____ 1. laws that enforced segregation

_____ 2. theatrical entertainment that featured a mixture of song, dance, and comedy

_____ 3. the movement of African Americans away from the rural South to cities, especially in the North

_____ 4. type of jazz music that blended African-American and European musical forms

_____ 5. immigrants arriving from southern and eastern Europe after 1900

B. Fill in the blanks with the correct term or name. Each term is used only once.

Homestead Act   imperialism
mass culture   yellow journalism
progressivism

1. A common culture experienced by large numbers of people is called
_____ .

2. _____ was the name given to a group of reform movements with related goals.

3. A policy of extending economic, political, or military control over other nations is called _____ .

4. The _____ was a law that offered free land to settlers to encourage western settlement.

5. A style of reporting the news that often uses exaggerated detail to arouse interest is called _____ .

Main Ideas

1. How were the growth of industry and the growth of cities related to each other?

_____

_____

2. Why did the increased popularity of newspapers contribute to the spread of an American mass culture?

_____

_____

3. What role did women have in the progressive era?

_____

_____

4. How did yellow journalism contribute to the outbreak of the Spanish-American War?

_____

_____

5. Why did the U.S. Senate refuse to ratify the Treaty of Versailles?

_____

_____

Thinking Critically

Answer the following questions on a separate sheet of paper.

1. Why do you think the hardships of life in the West led to more rights for women?

2. What did urban reformers, Populists, and progressives have in common?

Chapter **20** *Epilogue* *Section 1 (pages 569–573)*

Prosperity and the Great Depression

Before You Read

In the last chapter, you read how the United States helped Britain and France achieve victory in World War I.

In this section, you will learn how the stock market crash of 1929 and the Great Depression led to Franklin D. Roosevelt's New Deal.

As You Read

Use this diagram to take notes on the immediate events that led to the Great Depression.

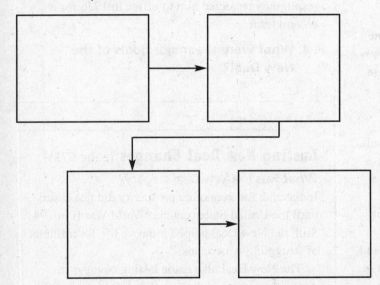

TERMS & NAMES

Warren G. Harding 29th U.S. president

Calvin Coolidge 30th U.S. president

jazz Lively style of music developed by African Americans

Harlem Renaissance Flourishing of African-American cultural activity

Great Depression Period of bad economic times lasting from 1929 to the start of World War II

Franklin D. Roosevelt 32nd U.S. president

New Deal Roosevelt's programs to fight the Depression

The Roaring Twenties' Business Boom

(pages 569–570)

What helped business to grow?

By the start of the 1920s, Americans were turning away from progressive reforms. Earlier in the century, presidents had sought to place tighter controls on business. Under presidents **Warren G. Harding** and **Calvin Coolidge,** the government put into practice pro-business policies. These policies made business growth easier and more profitable.

Improvements in methods of mass production made it possible to turn out products faster and cheaper. As a result, prices for many goods fell. At the same time, the nation's wealth grew. During the 1920s, the income of many workers grew. People had both more money to spend and more goods to buy.

1. How did improvements in mass production lead to lower prices for many goods?

_____

_____

The Rise of Popular Entertainment

(pages 570–571)

What was the Harlem Renaissance?

Americans made many sacrifices during World War I. After the war, Americans wanted to enjoy themselves. Radio, movies, and sports gained in popularity. The 1920s also introduced more Americans to a musical form called jazz. **Jazz** blended African and European musical traditions.

Literature and other art forms flourished during the 1920s. In the Harlem section of New York City, the 1920s was a time of great creativity for African-American artists. This movement was known as the **Harlem Renaissance**.

2. What activities did Americans enjoy during the 1920s?

_____

_____

Stock Market Crash and Great Depression (page 571)

What was the Great Depression?

During the 1920s, many Americans put their money in the stock market. They saw it as a safe, quick way to get rich. As a result, the stock market went up in value. Then, in October 1929, the stock market crashed.

The crash sparked a chain reaction. People rushed to get their money out of banks. As a result, many banks closed. Without banks to loan them money, many businesses shut down. This led to a sharp rise in unemployment. A time of great economic hardship followed. It was known as the **Great Depression**.

President Herbert Hoover took little action to end the crisis. He believed that providing government relief to the hungry and homeless would make Americans dependent on government handouts.

3. Why didn't President Hoover use federal relief to fight the Great Depression?

_____

_____

Roosevelt's New Deal (pages 572–573)

What was the New Deal?

In 1932, Americans elected **Franklin D. Roosevelt**

as president. He was also known as FDR. Unlike Hoover, Roosevelt took action to fight the economic crisis. FDR began a bold new program to end the Great Depression. It was called the **New Deal**.

Roosevelt's New Deal had three major goals, known as the "three R's": 1) relief programs for the hungry and jobless; 2) recovery programs to help agriculture and industry; 3) reform of the economy to make sure that such a deep economic crisis did not happen again.

Not all of FDR's policies worked. Still, most Americans viewed his programs as effective. As a result, they reelected him to office in 1936 for a second term.

4. What were the major goals of the New Deal?

_____

_____

Lasting New Deal Changes (page 573)

What was the New Deal's legacy?

In the end, full economic prosperity did not return until the United States entered World War II in 1941. Still, the New Deal helped improve life for millions of struggling Americans.

The New Deal also made lasting changes in American society and government. It increased the power of the federal government. In addition, the New Deal created programs that still exist today. They include Social Security, unemployment insurance, and other federal programs to care for the elderly, jobless, and needy.

5. Name two New Deal programs that exist today.

_____

_____

Chapter **20** Epilogue   Section 2 (pages 574-578)

The Rise of Dictators and World War II

Before You Read

In the last section, you read about the prosperity of the 1920s and the economic crisis of the 1930s.

In this section, you will learn how the rise of military dictators in the 1930s led to World War II.

As You Read

Use this diagram to take notes on the key events of World War II.

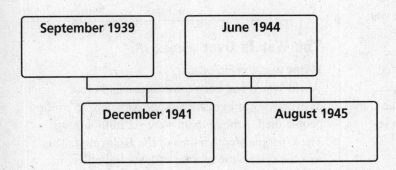

| September 1939 | | June 1944 |
| December 1941 | | August 1945 |

TERMS & NAMES

Benito Mussolini Ruler of Italy

fascism Political movement that preached intense nationalism and racism

Adolf Hitler Germany's dictator

Nazi Ruling party in Germany during the war

World War II Worldwide conflict between the Axis and Allied Powers

Dwight D. Eisenhower U.S. general and commander of the D-Day invasion

Holocaust Systematic mass murder of Jews and other minorities by the Nazis

Dictators Take Power (pages 574–575)

What *is fascism?*

During the 1930s, the Great Depression spread around the world. In Italy and Germany, dictators rose to power by promising to restore *prosperity*. In Italy, **Benito Mussolini** built a political movement called **fascism.** This is a system under which the government rules through terror and appeals to racism and nationalism. In Germany, **Adolf Hitler** and his National Socialist German Workers' or **Nazi** Party came to power in 1933.

In Japan, military leaders took control of the government. Meanwhile, dictator Joseph Stalin tightened his grip on power in the Soviet Union.

1. In what countries did dictators or military leaders seize power?

_____

_____

War Breaks Out in Europe; Surprise Attack on Pearl Harbor (pages 575–576)

Why *did America enter the war?*

Dictators sought to conquer land for their countries. On September 1, 1939, the Nazis invaded Poland. Two days later, Britain and France declared war on Germany. **World War II** had begun. On one side of the war were Italy, Germany and Japan. They were known as the Axis Powers. On the other side were Britain, France, and soon the Soviet Union. They were known as the Allied Powers.

By June 1940, Germany had conquered France. Hitler then tried to bomb Britain into surrendering. He failed to do so. Meanwhile, German forces invaded the Soviet Union in 1941 and began a long, intense battle with Soviet troops.

When war broke out, the United States remained *neutral*. However, Americans supported the Allies with weapons and other equipment. Then, in December 1941, the Japanese launched a surprise attack against the U.S. naval base in Pearl Harbor, Hawaii. America responded by entering the war on the side of the Allies.

2. Who were the main Axis Powers? The main Allied Powers?

_____

_____

The Home Front in America
(pages 576–577)

How did Americans help the war effort?
American citizens contributed greatly to the war effort. Many factories turned into defense plants. Workers produced tons of weapons and equipment for the war. In addition, Americans put up with wartime shortages so scarce goods could be redirected to military use.

With millions of men overseas, the war created many job opportunities for women and minorities. However, one minority group suffered during the war. Many citizens grew to distrust people of Japanese descent. As a result, thousands of Japanese Americans were forced to live in prison camps.

3. In what ways did Americans contribute to the war effort?

_____

War Continues in Europe and Asia
(pages 577–578)

Who was Dwight D. Eisenhower?
On June 6, 1944, the Allies invaded France in order to take Western Europe back from the Nazis. The

invasion was known as D-Day. It was led by U.S. General **Dwight D. Eisenhower.** Nearly a year later, in May 1945, Germany surrendered.

The Japanese continued to fight on. U.S. leaders worried that an invasion of Japan would cost many American lives. Instead, American bombers dropped atomic bombs on Japan in August 1945. Many Japanese citizens died. A month later, the Japanese surrendered.

4. Why did the U.S. decide against an invasion of Japan?

_____

_____

The War Is Over (page 578)

What was the Holocaust?
World War II had been the costliest and most destructive war in history. Approximately 55 million people died. Among them were six million Jews. These people were victims of the **Holocaust.** This was the systematic murder of Jews and other minorities by the Nazis.

After the war, the United States and other countries formed the United Nations. This is an international peacekeeping organization that replaced the League of Nations.

5. What is the United Nations?

_____

_____

_____

Name _____   Date _____

The Cold War

Before You Read

In the last section, you read about the events of World War II.

In this section, you will learn how the United States and the Soviet Union entered into an intense struggle for world power after the war.

As You Read

Use this diagram to take notes on examples of America's Cold War containment policy.

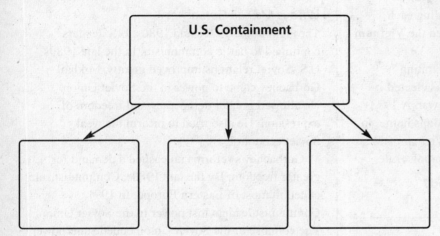

U.S. Containment

Harry S. Truman 33rd U.S. president

Cold War State of hostility between United States and Soviet Union but without direct military action

containment Effort to stop the spread of communism

John F. Kennedy 35th U.S. president

Lyndon B. Johnson 36th U.S. president

Vietnam War War between North and South Vietnam

Richard M. Nixon 37th U.S. president

Watergate scandal Attempt by Nixon and aides to cover up Watergate burglary

The Cold War Begins; The Korean War and McCarthyism (pages 579–580)

What *was the Cold War?*

The United States and the Soviet Union emerged from World War II as the globe's two superpowers. President **Harry S. Truman** feared that the Soviets wanted to spread communism around the world. He looked for ways to stop it. This struggle marked the start of the **Cold War** between the two countries. This was a state of hostility between the two nations but without any direct military action.

Truman's anti-Soviet policy was called **containment**. It sought to contain, or stop, the spread of communism. In 1950, Communist North Korea invaded American-backed South Korea. A United Nations force made up mostly of U.S. troops drove the North Koreans back into North Korea.

Back home, fear of communism allowed Senator Joseph McCarthy of Wisconsin to gain great power.

He accused many people of supporting communism. Many of his charges were proved to be unfounded. As a result, his power quickly faded.

1. What was the goal of Truman's anti-Soviet policy?

_____

_____

Nuclear Threat and Superpower Conflicts (pages 580–581)

What *happened in Cuba?*

In 1960, **John F. Kennedy** was elected president. He continued the Cold War. In 1962, Kennedy learned that the Soviets were supplying Cuba with missiles. In response, U.S. navy ships blockaded the island. The threat of nuclear war seemed very real.

The world waited to see if the Soviets would remove all missiles and missile bases from Cuba.

Finally, the Soviet Union agreed to remove them. In 1963, Kennedy was assassinated. **Lyndon B. Johnson** became president. Like his *predecessors,* Johnson fought communism.

2. How did the Cuban missile crisis end?

_____

_____

War in Vietnam (page 581)

***What** was the Vietnam War?*
In 1957, Communist North Vietnam and anti-Communist South Vietnam began fighting each other. In 1965, the United States entered the **Vietnam War** on the side of South Vietnam.

By 1968, the war had become a frustrating stalemate. **Richard M. Nixon,** who was elected president that year, pledged to end the war. A 1973 cease-fire finally brought American troops home. In 1975, North Vietnam defeated South Vietnam and brought the entire country under Communist rule.

3. How did the Vietnam War end?

_____

_____

Nixon as President (page 582)

***What** was the Watergate scandal?*
In the early 1970s, President Nixon took steps to improve relations with the Soviet Union and Communist China. In 1972, Nixon visited the two nations. The United States and the Soviet Union then signed an agreement limiting nuclear arms.

Nixon spent much of his second term dealing with what became known as the **Watergate scandal.** During Nixon's reelection campaign, some of his aides burglarized the Democratic Party headquarters in the Watergate building in Washington, D.C. An investigation showed that Nixon had ordered his staff to cover up White

House involvement in these crimes. In August 1974, Nixon resigned rather than face a possible impeachment.

4. How did President Nixon help to ease the tensions of the Cold War?

_____

_____

Foreign Policy of the 1970s and the 1980s; New Threats to the United States (pages 582–583)

***Who** is Mikhail Gorbachev?*
Throughout the 1970s and 1980s, U.S. leaders continued to battle communism. In the late 1980s, U.S.-Soviet relations improved greatly. Mikhail Gorbachev came to power in the Soviet Union. He allowed greater democracy and freedom of expression. He also tried to reform the weak Soviet economy.

Gorbachev's reforms unleashed a demand for greater freedom. By the late 1980s, Communist rule ended in most of Eastern Europe. In 1991, Communist leaders lost power in the Soviet Union. The collapse of the Soviet Union ended superpower rivalry and the Cold War.

After the Cold War ended, the United States faced new challenges. In 1990, Iraq invaded Kuwait. In 1991, the United States led a coalition to free Kuwait from Iraqi control.

In 2001, Americans faced the threat of terrorism. On September 11, terrorists crashed airplanes into the World Trade Center in New York City and the Pentagon outside Washington, D.C. Thousands died. While Americans mourned the deaths, they also began efforts to bring the terrorists to justice.

5. How did the Cold War come to an end?

_____

_____

Chapter **20** Epilogue   *Section 4 (pages 584–589)*

Life in America Since 1945

Before You Read

In the last section, you read about the events of the Cold War between the United States and the Soviet Union.

In this section, you will learn how civil rights, economic growth, and social change have dominated American life since World War II.

As You Read

Use this diagram to take notes on the groups that fought during the 1950s and 1960s for greater rights in American society.

TERMS & NAMES

baby boom Sharp increase in the U.S. birthrate following World War II

Dr. Martin Luther King, Jr. Leader of the civil rights movement

Great Society Name of President Lyndon Johnson's domestic programs

counterculture Group of Americans seeking a new way of living

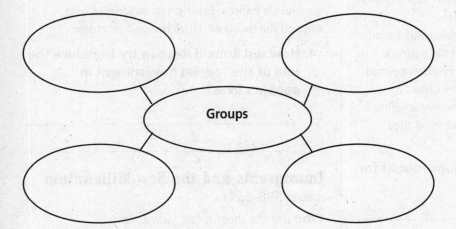

Groups

Economic Boom and Baby Boom

(pages 584–585)

***What** was the baby boom?*

After World War II, the U.S. economy boomed. During the late 1940s and the 1950s, the population also grew rapidly. This trend was known as the **baby boom.**

Not all Americans shared in the new prosperity, however. In the 1950s, African Americans and other minorities continued to face discrimination. So did many working women.

1. Which groups did not share in the prosperity of the 1950s?

_____

_____

The Civil Rights Movement; The Great Society (pages 585–586)

***Who** was Dr. Martin Luther King, Jr.?*

During the 1950s, African Americans began an organized effort to achieve equal rights in society. They challenged segregation laws in court. They also engaged in nonviolent protests. The leader of this movement was **Dr. Martin Luther King, Jr.**

The movement achieved many breakthroughs. For example, President Lyndon Johnson pushed a Civil Rights Act through Congress in 1964. It banned discrimination in public places.

In addition to promoting civil rights, President Johnson also fought to reduce poverty and expand medical care. These plans were part of his domestic programs, known as the **Great Society**.

2. What were some of the goals of the Great Society?

_____

_____

Rights for All; Youth Protests and the Counterculture (pages 586–587)

What *was the counterculture?*
During the 1960s, minorities and women also struggled for equal rights. Native Americans won greater land rights. Mexican Americans achieved greater economic and political rights. Meanwhile, a growing number of women organized to change laws that discriminated against their *gender.*

During the 1960s, many young Americans raised their voices in protest. They opposed the nation's involvement in the Vietnam War. They also opposed many of the beliefs and values held by older Americans. These groups of young people sought new ways of living. They became known as the **counterculture**.

3. During the 1960s, what groups fought for greater rights?

_____

_____

Reagan, Bush, and Conservatism; The Clinton Presidency; The 2000 Presidential Election (pages 587–588)

What *is a political conservative?*
Throughout the 1960s and 1970s, Democratic presidents favored a strong role for government in the economy and society. In 1980, Ronald Reagan became president. He was a political conservative. This meant that he believed in reducing the role of government in American life. Reagan sharply cut taxes. He also cut spending on social programs.

Reagan's successor was George Bush. He shared Reagan's conservative view. In the early 1990s, the country fell into a recession. As a result, Bush's popularity dropped. He was defeated in the 1992 presidential election by Democrat Bill Clinton, the governor of Arkansas.

During his two terms as president, Clinton focused on improving the economy. His second term in office was marred by scandal. Clinton was accused of having an improper relationship with a White House intern and lying under oath about it. The House of Representatives impeached him in December 1998. However, the Senate acquitted him on all charges.

The 2000 presidential election was extremely close. On the night of the election, Democrat Al Gore led Republican George W. Bush in the popular vote. But he did not have enough electoral votes to claim victory. The election was decided in Florida, where Bush led by a few hundred votes. For five weeks, both campaigns fought legal battles over recounts of the Florida ballots. Finally, the Supreme Court stopped the recounts. Bush became president.

4. How did Ronald Reagan try to reduce the role of the federal government in people's lives?

_____

_____

Immigrants and the New Millennium (pages 588–589)

Who *are the most recent immigrants?*
Throughout much of the later twentieth century, America continued to attract many immigrants. From 1981 to 1996, nearly 13.5 million people came to the United States. Many of these newcomers came from Latin America and Asia.

Immigrants from around the world have brought their unique cultures to America. However, they also have adopted American traditions. Most wear American clothes, adopt American customs, and learn English. They also share the American belief in the ideals of democracy and freedom. As the United States moves into the future, it will no doubt continue to change. Citizens of all colors and backgrounds will play a vital role in shaping what America will be.

5. From where have many of the recent immigrants to the United States come?

_____

_____

Chapter **20** _Epilogue_   _Review_

Glossary/After You Read

gender category based on someone's sex, either male or female

neutral taking neither side in a war

predecessor one who comes before

prosperity the condition of being wealthy

Terms & Names

A. Circle the name or phrase that best completes each sentence.

1. The _____ was a time of great economic hardship in America that lasted for much of the 1930s.
   Great Depression   New Deal   Cold War

2. The _____ was a group of programs aimed at ending the Great Depression.
   Great Society   Harlem Renaissance   New Deal

3. _____ led the Allied invasion of Europe known as D-Day.
   Adolf Hitler   Dwight D. Eisenhower   Benito Mussolini

4. An example of America's effort to stop the spread of communism was

   _____.
   the Vietnam War   World War II   the Watergate scandal

5. The leader of the nation's civil rights movement of the 1950s and 1960s was

   _____.
   Richard M. Nixon   Dr. Martin Luther King, Jr.   Lyndon Johnson

B. Write the letter of the name or term next to the description that explains it best.
   a. Holocaust
   b. Harlem Renaissance
   c. Great Society
   d. Cold War
   e. Franklin D. Roosevelt

   _____ 1. Flourishing of African-American culture in New York City during the 1920s

   _____ 2. President who worked to steer the nation out of the Great Depression

   _____ 3. Systematic murder of Jews and other minorities under Nazi rule

   _____ 4. State of hostility between the United States and the Soviet Union

   _____ 5. Name of President Johnson's domestic programs

Main Ideas

1. What were the three goals of FDR's New Deal?

_____

_____

2. What ended the war in the Pacific?

_____

_____

3. What were two examples of America's efforts to contain, or stop, the spread of communism?

_____

_____

_____

4. What was the Watergate scandal?

_____

_____

_____

5. How did Ronald Reagan attempt to reduce the role of government in American life?

_____

_____

Thinking Critically

Answer the following questions on a separate sheet of paper.

1. How were the Korean War and Vietnam War similar and different?

2. How important do you think it is for a nation to develop a single, unified culture?